CYCLOPS
SCOTT SUMMERS

EMMA FROST

TRIAGE
CHRISTOPHER MUSE

TEMPUS
EVA BELL

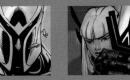
MAGNETO
ERIK LEHNSHERR

MAGIK
ILLYANA RASPUTIN

FABIO MEDIA

BENJAMIN DEEDS

VS. S.H.I.E.L.D.

BRIAN MICHAEL
BENDIS
WRITER

CHRIS
BACHALO
PENCILER, #19-22 & #25

KRIS
ANKA
ARTIST, #23-24

TIM
TOWNSEND

AL
VEY

JAIME
MENDOZA

MARK
IRWIN

VICTOR
OLAZABA

WAYNE
FAUCHER

JON
HOLDREDGE

MARC
DEERING

INKERS, #19-22 & #25

COVER ART: **CHRIS BACHALO & TIM TOWNSEND (#19-20, #22-23 & #25) AND ALEXANDER LOZANO (#21)**

CHRIS
BACHALO
COLORIST,(#19-22 & #25) WITH
JOSE VILLARRUBIA (#19 & #22)

VC'S JOE
CARAMAGNA
LETTERER

XANDER
JAROWEY
ASSISTANT EDITOR

MIKE
MARTS
EDITOR

COLLECTION EDITOR: **JENNIFER GRÜNWALD** ASSISTANT EDITOR: **SARAH BRUNSTAD**
ASSOCIATE MANAGING EDITOR: **ALEX STARBUCK** EDITOR, SPECIAL PROJECTS: **MARK D. BEAZLEY**
SENIOR EDITOR, SPECIAL PROJECTS: **JEFF YOUNGQUIST**
SVP PRINT, SALES & MARKETING: **DAVID GABRIEL** BOOK DESIGN: **JEFF POWELL & RODOLPHO MURAGUCHI**

EDITOR IN CHIEF: **AXEL ALONSO** CHIEF CREATIVE OFFICER: **JOE QUESADA**
PUBLISHER: **DAN BUCKLEY** EXECUTIVE PRODUCER: **ALAN FINE**

ANNY X-MEN VOL. 4: VS. S.H.I.E.L.D. Contains material originally published in magazine form as UNCANNY X-MEN #19-25. First printing 2014. ISBN# 978-0-7851-5489-1. Published by MARVEL WORLDWIDE, INC., a idiary of MARVEL ENTERTAINMENT, LLC. OFFICE OF PUBLICATION: 135 West 50th Street, New York, NY 10020. Copyright © 2014 Marvel Characters, Inc. All rights reserved. All characters featured in this issue and the ctive names and likenesses thereof, and all related indicia are trademarks of Marvel Characters, Inc. No similarity between any of the names, characters, persons, and/or institutions in this magazine with those of any or dead person or institution is intended, and any such similarity which may exist is purely coincidental. **Printed in the U.S.A.** ALAN FINE, EVP - Office of the President, Marvel Worldwide, Inc. and EVP & CMO Marvel acters B.V.; DAN BUCKLEY, Publisher & President - Print, Animation & Digital Divisions; JOE QUESADA, Chief Creative Officer; TOM BREVOORT, SVP of Publishing; DAVID BOGART, SVP of Operations & Procurement, shing; C.B. CEBULSKI, SVP of Creator & Content Development; DAVID GABRIEL, SVP Print, Sales & Marketing; JIM O'KEEFE, VP of Operations & Logistics; DAN CARR, Executive Director of Publishing Technology; SUSAN PI, Editorial Operations Manager; ALEX MORALES, Publishing Operations Manager; STAN LEE, Chairman Emeritus. For information regarding advertising in Marvel Comics or on Marvel.com, please contact Niza Disla, :tor of Marvel Partnerships, at ndisla@marvel.com. For Marvel subscription inquiries, please call 800-217-9158. **Manufactured between 7/18/2014 and 9/1/2014 by R.R. DONNELLEY, INC., SALEM, VA, USA.**

8 7 6 5 4 3 2 1

Born with genetic mutations that gave them abilities beyond those of normal humans, mutants are the next stage in evolution. As such, they are feared and hated by humanity. A group of mutants known as the X-Men fight for peaceful coexistence between mutants and humankind. But not all mutants see peaceful coexistence as a reality.

UNCANNY X-MEN

Cyclops is the public face of what he calls the new mutant revolution. Rededicating himself to the cause of protecting the mutant race, he has begun to gather and train a new generation of young mutants.

Recently, a new brand of Sentinels has been attacking the Uncanny X-Men at every turn. Cyclops has reason to believe S.H.I.E.L.D. is behind these attacks, and he has become increasingly wary of venturing outside the safe confines of the New Xavier School. While on a recent training mission, the new mutant Hijack unwittingly alerted S.H.I.E.L.D. to the students' location. Although they were able to escape, Hijack was expelled from the school for his reckless actions. But the question remains: Where are these new Sentinels coming from?

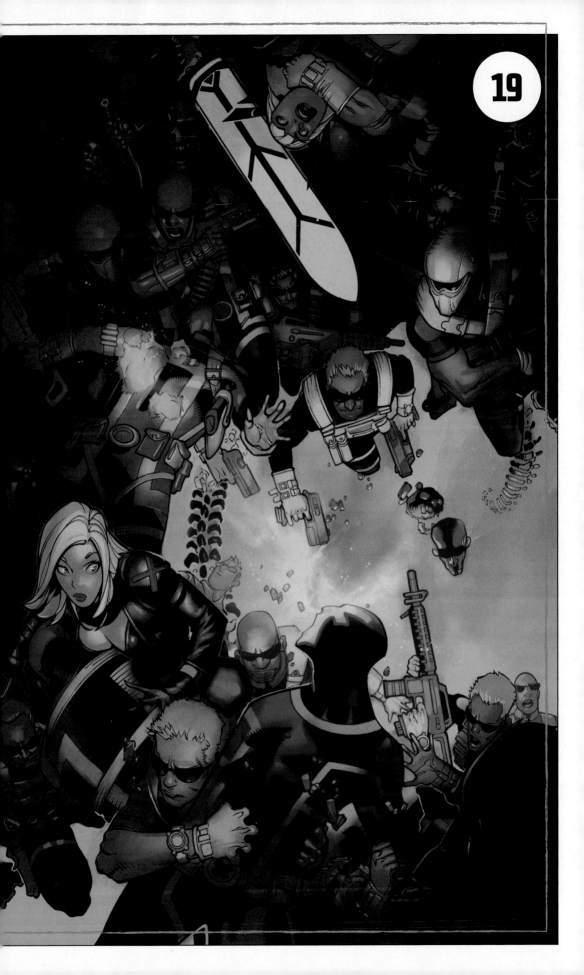

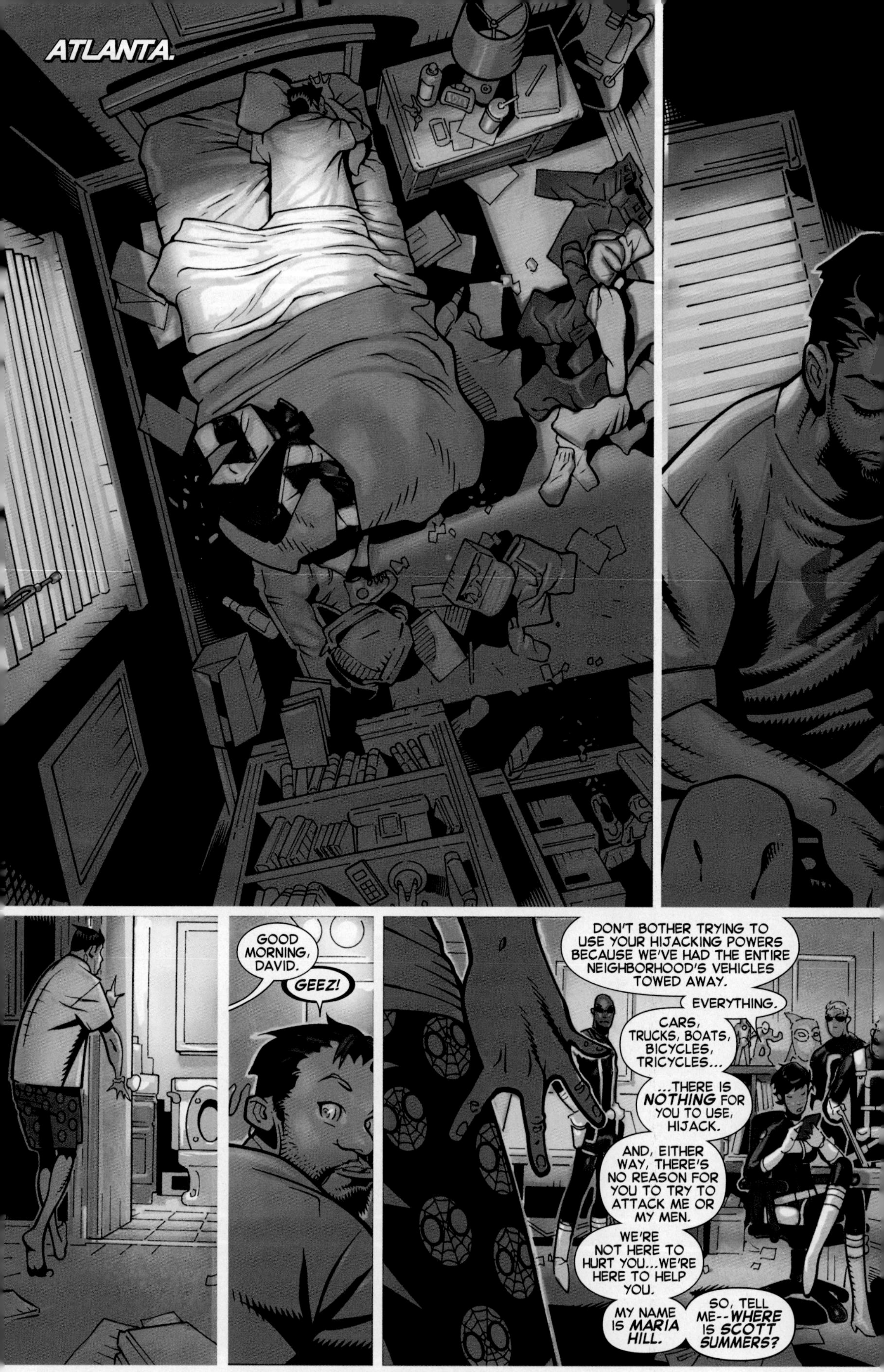
ATLANTA.
GOOD MORNING, DAVID.
GEEZ!
DON'T BOTHER TRYING TO USE YOUR HIJACKING POWERS BECAUSE WE'VE HAD THE ENTIRE NEIGHBORHOOD'S VEHICLES TOWED AWAY.
EVERYTHING.
CARS, TRUCKS, BOATS, BICYCLES, TRICYCLES...
...THERE IS NOTHING FOR YOU TO USE, HIJACK.
AND, EITHER WAY, THERE'S NO REASON FOR YOU TO TRY TO ATTACK ME OR MY MEN.
WE'RE NOT HERE TO HURT YOU...WE'RE HERE TO HELP YOU.
MY NAME IS MARIA HILL.
SO, TELL ME--WHERE IS SCOTT SUMMERS?

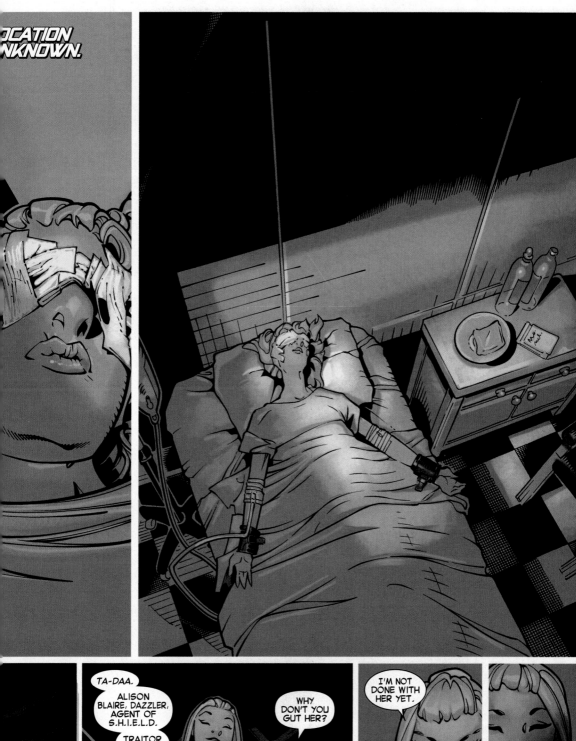

TA-DAA.

ALISON BLAIRE, DAZZLER, AGENT OF S.H.I.E.L.D.

TRAITOR TO HER PEOPLE.

WHY DON'T YOU GUT HER?

I'M NOT DONE WITH HER YET.

EVERYONE HAS A PURPOSE.

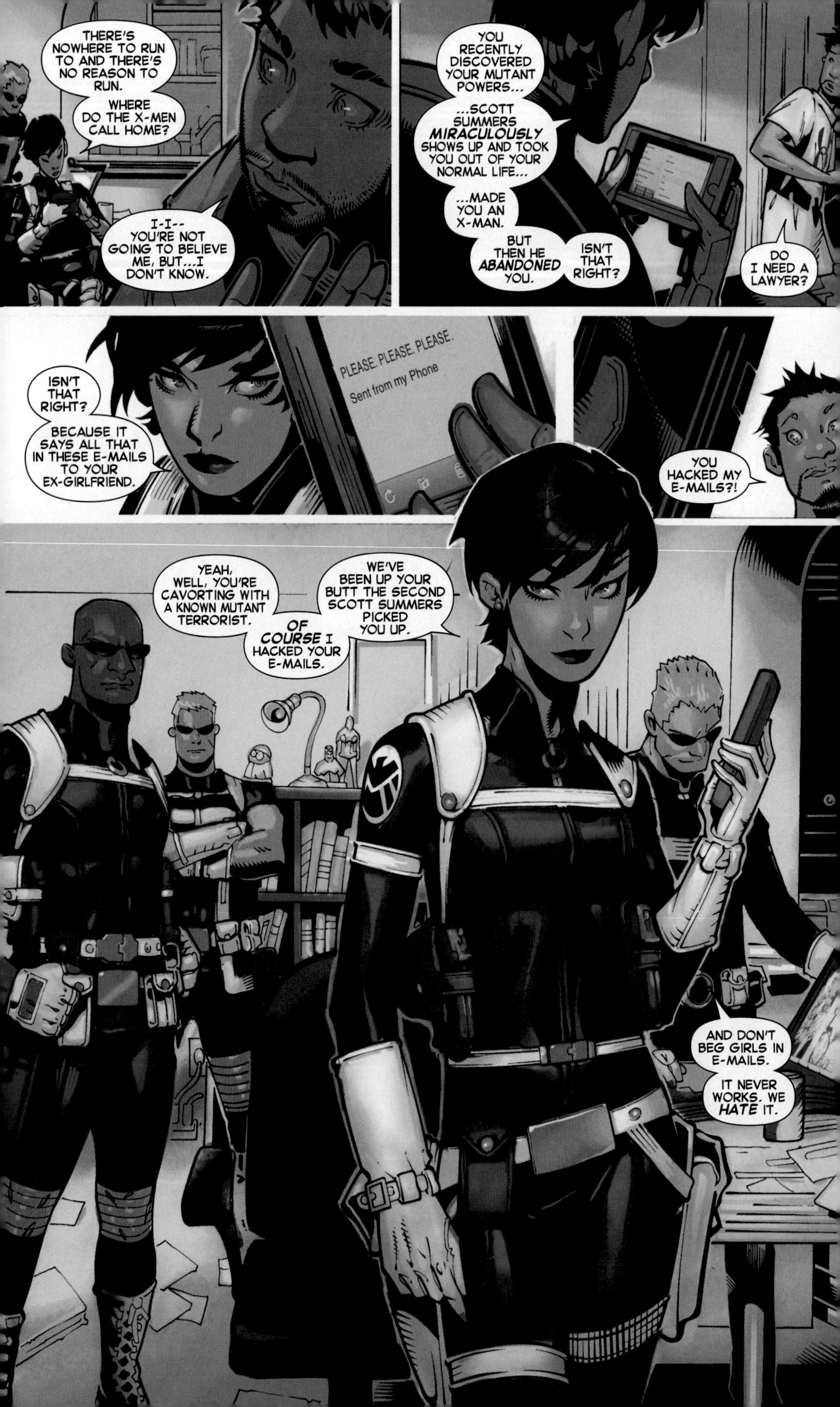
THERE'S NOWHERE TO RUN TO AND THERE'S NO REASON TO RUN.
WHERE DO THE X-MEN CALL HOME?
I-I-- YOU'RE NOT GOING TO BELIEVE ME, BUT...I DON'T KNOW.
YOU RECENTLY DISCOVERED YOUR MUTANT POWERS...
...SCOTT SUMMERS MIRACULOUSLY SHOWS UP AND TOOK YOU OUT OF YOUR NORMAL LIFE...
...MADE YOU AN X-MAN.
BUT THEN HE ABANDONED YOU.
ISN'T THAT RIGHT?
DO I NEED A LAWYER?
ISN'T THAT RIGHT?
BECAUSE IT SAYS ALL THAT IN THESE E-MAILS TO YOUR EX-GIRLFRIEND.
PLEASE. PLEASE. PLEASE.
Sent from my Phone
YOU HACKED MY E-MAILS?!
YEAH, WELL, YOU'RE CAVORTING WITH A KNOWN MUTANT TERRORIST.
OF COURSE I HACKED YOUR E-MAILS.
WE'VE BEEN UP YOUR BUTT THE SECOND SCOTT SUMMERS PICKED YOU UP.
AND DON'T BEG GIRLS IN E-MAILS.
IT NEVER WORKS. WE HATE IT.

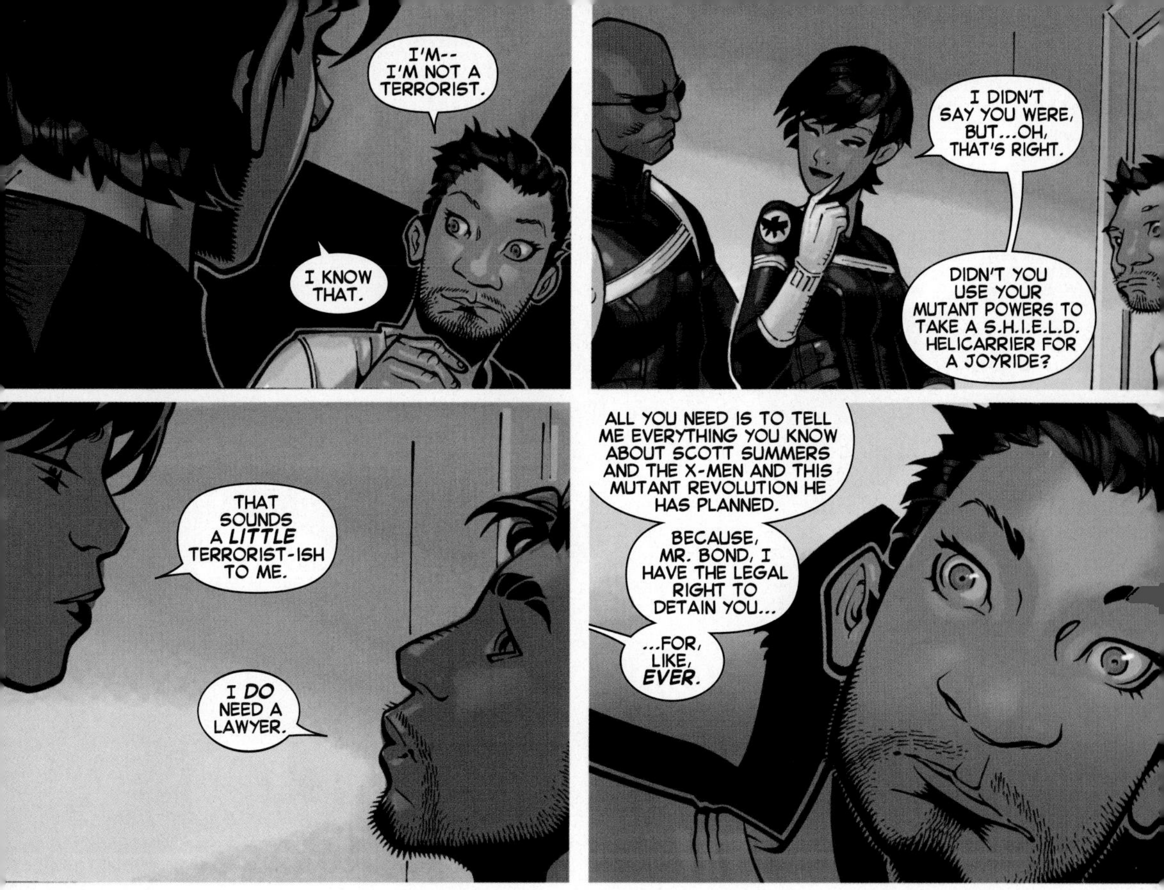
I'M-- I'M NOT A TERRORIST.
I KNOW THAT.
I DIDN'T SAY YOU WERE, BUT...OH, THAT'S RIGHT.
DIDN'T YOU USE YOUR MUTANT POWERS TO TAKE A S.H.I.E.L.D. HELICARRIER FOR A JOYRIDE?
THAT SOUNDS A LITTLE TERRORIST-ISH TO ME.
I DO NEED A LAWYER.
ALL YOU NEED IS TO TELL ME EVERYTHING YOU KNOW ABOUT SCOTT SUMMERS AND THE X-MEN AND THIS MUTANT REVOLUTION HE HAS PLANNED.
BECAUSE, MR. BOND, I HAVE THE LEGAL RIGHT TO DETAIN YOU...
...FOR, LIKE, EVER.

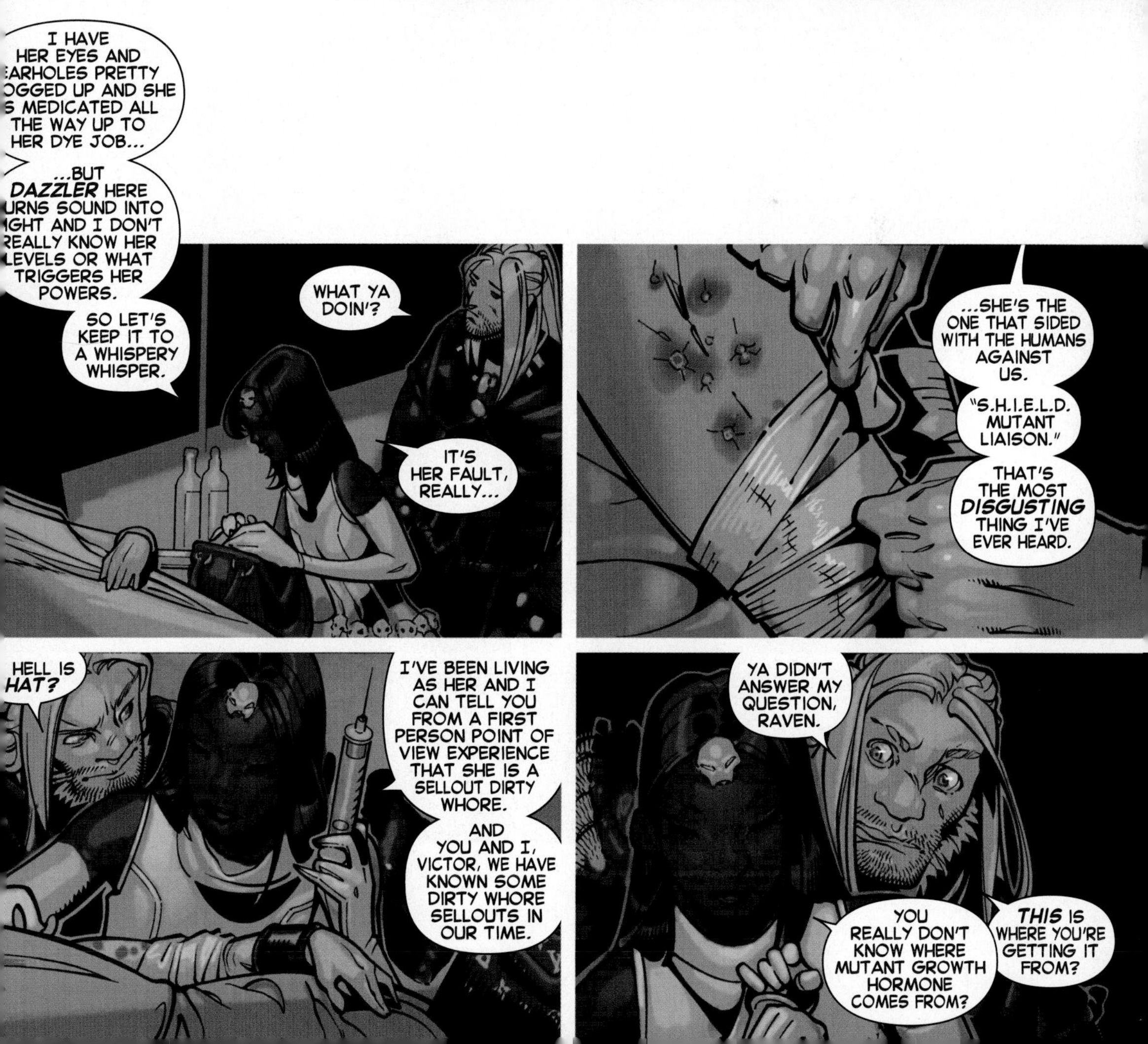
I HAVE HER EYES AND EARHOLES PRETTY OGGED UP AND SHE S MEDICATED ALL THE WAY UP TO HER DYE JOB...
...BUT DAZZLER HERE URNS SOUND INTO IGHT AND I DON'T REALLY KNOW HER LEVELS OR WHAT TRIGGERS HER POWERS.
SO LET'S KEEP IT TO A WHISPERY WHISPER.
WHAT YA DOIN'?
IT'S HER FAULT, REALLY...
...SHE'S THE ONE THAT SIDED WITH THE HUMANS AGAINST US.
"S.H.I.E.L.D. MUTANT LIAISON."
THAT'S THE MOST DISGUSTING THING I'VE EVER HEARD.
HELL IS HAT?
I'VE BEEN LIVING AS HER AND I CAN TELL YOU FROM A FIRST PERSON POINT OF VIEW EXPERIENCE THAT SHE IS A SELLOUT DIRTY WHORE.
AND YOU AND I, VICTOR, WE HAVE KNOWN SOME DIRTY WHORE SELLOUTS IN OUR TIME.
YA DIDN'T ANSWER MY QUESTION, RAVEN.
THIS IS WHERE YOU'RE GETTING IT FROM?
YOU REALLY DON'T KNOW WHERE MUTANT GROWTH HORMONE COMES FROM?

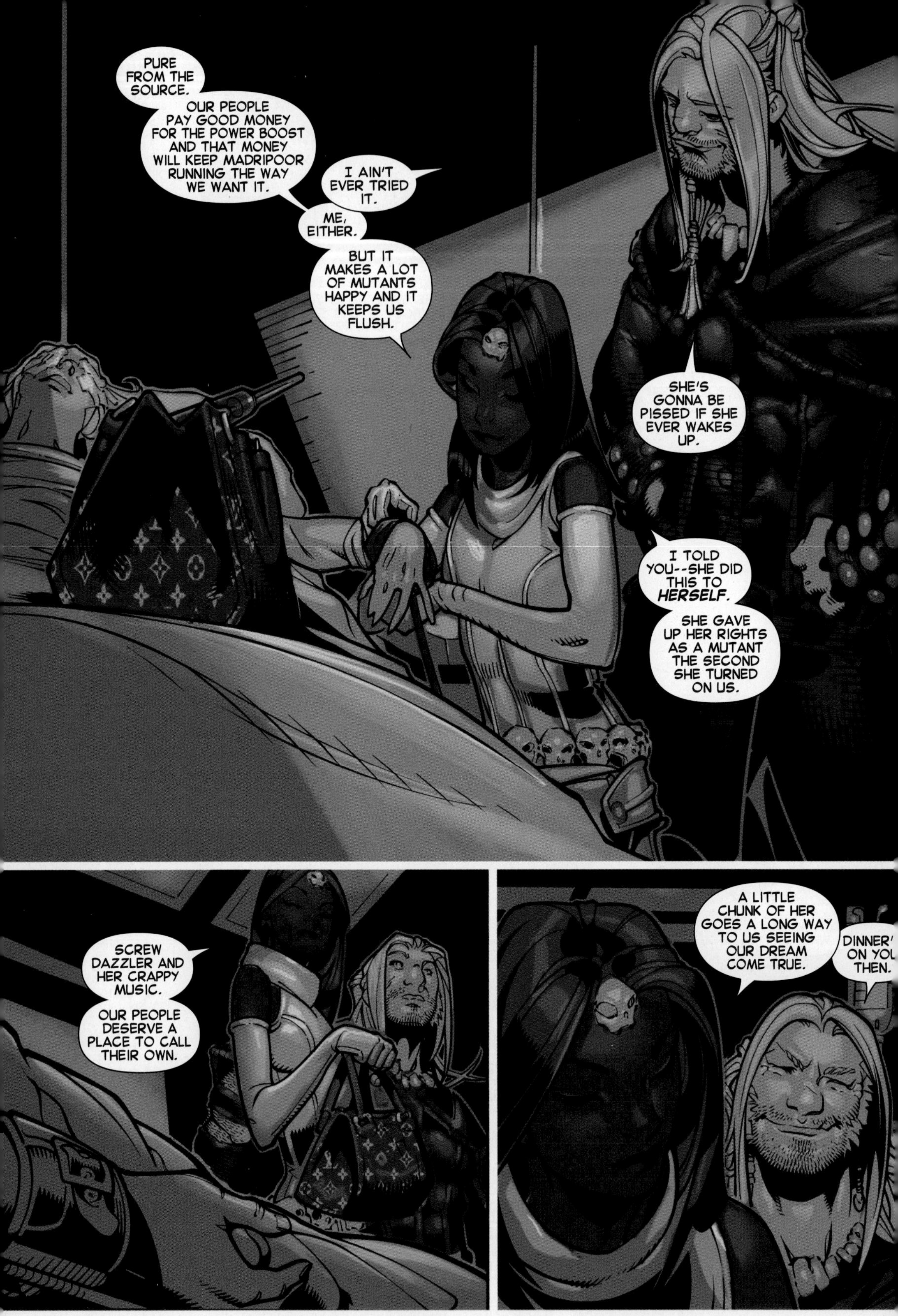
PURE FROM THE SOURCE.
OUR PEOPLE PAY GOOD MONEY FOR THE POWER BOOST AND THAT MONEY WILL KEEP MADRIPOOR RUNNING THE WAY WE WANT IT.
I AIN'T EVER TRIED IT.
ME, EITHER.
BUT IT MAKES A LOT OF MUTANTS HAPPY AND IT KEEPS US FLUSH.
SHE'S GONNA BE PISSED IF SHE EVER WAKES UP.
I TOLD YOU--SHE DID THIS TO HERSELF.
SHE GAVE UP HER RIGHTS AS A MUTANT THE SECOND SHE TURNED ON US.
SCREW DAZZLER AND HER CRAPPY MUSIC.
OUR PEOPLE DESERVE A PLACE TO CALL THEIR OWN.
A LITTLE CHUNK OF HER GOES A LONG WAY TO US SEEING OUR DREAM COME TRUE.
DINNER'S ON YOU THEN.

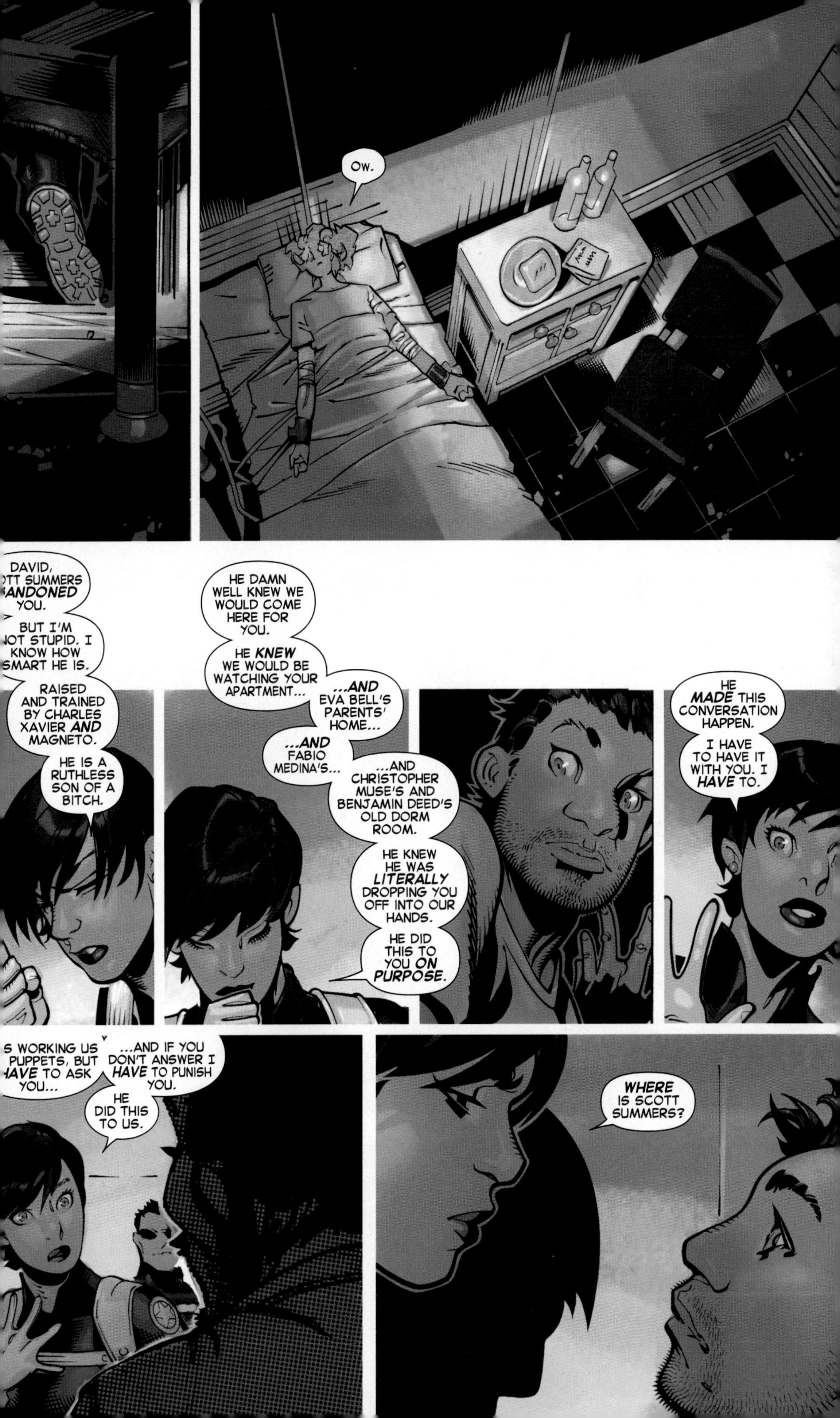
OW.
DAVID, OTT SUMMERS ANDONED YOU.
BUT I'M OT STUPID. I KNOW HOW SMART HE IS.
RAISED AND TRAINED BY CHARLES XAVIER AND MAGNETO.
HE IS A RUTHLESS SON OF A BITCH.
HE DAMN WELL KNEW WE WOULD COME HERE FOR YOU.
HE KNEW WE WOULD BE WATCHING YOUR APARTMENT...
...AND EVA BELL'S PARENTS' HOME...
...AND FABIO MEDINA'S...
...AND CHRISTOPHER MUSE'S AND BENJAMIN DEED'S OLD DORM ROOM.
HE KNEW HE WAS LITERALLY DROPPING YOU OFF INTO OUR HANDS.
HE DID THIS TO YOU ON PURPOSE.
HE MADE THIS CONVERSATION HAPPEN.
I HAVE TO HAVE IT WITH YOU. I HAVE TO.
S WORKING US PUPPETS, BUT HAVE TO ASK YOU...
...AND IF YOU DON'T ANSWER I HAVE TO PUNISH YOU.
HE DID THIS TO US.
WHERE IS SCOTT SUMMERS?

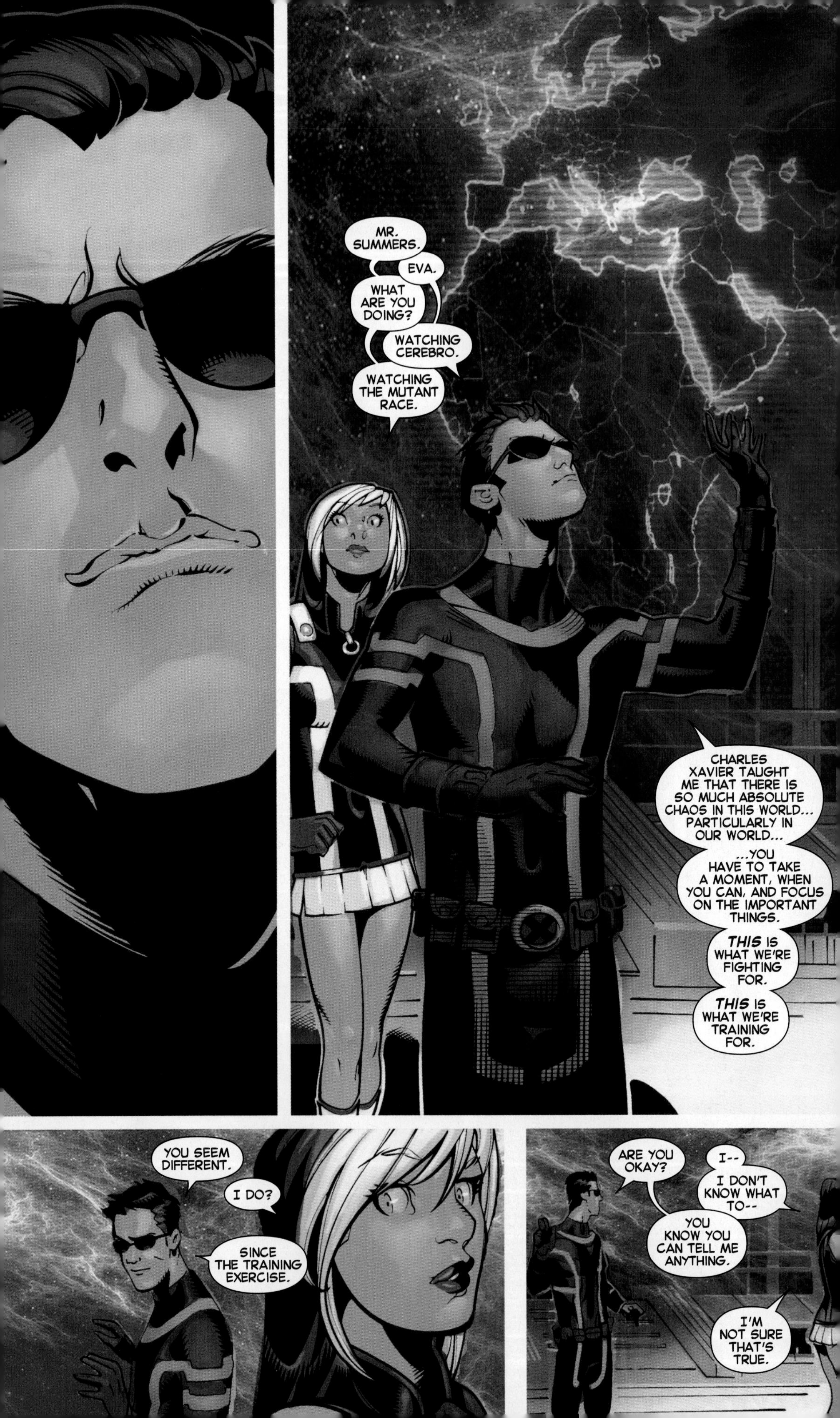
MR. SUMMERS.
EVA.
WHAT ARE YOU DOING?
WATCHING CEREBRO.
WATCHING THE MUTANT RACE.
CHARLES XAVIER TAUGHT ME THAT THERE IS SO MUCH ABSOLUTE CHAOS IN THIS WORLD... PARTICULARLY IN OUR WORLD...
...YOU HAVE TO TAKE A MOMENT, WHEN YOU CAN, AND FOCUS ON THE IMPORTANT THINGS.
THIS IS WHAT WE'RE FIGHTING FOR.
THIS IS WHAT WE'RE TRAINING FOR.
YOU SEEM DIFFERENT.
I DO?
SINCE THE TRAINING EXERCISE.
ARE YOU OKAY?
I--
I DON'T KNOW WHAT TO--
YOU KNOW YOU CAN TELL ME ANYTHING.
I'M NOT SURE THAT'S TRUE.

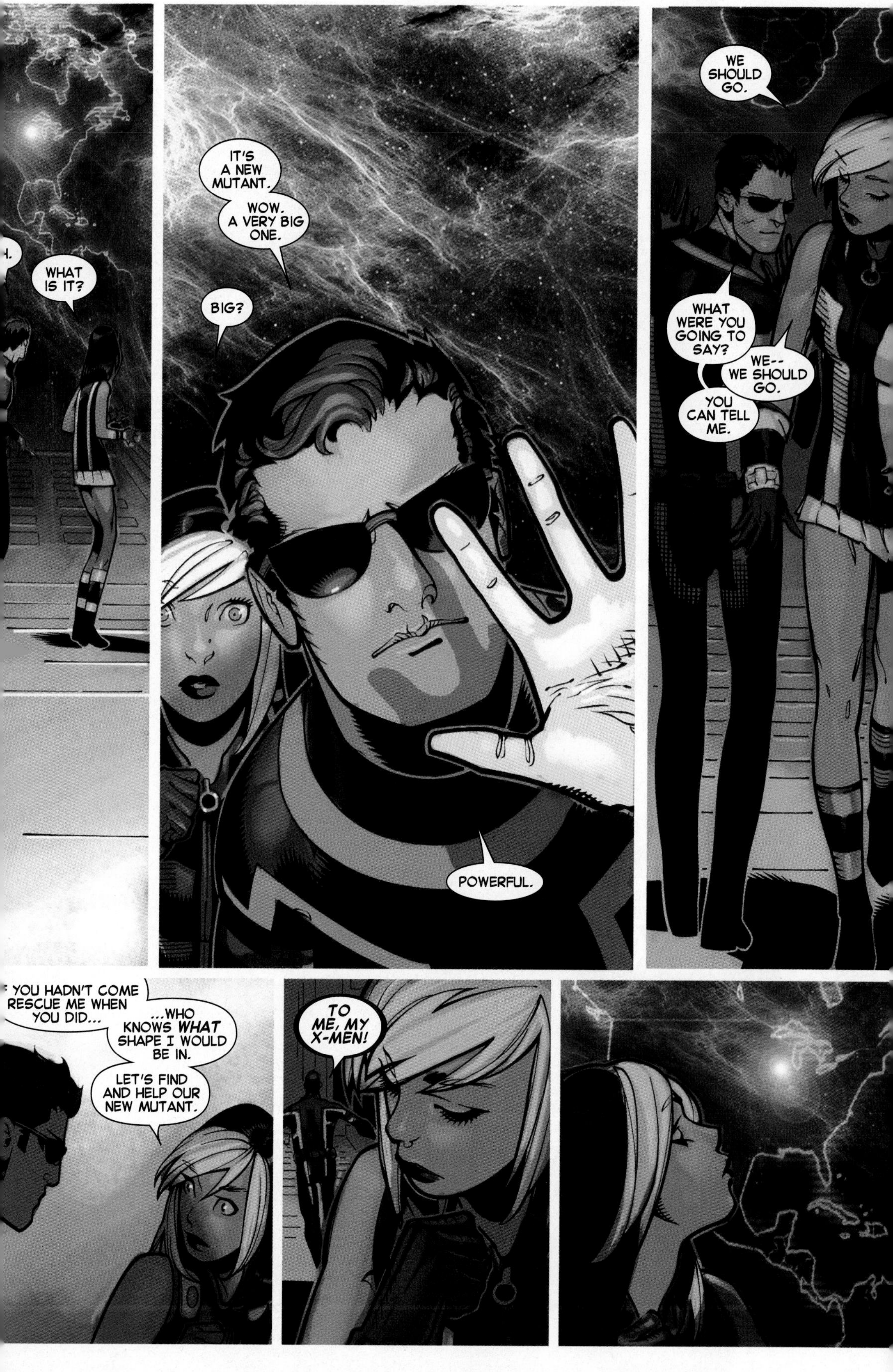
WHAT IS IT?
IT'S A NEW MUTANT.
WOW. A VERY BIG ONE.
BIG?
POWERFUL.
WE SHOULD GO.
WHAT WERE YOU GOING TO SAY?
WE-- WE SHOULD GO.
YOU CAN TELL ME.
F YOU HADN'T COME RESCUE ME WHEN YOU DID...
...WHO KNOWS *WHAT* SHAPE I WOULD BE IN.
LET'S FIND AND HELP OUR NEW MUTANT.
TO ME, MY X-MEN!

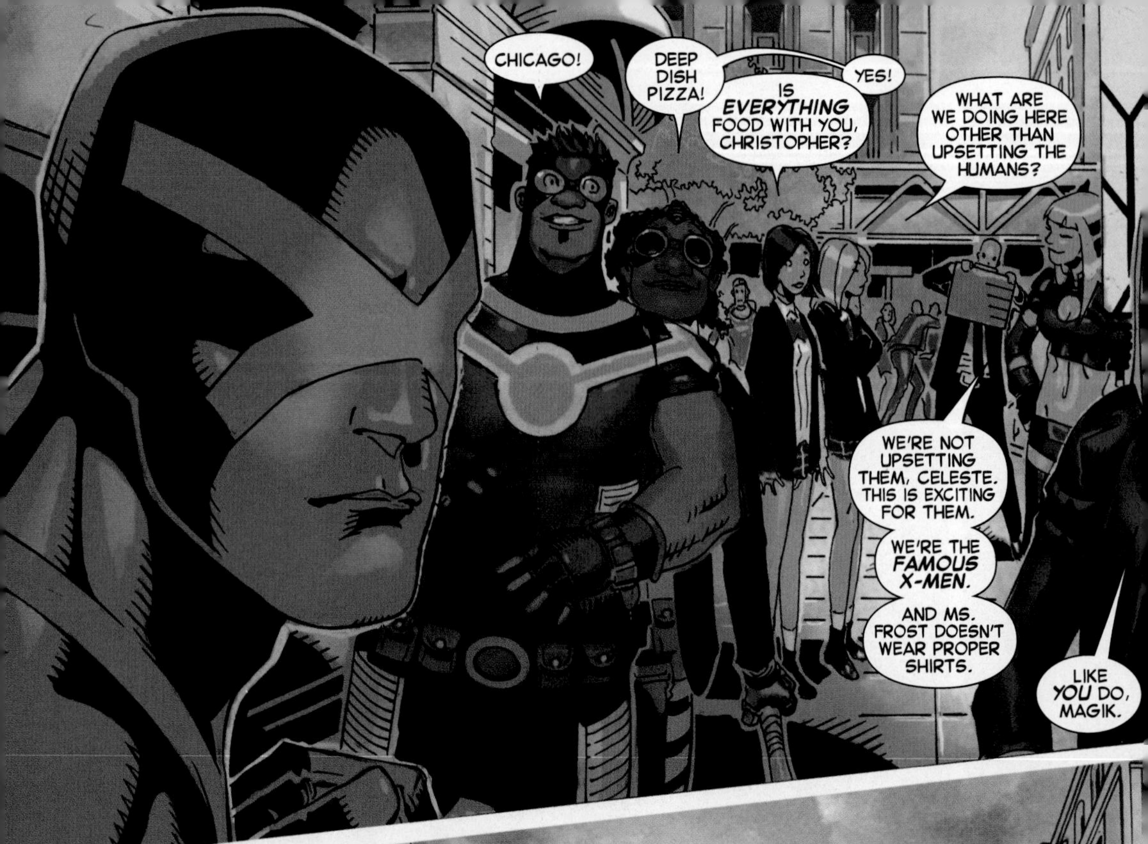
CHICAGO!
DEEP DISH PIZZA!
YES!
IS EVERYTHING FOOD WITH YOU, CHRISTOPHER?
WHAT ARE WE DOING HERE OTHER THAN UPSETTING THE HUMANS?
WE'RE NOT UPSETTING THEM, CELESTE. THIS IS EXCITING FOR THEM.
WE'RE THE FAMOUS X-MEN.
AND MS. FROST DOESN'T WEAR PROPER SHIRTS.
LIKE YOU DO, MAGIK.

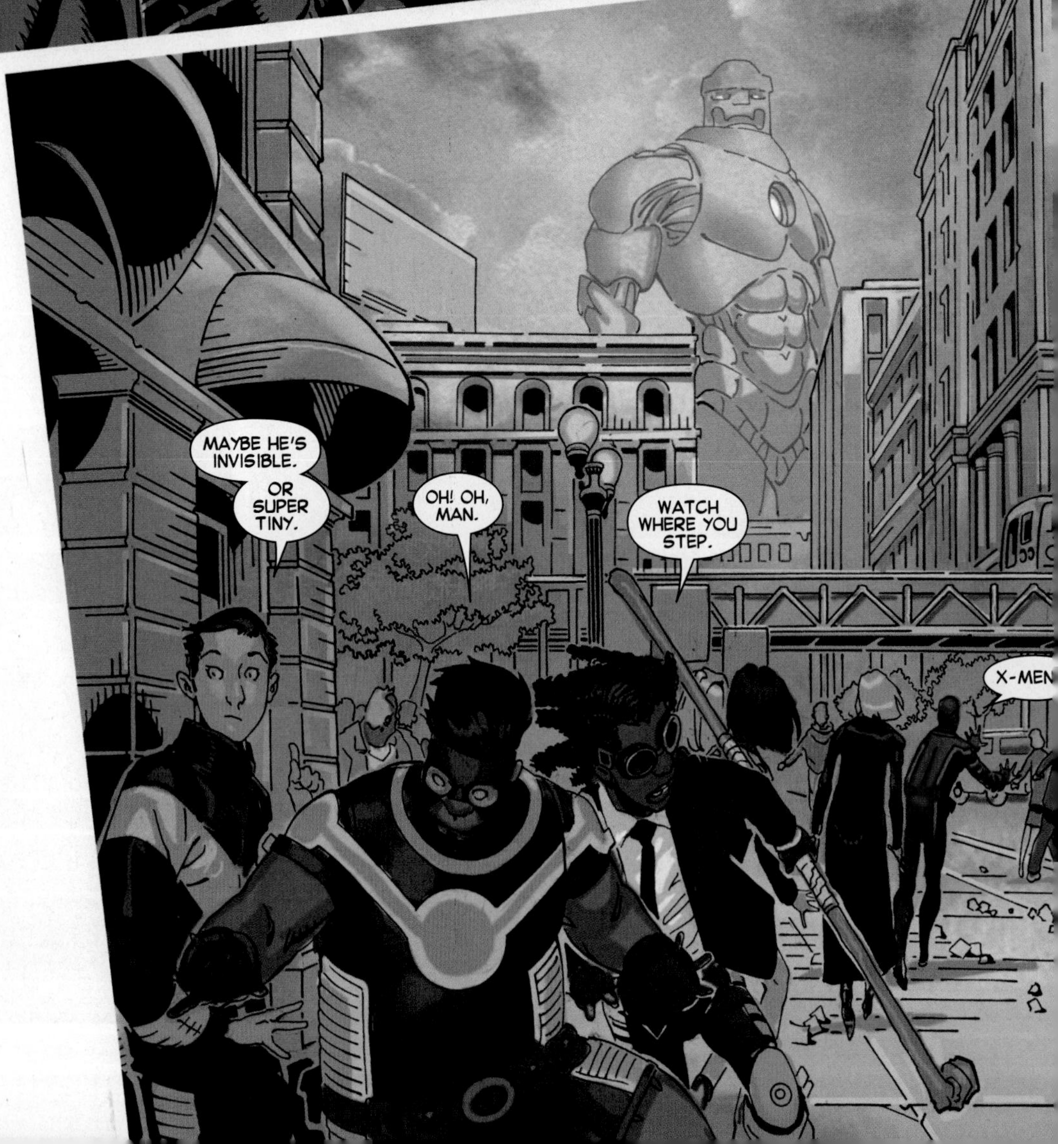
MAYBE HE'S INVISIBLE.
OR SUPER TINY.
OH! OH, MAN.
WATCH WHERE YOU STEP.
X-MEN

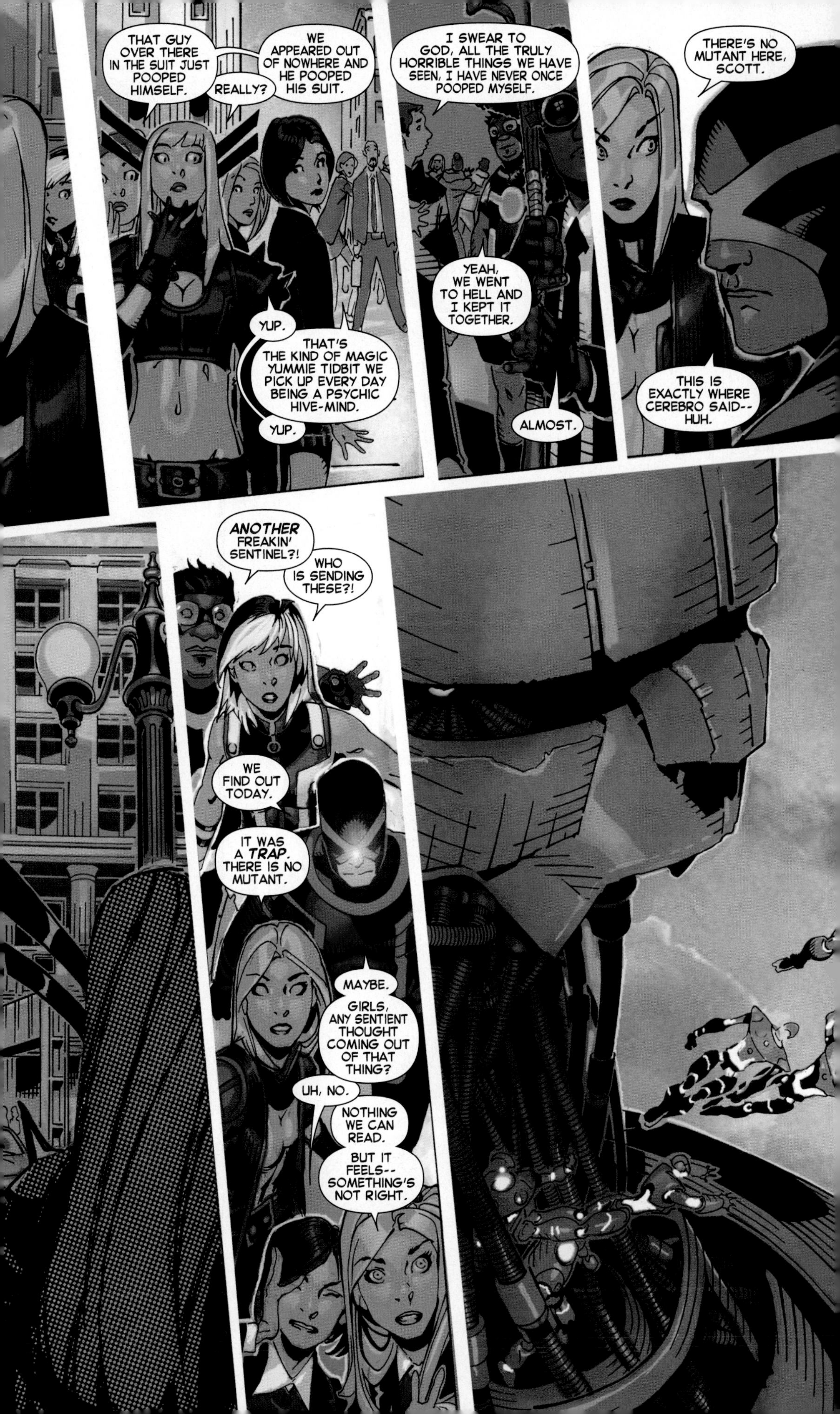
THAT GUY OVER THERE IN THE SUIT JUST POOPED HIMSELF.
REALLY?
WE APPEARED OUT OF NOWHERE AND HE POOPED HIS SUIT.
YUP.
THAT'S THE KIND OF MAGIC YUMMIE TIDBIT WE PICK UP EVERY DAY BEING A PSYCHIC HIVE-MIND.
YUP.
I SWEAR TO GOD, ALL THE TRULY HORRIBLE THINGS WE HAVE SEEN, I HAVE NEVER ONCE POOPED MYSELF.
YEAH, WE WENT TO HELL AND I KEPT IT TOGETHER.
ALMOST.
THERE'S NO MUTANT HERE, SCOTT.
THIS IS EXACTLY WHERE CEREBRO SAID-- HUH.
ANOTHER FREAKIN' SENTINEL?!
WHO IS SENDING THESE?!
WE FIND OUT TODAY.
IT WAS A TRAP. THERE IS NO MUTANT.
MAYBE.
GIRLS, ANY SENTIENT THOUGHT COMING OUT OF THAT THING?
UH, NO.
NOTHING WE CAN READ.
BUT IT FEELS-- SOMETHING'S NOT RIGHT.

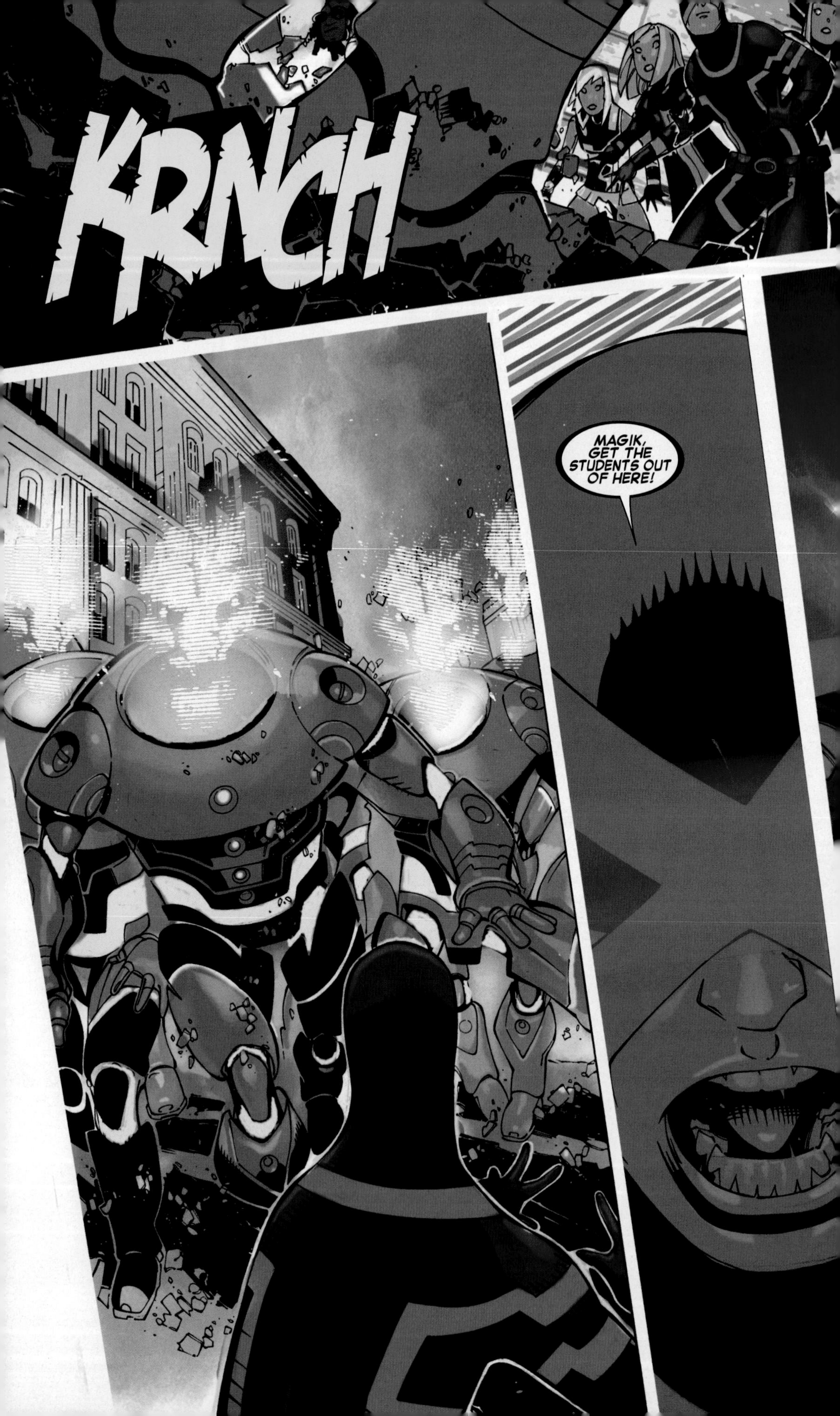
KRNCH
MAGIK, GET THE STUDENTS OUT OF HERE!

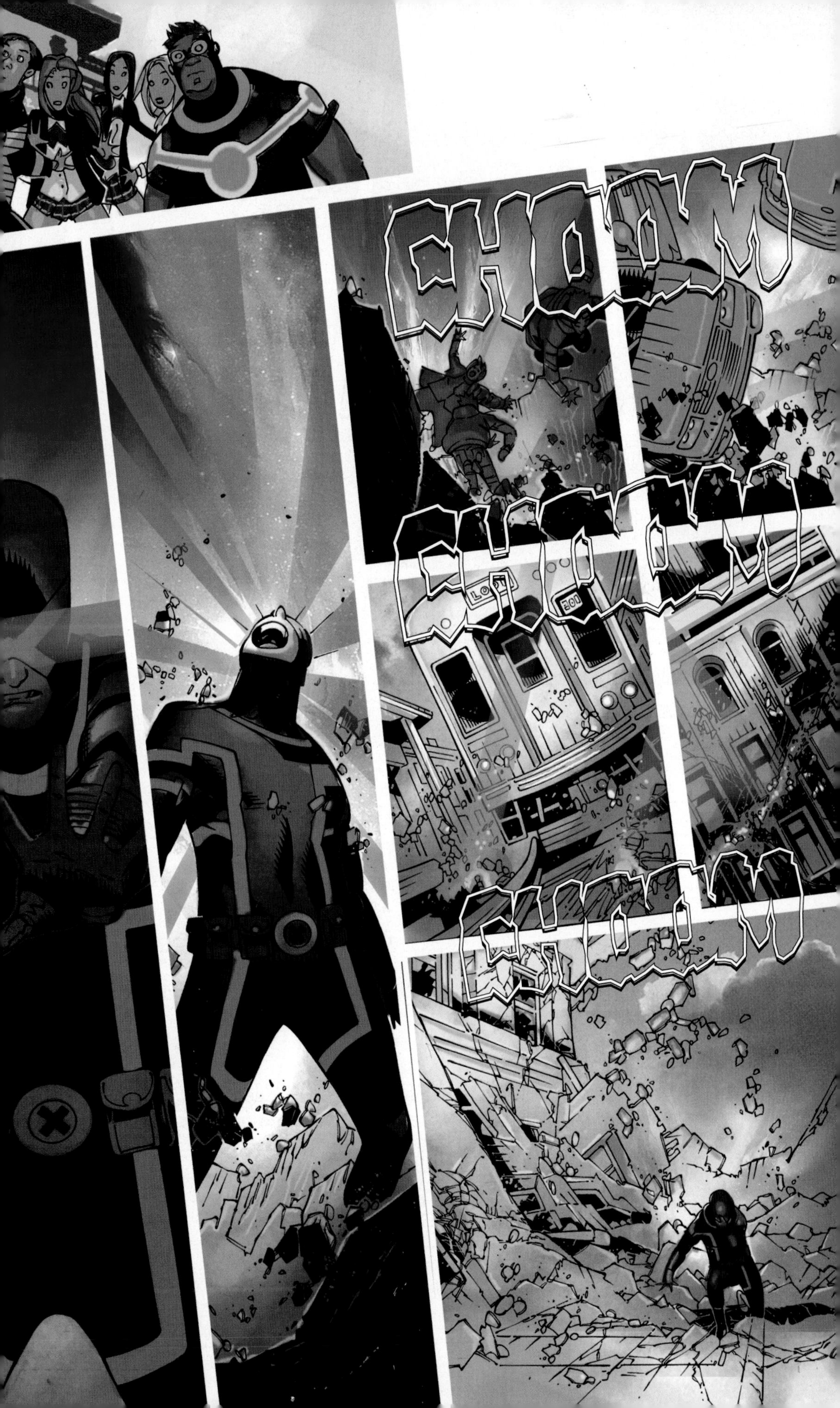
CHOOOM
CHOOOM
CHOOOM

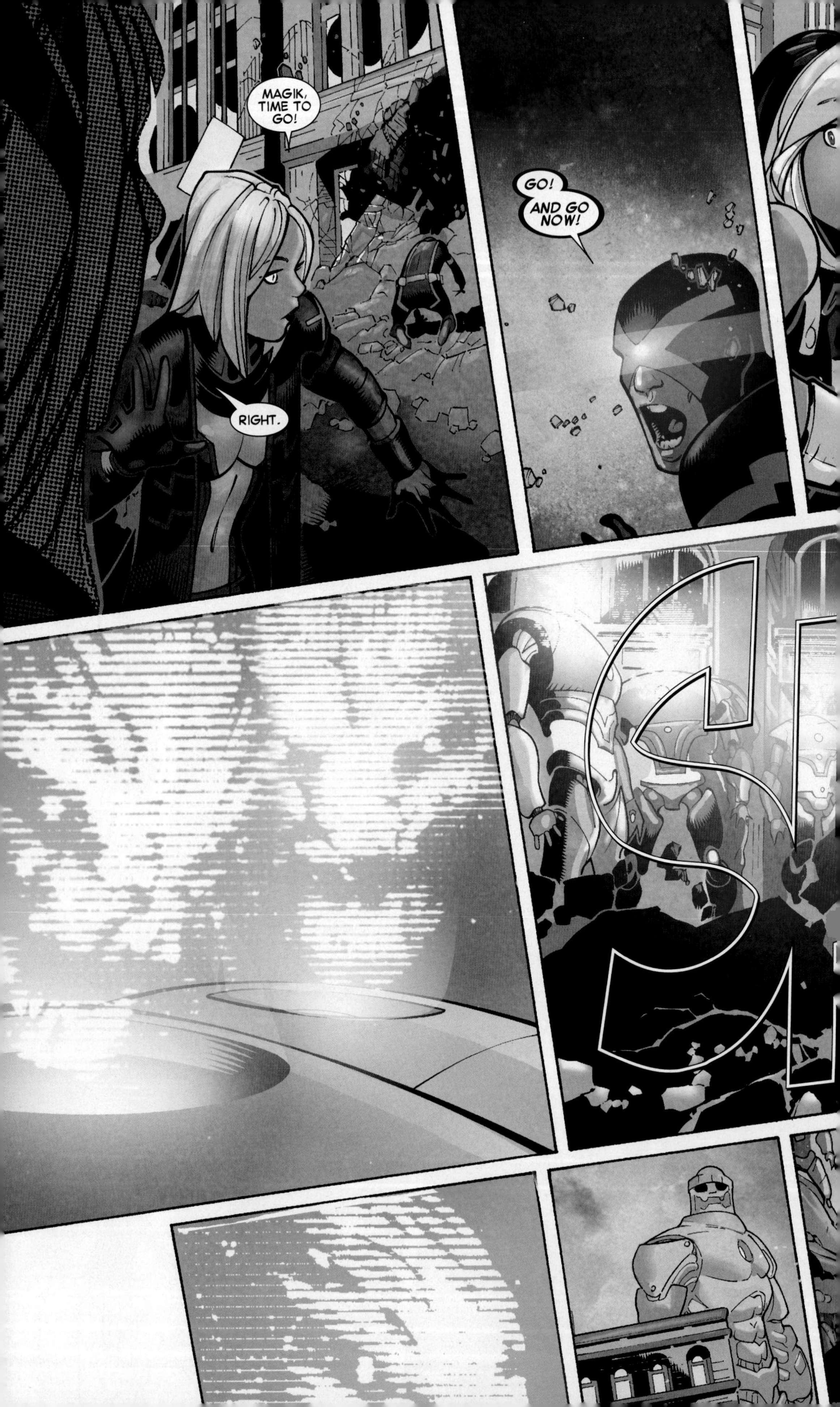
MAGIK, TIME TO GO!
RIGHT.
GO! AND GO NOW!

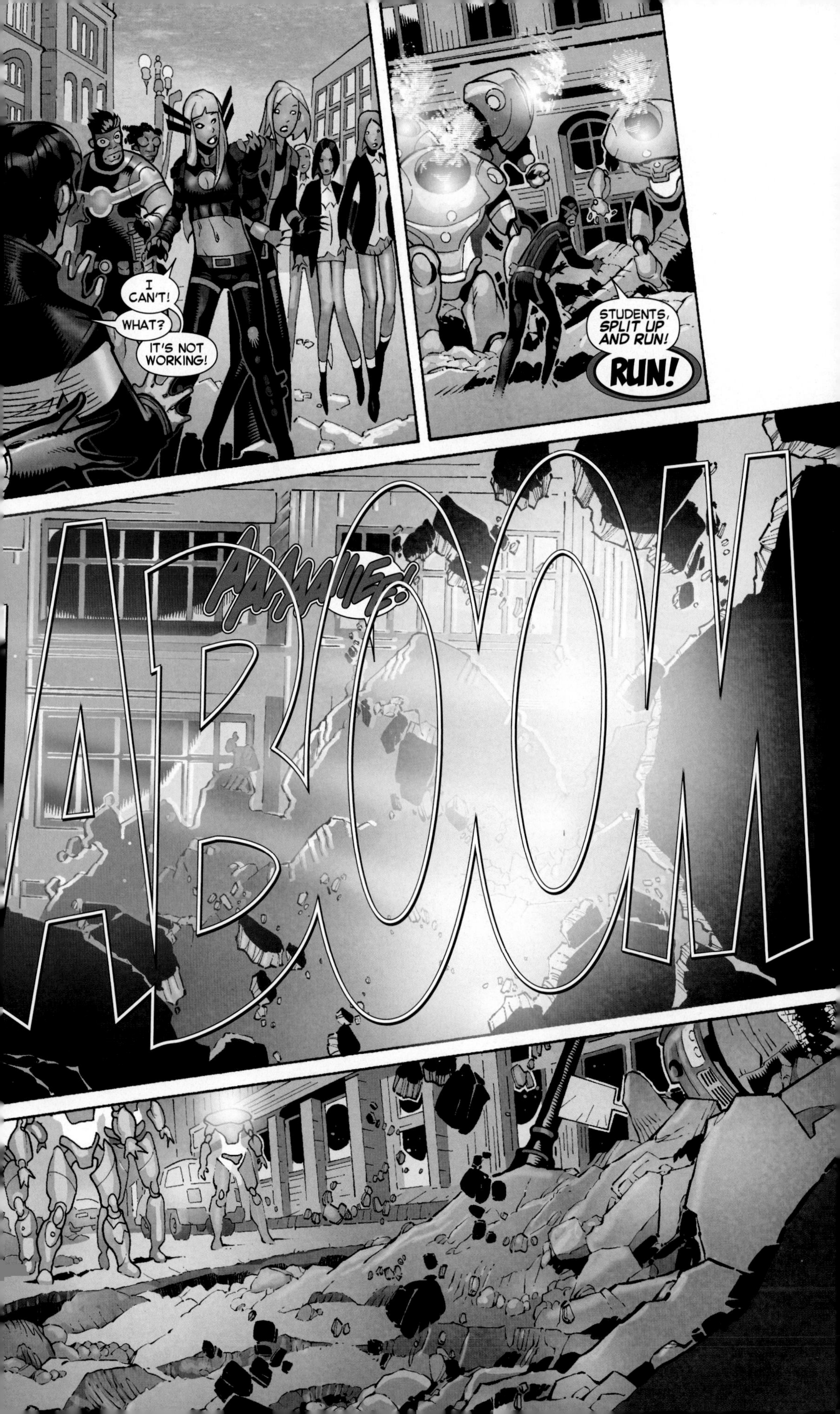
I CAN'T!
WHAT?
IT'S NOT WORKING!
STUDENTS, SPLIT UP AND RUN!
RUN!
AAAAAIIEEE!
ABOOM

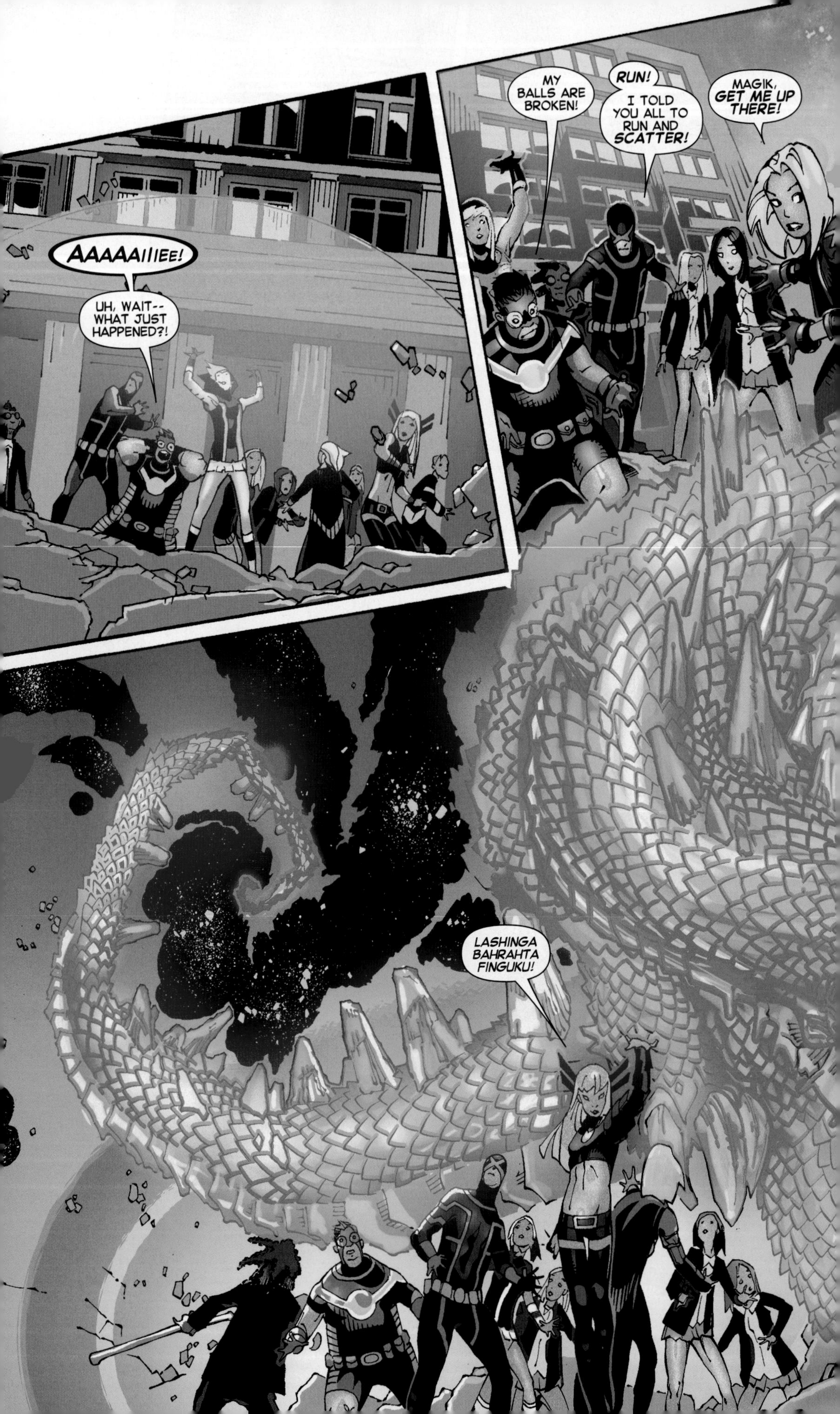
AAAAAIIIEE!
UH, WAIT-- WHAT JUST HAPPENED?!
MY BALLS ARE BROKEN!
RUN! I TOLD YOU ALL TO RUN AND SCATTER!
MAGIK, GET ME UP THERE!
LASHINGA BAHRAHTA FINGUKU!

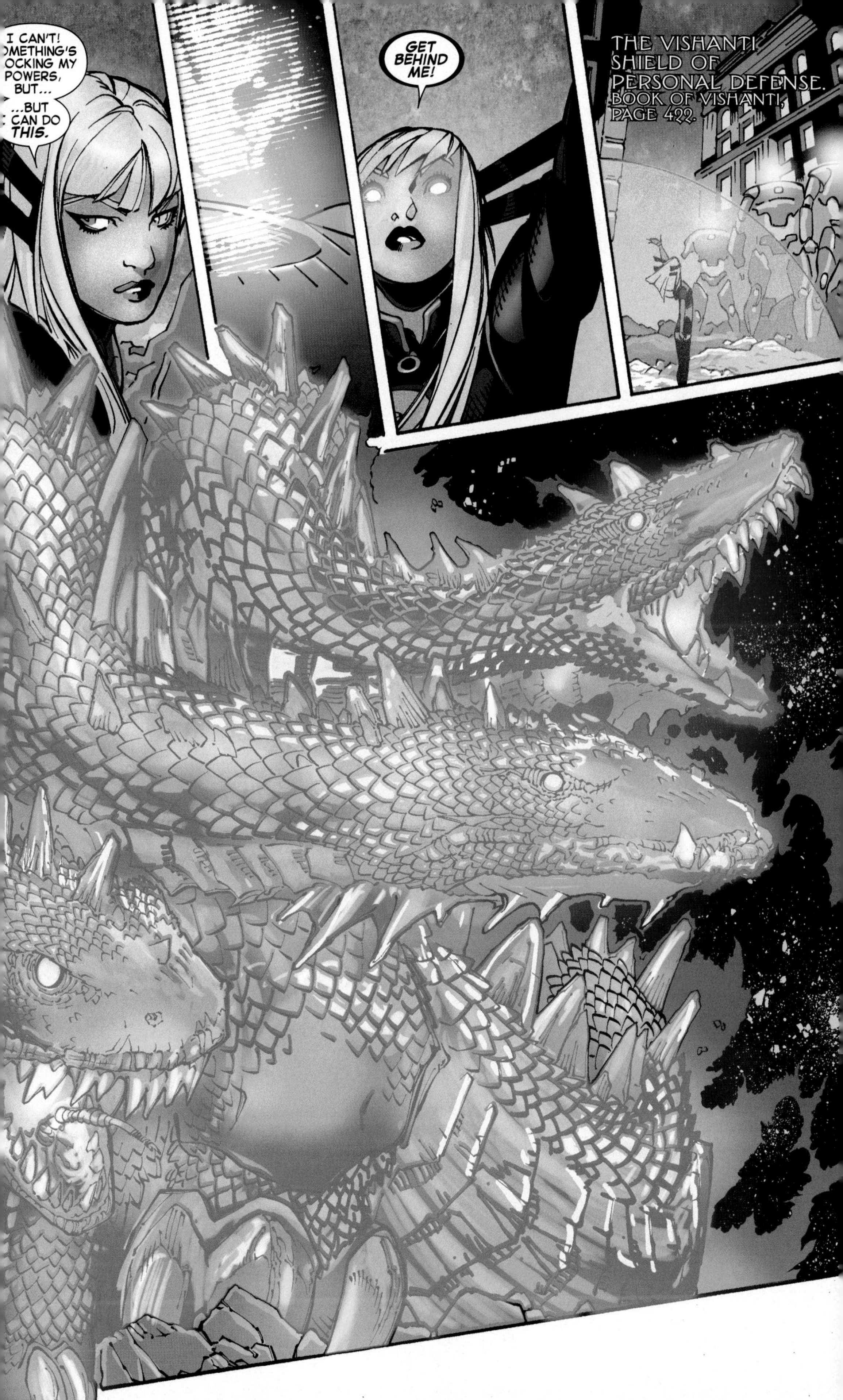
I CAN'T! OMETHING'S OCKING MY POWERS, BUT...
...BUT CAN DO THIS.
GET BEHIND ME!
THE VISHANTI SHIELD OF PERSONAL DEFENSE. BOOK OF VISHANTI, PAGE 422.

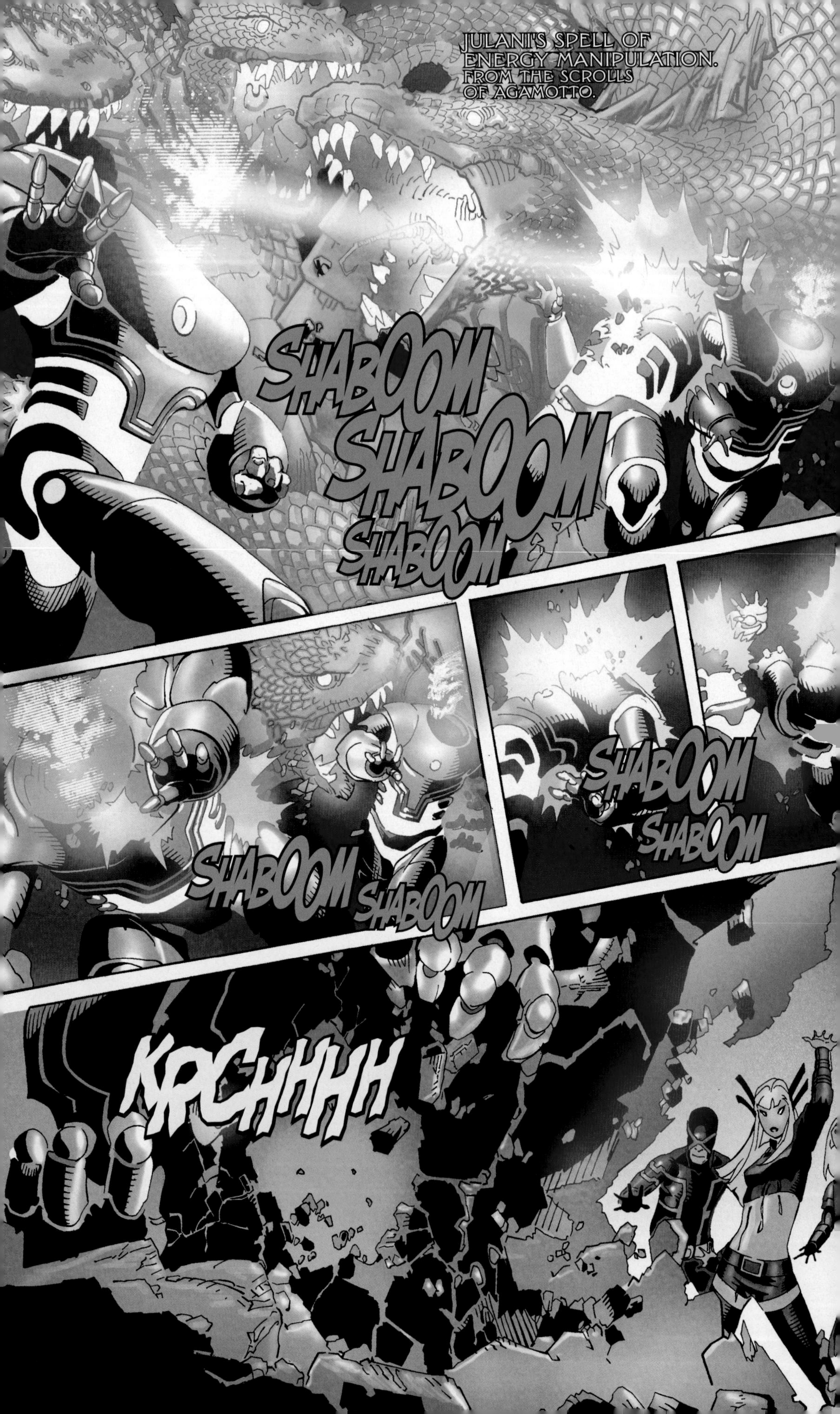
JULANI'S SPELL OF ENERGY MANIPULATION. FROM THE SCROLLS OF AGAMOTTO.
SHABOOM
SHABOOM
SHABOOM
SHABOOM
SHABOOM
SHABOOM
SHABOOM
KRCHHHH

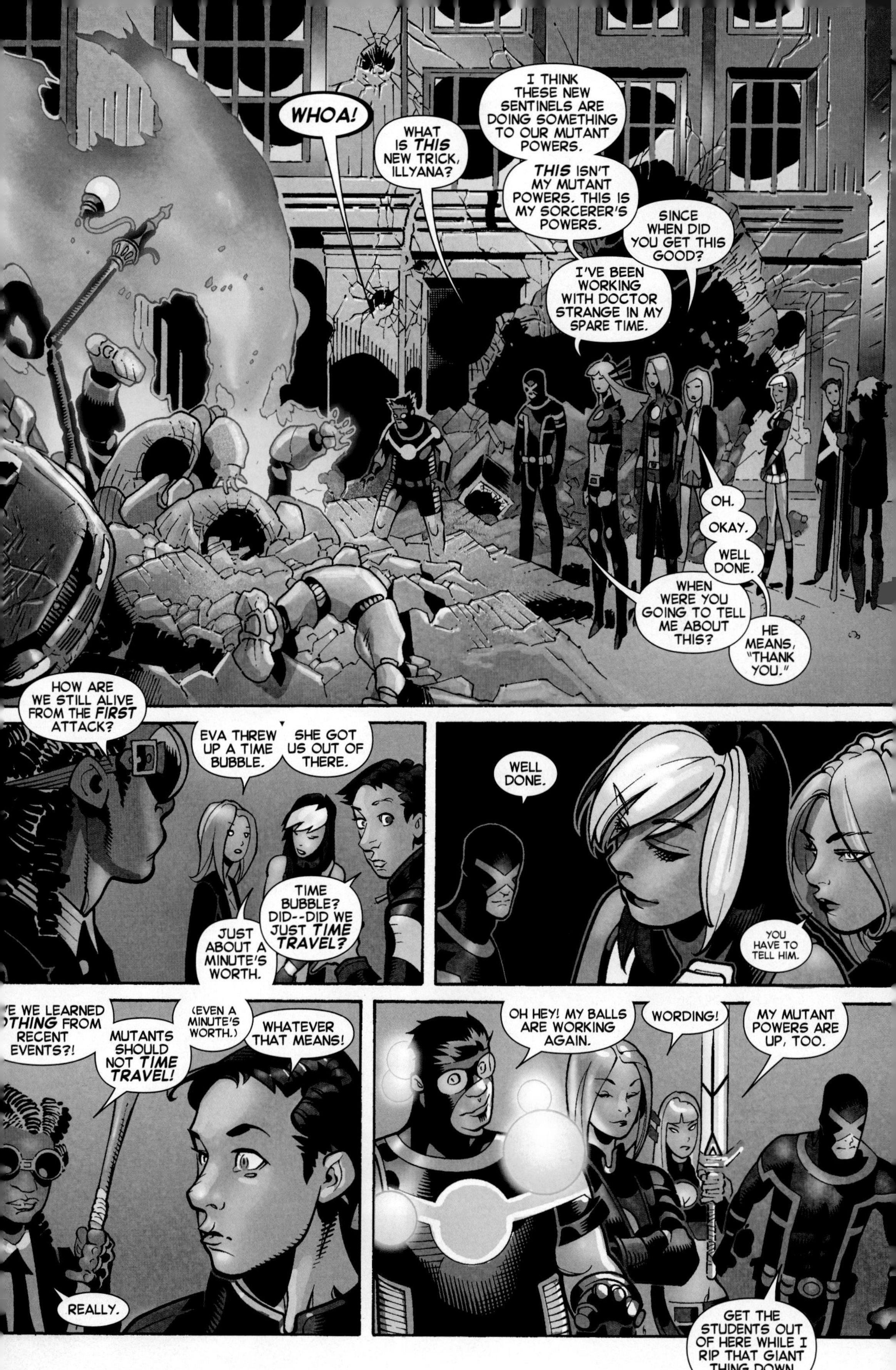
WHOA!
WHAT IS THIS NEW TRICK, ILLYANA?
I THINK THESE NEW SENTINELS ARE DOING SOMETHING TO OUR MUTANT POWERS.
THIS ISN'T MY MUTANT POWERS. THIS IS MY SORCERER'S POWERS.
SINCE WHEN DID YOU GET THIS GOOD?
I'VE BEEN WORKING WITH DOCTOR STRANGE IN MY SPARE TIME.
OH.
OKAY.
WELL DONE.
WHEN WERE YOU GOING TO TELL ME ABOUT THIS?
HE MEANS, "THANK YOU."
HOW ARE WE STILL ALIVE FROM THE FIRST ATTACK?
EVA THREW UP A TIME BUBBLE.
SHE GOT US OUT OF THERE.
TIME BUBBLE? DID--DID WE JUST TIME TRAVEL?
JUST ABOUT A MINUTE'S WORTH.
WELL DONE.
YOU HAVE TO TELL HIM.
'E WE LEARNED THING FROM RECENT EVENTS?!
MUTANTS SHOULD NOT TIME TRAVEL!
(EVEN A MINUTE'S WORTH.)
WHATEVER THAT MEANS!
REALLY.
OH HEY! MY BALLS ARE WORKING AGAIN.
WORDING!
MY MUTANT POWERS ARE UP, TOO.
GET THE STUDENTS OUT OF HERE WHILE I RIP THAT GIANT THING DOWN TO THE--

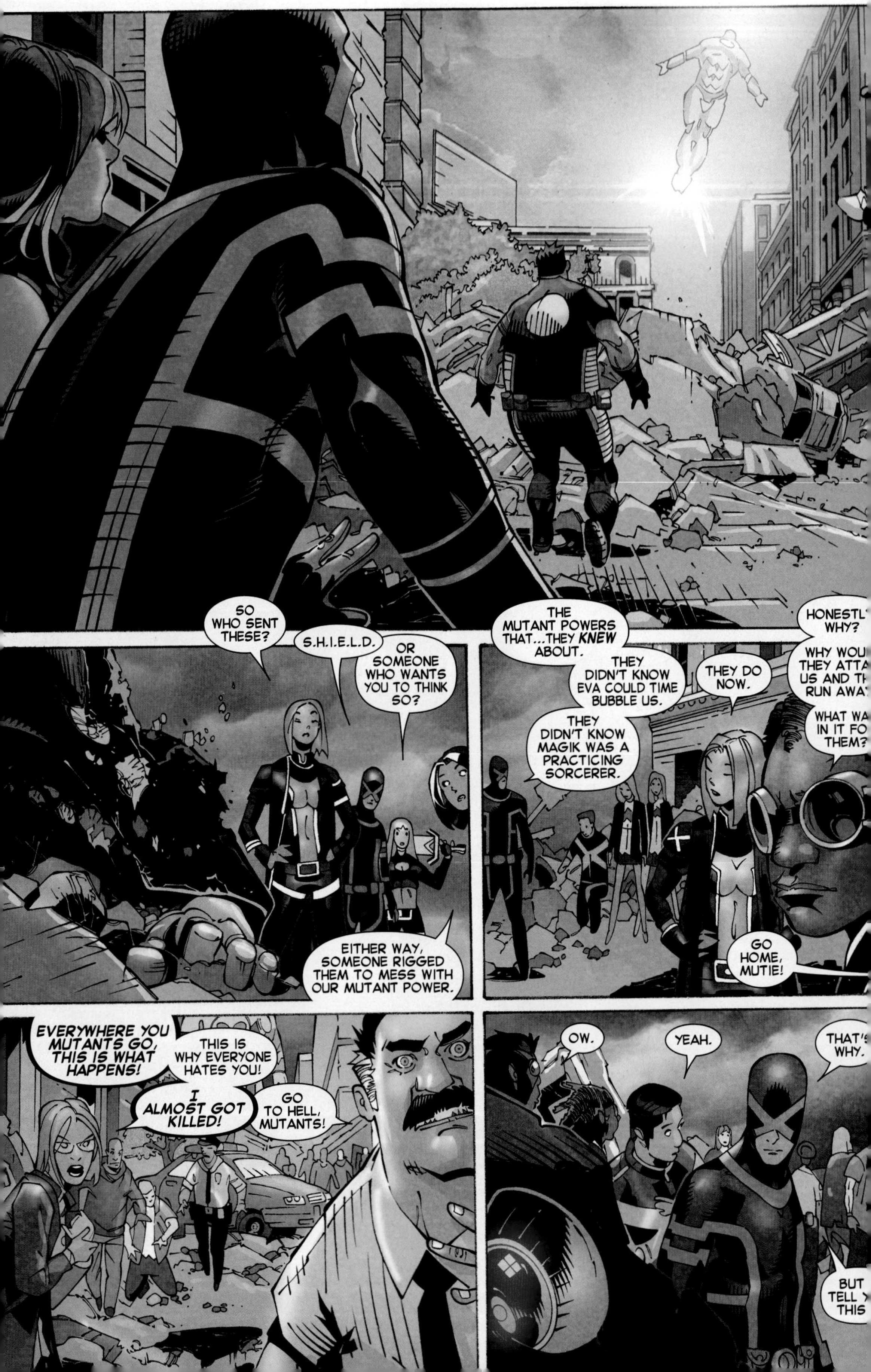
SO WHO SENT THESE?
S.H.I.E.L.D.
OR SOMEONE WHO WANTS YOU TO THINK SO?
EITHER WAY, SOMEONE RIGGED THEM TO MESS WITH OUR MUTANT POWER.
THE MUTANT POWERS THAT...THEY *KNEW* ABOUT.
THEY DIDN'T KNOW EVA COULD TIME BUBBLE US.
THEY DIDN'T KNOW MAGIK WAS A PRACTICING SORCERER.
THEY DO NOW.
HONESTL WHY?
WHY WOU THEY ATTA US AND TH RUN AWA
WHAT WA IN IT FO THEM?
GO HOME, MUTIE!
EVERYWHERE YOU MUTANTS GO, THIS IS WHAT HAPPENS!
THIS IS WHY EVERYONE HATES YOU!
I ALMOST GOT KILLED!
GO TO HELL, MUTANTS!
OW.
YEAH.
THAT'S WHY.
BUT TELL Y THIS

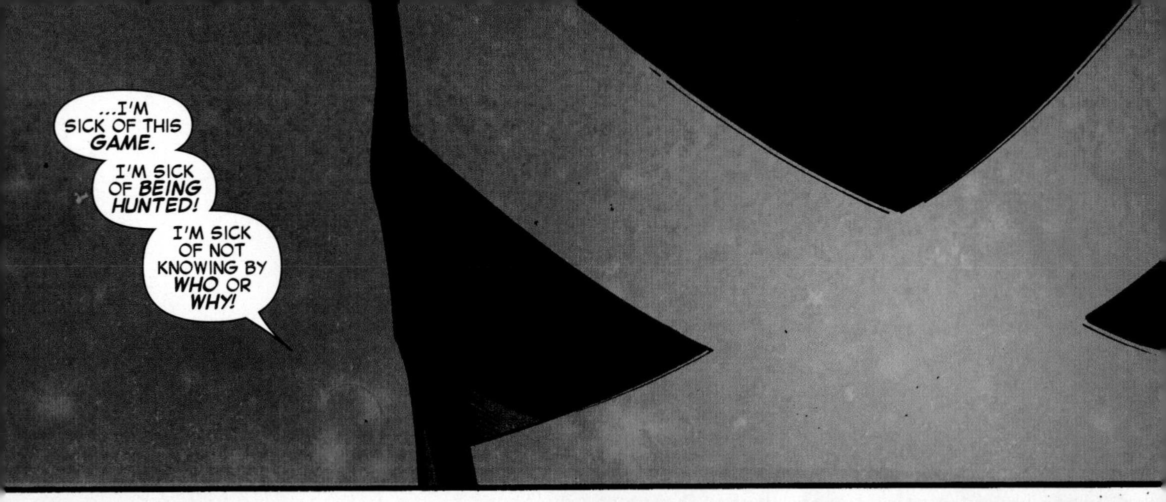

...I'M SICK OF THIS GAME.
I'M SICK OF BEING HUNTED!
I'M SICK OF NOT KNOWING BY WHO OR WHY!

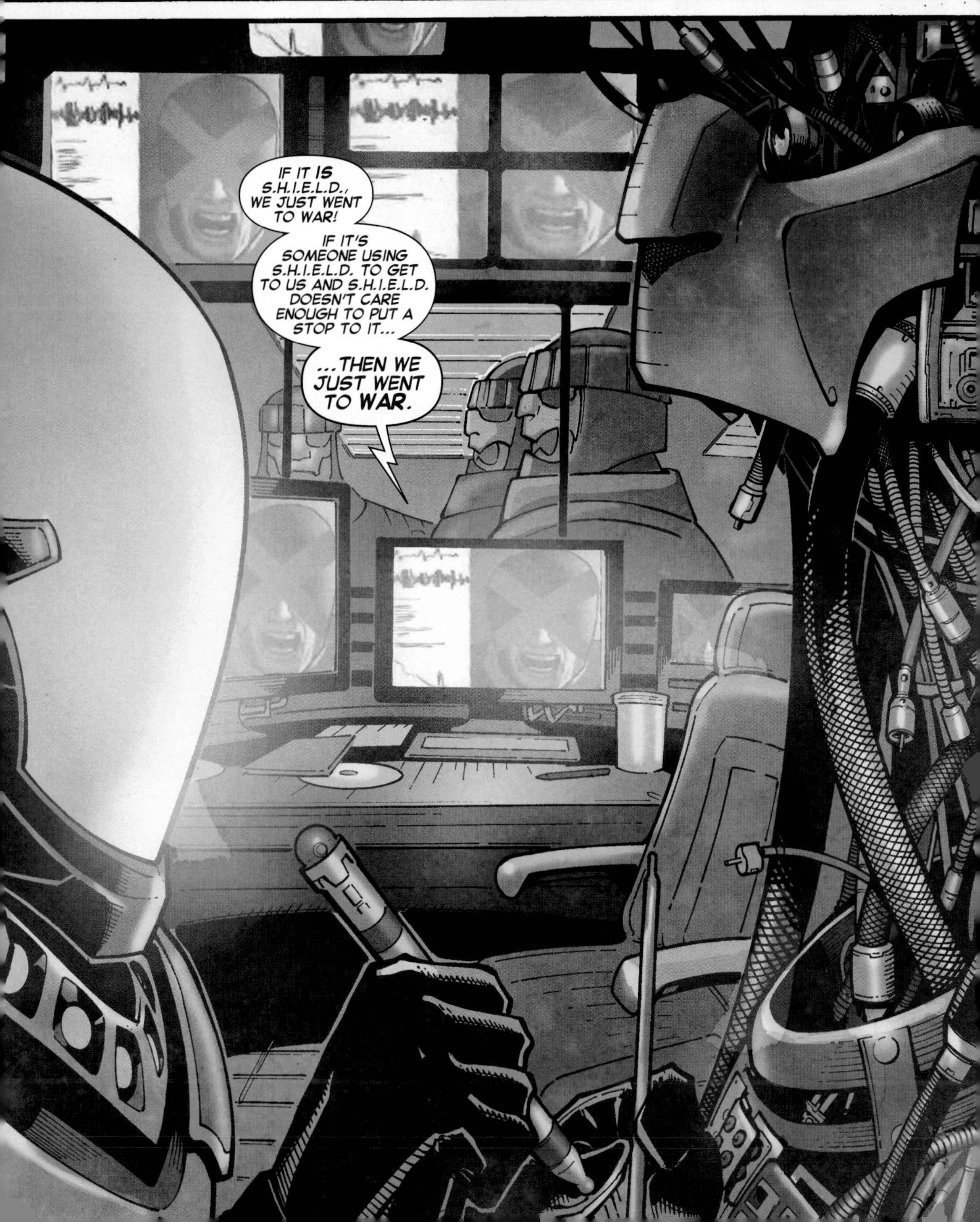

IF IT IS S.H.I.E.L.D., WE JUST WENT TO WAR!
IF IT'S SOMEONE USING S.H.I.E.L.D. TO GET TO US AND S.H.I.E.L.D. DOESN'T CARE ENOUGH TO PUT A STOP TO IT...
...THEN WE JUST WENT TO WAR.

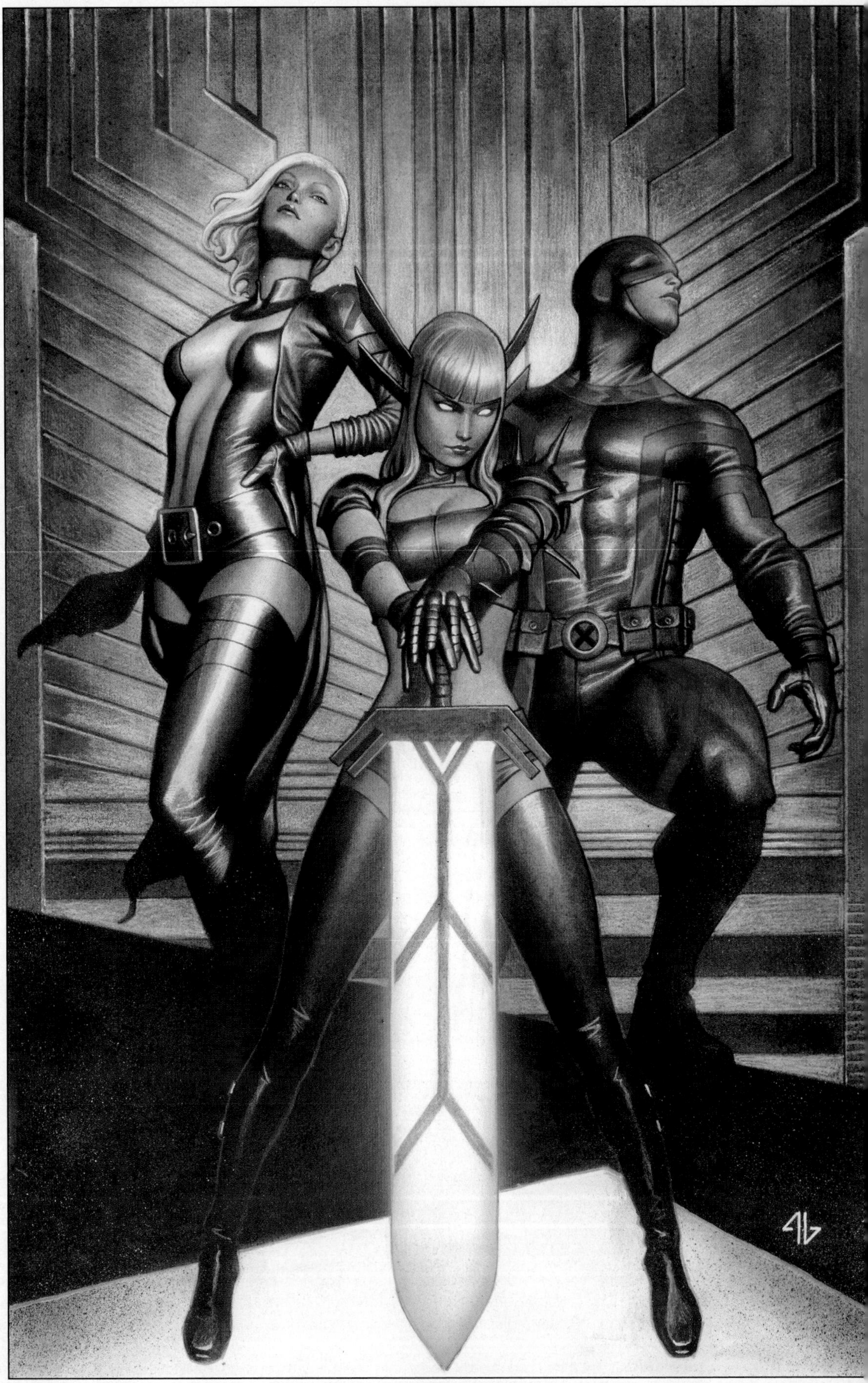

UNCANNY X-MEN #20 VARIANT
BY ADI GRANOV

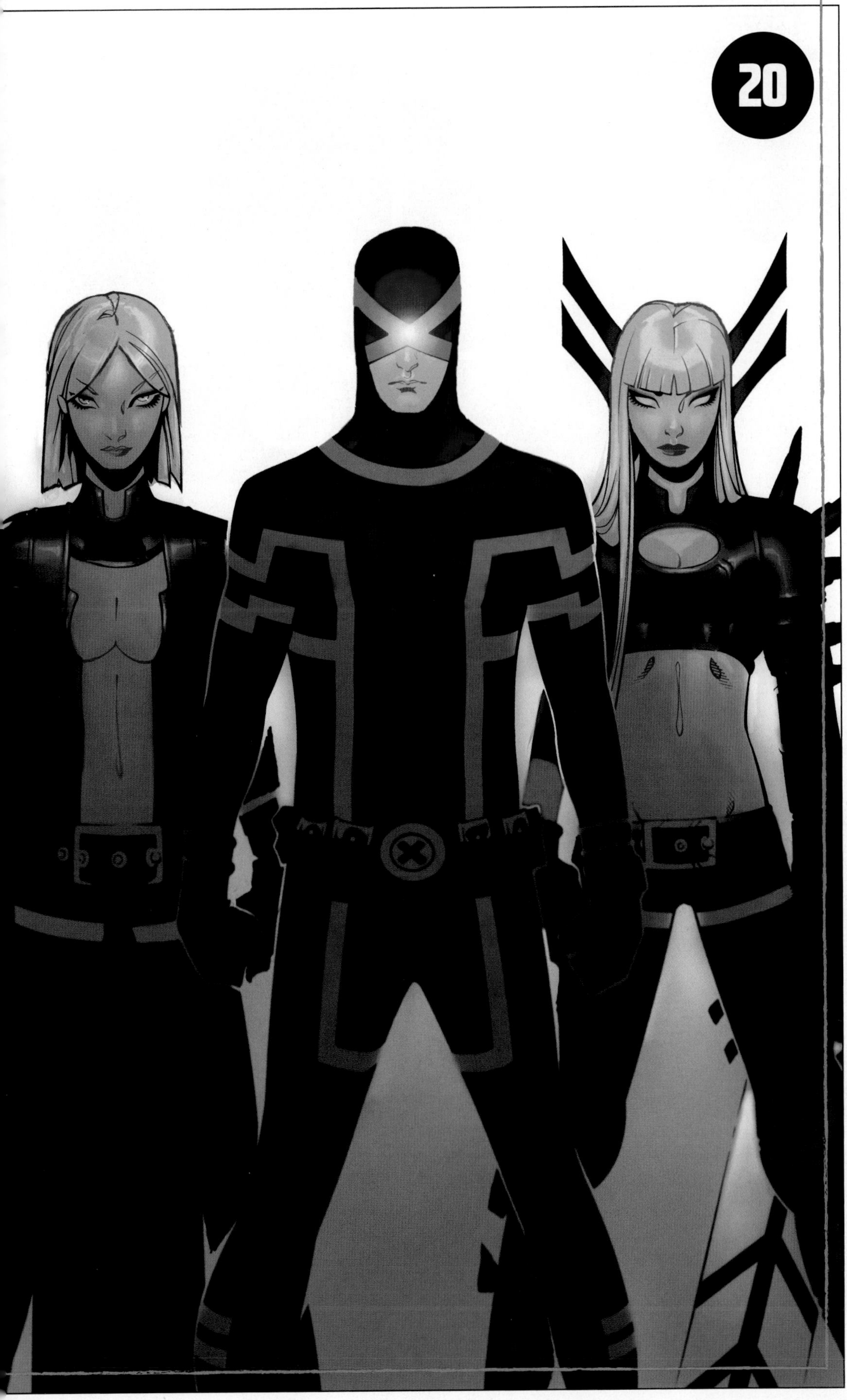
20

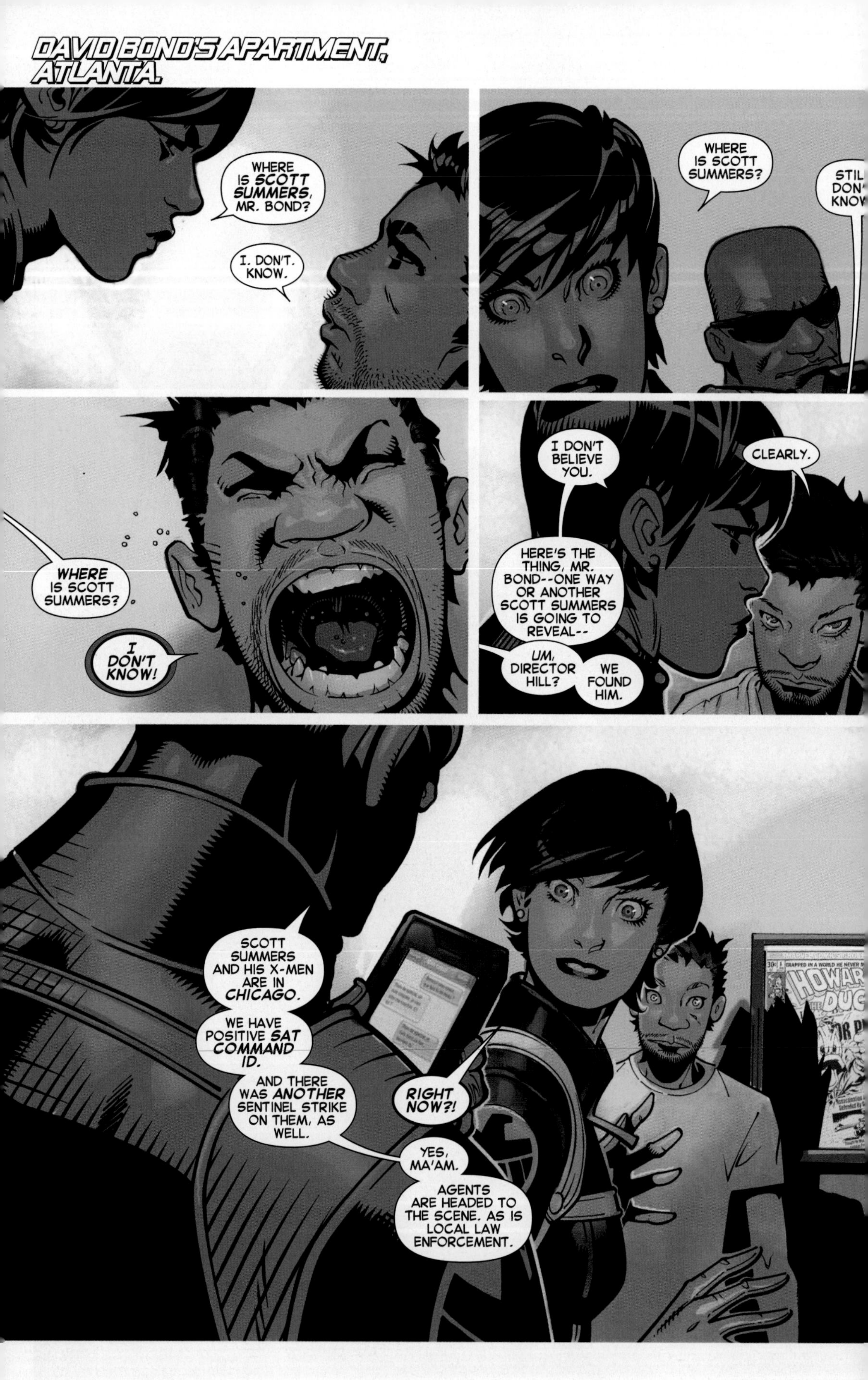
DAVID BOND'S APARTMENT, ATLANTA.
WHERE IS SCOTT SUMMERS, MR. BOND?
I. DON'T. KNOW.
WHERE IS SCOTT SUMMERS?
WHERE IS SCOTT SUMMERS?
I DON'T KNOW!
I DON'T BELIEVE YOU.
CLEARLY.
HERE'S THE THING, MR. BOND--ONE WAY OR ANOTHER SCOTT SUMMERS IS GOING TO REVEAL--
UM, DIRECTOR HILL?
WE FOUND HIM.
SCOTT SUMMERS AND HIS X-MEN ARE IN CHICAGO.
WE HAVE POSITIVE SAT COMMAND ID.
AND THERE WAS ANOTHER SENTINEL STRIKE ON THEM, AS WELL.
RIGHT NOW?!
YES, MA'AM.
AGENTS ARE HEADED TO THE SCENE. AS IS LOCAL LAW ENFORCEMENT.

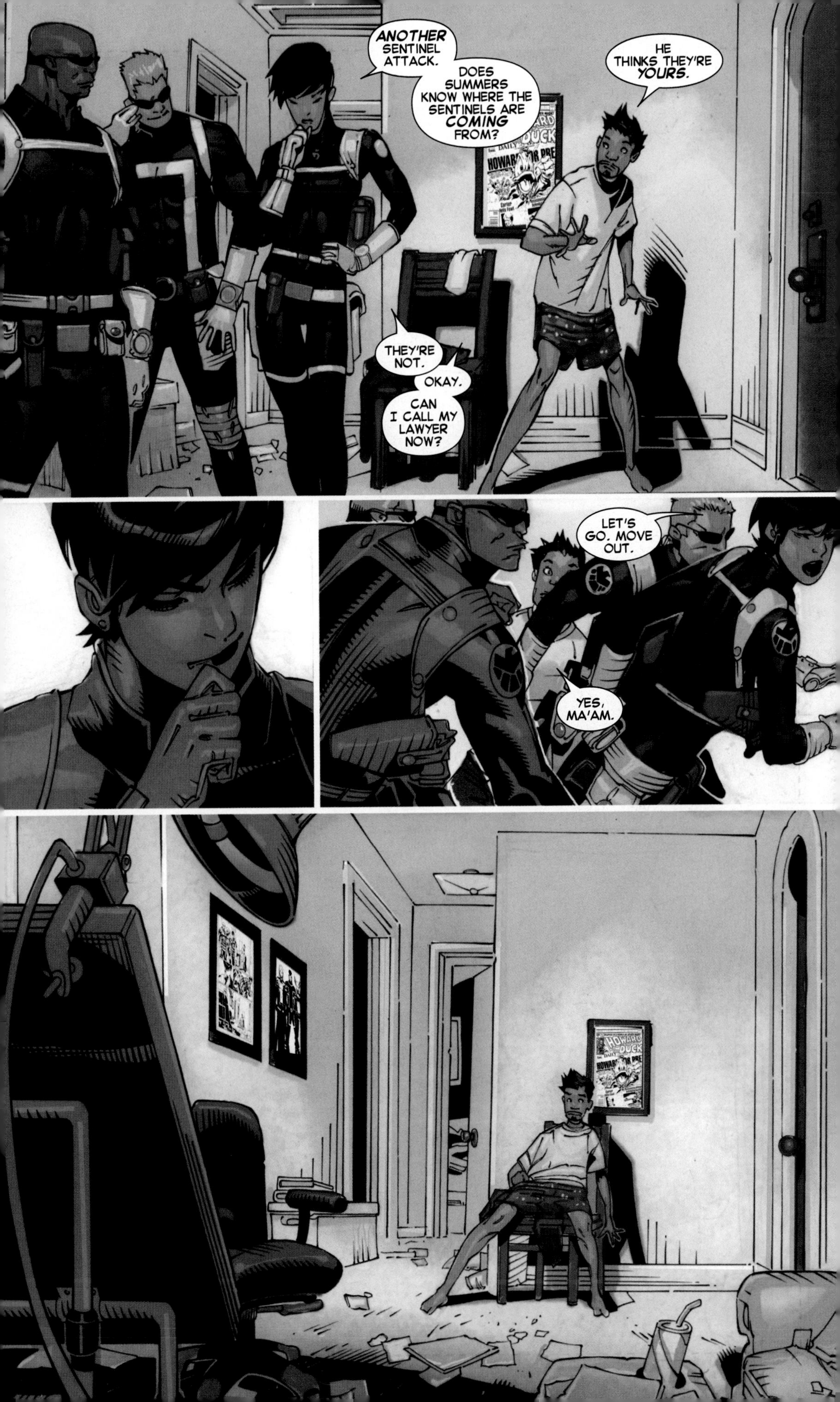
ANOTHER SENTINEL ATTACK.
DOES SUMMERS KNOW WHERE THE SENTINELS ARE COMING FROM?
HE THINKS THEY'RE YOURS.
THEY'RE NOT.
OKAY.
CAN I CALL MY LAWYER NOW?
LET'S GO. MOVE OUT.
YES, MA'AM.

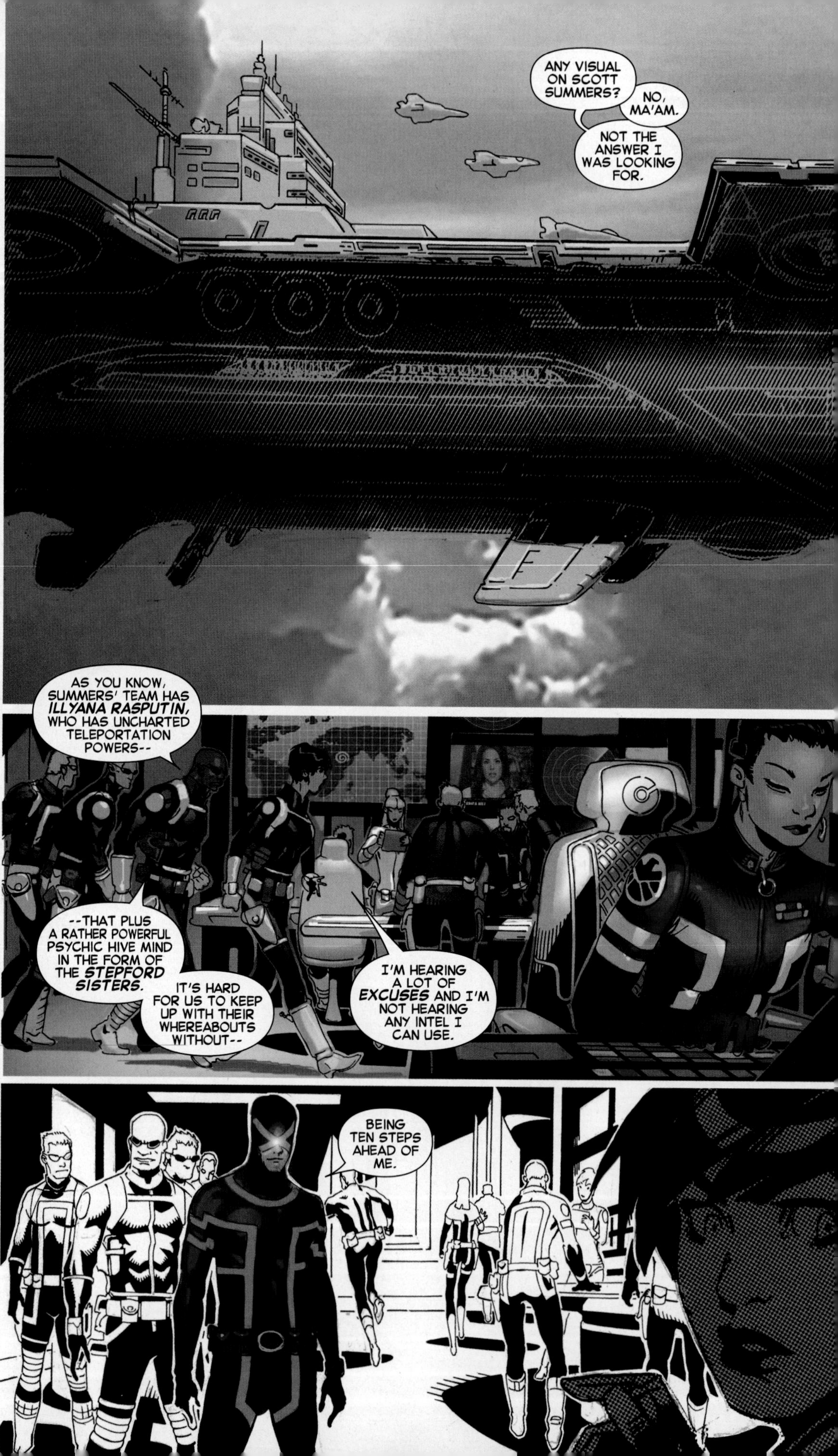
ANY VISUAL ON SCOTT SUMMERS?
NO, MA'AM.
NOT THE ANSWER I WAS LOOKING FOR.
AS YOU KNOW, SUMMERS' TEAM HAS ILLYANA RASPUTIN, WHO HAS UNCHARTED TELEPORTATION POWERS--
--THAT PLUS A RATHER POWERFUL PSYCHIC HIVE MIND IN THE FORM OF THE STEPFORD SISTERS.
IT'S HARD FOR US TO KEEP UP WITH THEIR WHEREABOUTS WITHOUT--
I'M HEARING A LOT OF EXCUSES AND I'M NOT HEARING ANY INTEL I CAN USE.
BEING TEN STEPS AHEAD OF ME.

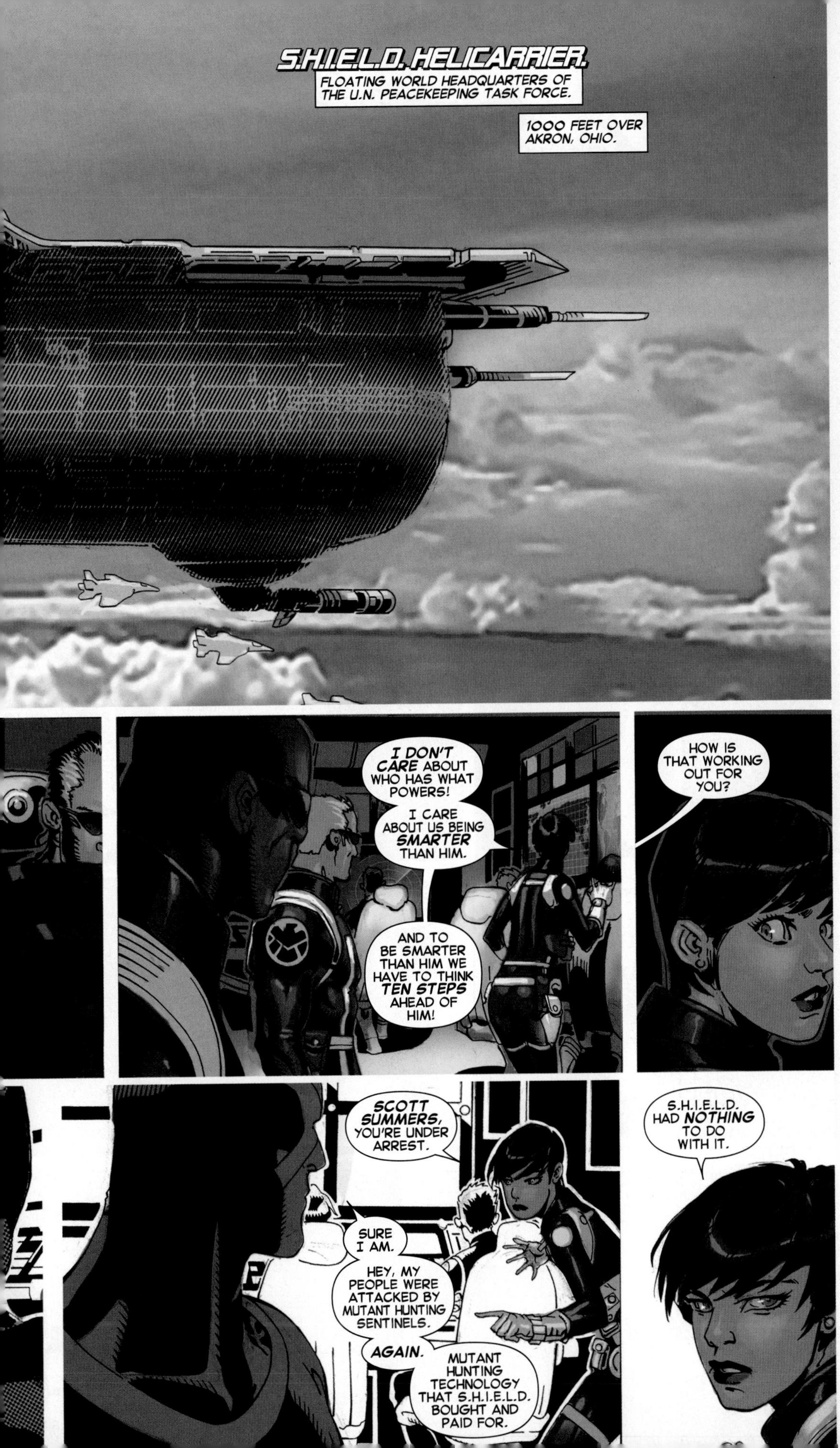

S.H.I.E.L.D. HELICARRIER.
FLOATING WORLD HEADQUARTERS OF THE U.N. PEACEKEEPING TASK FORCE.
1000 FEET OVER AKRON, OHIO.
I DON'T CARE ABOUT WHO HAS WHAT POWERS!
I CARE ABOUT US BEING SMARTER THAN HIM.
AND TO BE SMARTER THAN HIM WE HAVE TO THINK TEN STEPS AHEAD OF HIM!
HOW IS THAT WORKING OUT FOR YOU?
SCOTT SUMMERS, YOU'RE UNDER ARREST.
SURE I AM.
HEY, MY PEOPLE WERE ATTACKED BY MUTANT HUNTING SENTINELS.
AGAIN.
MUTANT HUNTING TECHNOLOGY THAT S.H.I.E.L.D. BOUGHT AND PAID FOR.
S.H.I.E.L.D. HAD NOTHING TO DO WITH IT.

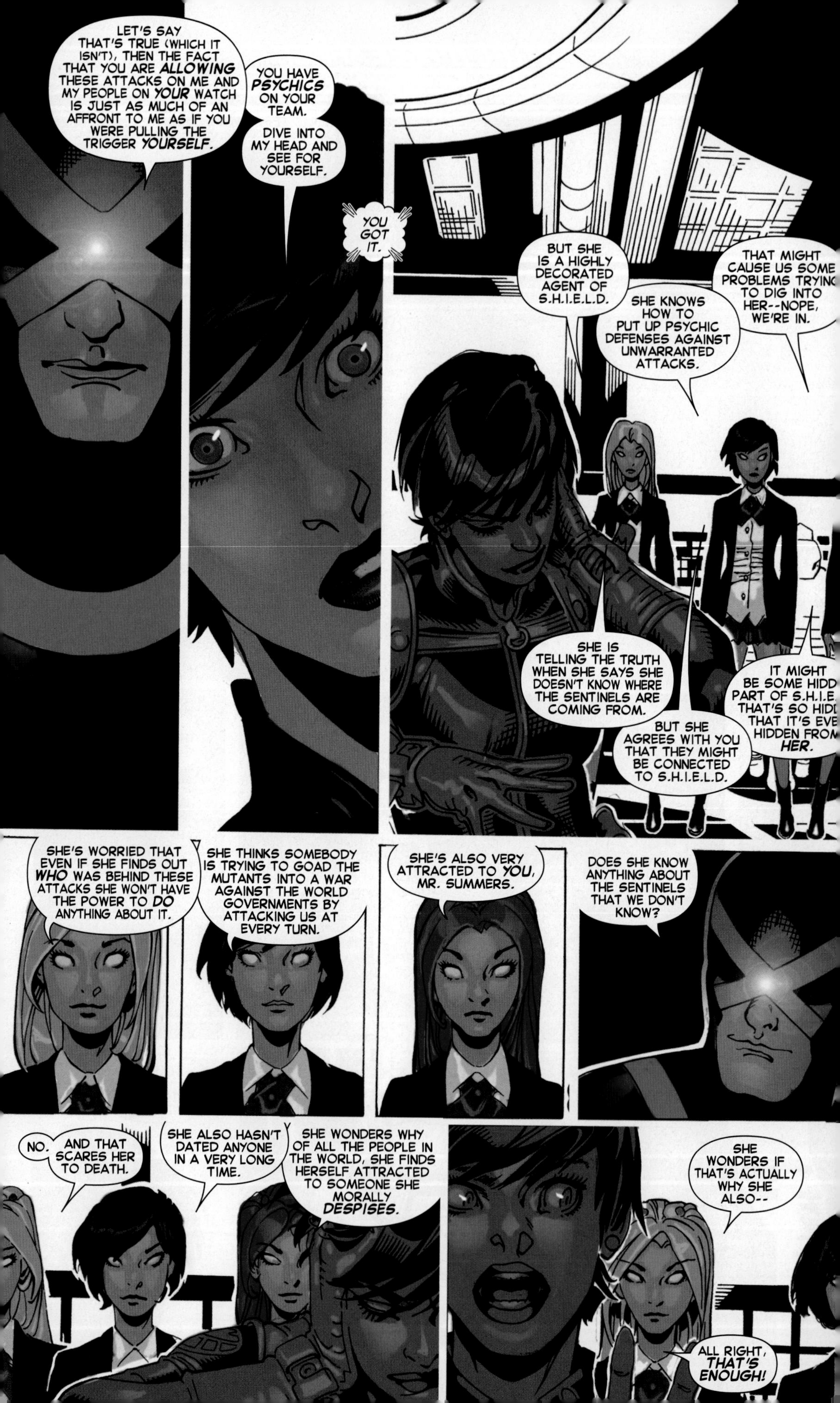

LET'S SAY THAT'S TRUE (WHICH IT ISN'T), THEN THE FACT THAT YOU ARE ALLOWING THESE ATTACKS ON ME AND MY PEOPLE ON YOUR WATCH IS JUST AS MUCH OF AN AFFRONT TO ME AS IF YOU WERE PULLING THE TRIGGER YOURSELF.
YOU HAVE PSYCHICS ON YOUR TEAM.
DIVE INTO MY HEAD AND SEE FOR YOURSELF.
YOU GOT IT.
BUT SHE IS A HIGHLY DECORATED AGENT OF S.H.I.E.L.D.
SHE KNOWS HOW TO PUT UP PSYCHIC DEFENSES AGAINST UNWARRANTED ATTACKS.
THAT MIGHT CAUSE US SOME PROBLEMS TRYING TO DIG INTO HER--NOPE, WE'RE IN.
SHE IS TELLING THE TRUTH WHEN SHE SAYS SHE DOESN'T KNOW WHERE THE SENTINELS ARE COMING FROM.
BUT SHE AGREES WITH YOU THAT THEY MIGHT BE CONNECTED TO S.H.I.E.L.D.
IT MIGHT BE SOME HIDD PART OF S.H.I.E. THAT'S SO HIDD THAT IT'S EVE HIDDEN FROM HER.
SHE'S WORRIED THAT EVEN IF SHE FINDS OUT WHO WAS BEHIND THESE ATTACKS SHE WON'T HAVE THE POWER TO DO ANYTHING ABOUT IT.
SHE THINKS SOMEBODY IS TRYING TO GOAD THE MUTANTS INTO A WAR AGAINST THE WORLD GOVERNMENTS BY ATTACKING US AT EVERY TURN.
SHE'S ALSO VERY ATTRACTED TO YOU, MR. SUMMERS.
DOES SHE KNOW ANYTHING ABOUT THE SENTINELS THAT WE DON'T KNOW?
NO.
AND THAT SCARES HER TO DEATH.
SHE ALSO HASN'T DATED ANYONE IN A VERY LONG TIME.
SHE WONDERS WHY OF ALL THE PEOPLE IN THE WORLD, SHE FINDS HERSELF ATTRACTED TO SOMEONE SHE MORALLY DESPISES.
SHE WONDERS IF THAT'S ACTUALLY WHY SHE ALSO--
ALL RIGHT, THAT'S ENOUGH!

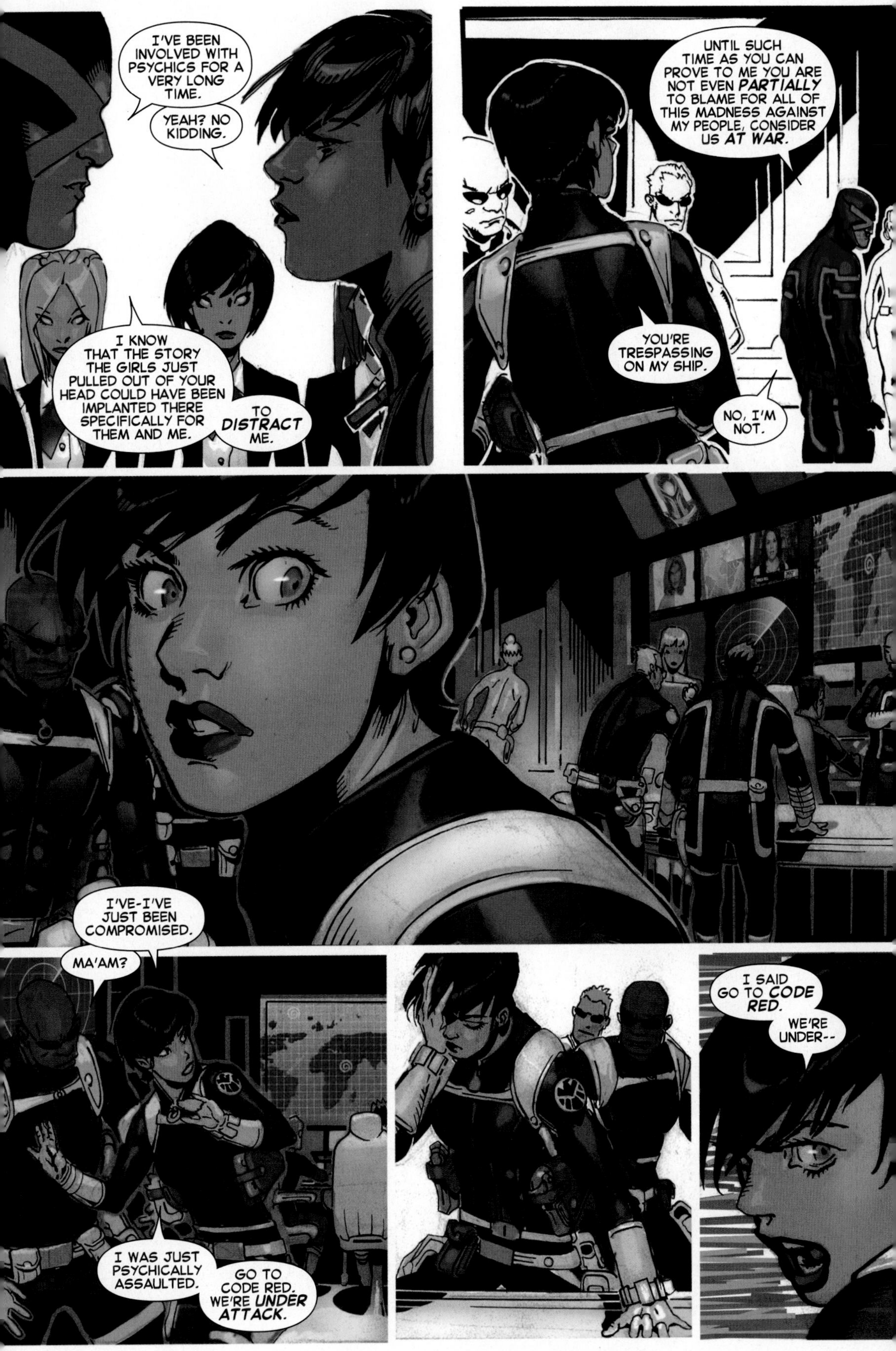

I'VE BEEN INVOLVED WITH PSYCHICS FOR A VERY LONG TIME.
YEAH? NO KIDDING.
I KNOW THAT THE STORY THE GIRLS JUST PULLED OUT OF YOUR HEAD COULD HAVE BEEN IMPLANTED THERE SPECIFICALLY FOR THEM AND ME.
TO DISTRACT ME.
UNTIL SUCH TIME AS YOU CAN PROVE TO ME YOU ARE NOT EVEN PARTIALLY TO BLAME FOR ALL OF THIS MADNESS AGAINST MY PEOPLE, CONSIDER US AT WAR.
YOU'RE TRESPASSING ON MY SHIP.
NO, I'M NOT.
I'VE-I'VE JUST BEEN COMPROMISED.
MA'AM?
I WAS JUST PSYCHICALLY ASSAULTED.
GO TO CODE RED. WE'RE UNDER ATTACK.
I SAID GO TO CODE RED.
WE'RE UNDER--

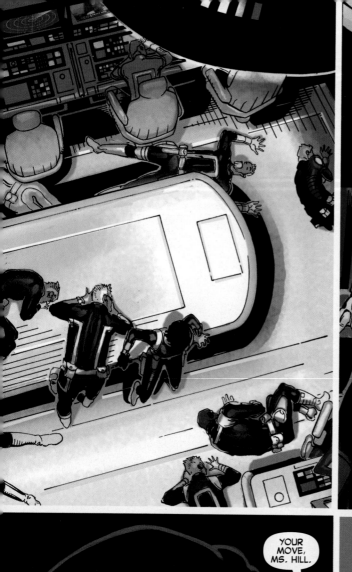

YOUR MOVE, MS. HILL.

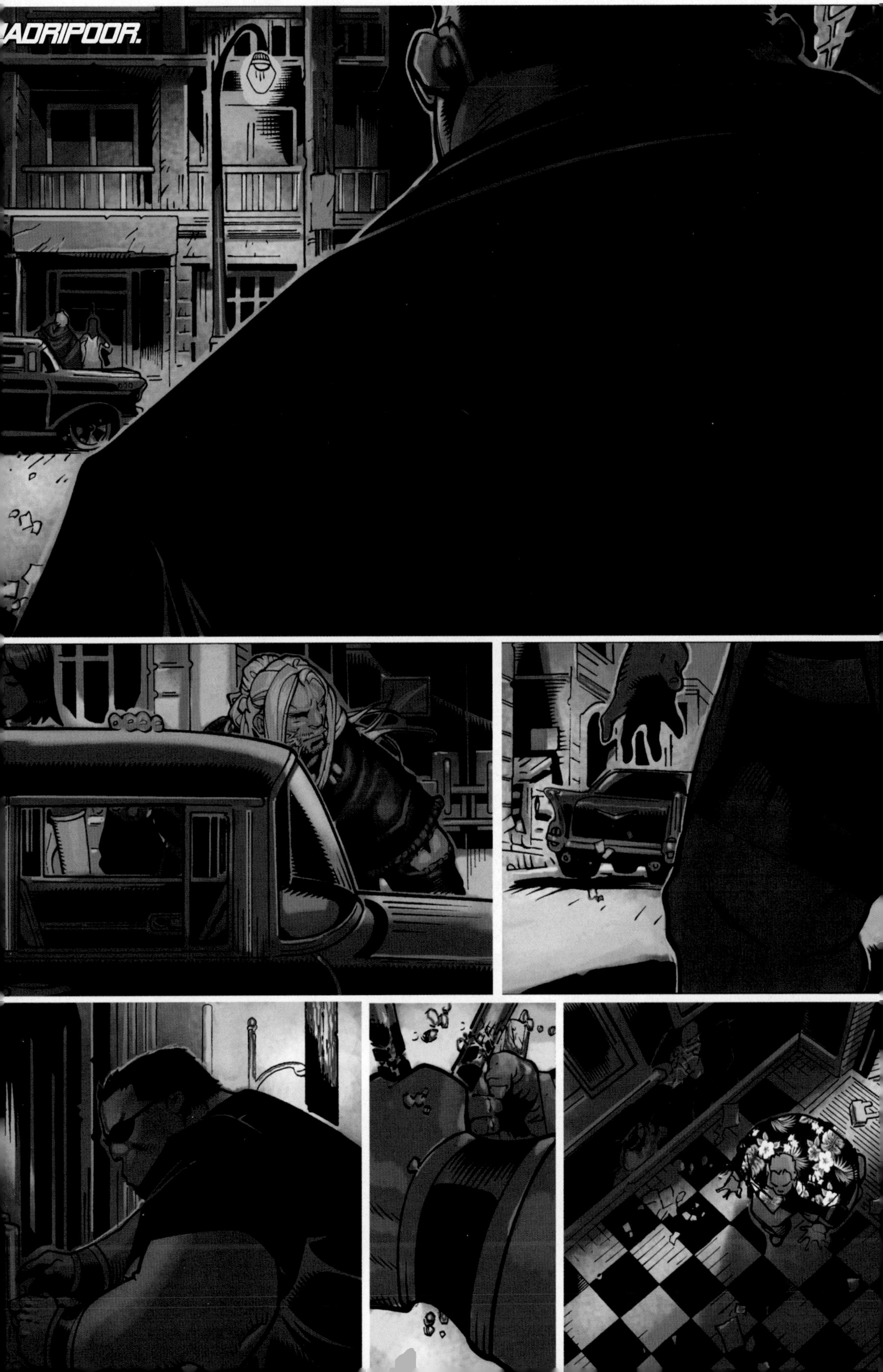
ADRIPOOR.

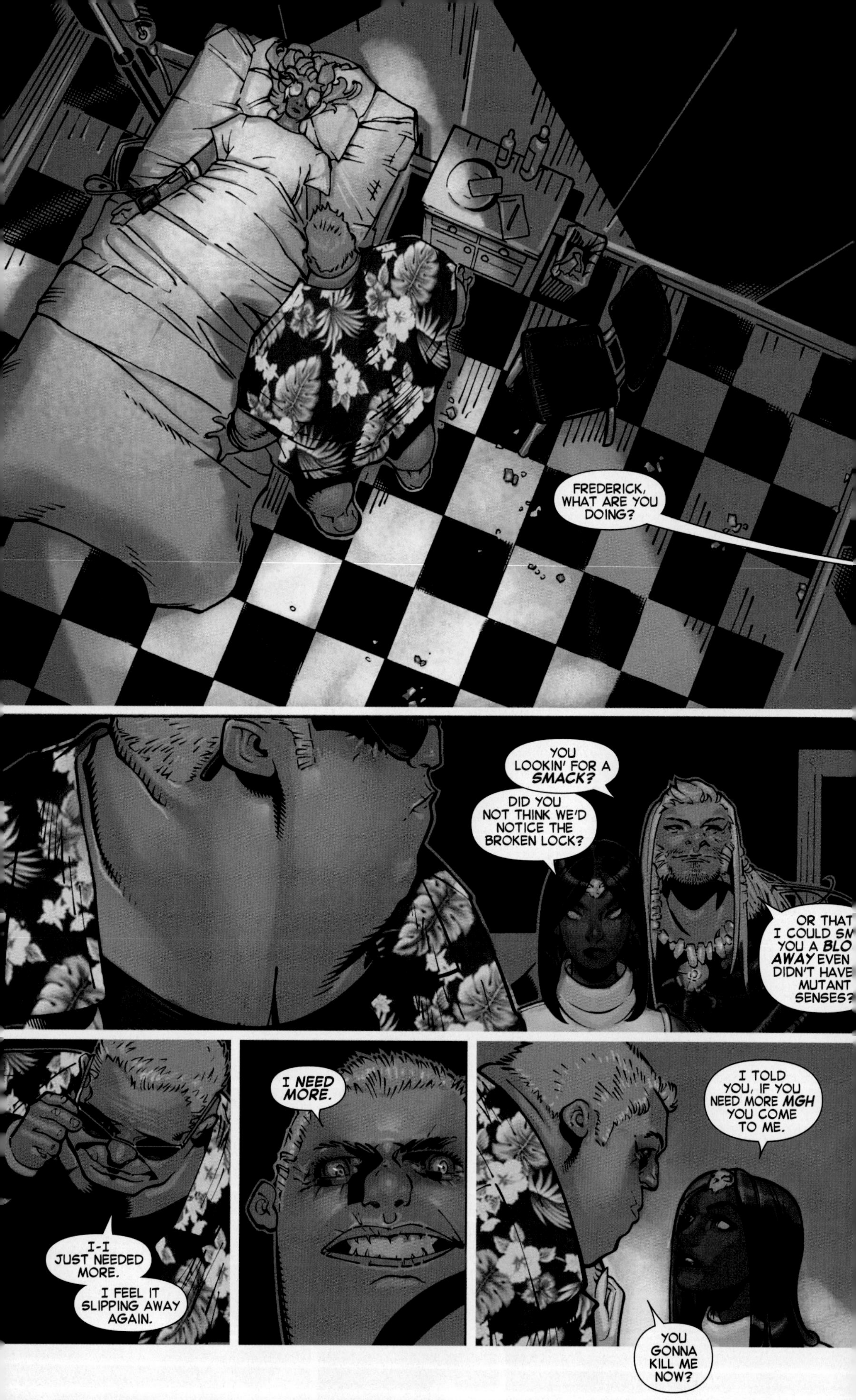
FREDERICK, WHAT ARE YOU DOING?
YOU LOOKIN' FOR A *SMACK?*
DID YOU NOT THINK WE'D NOTICE THE BROKEN LOCK?
OR THAT I COULD SM YOU A *BLO AWAY* EVEN DIDN'T HAVE MUTANT SENSES?
I-I JUST NEEDED MORE.
I FEEL IT SLIPPING AWAY AGAIN.
I *NEED MORE.*
I TOLD YOU, IF YOU NEED MORE *MGH* YOU COME TO ME.
YOU GONNA KILL ME NOW?

ALL YOU HAVE TO DO IS ASK.

WE'RE A TEAM. WE'RE A *FAMILY*.

I *WANT* YOU TO BE AS POWERFUL AS YOU CAN BE.

GOD CREATED YOU AS THE BLOB. YOU *DESERVE* YOUR POWER.

IT'S NOT YOUR FAULT THAT THE CRAZY WORLD TOOK THOSE POWERS AWAY FROM YOU.

BUT YOU NEED TO *TRUST* ME.

I-I DO.

THIS IS NOT TRUST, FREDERICK.

I-I-I-I JUST DIDN'T KNOW WHERE YOU WERE GETTING IT FROM.

I DIDN'T KNOW IF--

AND NOW THAT YOU DO, DOES IT *MATTER?*

DAZZLER BETRAYED OUR PEOPLE.

INSTEAD OF LETTING VICTOR HERE *GUT* HER FOR HER SINS...SHE'S SUPPLYING US WITH EVERYTHING WE NEED TO MAKE THIS ISLAND A TRUE MUTANT UTOPIA.

AND TO KEEP YOU THE WAY YOU HAVE BEEN AND SHOULD BE ACCUSTOMED TO BEING.

I'M SORRY.

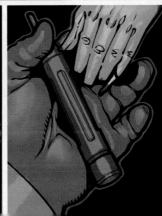

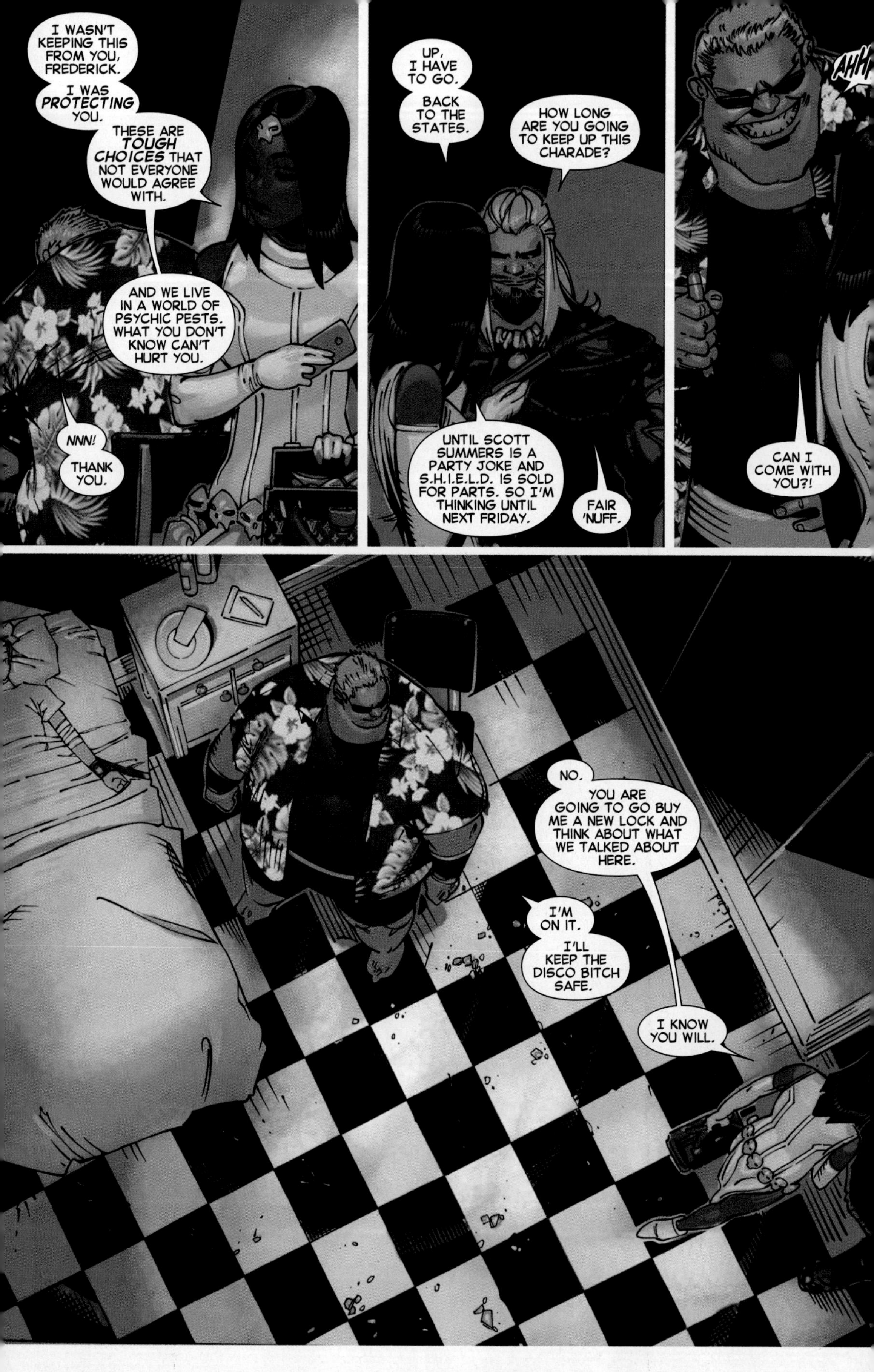
I WASN'T KEEPING THIS FROM YOU, FREDERICK.
I WAS *PROTECTING* YOU.
THESE ARE *TOUGH CHOICES* THAT NOT EVERYONE WOULD AGREE WITH.
AND WE LIVE IN A WORLD OF PSYCHIC PESTS. WHAT YOU DON'T KNOW CAN'T HURT YOU.
NNN!
THANK YOU.
UP, I HAVE TO GO.
BACK TO THE STATES.
HOW LONG ARE YOU GOING TO KEEP UP THIS CHARADE?
UNTIL SCOTT SUMMERS IS A PARTY JOKE AND S.H.I.E.L.D. IS SOLD FOR PARTS. SO I'M THINKING UNTIL NEXT FRIDAY.
FAIR 'NUFF.
AHH
CAN I COME WITH YOU?!
NO.
YOU ARE GOING TO GO BUY ME A NEW LOCK AND THINK ABOUT WHAT WE TALKED ABOUT HERE.
I'M ON IT.
I'LL KEEP THE DISCO BITCH SAFE.
I KNOW YOU WILL.

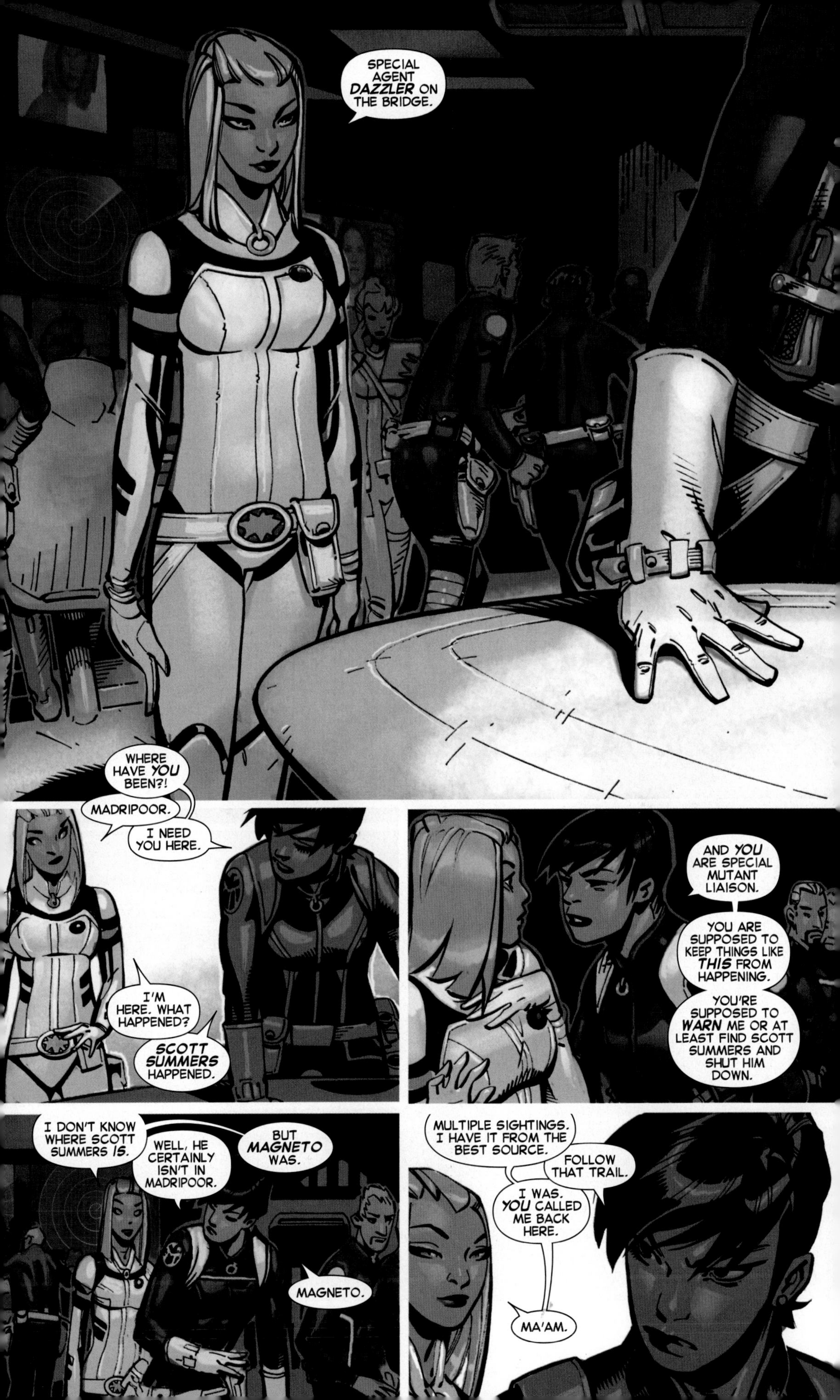
SPECIAL AGENT DAZZLER ON THE BRIDGE.
WHERE HAVE YOU BEEN?!
MADRIPOOR.
I NEED YOU HERE.
I'M HERE. WHAT HAPPENED?
SCOTT SUMMERS HAPPENED.
AND YOU ARE SPECIAL MUTANT LIAISON.
YOU ARE SUPPOSED TO KEEP THINGS LIKE THIS FROM HAPPENING.
YOU'RE SUPPOSED TO WARN ME OR AT LEAST FIND SCOTT SUMMERS AND SHUT HIM DOWN.
I DON'T KNOW WHERE SCOTT SUMMERS IS.
WELL, HE CERTAINLY ISN'T IN MADRIPOOR.
BUT MAGNETO WAS.
MAGNETO.
MULTIPLE SIGHTINGS. I HAVE IT FROM THE BEST SOURCE.
FOLLOW THAT TRAIL.
I WAS. YOU CALLED ME BACK HERE.
MA'AM.

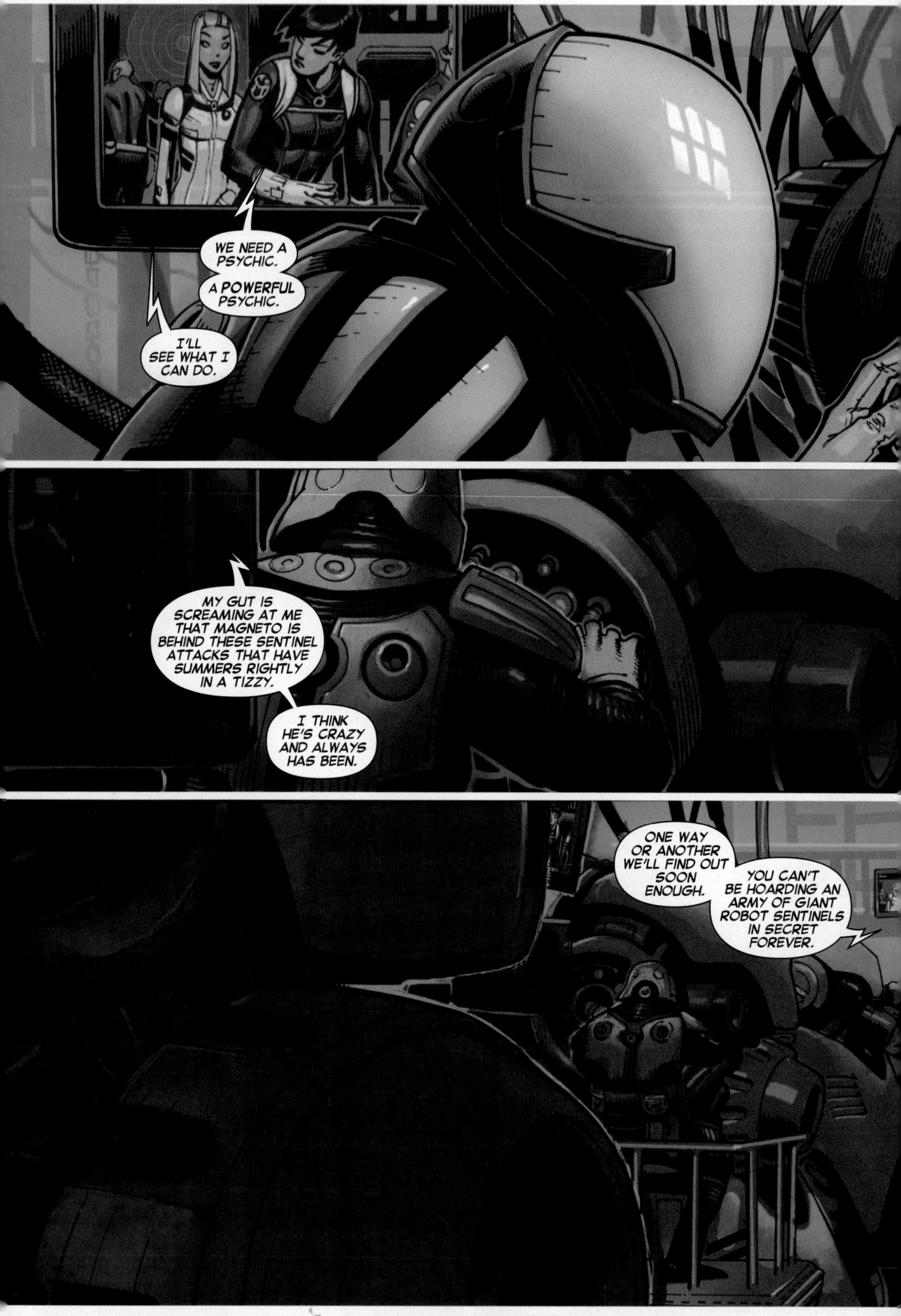
WE NEED A PSYCHIC.
A POWERFUL PSYCHIC.
I'LL SEE WHAT I CAN DO.
MY GUT IS SCREAMING AT ME THAT MAGNETO IS BEHIND THESE SENTINEL ATTACKS THAT HAVE SUMMERS RIGHTLY IN A TIZZY.
I THINK HE'S CRAZY AND ALWAYS HAS BEEN.
ONE WAY OR ANOTHER WE'LL FIND OUT SOON ENOUGH.
YOU CAN'T BE HOARDING AN ARMY OF GIANT ROBOT SENTINELS IN SECRET FOREVER.

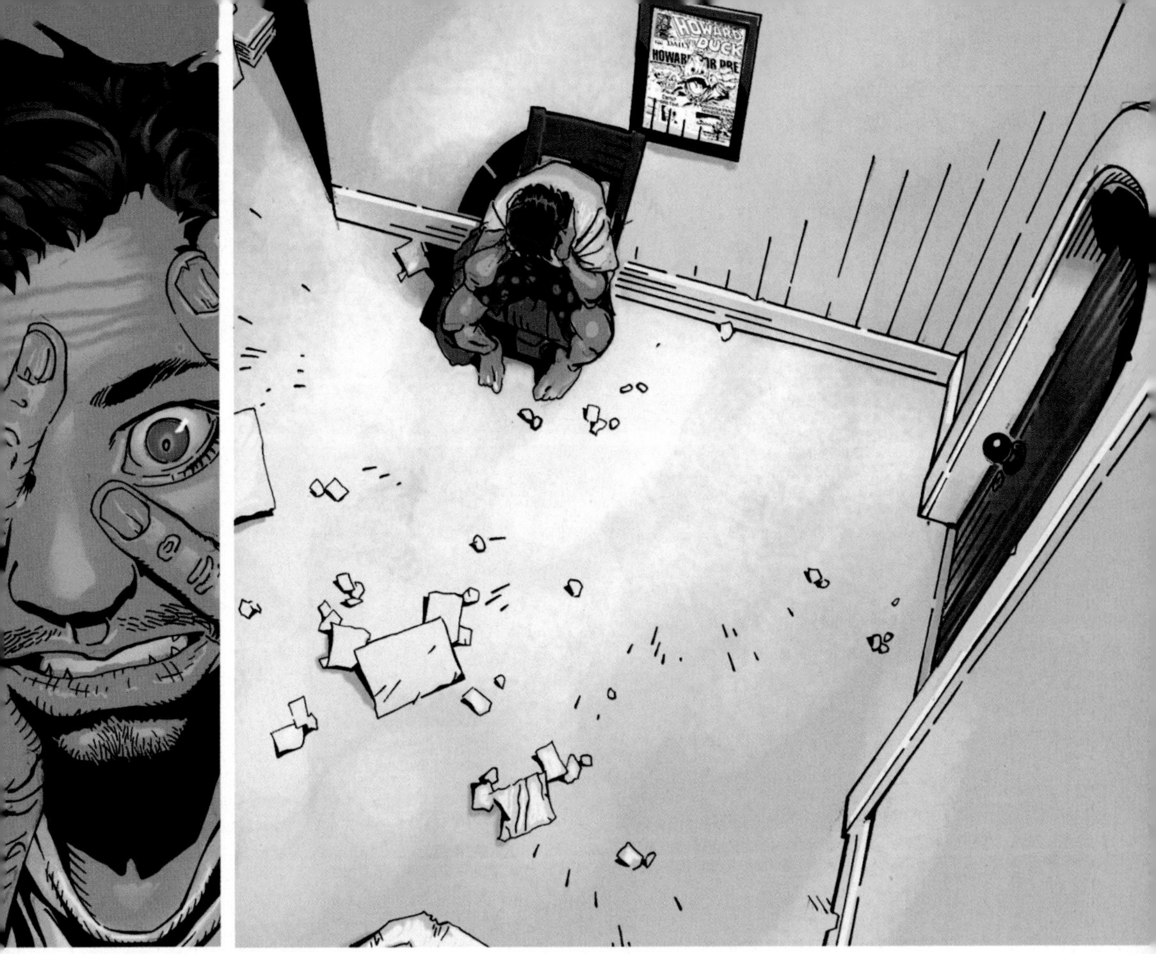

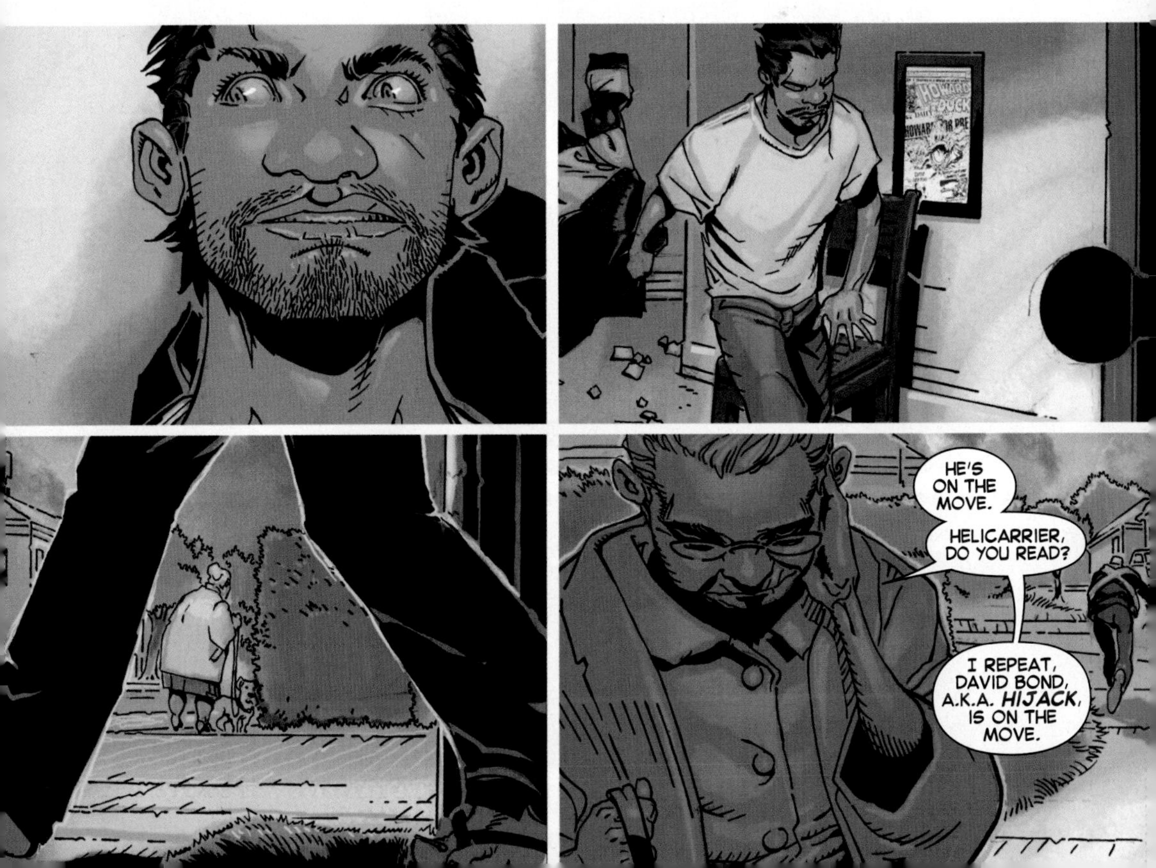
HE'S ON THE MOVE.
HELICARRIER, DO YOU READ?
I REPEAT, DAVID BOND, A.K.A. HIJACK, IS ON THE MOVE.

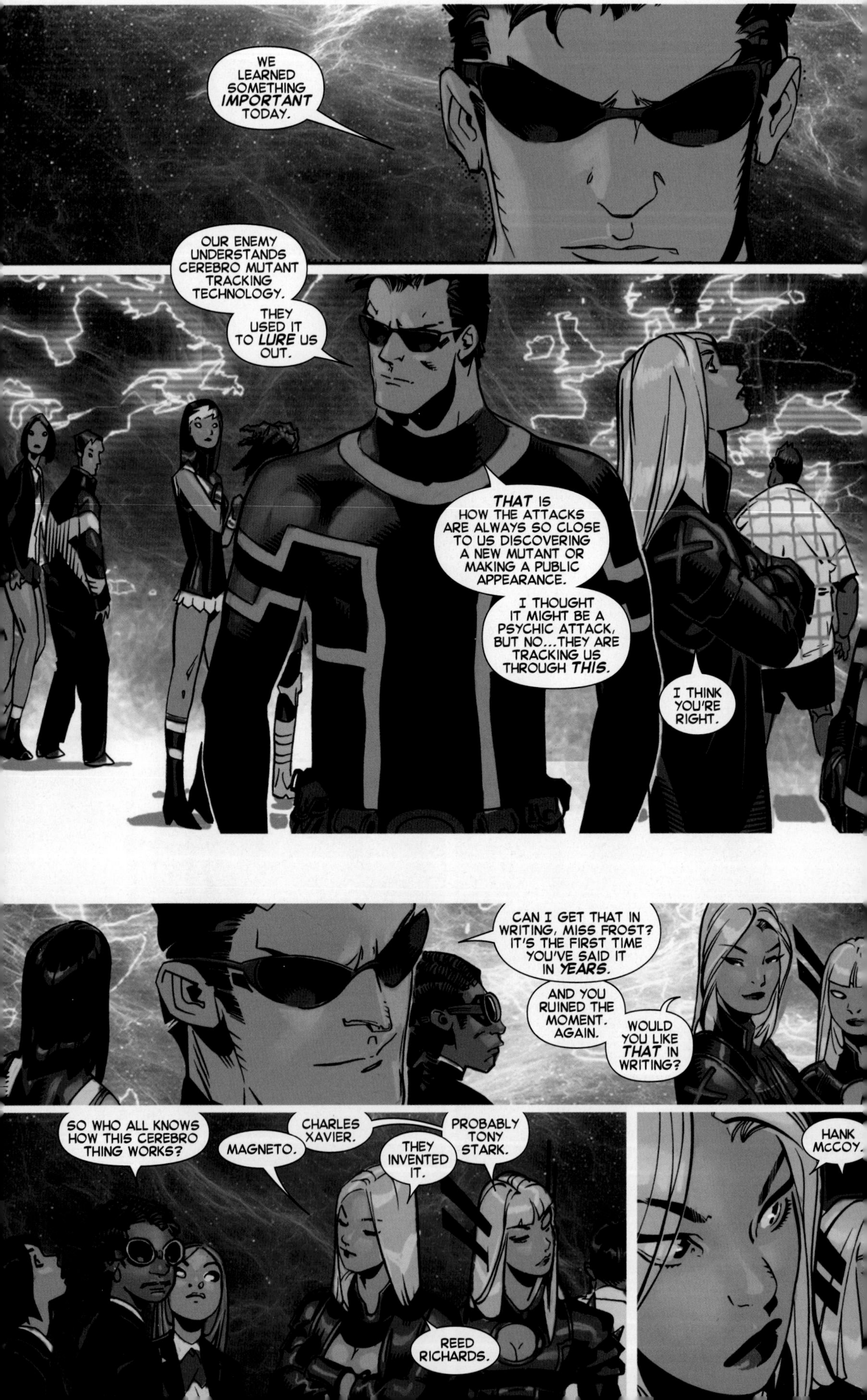

WE LEARNED SOMETHING *IMPORTANT* TODAY.
OUR ENEMY UNDERSTANDS CEREBRO MUTANT TRACKING TECHNOLOGY.
THEY USED IT TO *LURE* US OUT.
THAT IS HOW THE ATTACKS ARE ALWAYS SO CLOSE TO US DISCOVERING A NEW MUTANT OR MAKING A PUBLIC APPEARANCE.
I THOUGHT IT MIGHT BE A PSYCHIC ATTACK, BUT NO...THEY ARE TRACKING US THROUGH *THIS*.
I THINK YOU'RE RIGHT.
CAN I GET THAT IN WRITING, MISS FROST? IT'S THE FIRST TIME YOU'VE SAID IT IN *YEARS*.
AND YOU RUINED THE MOMENT. AGAIN.
WOULD YOU LIKE *THAT* IN WRITING?
SO WHO ALL KNOWS HOW THIS CEREBRO THING WORKS?
MAGNETO.
CHARLES XAVIER.
THEY INVENTED IT.
PROBABLY TONY STARK.
REED RICHARDS.
HANK McCOY.

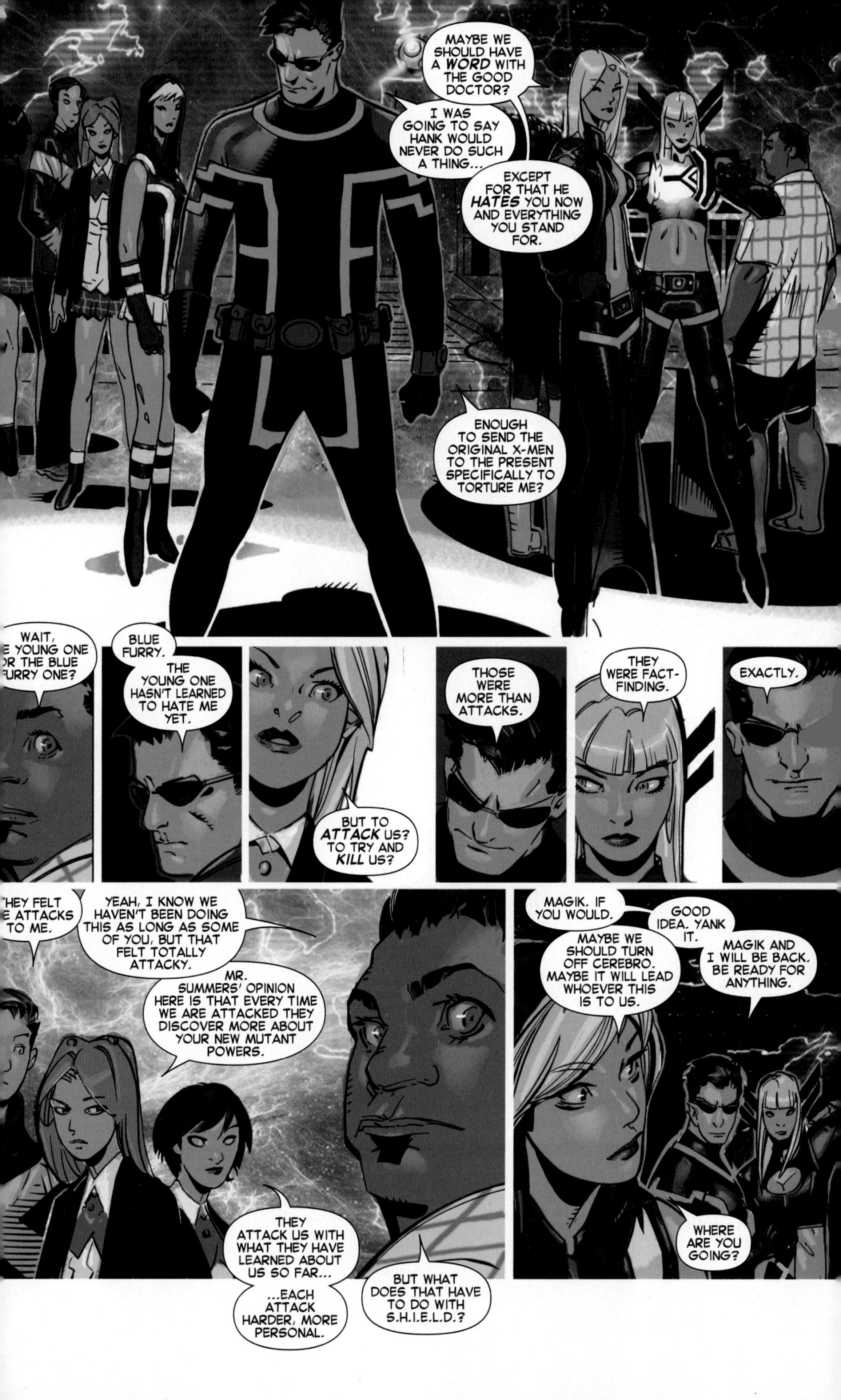
MAYBE WE SHOULD HAVE A *WORD* WITH THE GOOD DOCTOR?
I WAS GOING TO SAY HANK WOULD NEVER DO SUCH A THING...
EXCEPT FOR THAT HE *HATES* YOU NOW AND EVERYTHING YOU STAND FOR.
ENOUGH TO SEND THE ORIGINAL X-MEN TO THE PRESENT SPECIFICALLY TO TORTURE ME?
WAIT, E YOUNG ONE R THE BLUE URRY ONE?
BLUE FURRY.
THE YOUNG ONE HASN'T LEARNED TO HATE ME YET.
BUT TO *ATTACK* US? TO TRY AND *KILL* US?
THOSE WERE MORE THAN ATTACKS.
THEY WERE FACT-FINDING.
EXACTLY.
HEY FELT E ATTACKS TO ME.
YEAH, I KNOW WE HAVEN'T BEEN DOING THIS AS LONG AS SOME OF YOU, BUT THAT FELT TOTALLY ATTACKY.
MR. SUMMERS' OPINION HERE IS THAT EVERY TIME WE ARE ATTACKED THEY DISCOVER MORE ABOUT YOUR NEW MUTANT POWERS.
THEY ATTACK US WITH WHAT THEY HAVE LEARNED ABOUT US SO FAR...
...EACH ATTACK HARDER, MORE PERSONAL.
BUT WHAT DOES THAT HAVE TO DO WITH S.H.I.E.L.D.?
MAGIK. IF YOU WOULD.
GOOD IDEA. YANK IT.
MAYBE WE SHOULD TURN OFF CEREBRO. MAYBE IT WILL LEAD WHOEVER THIS IS TO US.
MAGIK AND I WILL BE BACK. BE READY FOR ANYTHING.
WHERE ARE YOU GOING?

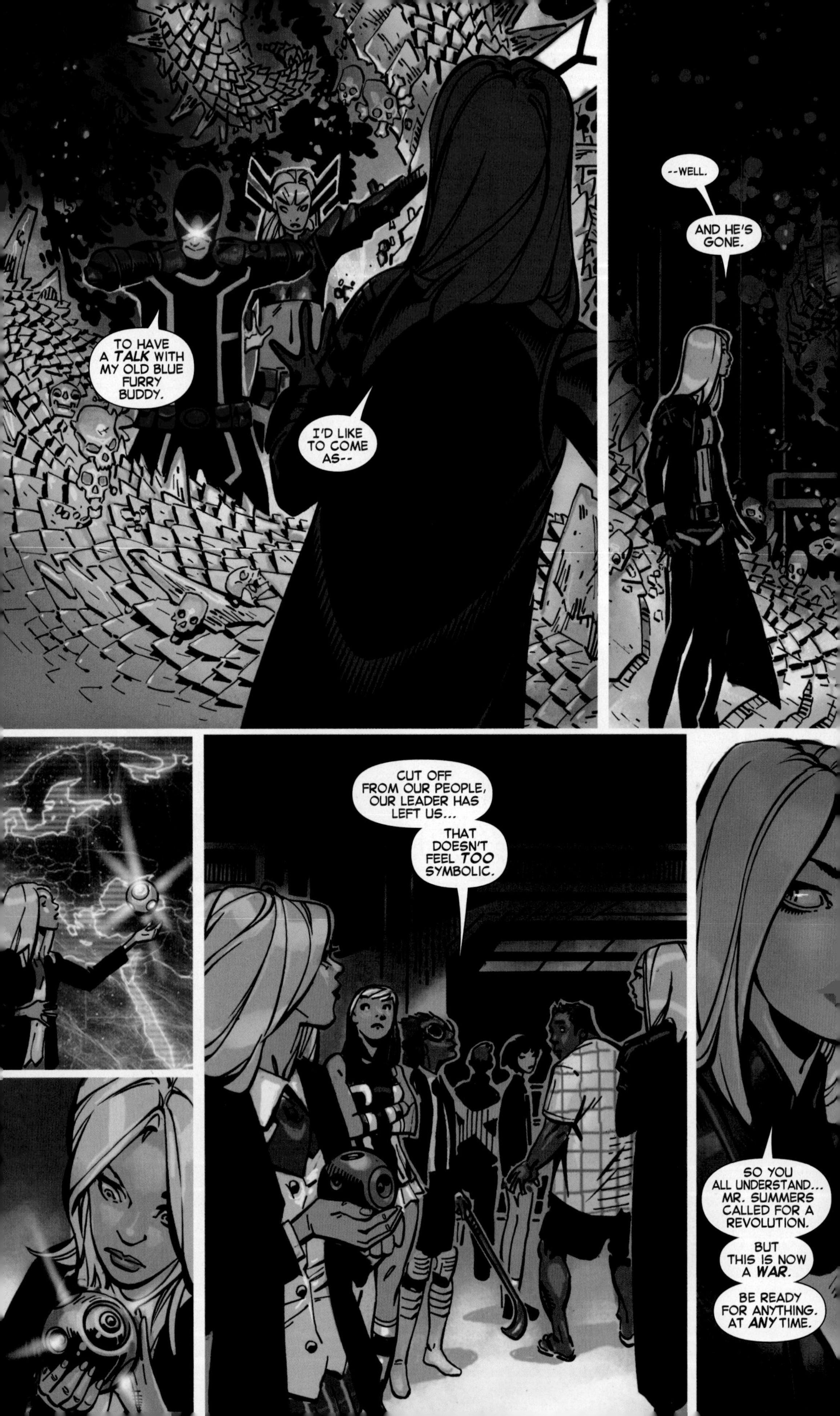

I'D LIKE TO COME AS--
TO HAVE A TALK WITH MY OLD BLUE FURRY BUDDY.
--WELL.
AND HE'S GONE.
CUT OFF FROM OUR PEOPLE, OUR LEADER HAS LEFT US...
THAT DOESN'T FEEL TOO SYMBOLIC.
SO YOU ALL UNDERSTAND... MR. SUMMERS CALLED FOR A REVOLUTION.
BUT THIS IS NOW A WAR.
BE READY FOR ANYTHING. AT ANY TIME.

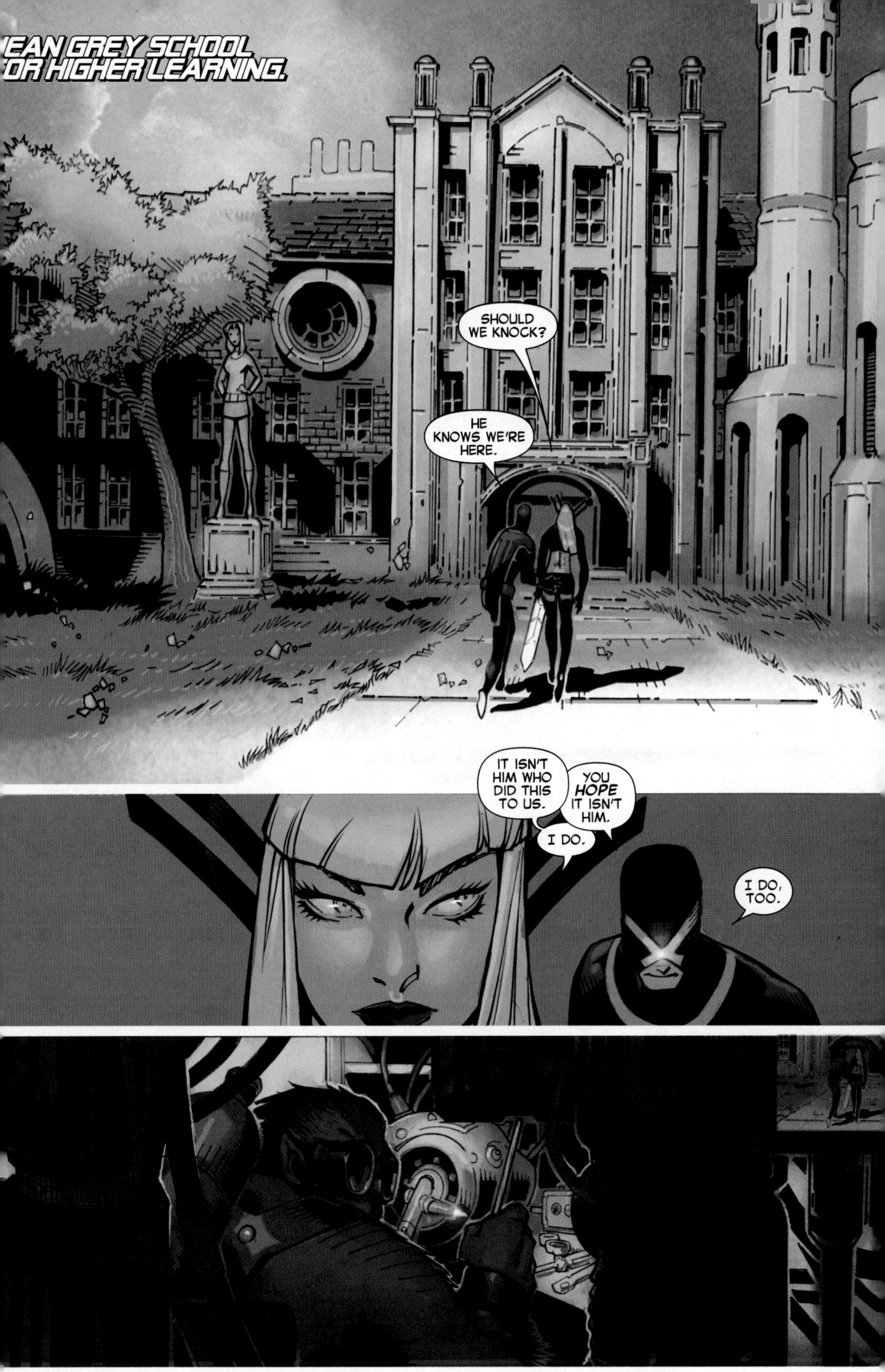
EAN GREY SCHOOL
OR HIGHER LEARNING.
SHOULD WE KNOCK?
HE KNOWS WE'RE HERE.
IT ISN'T HIM WHO DID THIS TO US.
YOU HOPE IT ISN'T HIM.
I DO.
I DO, TOO.

SCOTT, ILLYANA. PLEASE, PLEASE GO AWAY.
LET US TEACH OUR STUDENTS IN PEACE.
I'M HERE TO TALK TO HENRY.
YOU ALREADY HAVE A HENRY TO TALK TO! GO TALK TO YOURS.
IT'S GOOD TO SEE YOU, ORORO.
I REALLY DO MISS YOU.
WHAT DID HANK DO?
YOU MEAN WHAT DID HANK DO NOW.
DID YOU SEE WHAT HAPPENED TO US IN CHICAGO?
ONLY THE NEWS REPORTS.
HEY, IT'S A REUNION!
WELL, IT WAS GOOD SEEING YOU ALL, BYE.
CAN I SEE YOUR LAB, HENRY?
CAN I SEE WHAT YOU'RE WORKING ON?
EXCUSE ME?
HOW ARE YOU FEELING?
FINE.
BECAUSE YOU WERE DYING. BUT NOW YOU'RE FINE.
AND CHARLES XAVIER WAS ALIVE ONCE.
THINGS CHANGE.
WHAT IS THIS?
WE'VE BEEN UNDER ATTACK.
AND THE ATTACKER IS USING CEREBRO TO DO IT.
ONLY A FEW PEOPLE ON THE PLANET EVEN KNOW IT EXISTS LET ALONE KNOW HOW TO WORK IT.
HOW DARE YOU?
I KNOW YOU'LL NEVER FORGIVE ME FOR THE DEATH OF XAVIER BUT MY STUDENTS ARE JUST AS IMPORTANT AS YOURS ARE.
HOW DARE YOU?!
THEY ARE OUR FUTURE. THEY WILL SUCCEED WHERE YOU AND I HAVE FAILED.
LET ORORO INTO YOUR LAB.
OPEN YOUR FILES.
PROVE YOUR INNOCENCE AND I'LL GLADLY APOLOGIZE.
BUT I KNOW YOU, HENRY, AND I KNOW--
WHAT?
--SOMETHING IS--

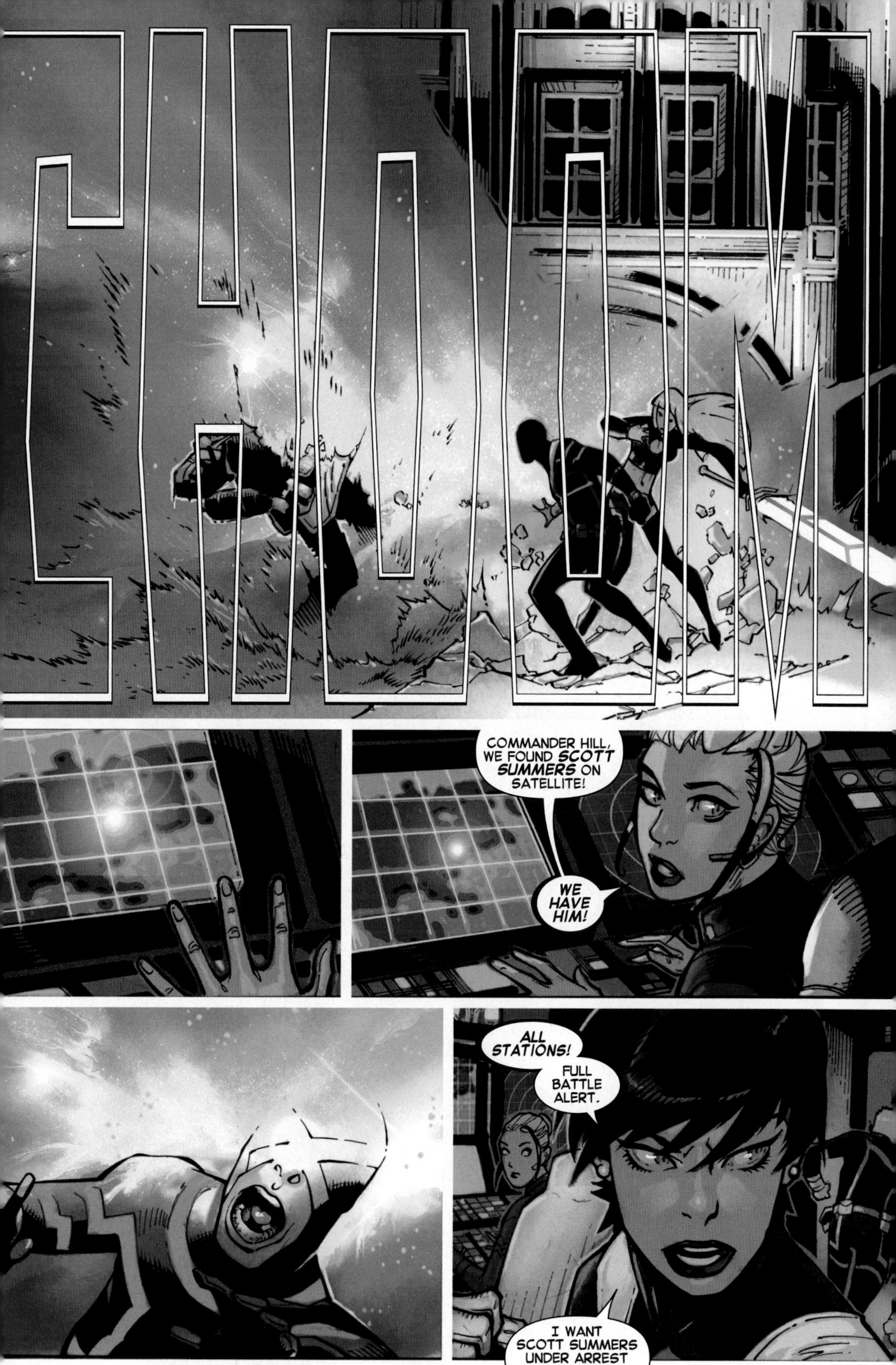
SHOOOM
COMMANDER HILL, WE FOUND SCOTT SUMMERS ON SATELLITE!
WE HAVE HIM!
ALL STATIONS!
FULL BATTLE ALERT.
I WANT SCOTT SUMMERS UNDER ARREST AND IN PRISON TONIGHT!

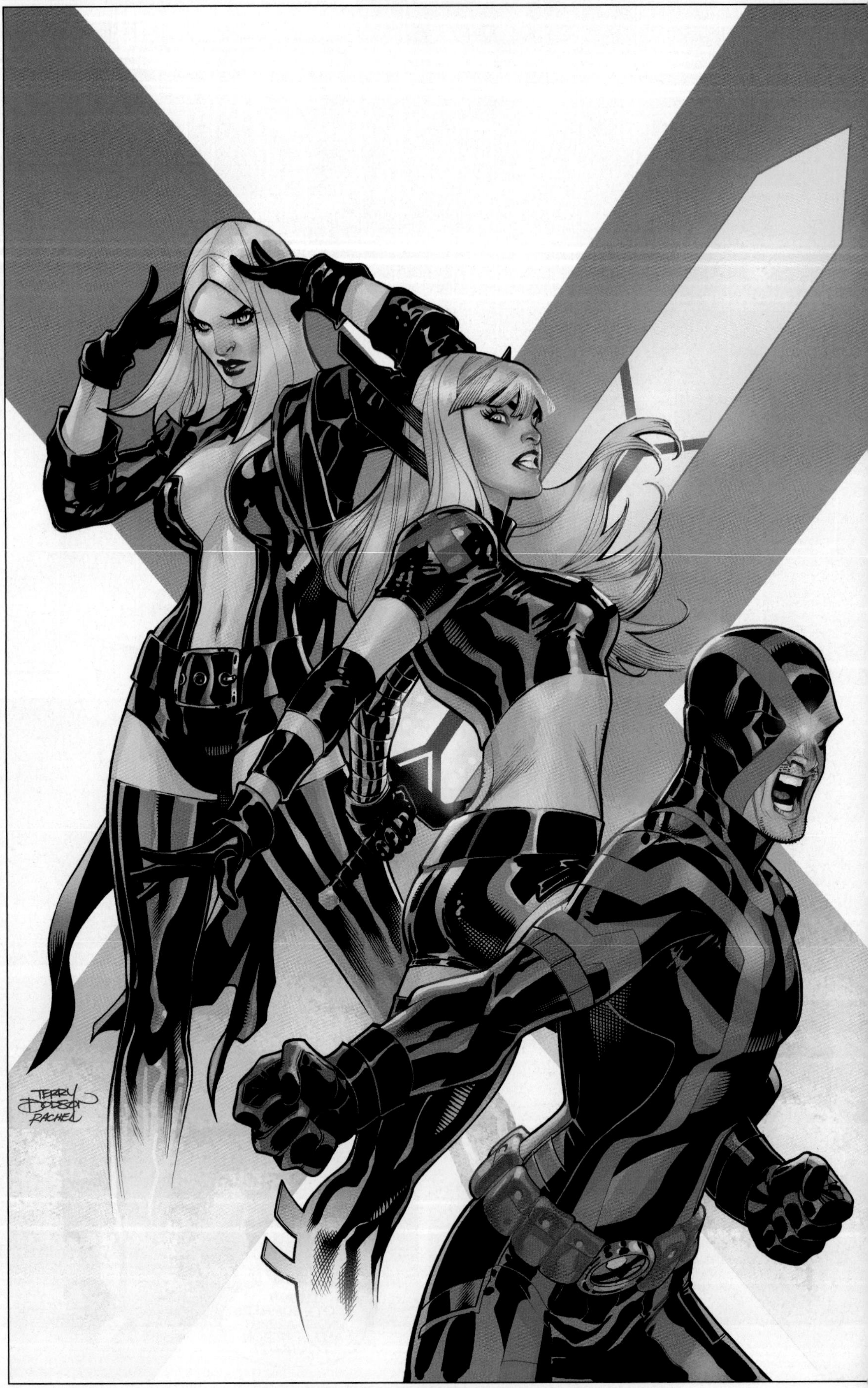
TERRY DODSON RACHEL

UNCANNY X-MEN #21 VARIANT

BY TERRY DODSON & RACHEL DODSON

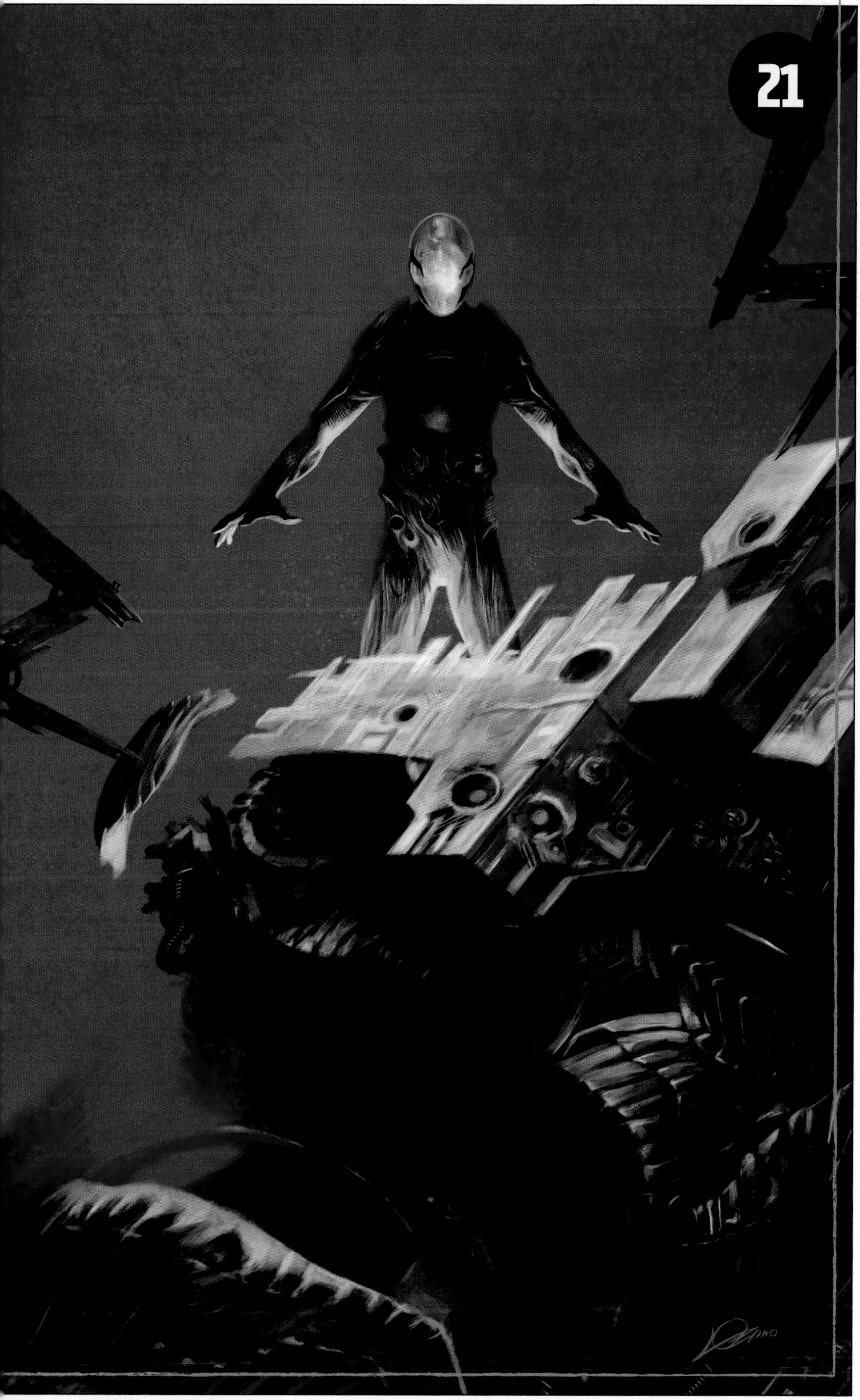
21

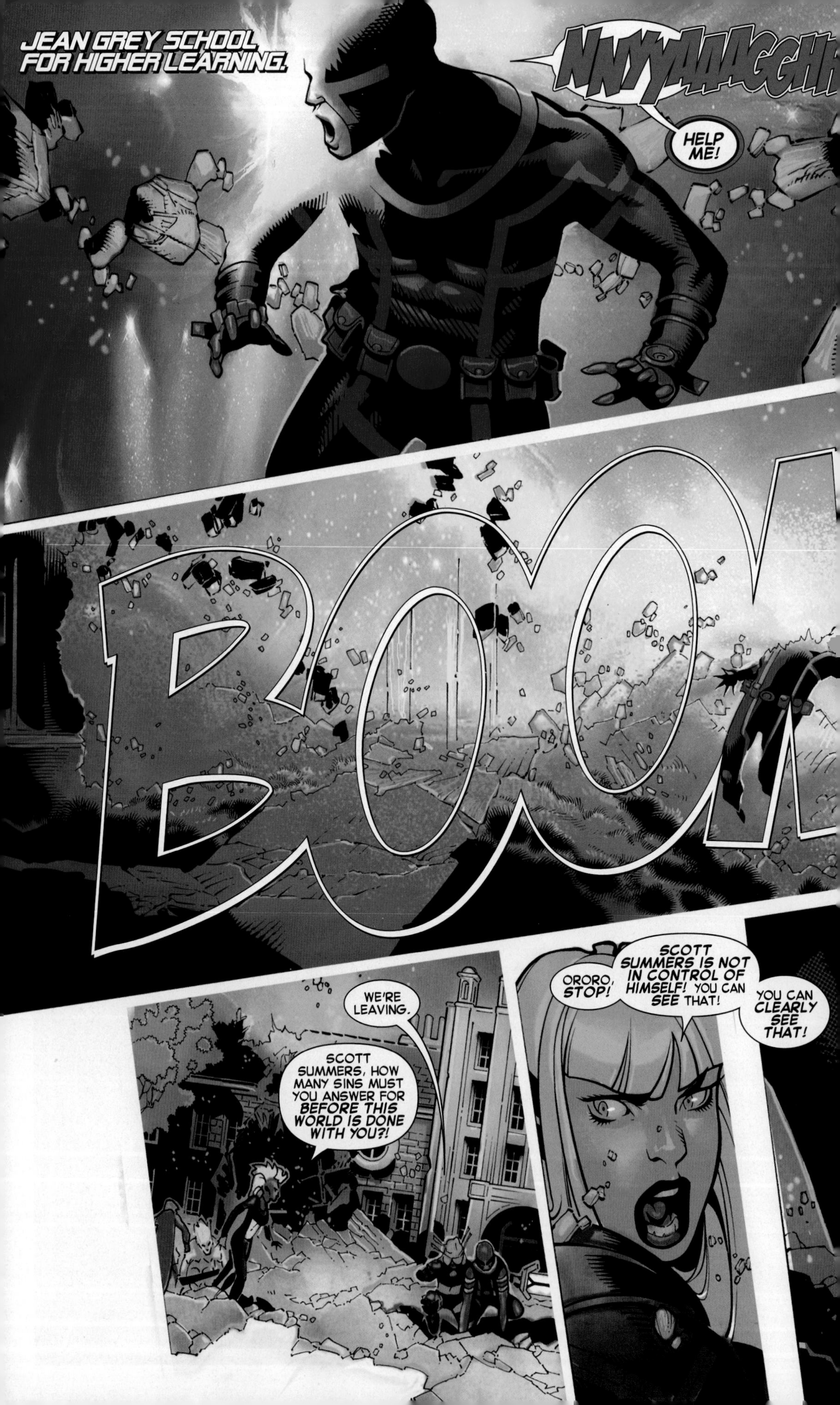
JEAN GREY SCHOOL FOR HIGHER LEARNING.
NNYYAAAAGGHH
HELP ME!
BOOM
WE'RE LEAVING.
SCOTT SUMMERS, HOW MANY SINS MUST YOU ANSWER FOR BEFORE THIS WORLD IS DONE WITH YOU?!
ORORO, STOP!
SCOTT SUMMERS IS NOT IN CONTROL OF HIMSELF! YOU CAN SEE THAT!
YOU CAN CLEARLY SEE THAT!

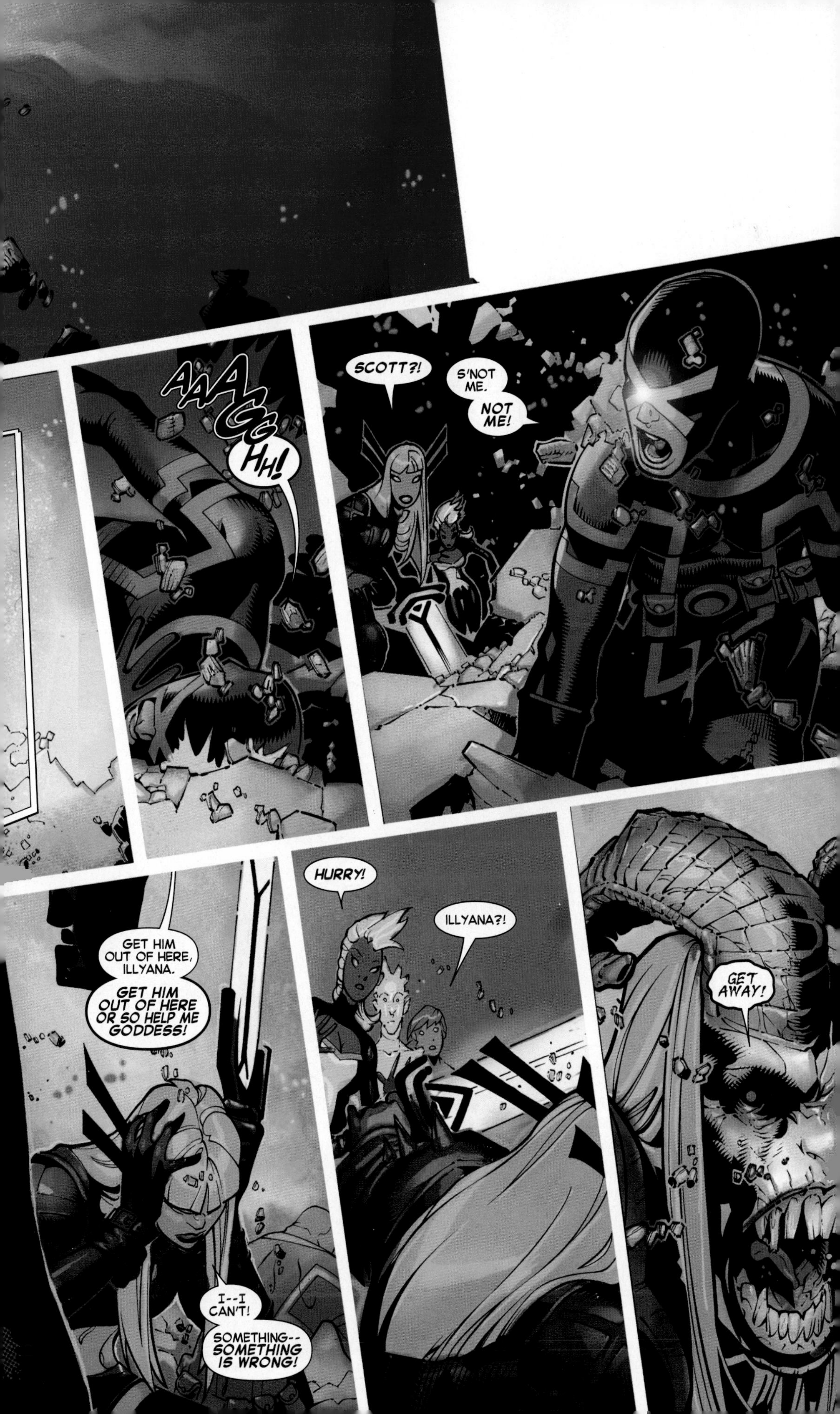
AAAGGHH!
SCOTT?!
S'NOT ME.
NOT ME!
GET HIM OUT OF HERE, ILLYANA.
GET HIM OUT OF HERE OR SO HELP ME GODDESS!
I--I CAN'T!
SOMETHING-- SOMETHING IS WRONG!
HURRY!
ILLYANA?!
GET AWAY!

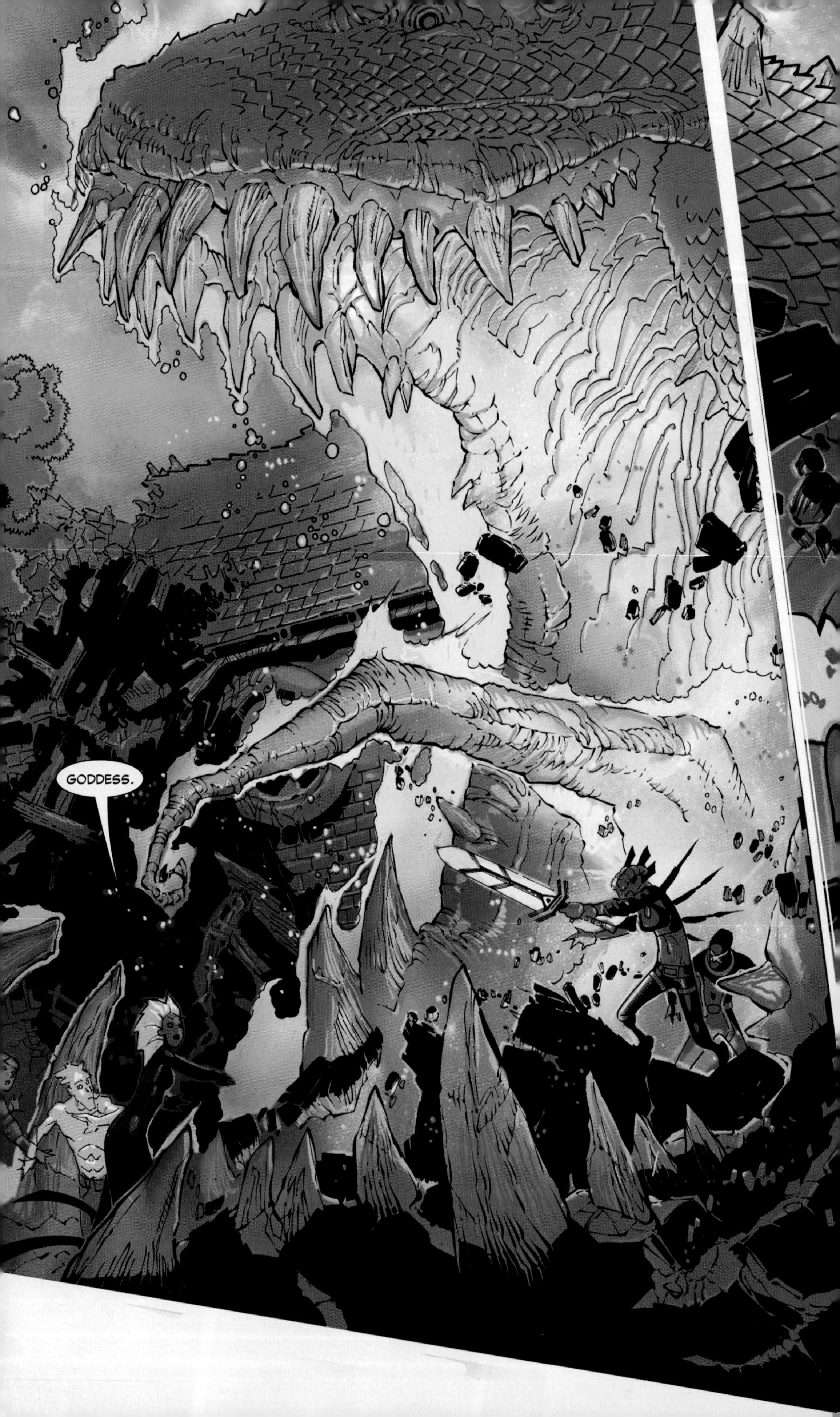
GODDESS.

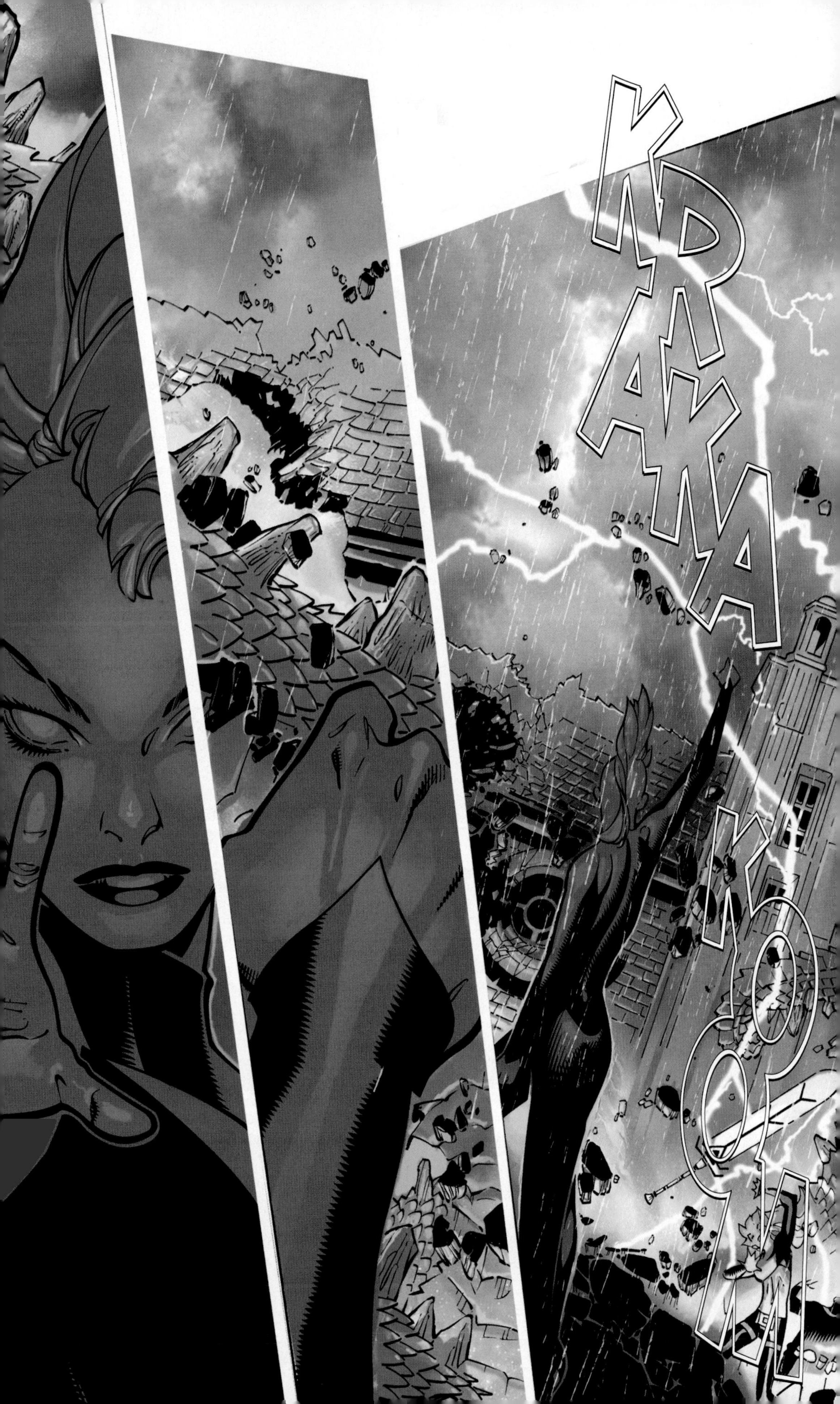
KRAKKA
KOOM

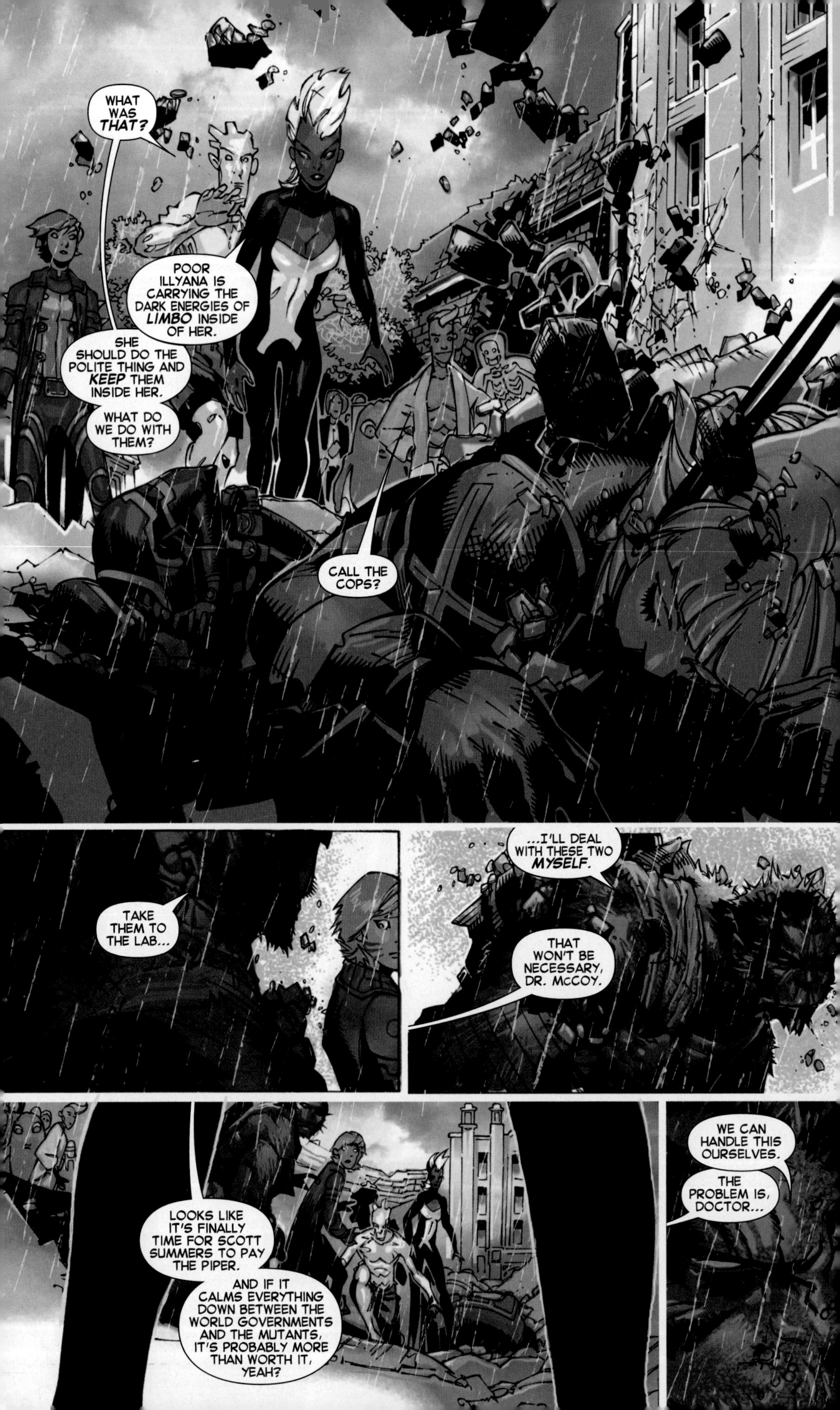

WHAT WAS *THAT?*
POOR ILLYANA IS CARRYING THE DARK ENERGIES OF *LIMBO* INSIDE OF HER.
SHE SHOULD DO THE POLITE THING AND *KEEP* THEM INSIDE HER.
WHAT DO WE DO WITH THEM?
CALL THE COPS?
TAKE THEM TO THE LAB...
...I'LL DEAL WITH THESE TWO *MYSELF*.
THAT WON'T BE NECESSARY, DR. McCOY.
LOOKS LIKE IT'S FINALLY TIME FOR SCOTT SUMMERS TO PAY THE PIPER.
AND IF IT CALMS EVERYTHING DOWN BETWEEN THE WORLD GOVERNMENTS AND THE MUTANTS, IT'S PROBABLY MORE THAN WORTH IT, YEAH?
WE CAN HANDLE THIS OURSELVES.
THE PROBLEM IS, DOCTOR...

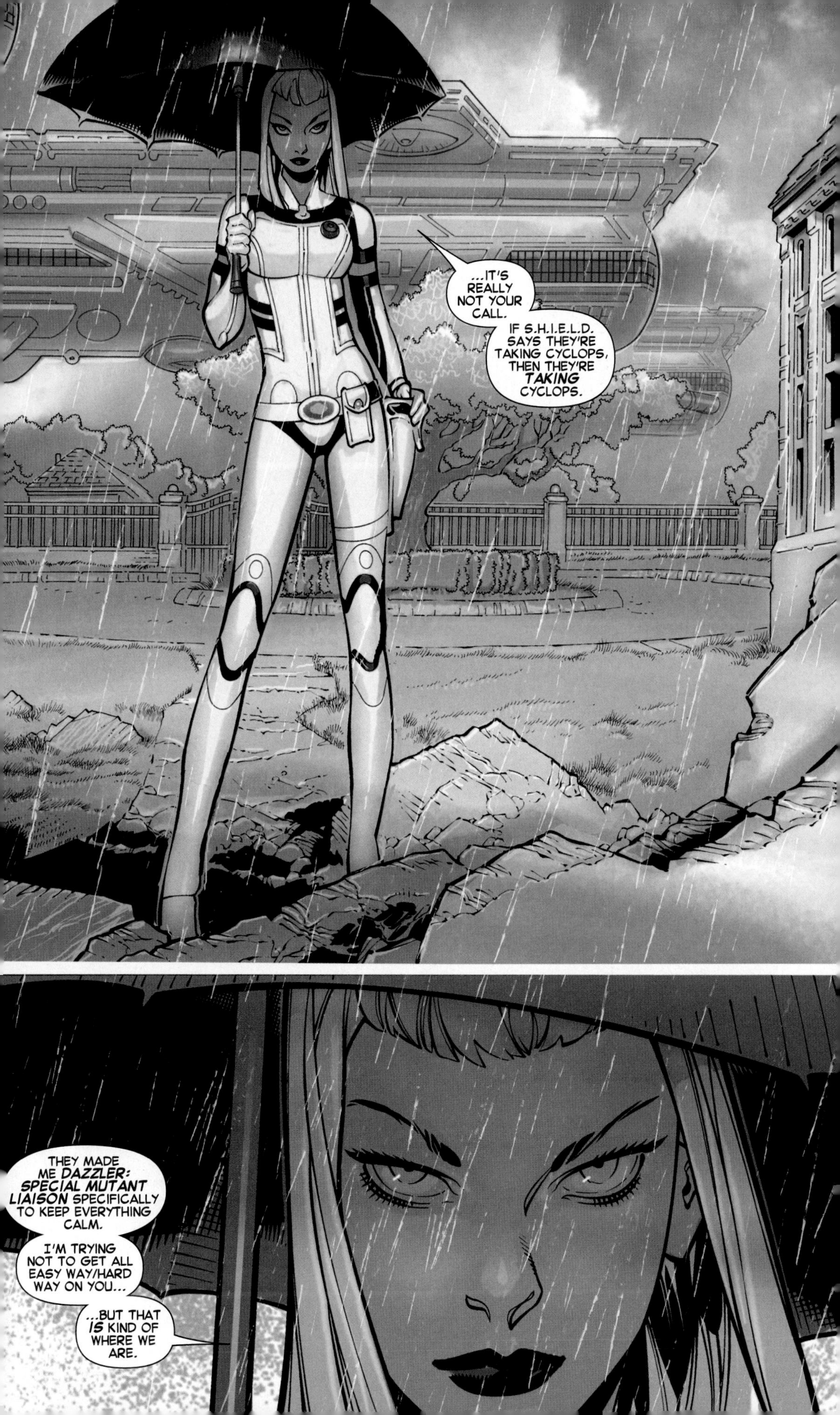
...IT'S REALLY NOT YOUR CALL.
IF S.H.I.E.L.D. SAYS THEY'RE TAKING CYCLOPS, THEN THEY'RE *TAKING* CYCLOPS.
THEY MADE ME *DAZZLER: SPECIAL MUTANT LIAISON* SPECIFICALLY TO KEEP EVERYTHING CALM.
I'M TRYING NOT TO GET ALL EASY WAY/HARD WAY ON YOU...
...BUT THAT *IS* KIND OF WHERE WE ARE.

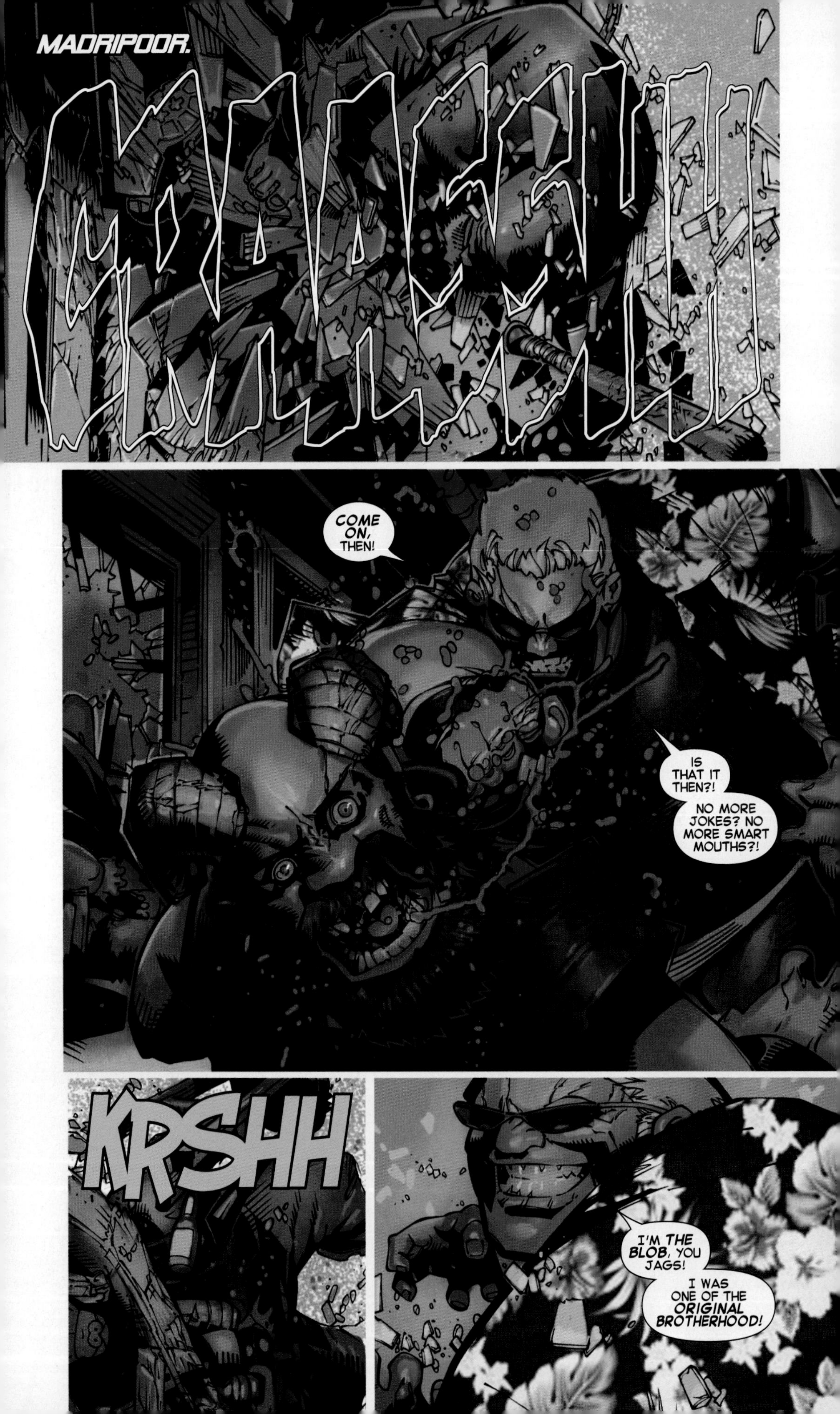
MADRIPOOR.
COME ON, THEN!
IS THAT IT THEN?!
NO MORE JOKES? NO MORE SMART MOUTHS?!
KRSHH
I'M THE BLOB, YOU JAGS!
I WAS ONE OF THE ORIGINAL BROTHERHOOD!

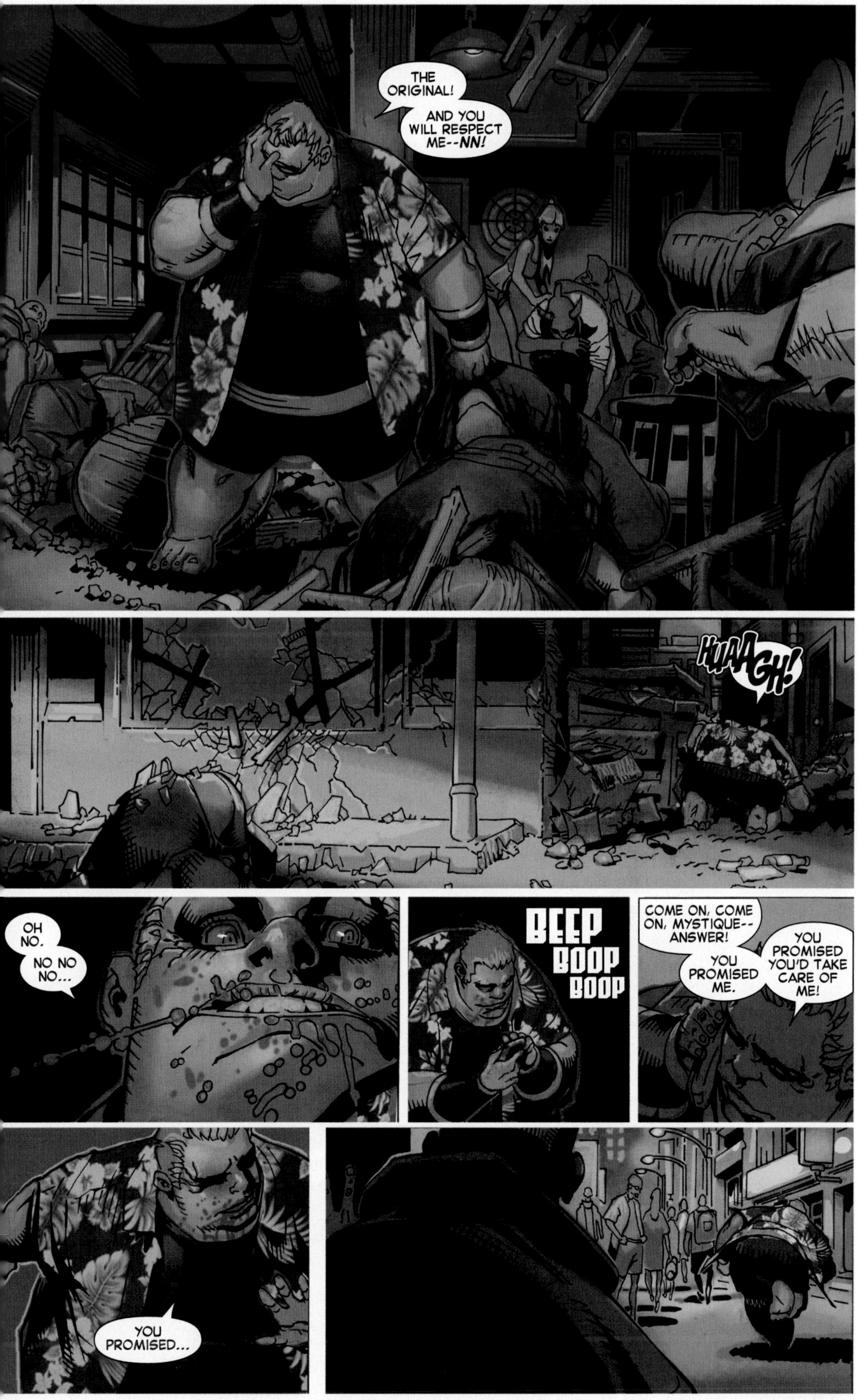
THE ORIGINAL!
AND YOU WILL RESPECT ME--NN!
HUAAAGH!
OH NO.
NO NO NO...
BEEP BOOP BOOP
COME ON, COME ON, MYSTIQUE--ANSWER!
YOU PROMISED ME.
YOU PROMISED YOU'D TAKE CARE OF ME!
YOU PROMISED...

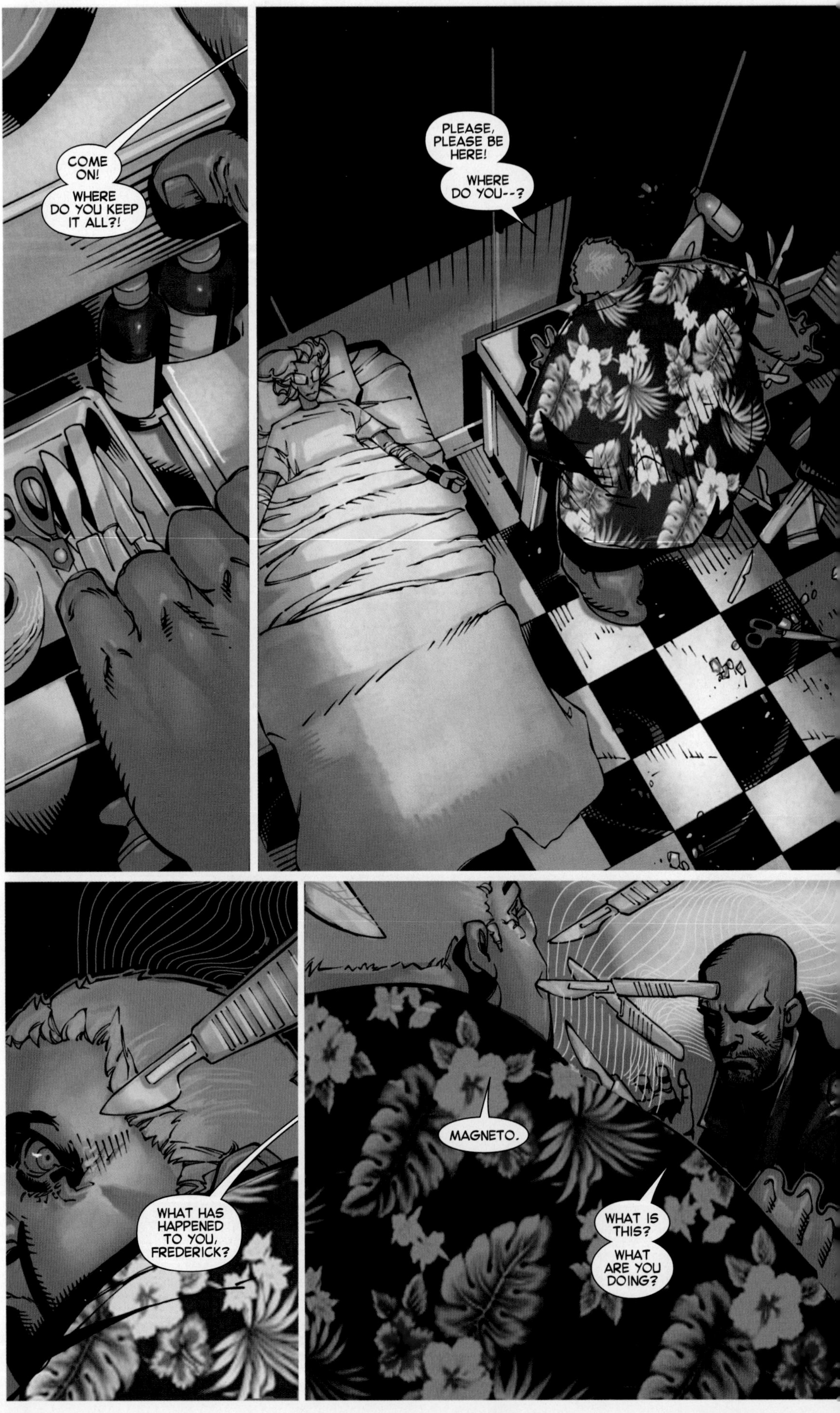
COME ON!
WHERE DO YOU KEEP IT ALL?!
PLEASE, PLEASE BE HERE!
WHERE DO YOU--?
WHAT HAS HAPPENED TO YOU, FREDERICK?
MAGNETO.
WHAT IS THIS?
WHAT ARE YOU DOING?

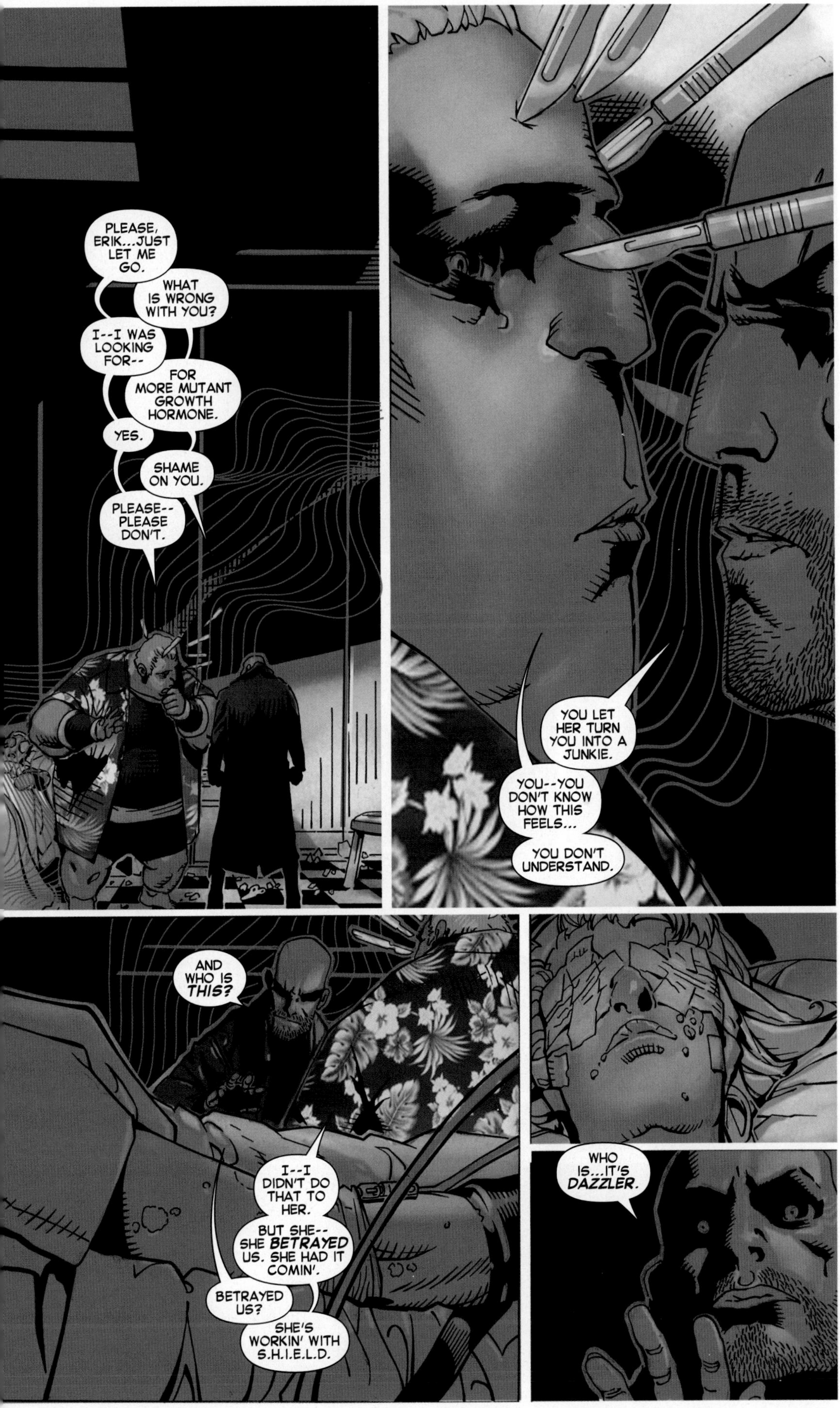
PLEASE, ERIK...JUST LET ME GO.
WHAT IS WRONG WITH YOU?
I--I WAS LOOKING FOR--
FOR MORE MUTANT GROWTH HORMONE.
YES.
SHAME ON YOU.
PLEASE--PLEASE DON'T.
YOU LET HER TURN YOU INTO A JUNKIE.
YOU--YOU DON'T KNOW HOW THIS FEELS...
YOU DON'T UNDERSTAND.
AND WHO IS *THIS?*
I--I DIDN'T DO THAT TO HER.
BUT SHE--SHE *BETRAYED* US. SHE HAD IT COMIN'.
BETRAYED US?
SHE'S WORKIN' WITH S.H.I.E.L.D.
WHO IS...IT'S *DAZZLER*.

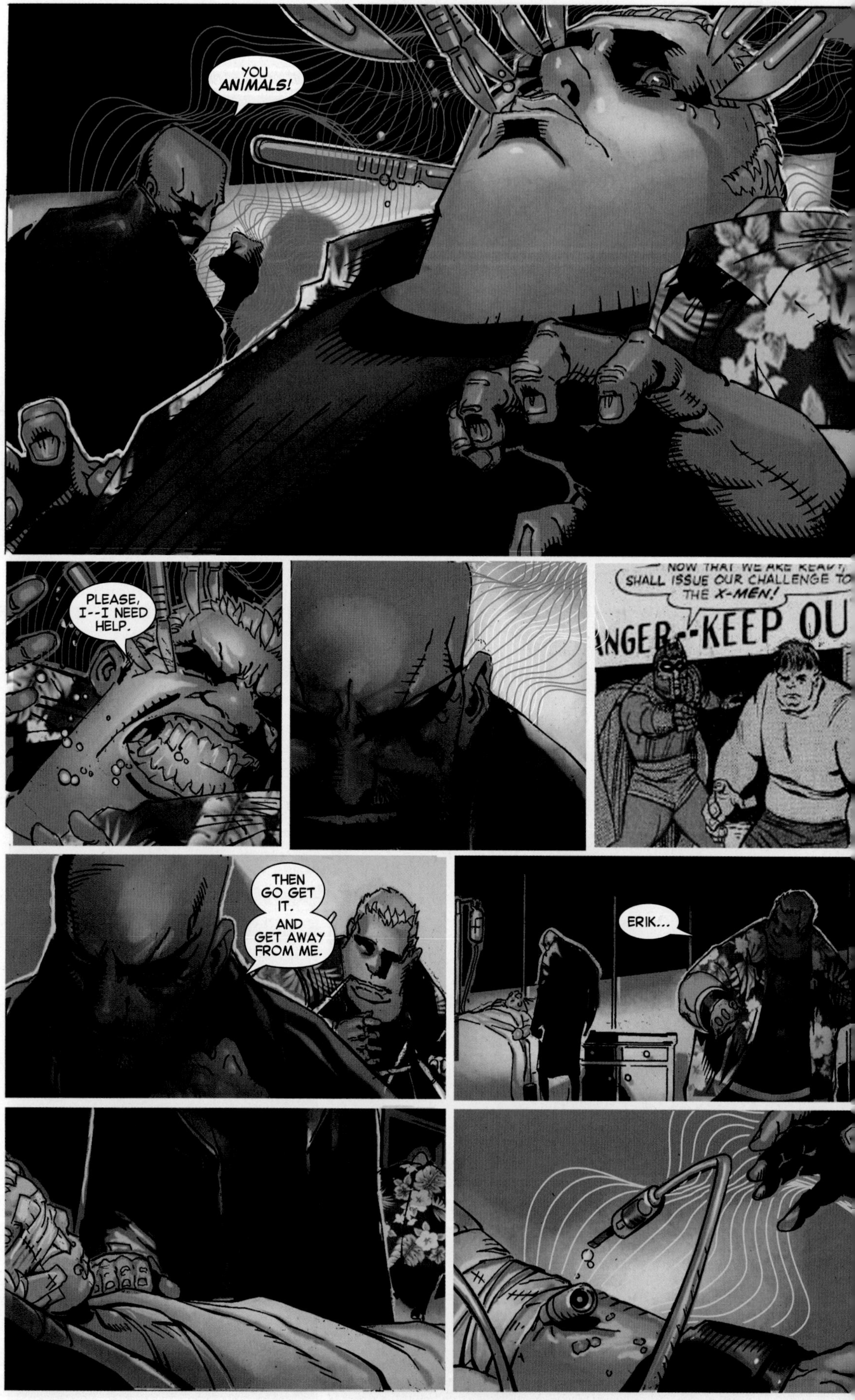
YOU ANIMALS!
PLEASE, I--I NEED HELP.
NOW THAT WE ARE READY, SHALL ISSUE OUR CHALLENGE TO THE X-MEN!
-KEEP OU
THEN GO GET IT.
AND GET AWAY FROM ME.
ERIK...

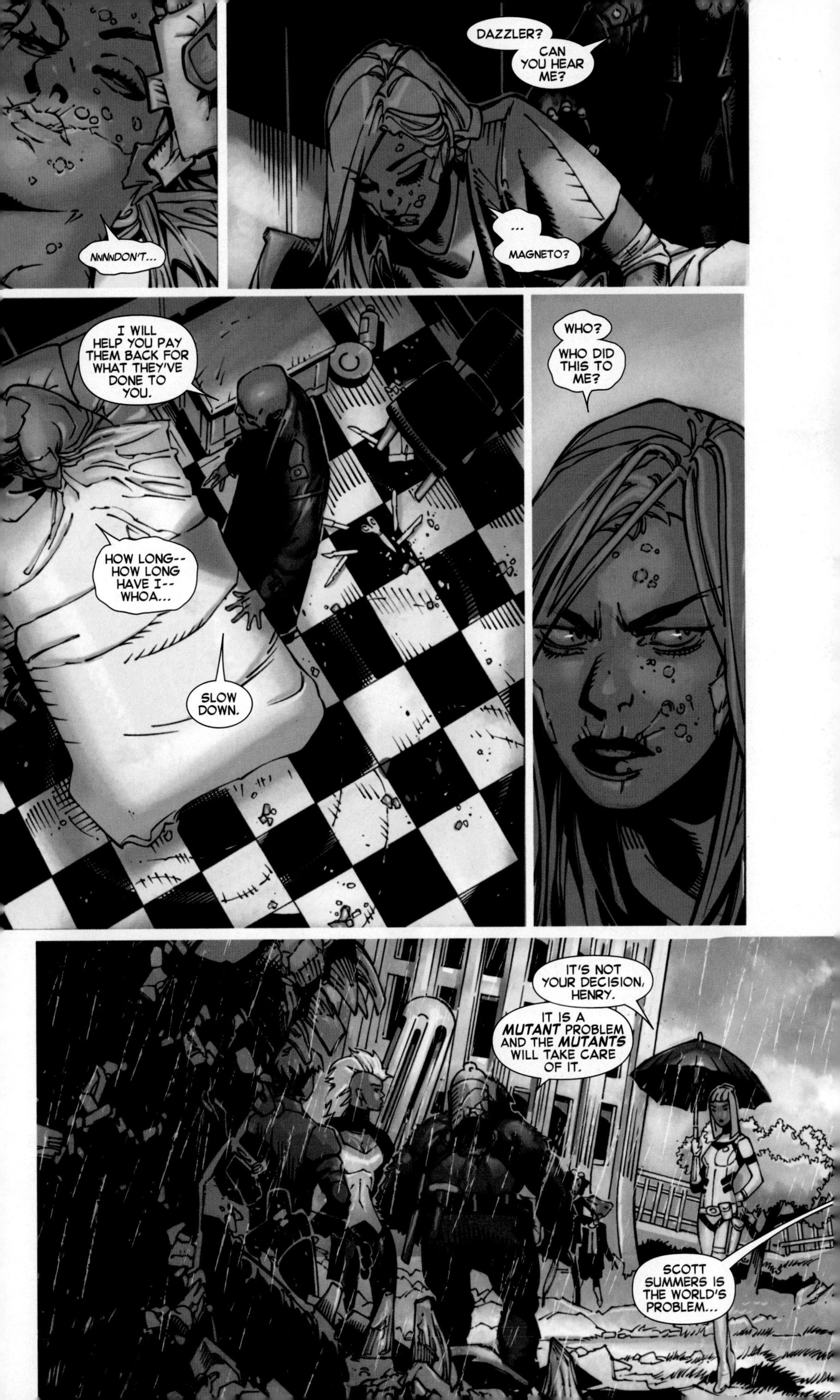
NNNNDON'T...
DAZZLER?
CAN YOU HEAR ME?
...
MAGNETO?
I WILL HELP YOU PAY THEM BACK FOR WHAT THEY'VE DONE TO YOU.
HOW LONG--HOW LONG HAVE I--WHOA...
SLOW DOWN.
WHO?
WHO DID THIS TO ME?
IT'S NOT YOUR DECISION, HENRY.
IT IS A MUTANT PROBLEM AND THE MUTANTS WILL TAKE CARE OF IT.
SCOTT SUMMERS IS THE WORLD'S PROBLEM...

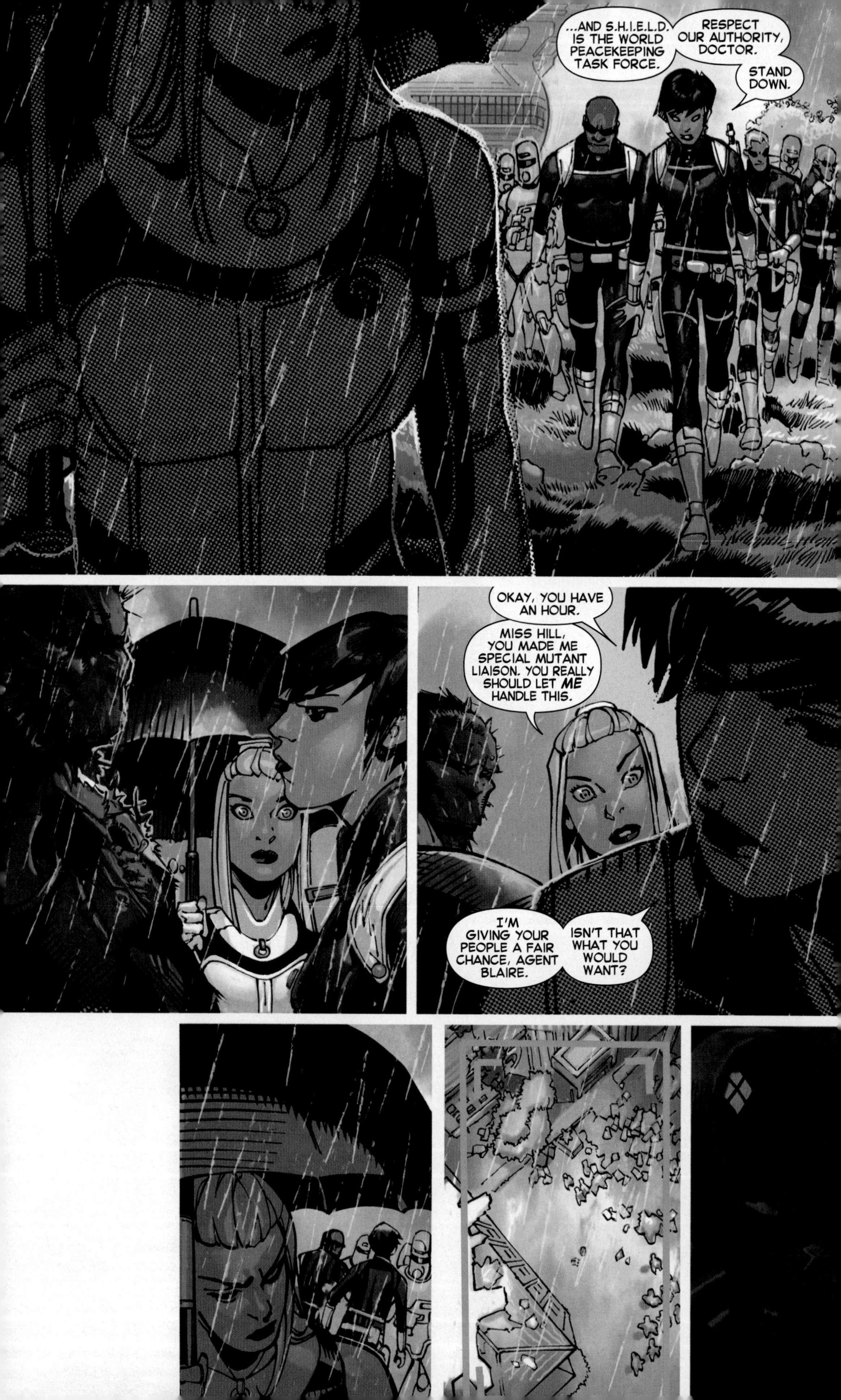

...AND S.H.I.E.L.D. IS THE WORLD PEACEKEEPING TASK FORCE.
RESPECT OUR AUTHORITY, DOCTOR.
STAND DOWN.
OKAY, YOU HAVE AN HOUR.
MISS HILL, YOU MADE ME SPECIAL MUTANT LIAISON. YOU REALLY SHOULD LET ME HANDLE THIS.
I'M GIVING YOUR PEOPLE A FAIR CHANCE, AGENT BLAIRE.
ISN'T THAT WHAT YOU WOULD WANT?

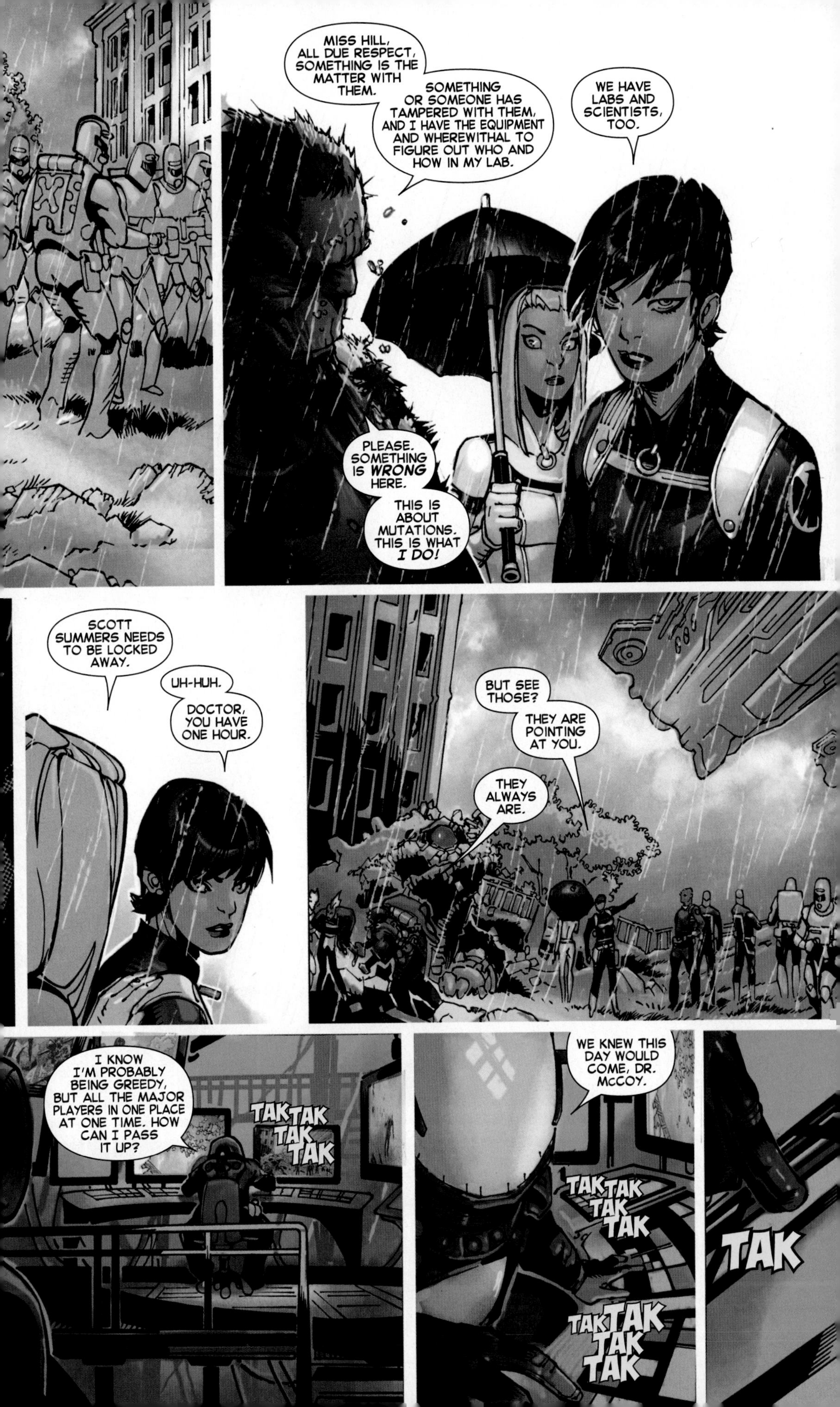
MISS HILL, ALL DUE RESPECT, SOMETHING IS THE MATTER WITH THEM.
SOMETHING OR SOMEONE HAS TAMPERED WITH THEM, AND I HAVE THE EQUIPMENT AND WHEREWITHAL TO FIGURE OUT WHO AND HOW IN MY LAB.
WE HAVE LABS AND SCIENTISTS, TOO.
PLEASE. SOMETHING IS *WRONG* HERE.
THIS IS ABOUT MUTATIONS. THIS IS WHAT *I DO!*
SCOTT SUMMERS NEEDS TO BE LOCKED AWAY.
UH-HUH.
DOCTOR, YOU HAVE ONE HOUR.
BUT SEE THOSE?
THEY ARE POINTING AT YOU.
THEY ALWAYS ARE.
I KNOW I'M PROBABLY BEING GREEDY, BUT ALL THE MAJOR PLAYERS IN ONE PLACE AT ONE TIME. HOW CAN I PASS IT UP?
TAK TAK TAK TAK
WE KNEW THIS DAY WOULD COME, DR. McCOY.
TAK TAK TAK TAK
TAK TAK TAK TAK
TAK

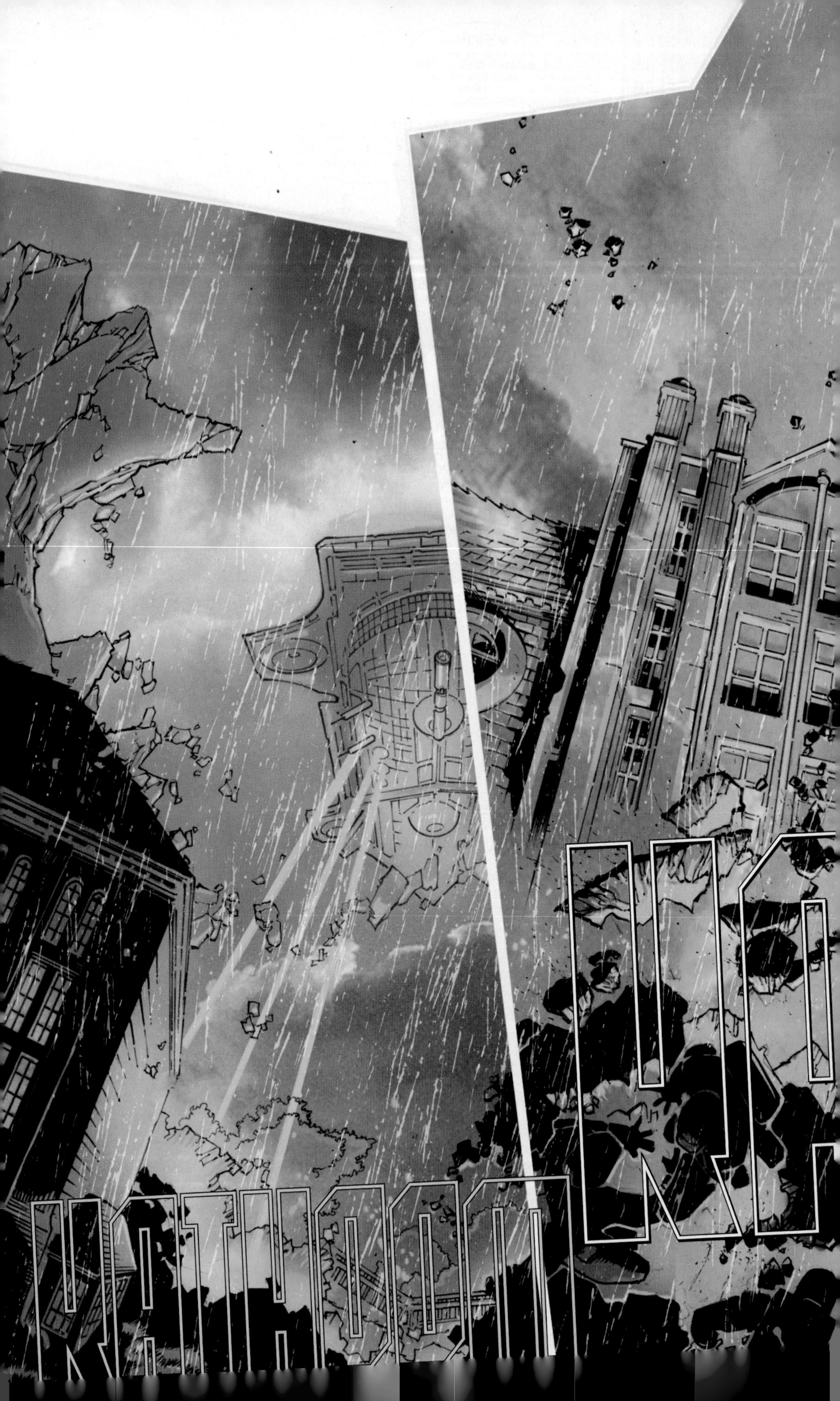

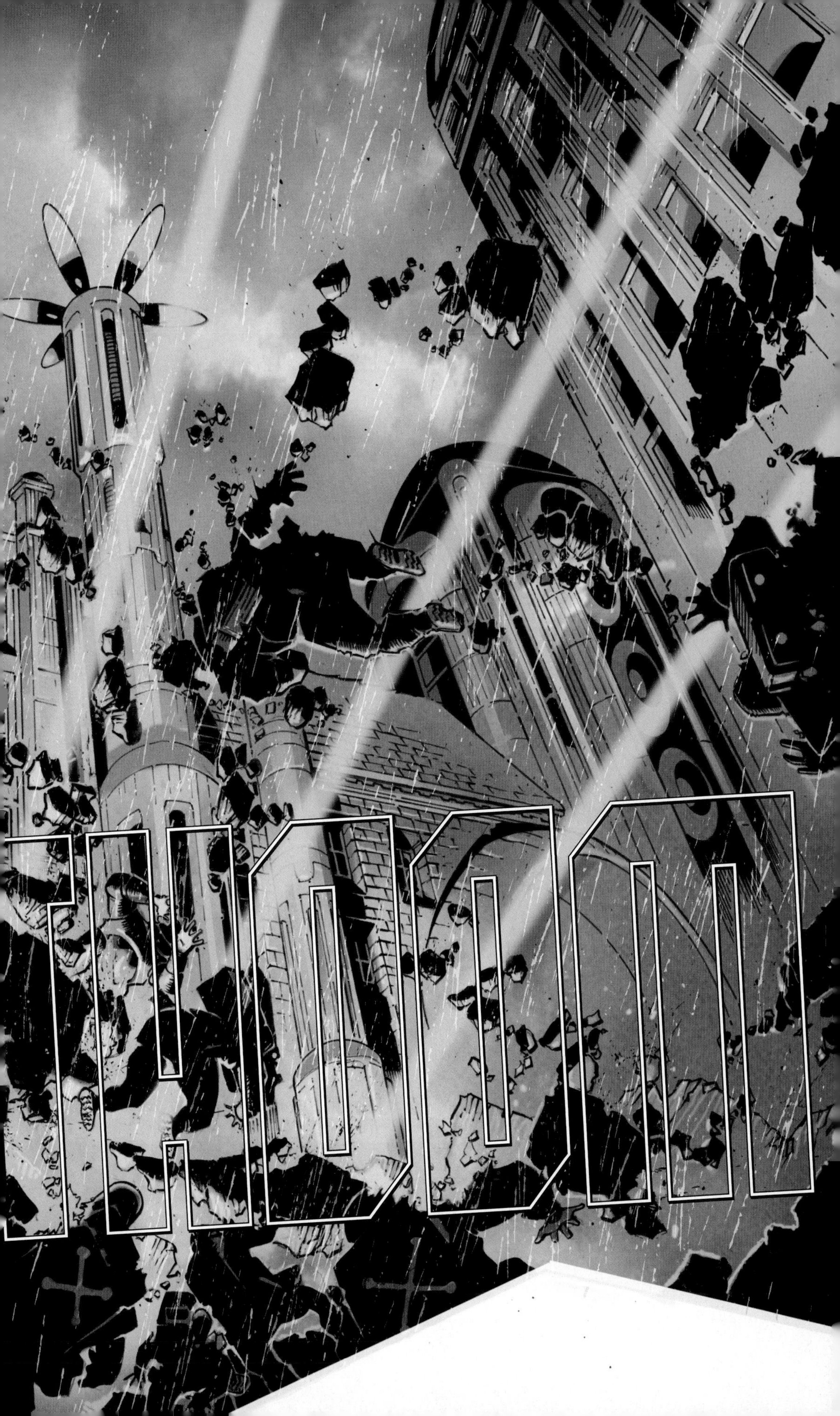
THOOM

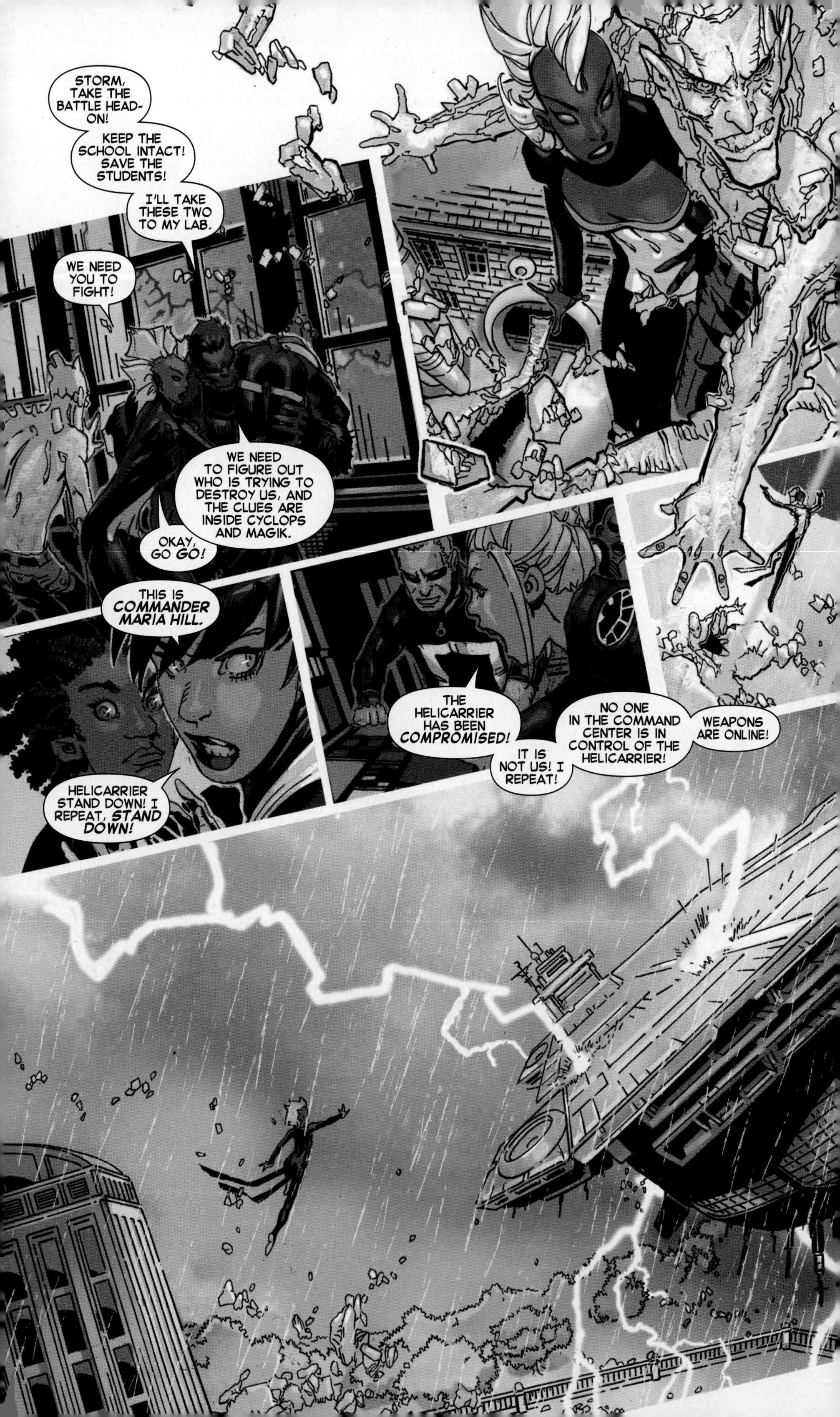

STORM, TAKE THE BATTLE HEAD-ON!
KEEP THE SCHOOL INTACT! SAVE THE STUDENTS!
I'LL TAKE THESE TWO TO MY LAB.
WE NEED YOU TO FIGHT!
WE NEED TO FIGURE OUT WHO IS TRYING TO DESTROY US, AND THE CLUES ARE INSIDE CYCLOPS AND MAGIK.
OKAY, GO GO!
THIS IS COMMANDER MARIA HILL.
HELICARRIER STAND DOWN! I REPEAT, STAND DOWN!
THE HELICARRIER HAS BEEN COMPROMISED!
IT IS NOT US! I REPEAT!
NO ONE IN THE COMMAND CENTER IS IN CONTROL OF THE HELICARRIER!
WEAPONS ARE ONLINE!

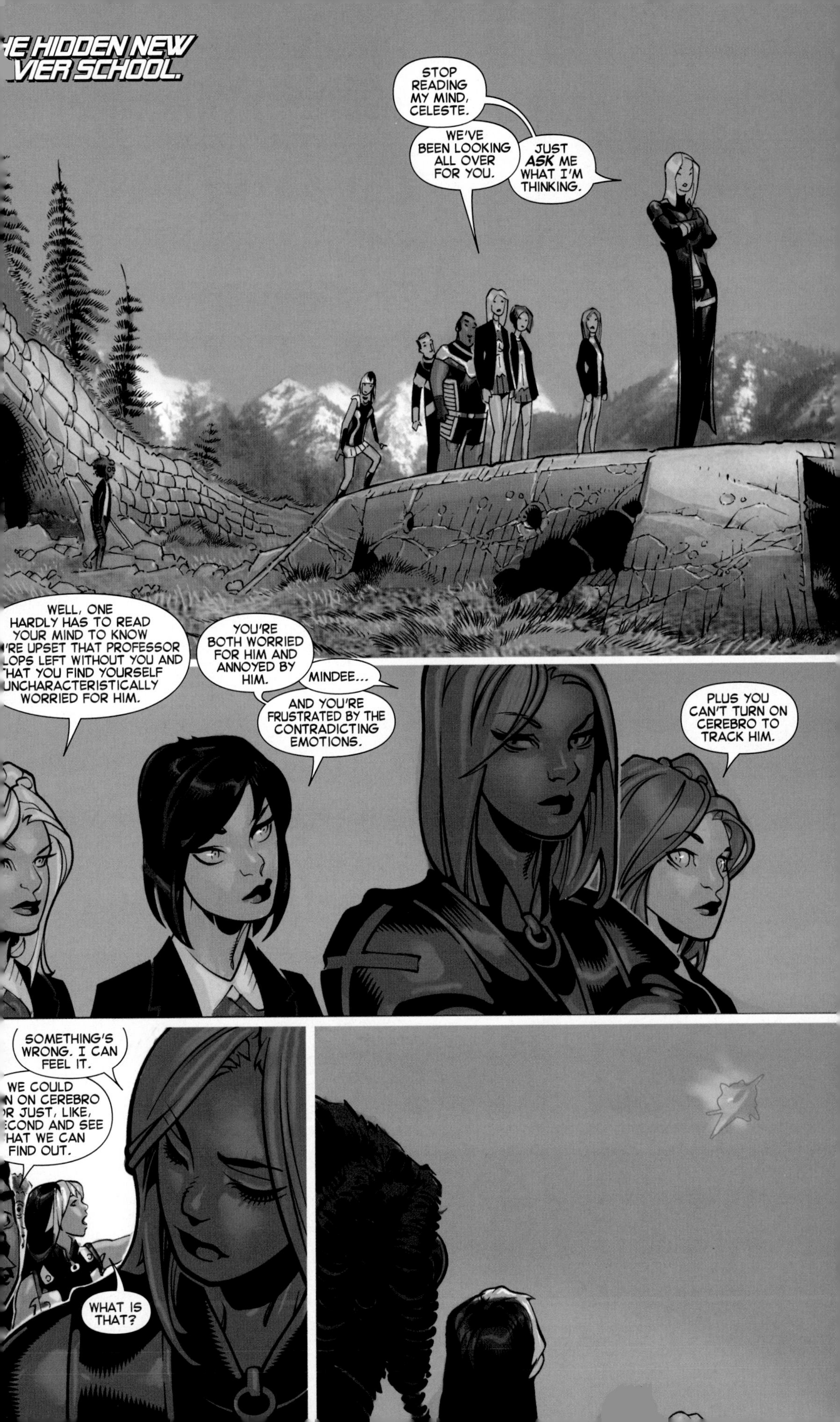

HE HIDDEN NEW
VIER SCHOOL.
STOP READING MY MIND, CELESTE.
JUST ASK ME WHAT I'M THINKING.
WE'VE BEEN LOOKING ALL OVER FOR YOU.
WELL, ONE HARDLY HAS TO READ YOUR MIND TO KNOW 'RE UPSET THAT PROFESSOR LOPS LEFT WITHOUT YOU AND HAT YOU FIND YOURSELF UNCHARACTERISTICALLY WORRIED FOR HIM.
YOU'RE BOTH WORRIED FOR HIM AND ANNOYED BY HIM.
MINDEE...
AND YOU'RE FRUSTRATED BY THE CONTRADICTING EMOTIONS.
PLUS YOU CAN'T TURN ON CEREBRO TO TRACK HIM.
SOMETHING'S WRONG. I CAN FEEL IT.
WE COULD N ON CEREBRO R JUST, LIKE, ECOND AND SEE HAT WE CAN FIND OUT.
WHAT IS THAT?

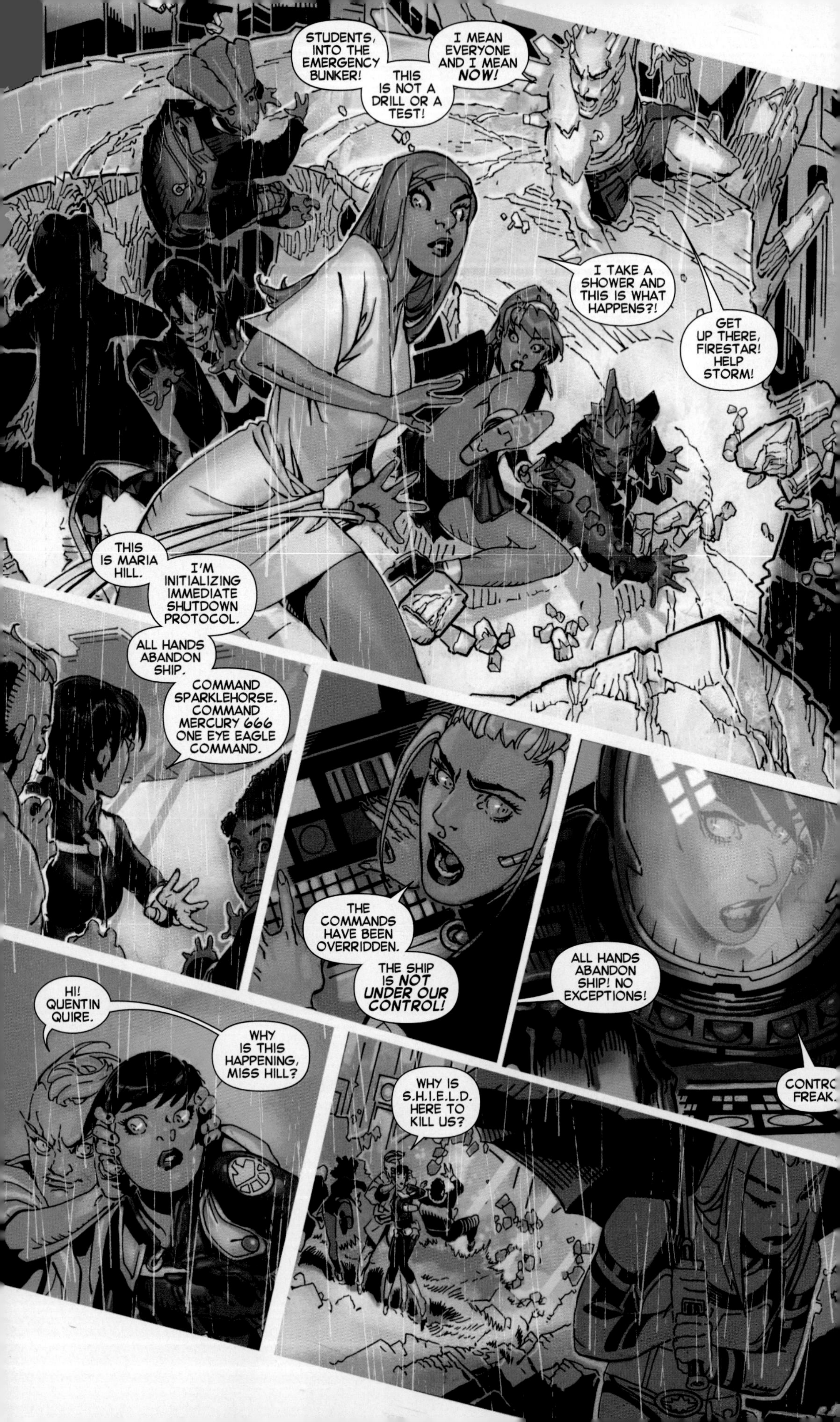
STUDENTS, INTO THE EMERGENCY BUNKER!
I MEAN EVERYONE AND I MEAN NOW!
THIS IS NOT A DRILL OR A TEST!
I TAKE A SHOWER AND THIS IS WHAT HAPPENS?!
GET UP THERE, FIRESTAR! HELP STORM!
THIS IS MARIA HILL.
I'M INITIALIZING IMMEDIATE SHUTDOWN PROTOCOL.
ALL HANDS ABANDON SHIP.
COMMAND SPARKLEHORSE. COMMAND MERCURY 666 ONE EYE EAGLE COMMAND.
THE COMMANDS HAVE BEEN OVERRIDDEN.
THE SHIP IS NOT UNDER OUR CONTROL!
ALL HANDS ABANDON SHIP! NO EXCEPTIONS!
HI! QUENTIN QUIRE.
WHY IS THIS HAPPENING, MISS HILL?
WHY IS S.H.I.E.L.D. HERE TO KILL US?
CONTRO FREAK.

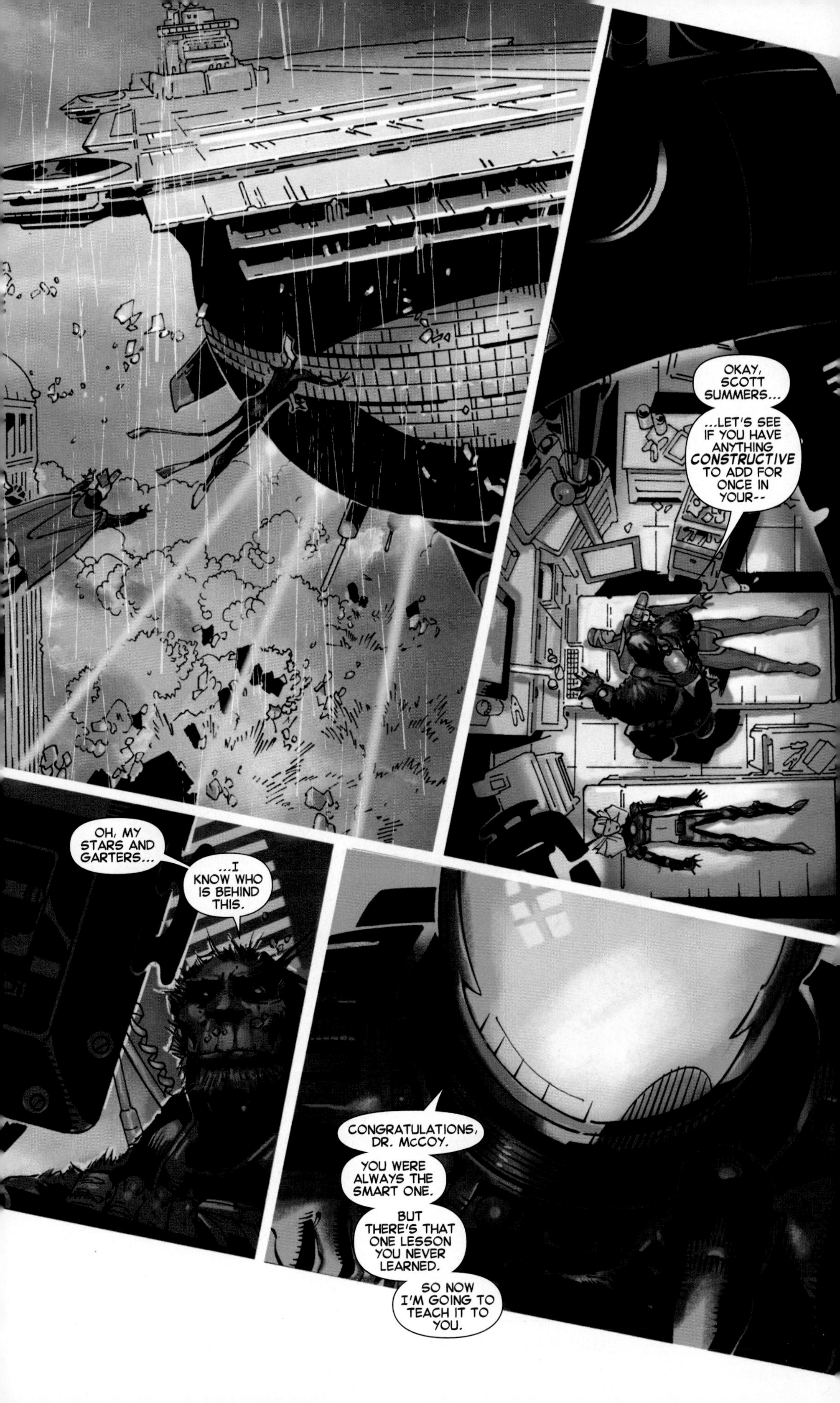
OKAY, SCOTT SUMMERS...
...LET'S SEE IF YOU HAVE ANYTHING *CONSTRUCTIVE* TO ADD FOR ONCE IN YOUR--
OH, MY STARS AND GARTERS...
...I KNOW WHO IS BEHIND THIS.
CONGRATULATIONS, DR. McCOY.
YOU WERE ALWAYS THE SMART ONE.
BUT THERE'S THAT ONE LESSON YOU NEVER LEARNED.
SO NOW I'M GOING TO TEACH IT TO YOU.

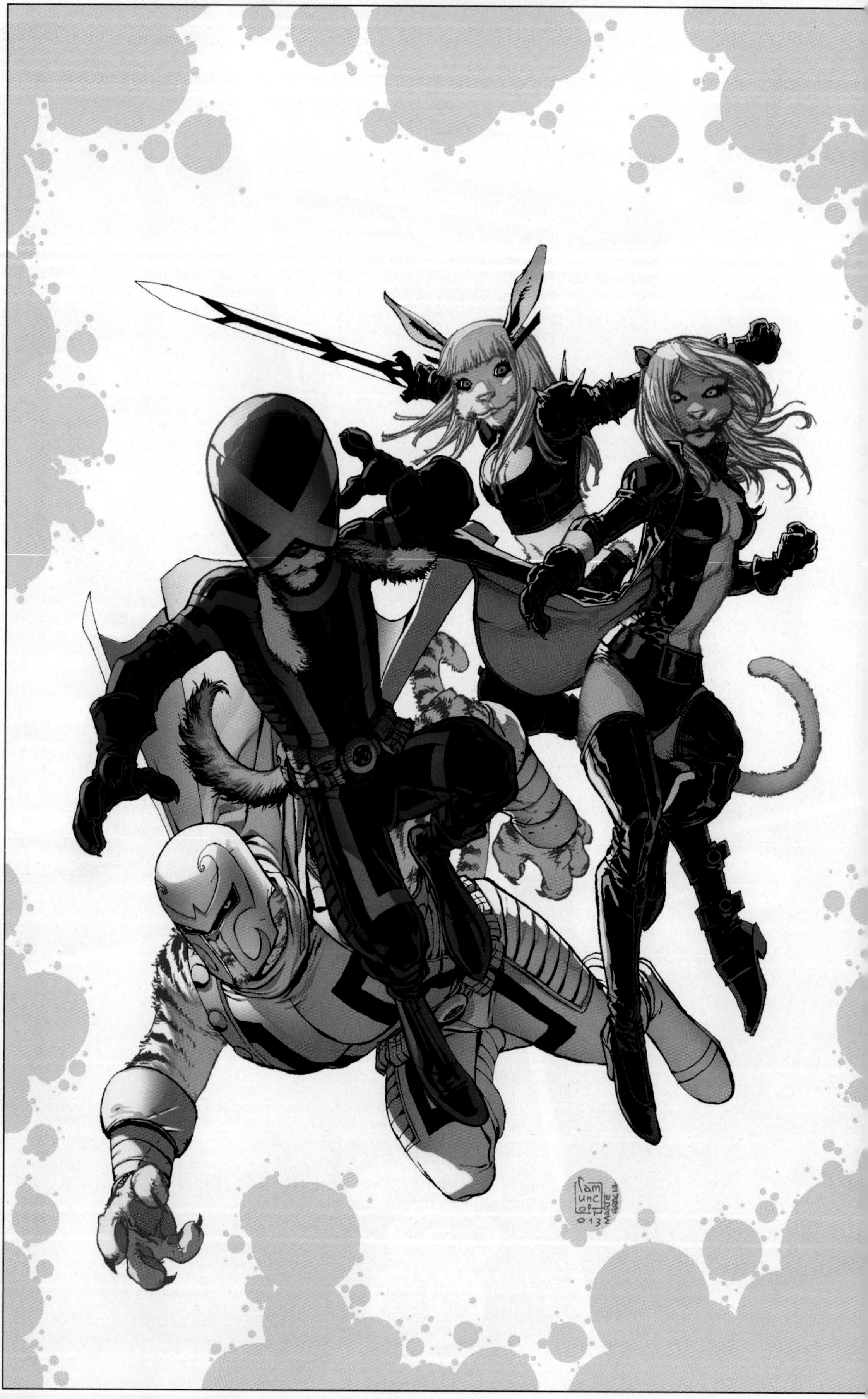
Camuncoli 013
Marte Gracia

UNCANNY X-MEN #19 ANIMAL VARIANT
BY GIUSEPPE CAMUNCOLI & MARTE GRACIA

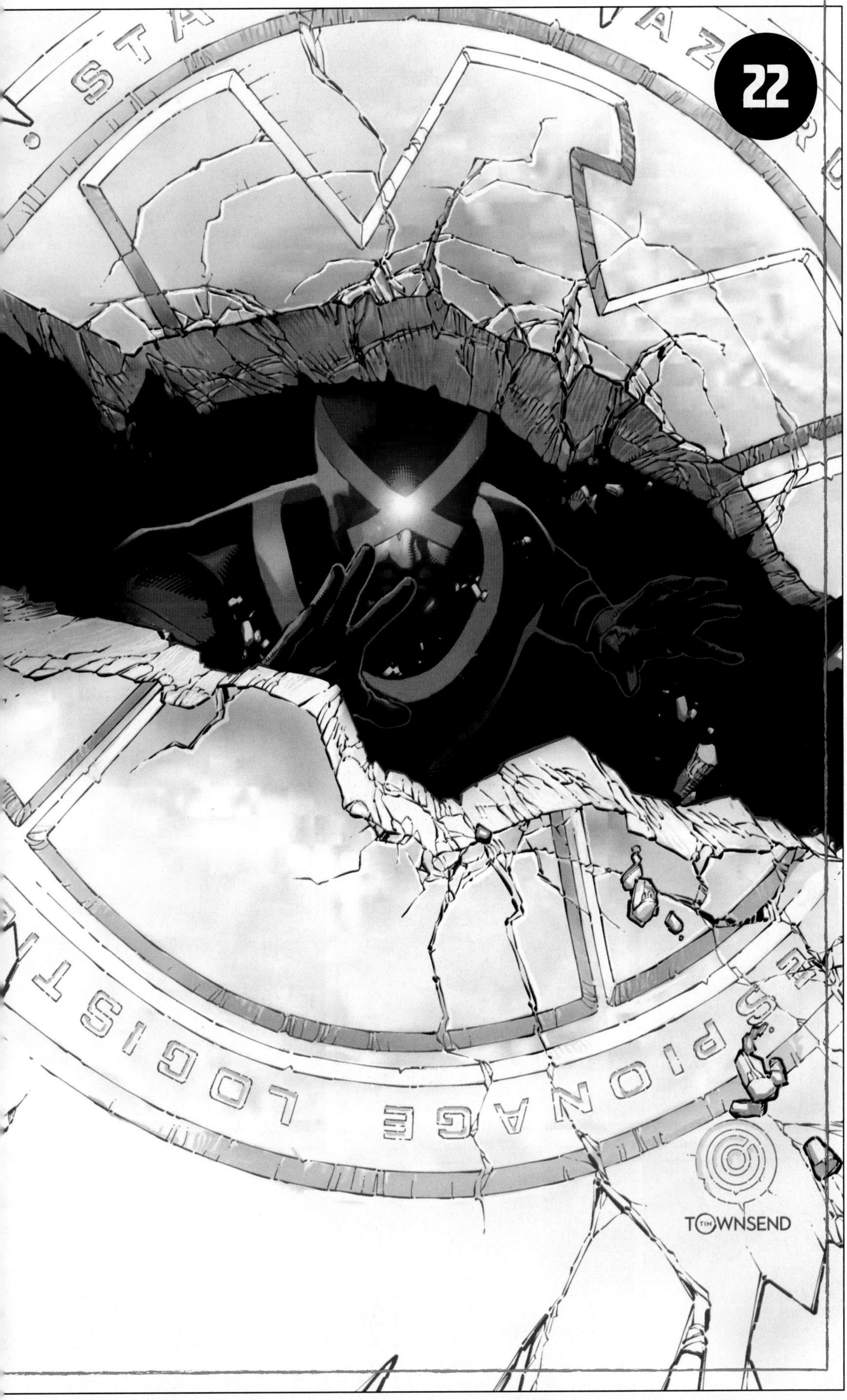
22
TOWNSEND

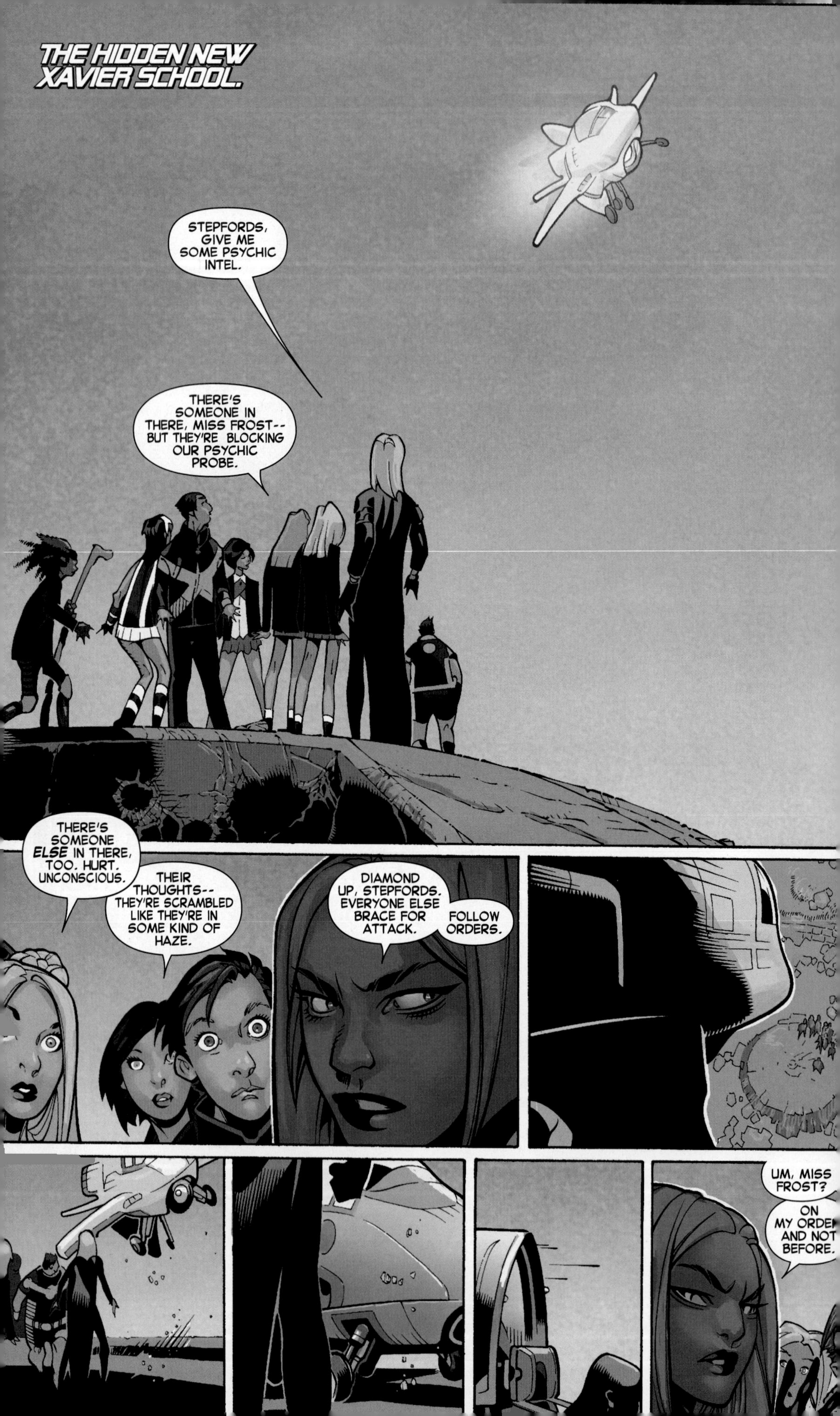
THE HIDDEN NEW XAVIER SCHOOL.
STEPFORDS, GIVE ME SOME PSYCHIC INTEL.
THERE'S SOMEONE IN THERE, MISS FROST-- BUT THEY'RE BLOCKING OUR PSYCHIC PROBE.
THERE'S SOMEONE ELSE IN THERE, TOO. HURT. UNCONSCIOUS.
THEIR THOUGHTS-- THEY'RE SCRAMBLED LIKE THEY'RE IN SOME KIND OF HAZE.
DIAMOND UP, STEPFORDS. EVERYONE ELSE BRACE FOR ATTACK.
FOLLOW ORDERS.
UM, MISS FROST?
ON MY ORDE
AND NOT BEFORE.

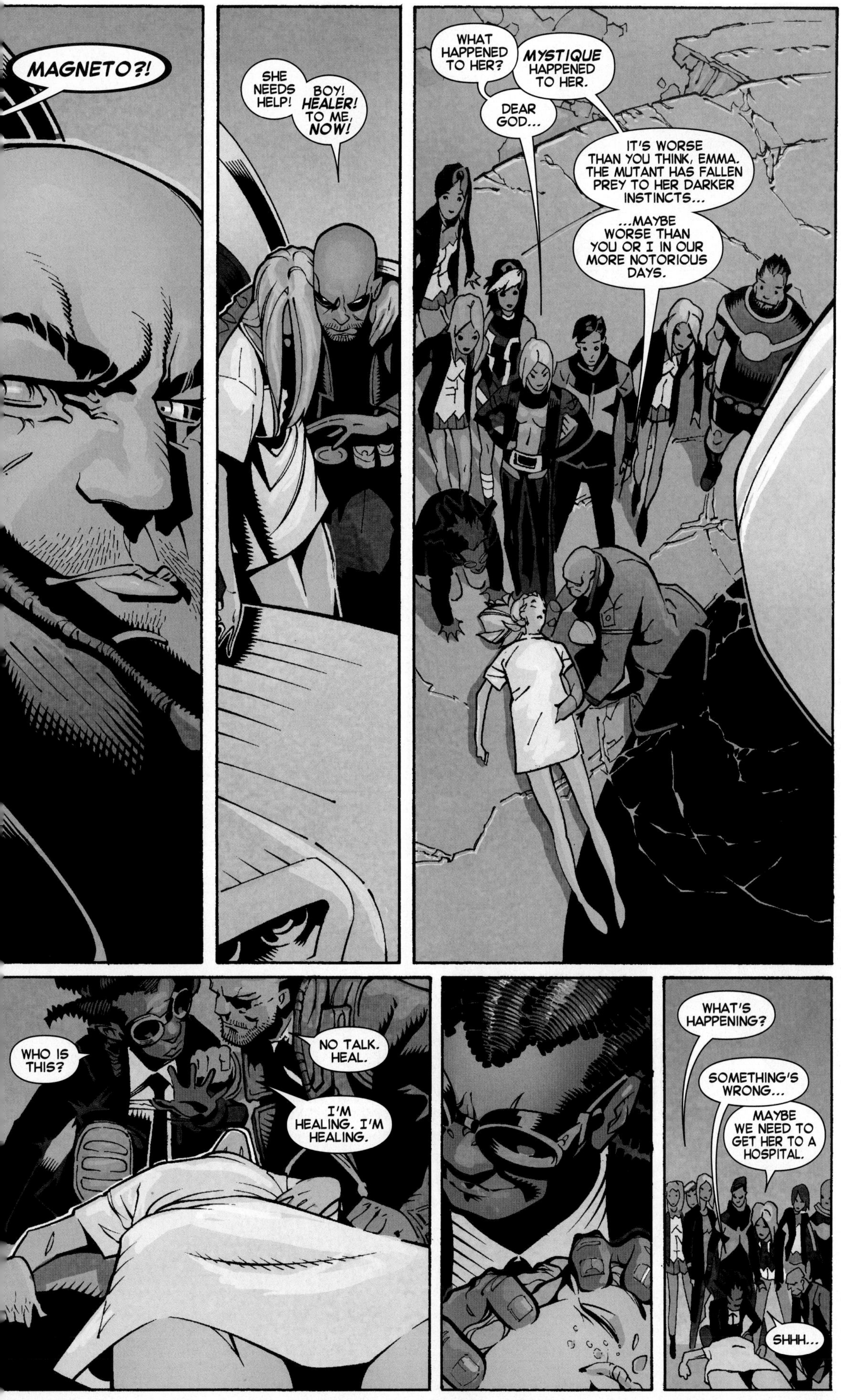
MAGNETO?!
SHE NEEDS HELP!
BOY! HEALER! TO ME, NOW!
WHAT HAPPENED TO HER?
MYSTIQUE HAPPENED TO HER.
DEAR GOD...
IT'S WORSE THAN YOU THINK, EMMA. THE MUTANT HAS FALLEN PREY TO HER DARKER INSTINCTS...
...MAYBE WORSE THAN YOU OR I IN OUR MORE NOTORIOUS DAYS.
WHO IS THIS?
NO TALK. HEAL.
I'M HEALING. I'M HEALING.
WHAT'S HAPPENING?
SOMETHING'S WRONG...
MAYBE WE NEED TO GET HER TO A HOSPITAL.
SHHH...

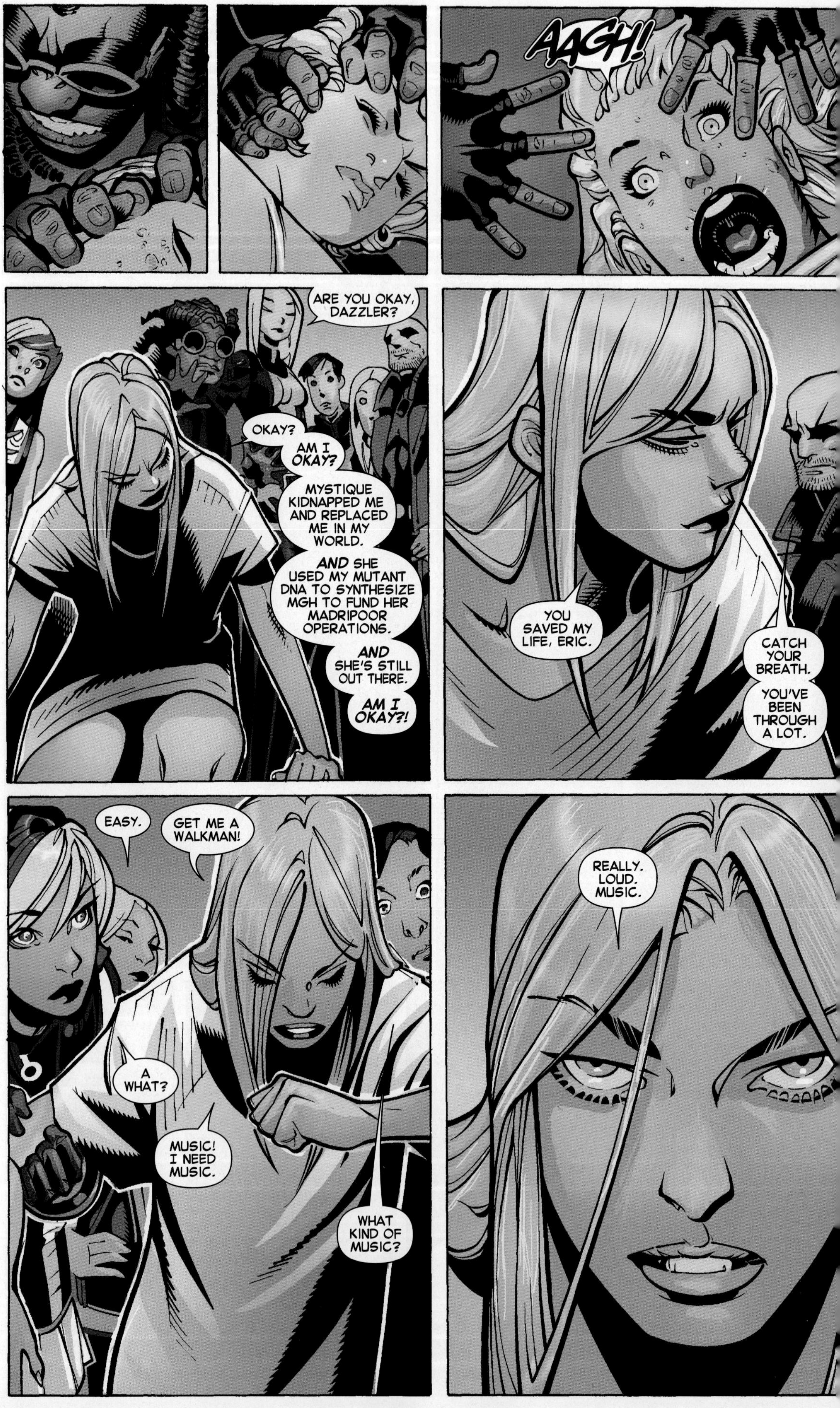
AAGH!
ARE YOU OKAY, DAZZLER?
OKAY?
AM I OKAY?
MYSTIQUE KIDNAPPED ME AND REPLACED ME IN MY WORLD.
AND SHE USED MY MUTANT DNA TO SYNTHESIZE MGH TO FUND HER MADRIPOOR OPERATIONS.
AND SHE'S STILL OUT THERE.
AM I OKAY?!
YOU SAVED MY LIFE, ERIC.
CATCH YOUR BREATH.
YOU'VE BEEN THROUGH A LOT.
EASY.
GET ME A WALKMAN!
A WHAT?
MUSIC! I NEED MUSIC.
WHAT KIND OF MUSIC?
REALLY. LOUD. MUSIC.

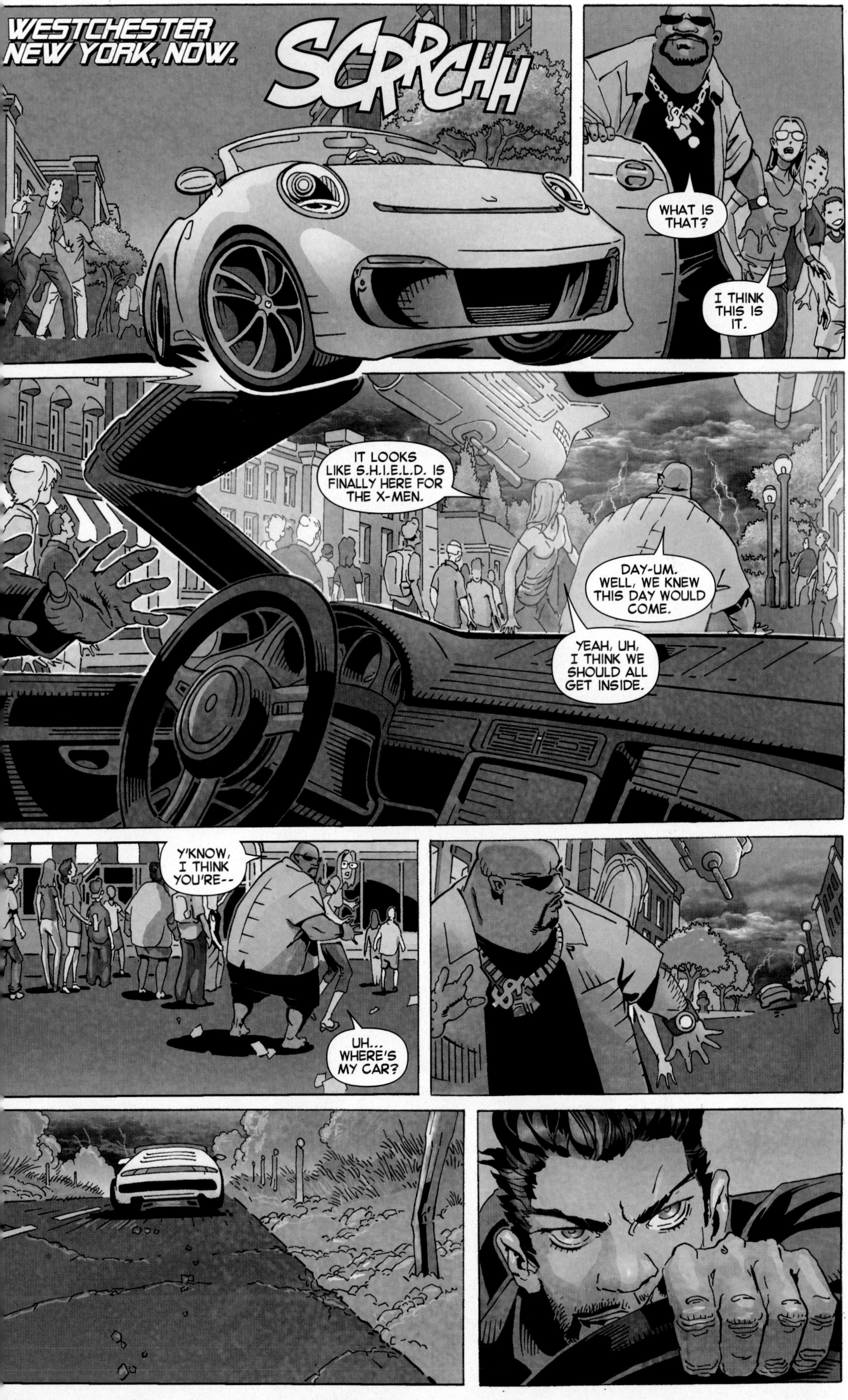
WESTCHESTER NEW YORK, NOW.
SCRRCHH
WHAT IS THAT?
I THINK THIS IS IT.
IT LOOKS LIKE S.H.I.E.L.D. IS FINALLY HERE FOR THE X-MEN.
DAY-UM. WELL, WE KNEW THIS DAY WOULD COME.
YEAH, UH, I THINK WE SHOULD ALL GET INSIDE.
Y'KNOW, I THINK YOU'RE--
UH... WHERE'S MY CAR?

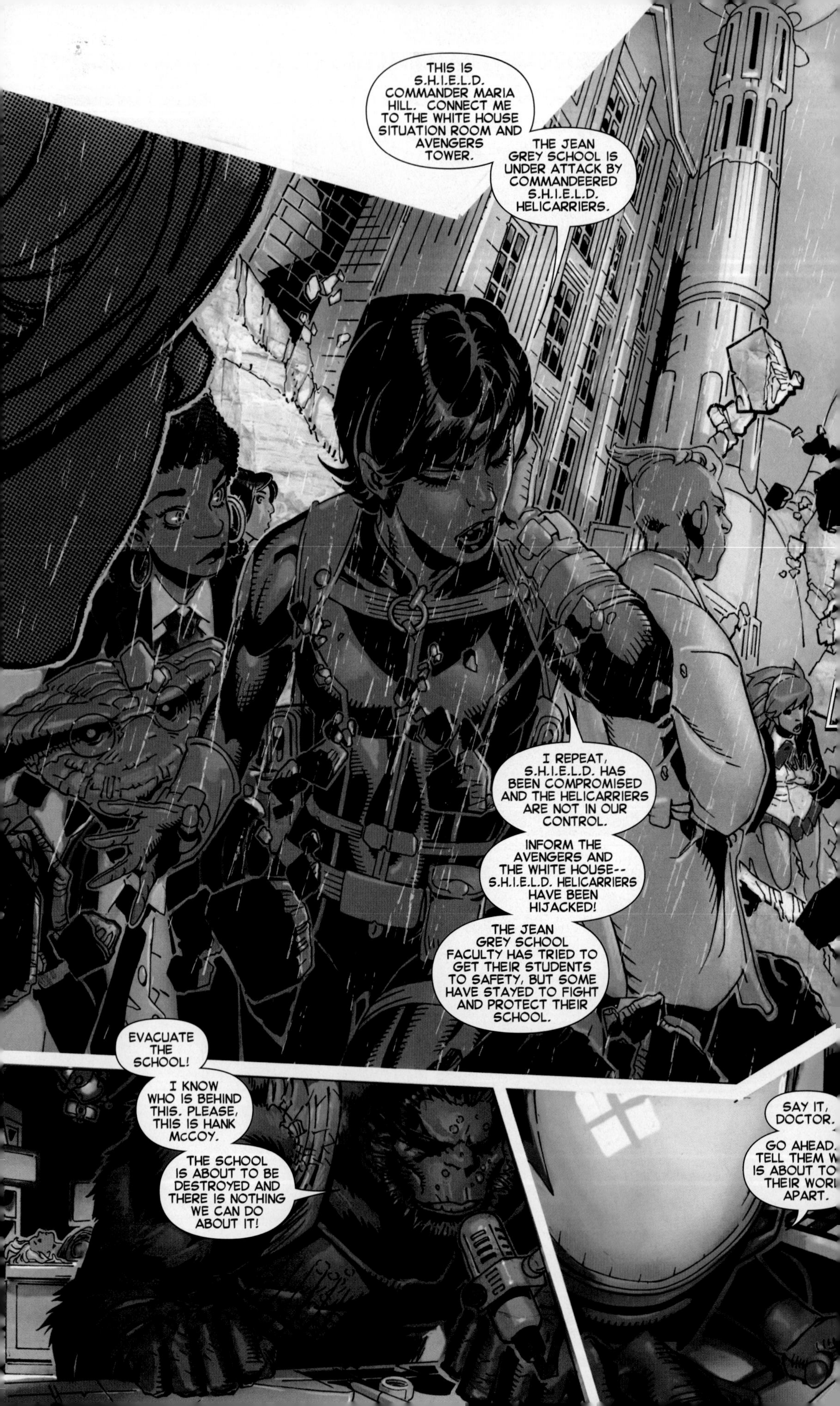
THIS IS S.H.I.E.L.D. COMMANDER MARIA HILL. CONNECT ME TO THE WHITE HOUSE SITUATION ROOM AND AVENGERS TOWER.
THE JEAN GREY SCHOOL IS UNDER ATTACK BY COMMANDEERED S.H.I.E.L.D. HELICARRIERS.
I REPEAT, S.H.I.E.L.D. HAS BEEN COMPROMISED AND THE HELICARRIERS ARE NOT IN OUR CONTROL.
INFORM THE AVENGERS AND THE WHITE HOUSE-- S.H.I.E.L.D. HELICARRIERS HAVE BEEN HIJACKED!
THE JEAN GREY SCHOOL FACULTY HAS TRIED TO GET THEIR STUDENTS TO SAFETY, BUT SOME HAVE STAYED TO FIGHT AND PROTECT THEIR SCHOOL.
EVACUATE THE SCHOOL!
I KNOW WHO IS BEHIND THIS. PLEASE, THIS IS HANK McCOY.
THE SCHOOL IS ABOUT TO BE DESTROYED AND THERE IS NOTHING WE CAN DO ABOUT IT!
SAY IT, DOCTOR.

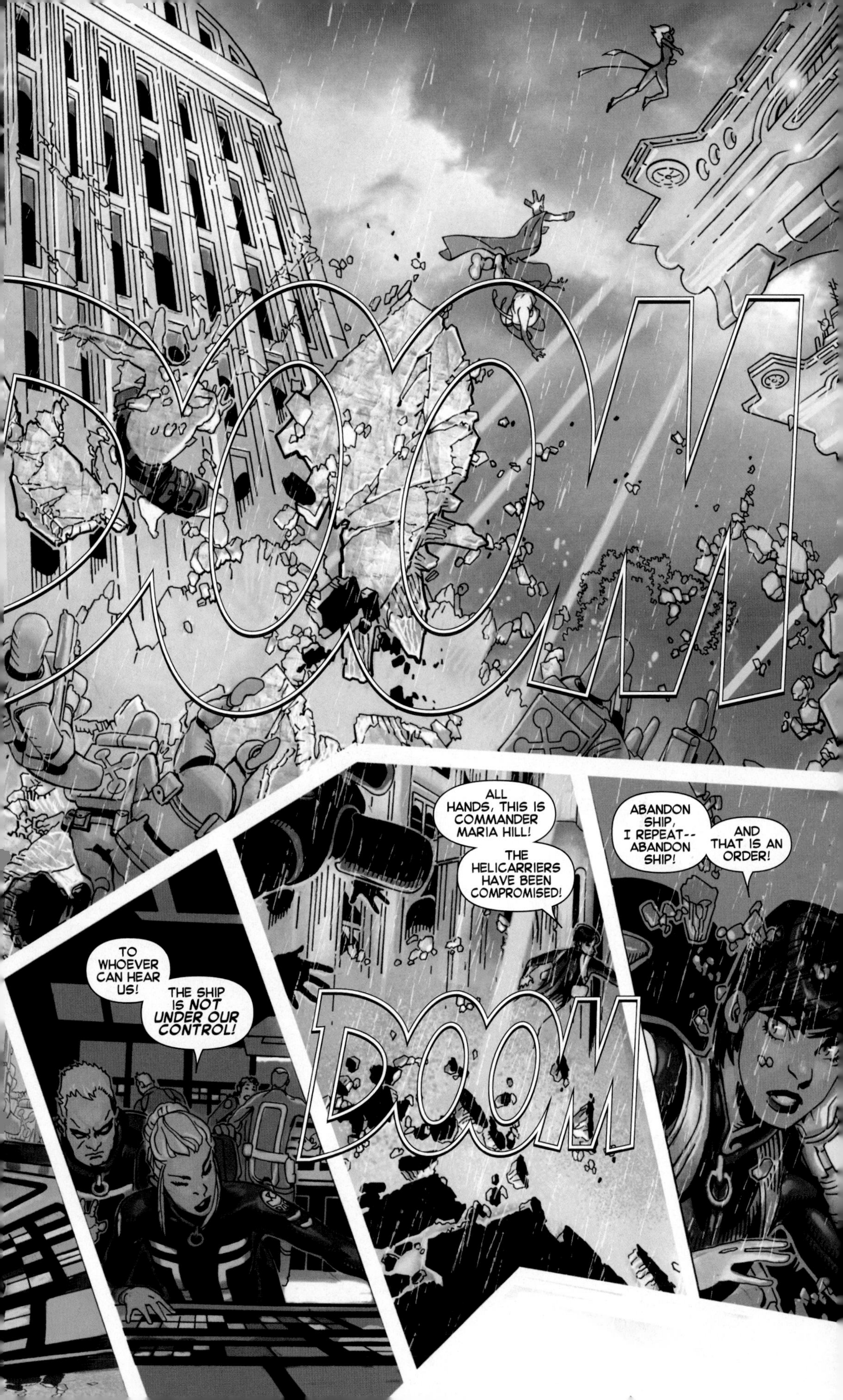
DOOOM
ALL HANDS, THIS IS COMMANDER MARIA HILL!
THE HELICARRIERS HAVE BEEN COMPROMISED!
ABANDON SHIP, I REPEAT--ABANDON SHIP!
AND THAT IS AN ORDER!
TO WHOEVER CAN HEAR US!
THE SHIP IS NOT UNDER OUR CONTROL!
DOOM

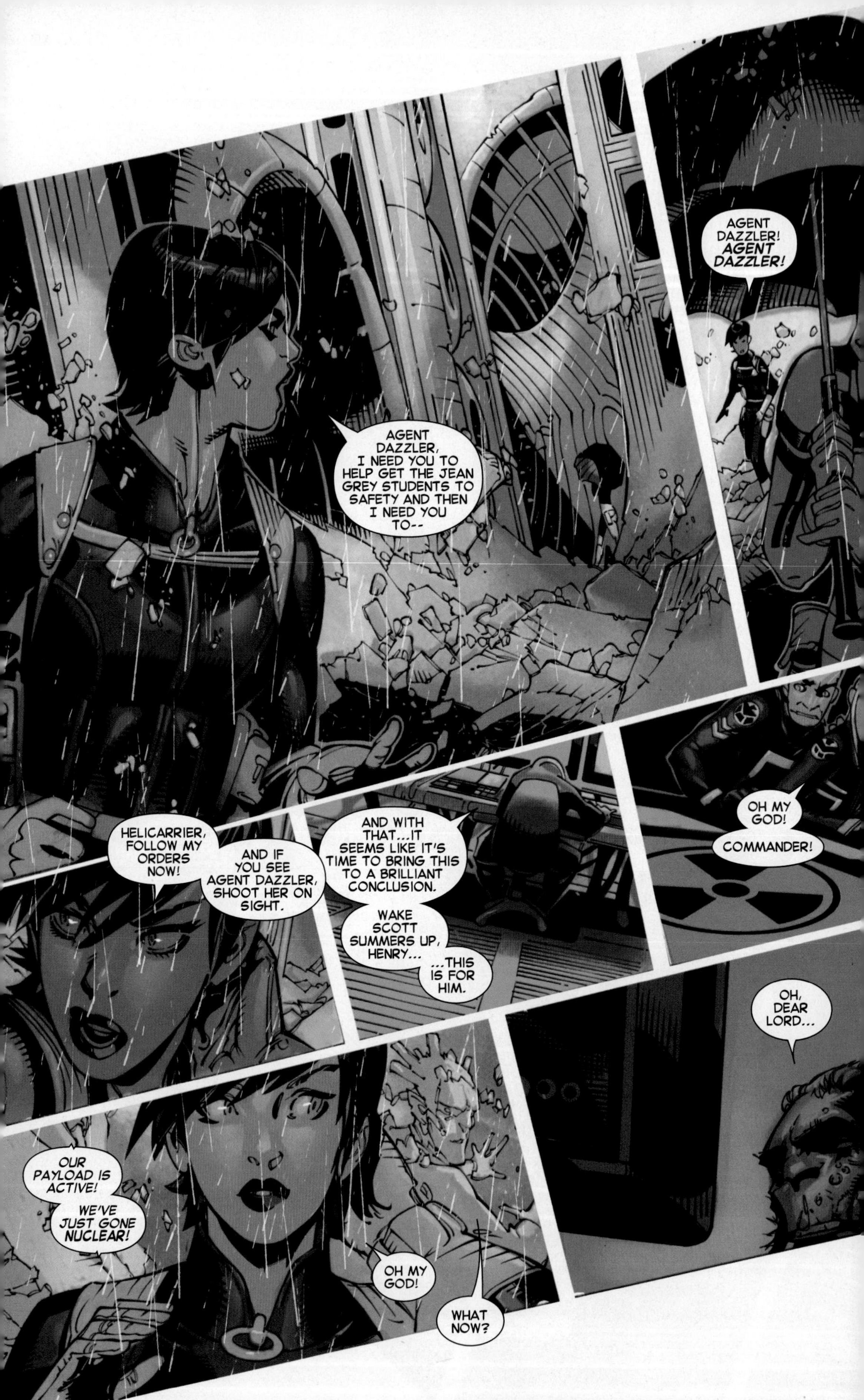
AGENT DAZZLER, I NEED YOU TO HELP GET THE JEAN GREY STUDENTS TO SAFETY AND THEN I NEED YOU TO--
AGENT DAZZLER! AGENT DAZZLER!
HELICARRIER, FOLLOW MY ORDERS NOW!
AND IF YOU SEE AGENT DAZZLER, SHOOT HER ON SIGHT.
AND WITH THAT...IT SEEMS LIKE IT'S TIME TO BRING THIS TO A BRILLIANT CONCLUSION.
WAKE SCOTT SUMMERS UP, HENRY...
...THIS IS FOR HIM.
OH MY GOD!
COMMANDER!
OUR PAYLOAD IS ACTIVE!
WE'VE JUST GONE NUCLEAR!
OH, DEAR LORD...
OH MY GOD!
WHAT NOW?

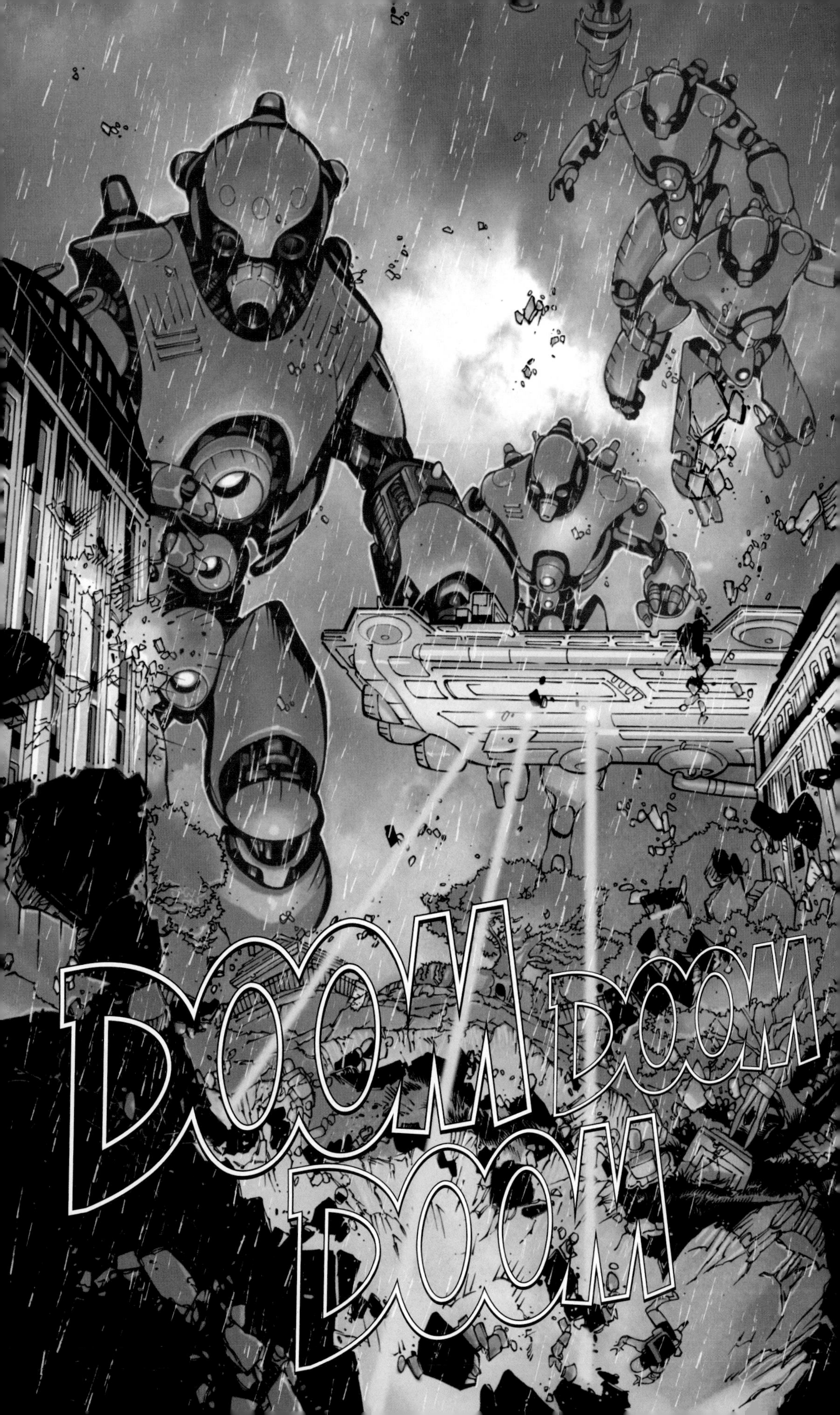
DOOM DOOM
DOOM

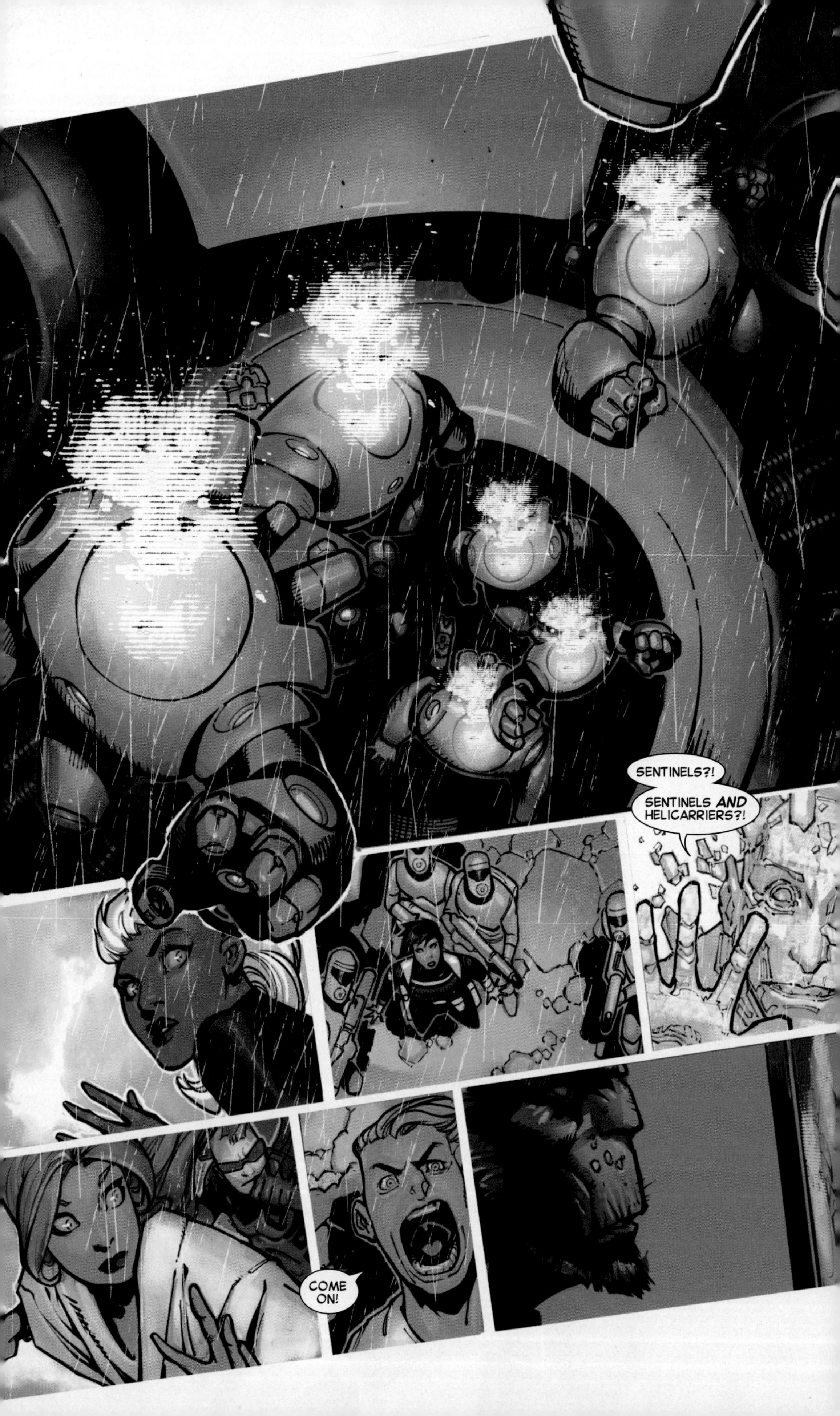
SENTINELS?!
SENTINELS AND HELICARRIERS?!
COME ON!

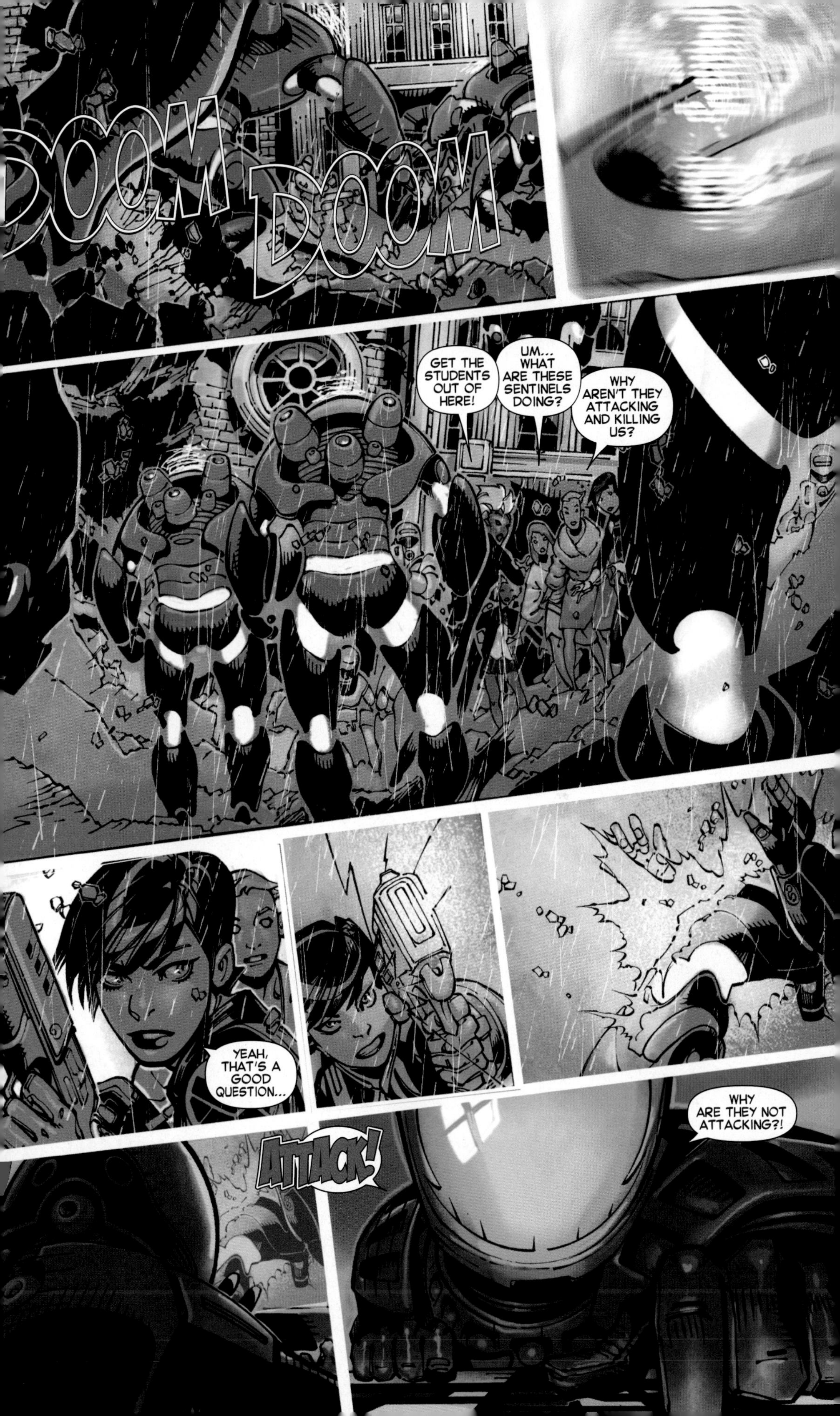
DOOM DOOM
GET THE STUDENTS OUT OF HERE!
UM... WHAT ARE THESE SENTINELS DOING?
WHY AREN'T THEY ATTACKING AND KILLING US?
YEAH, THAT'S A GOOD QUESTION...
WHY ARE THEY NOT ATTACKING?!
ATTACK!

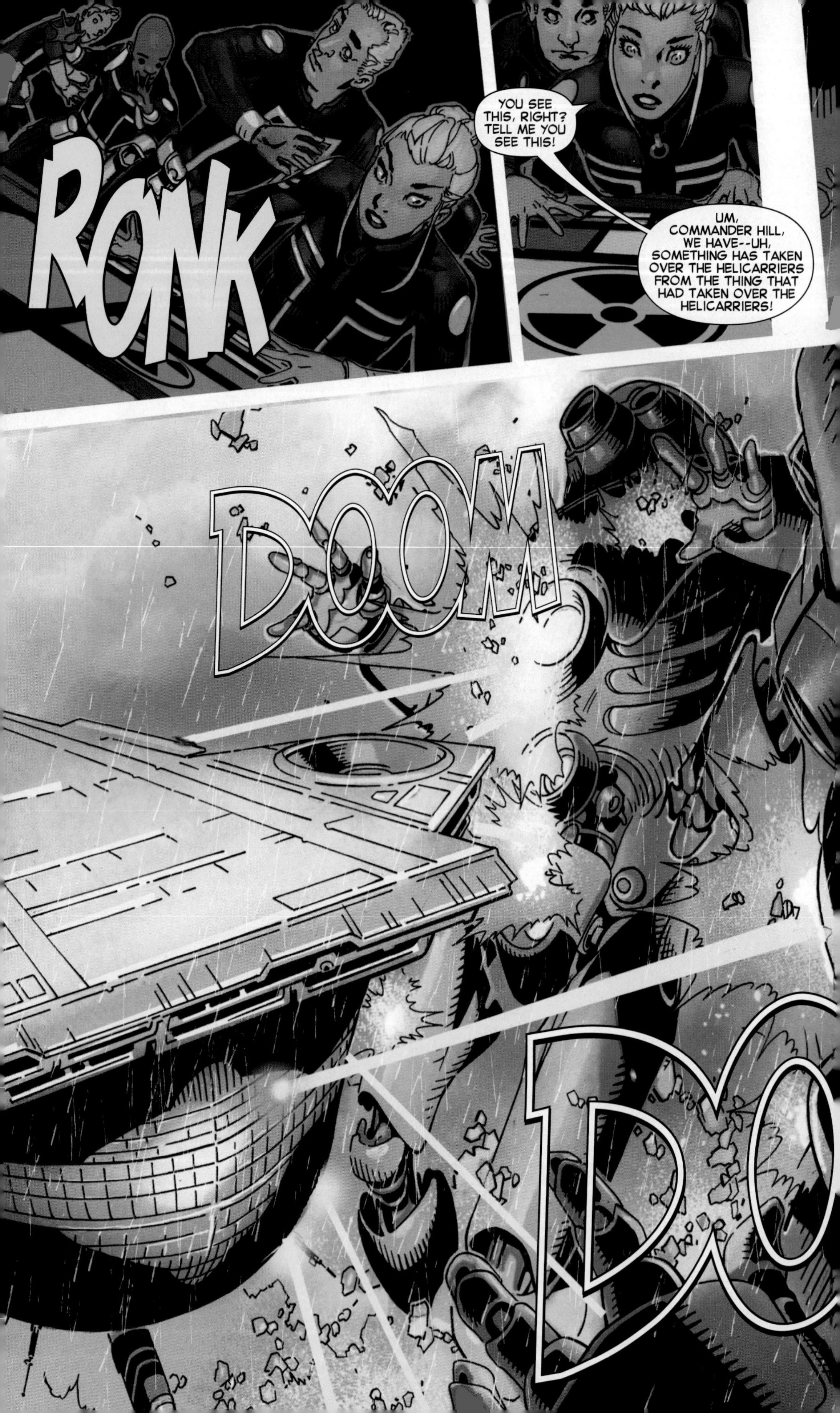
RONK
YOU SEE THIS, RIGHT? TELL ME YOU SEE THIS!
UM, COMMANDER HILL, WE HAVE--UH, SOMETHING HAS TAKEN OVER THE HELICARRIERS FROM THE THING THAT HAD TAKEN OVER THE HELICARRIERS!
DOOM
DO

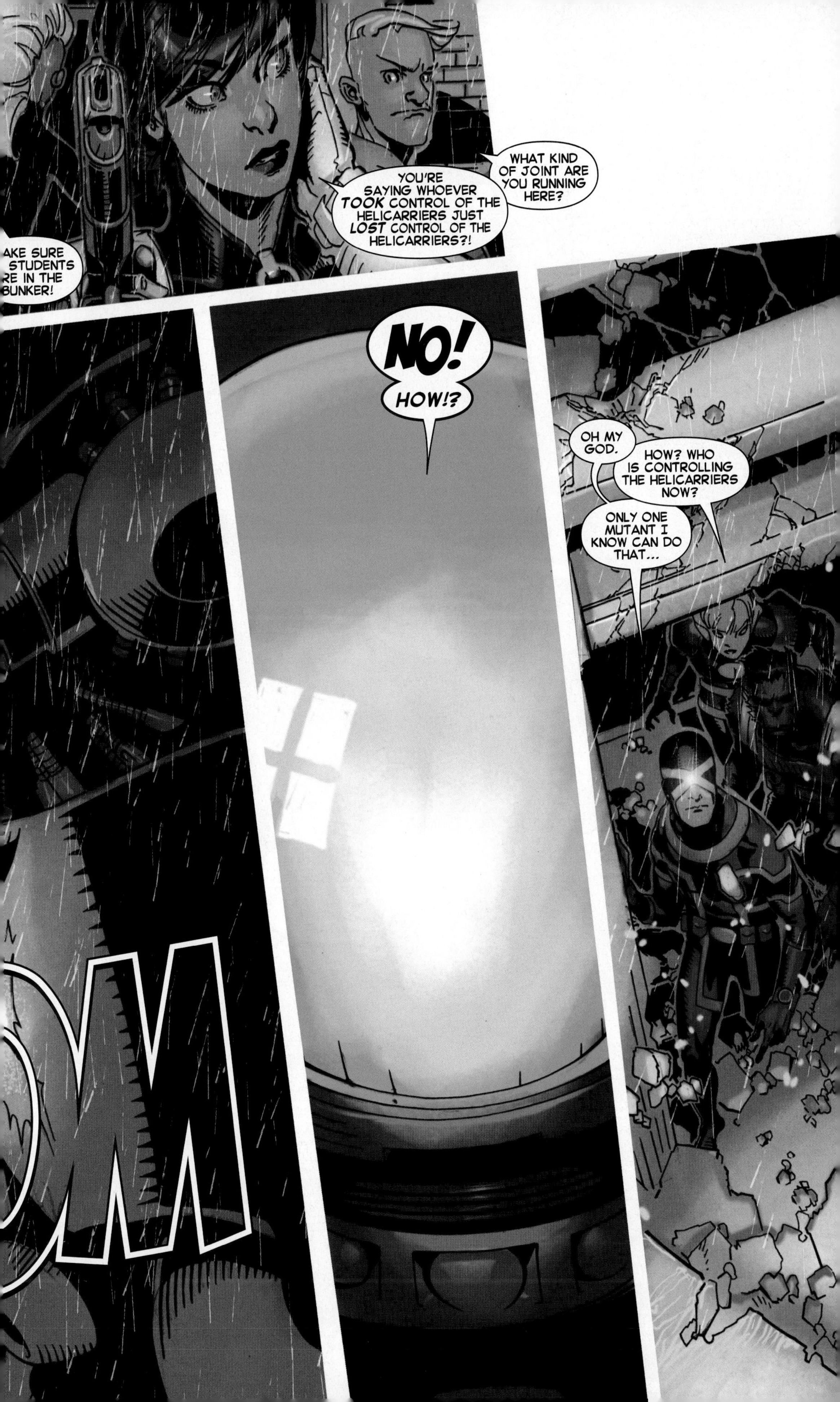

AKE SURE
STUDENTS
RE IN THE
BUNKER!
YOU'RE SAYING WHOEVER TOOK CONTROL OF THE HELICARRIERS JUST LOST CONTROL OF THE HELICARRIERS?!
WHAT KIND OF JOINT ARE YOU RUNNING HERE?
NO!
HOW!?
OH MY GOD.
HOW? WHO IS CONTROLLING THE HELICARRIERS NOW?
ONLY ONE MUTANT I KNOW CAN DO THAT...

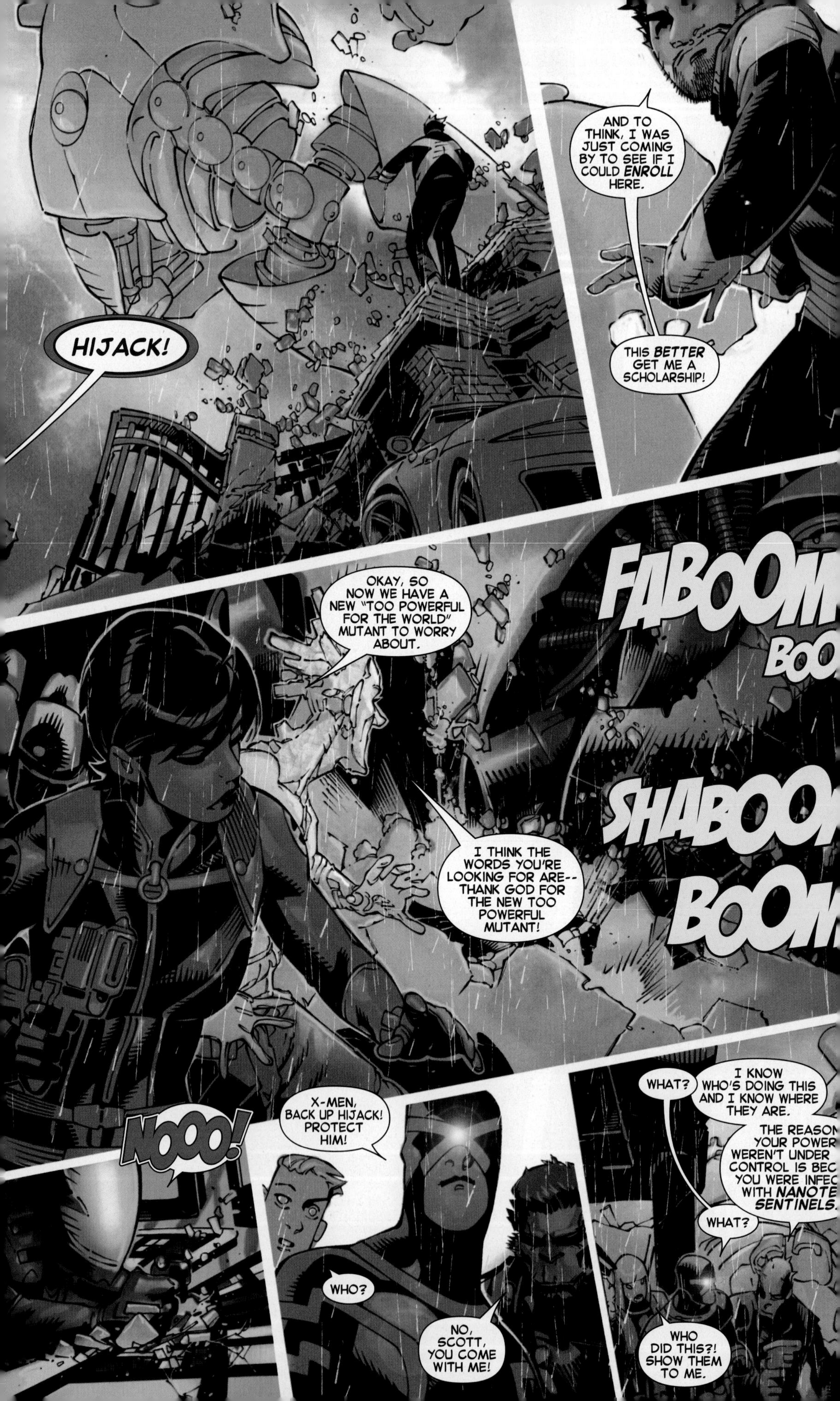
HIJACK!
AND TO THINK, I WAS JUST COMING BY TO SEE IF I COULD ENROLL HERE.
THIS BETTER GET ME A SCHOLARSHIP!
OKAY, SO NOW WE HAVE A NEW "TOO POWERFUL FOR THE WORLD" MUTANT TO WORRY ABOUT.
FABOOM
I THINK THE WORDS YOU'RE LOOKING FOR ARE-- THANK GOD FOR THE NEW TOO POWERFUL MUTANT!
NOOO!
X-MEN, BACK UP HIJACK! PROTECT HIM!
WHO?
NO, SCOTT, YOU COME WITH ME!
WHAT?
I KNOW WHO'S DOING THIS AND I KNOW WHERE THEY ARE.
WHAT?
WHO DID THIS?! SHOW THEM TO ME.

IT'S
ADVANCED TECH.
YEARS AHEAD OF
WHERE THEY ARE NOW...
BUT DEFINITELY
WHERE IT IS ALL
GOING.

I SHUT
THEM DOWN IN YOUR
SYSTEM. YOU CAN
LOOK FORWARD TO
SOME NASTY
DIARRHEA.

BUT IT HAD
A VERY POTENT
SIGNATURE.

I CAN,
AND HAVE, TRACED
IT BACK TO ITS OWNER.
AND I KNOW WHO IT
IS AND WHERE
THEY ARE.

SHOW
ME!

MAGIK,
NO--WE NEED
BACKUP!

BUT--

GET
EVERYONE
AND GET
BACK
HERE!

WHO?!
WHO
IS IT?

NEW
SECRET
XAVIER
SCHOOL.

WHERE ARE WE
GOING, MISS
FROST?

WE ARE
GOING TO FIND
AND HELP SCOTT
SUMMERS AND
ILLYANA.

I
SHALL JOIN
YOU.

YEAH,
YOU SHALL,
MAGNETO.
WE NEED
BOTH OF YOU.
DAZZLER, ARE
YOU UP FOR
THIS?

THAT'S
ALL I
AM!

AND
NOW MAGIK,
APPEARING
OUT OF
NOWHERE.

OH GOOD,
MAGNETO,
DAZZLER...WE NEED
ALL THE HELP WE
CAN GET.

WHAT
IS IT?

S.H.I.E.L.D.
VERSUS THE
X-MEN. COME
WITH ME.

EVERYONE
READY?

YES! GO!
NOW!

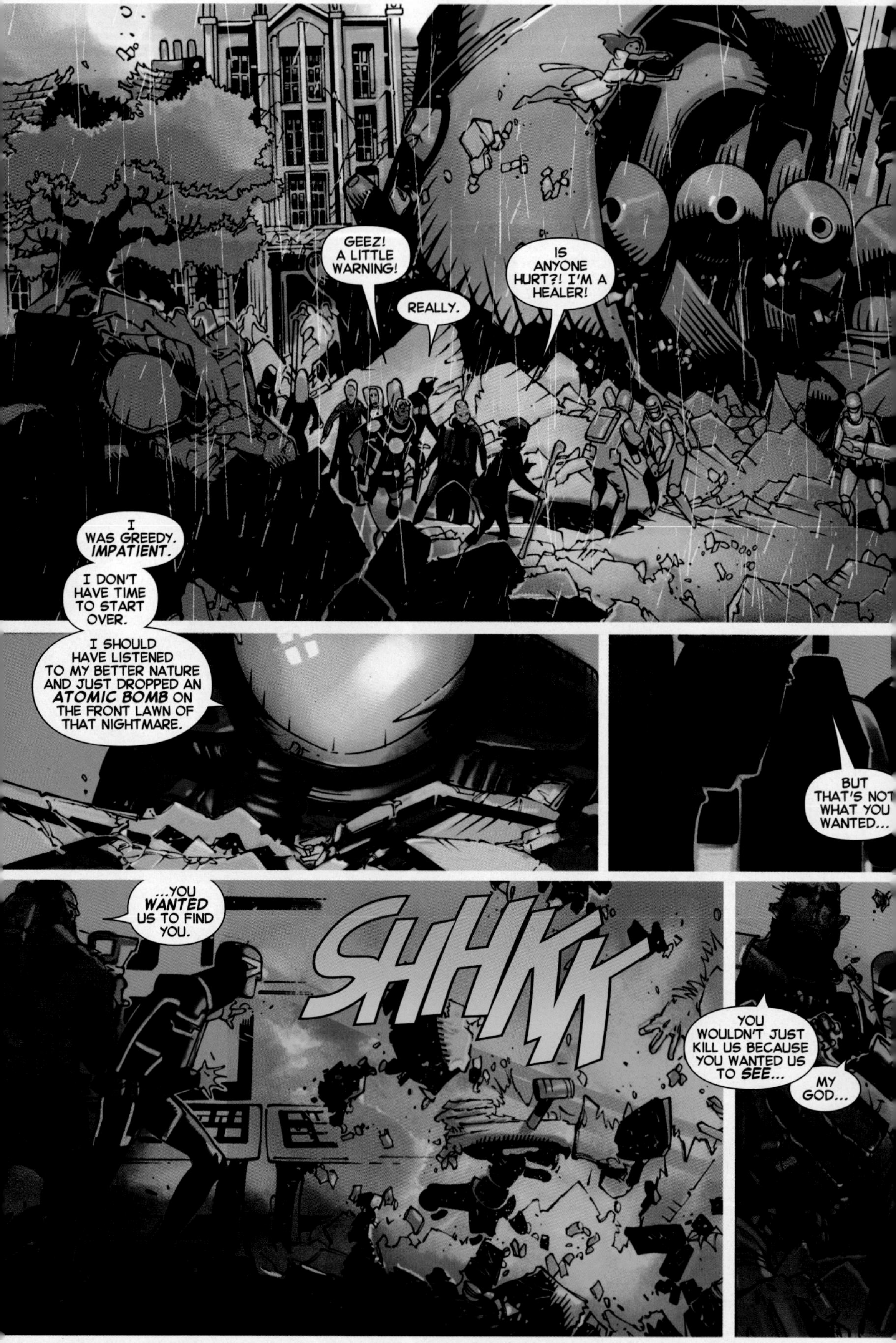

GEEZ! A LITTLE WARNING!
REALLY.
IS ANYONE HURT?! I'M A HEALER!
I WAS GREEDY. IMPATIENT.
I DON'T HAVE TIME TO START OVER.
I SHOULD HAVE LISTENED TO MY BETTER NATURE AND JUST DROPPED AN ATOMIC BOMB ON THE FRONT LAWN OF THAT NIGHTMARE.
BUT THAT'S NOT WHAT YOU WANTED...
...YOU WANTED US TO FIND YOU.
SHHKK
YOU WOULDN'T JUST KILL US BECAUSE YOU WANTED US TO SEE...
MY GOD...

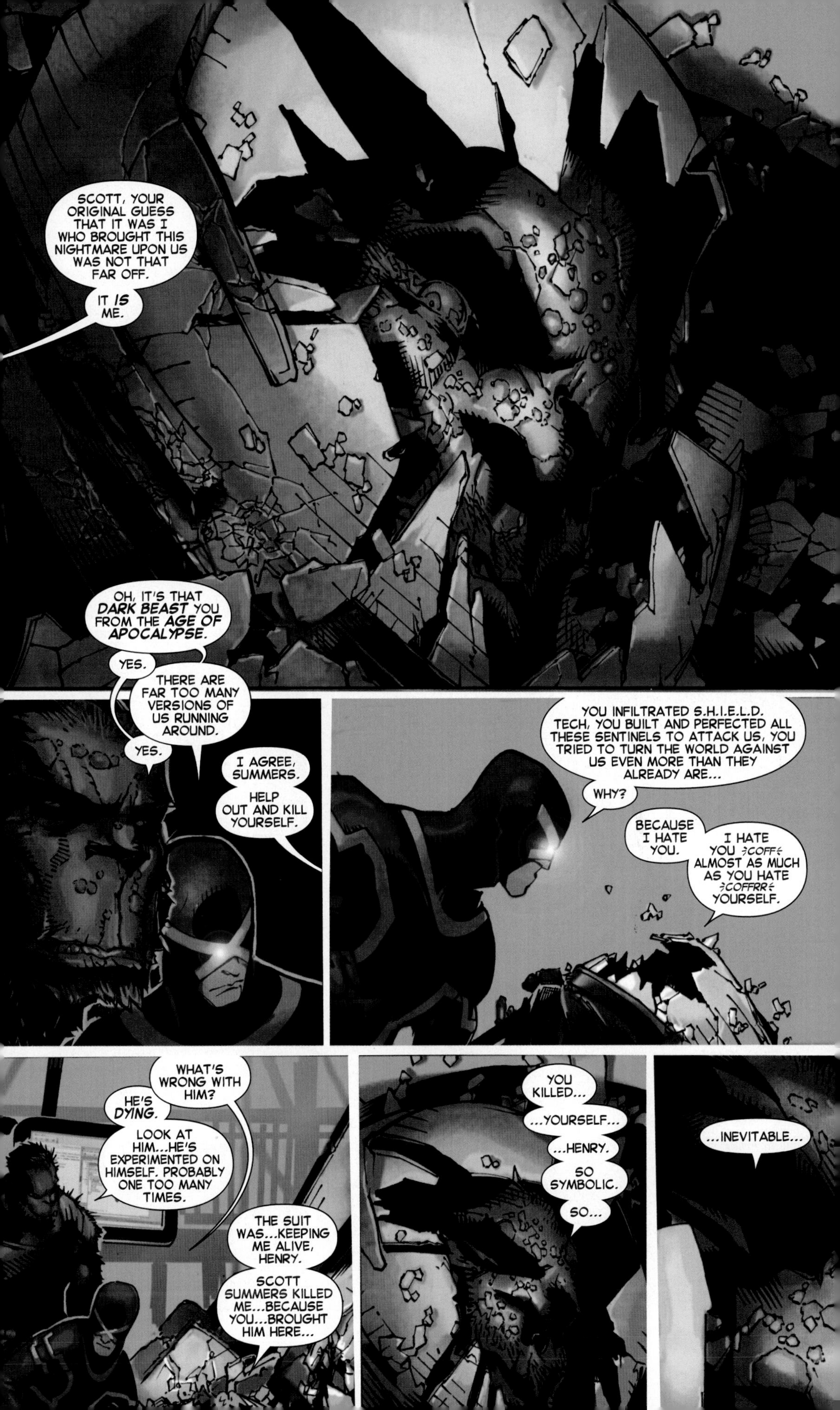

SCOTT, YOUR ORIGINAL GUESS THAT IT WAS I WHO BROUGHT THIS NIGHTMARE UPON US WAS NOT THAT FAR OFF.
IT *IS* ME.
OH, IT'S THAT ***DARK BEAST*** YOU FROM THE ***AGE OF APOCALYPSE***.
YES.
THERE ARE FAR TOO MANY VERSIONS OF US RUNNING AROUND.
YES.
I AGREE, SUMMERS.
HELP OUT AND KILL YOURSELF.
YOU INFILTRATED S.H.I.E.L.D. TECH, YOU BUILT AND PERFECTED ALL THESE SENTINELS TO ATTACK US, YOU TRIED TO TURN THE WORLD AGAINST US EVEN MORE THAN THEY ALREADY ARE...
WHY?
BECAUSE I HATE YOU.
I HATE YOU *COFF* ALMOST AS MUCH AS YOU HATE *COFFRR* YOURSELF.
WHAT'S WRONG WITH HIM?
HE'S *DYING*.
LOOK AT HIM...HE'S EXPERIMENTED ON HIMSELF. PROBABLY ONE TOO MANY TIMES.
THE SUIT WAS...KEEPING ME ALIVE, HENRY.
SCOTT SUMMERS KILLED ME...BECAUSE YOU...BROUGHT HIM HERE...
YOU KILLED...
...YOURSELF...
...HENRY.
SO SYMBOLIC.
SO...
...INEVITABLE...

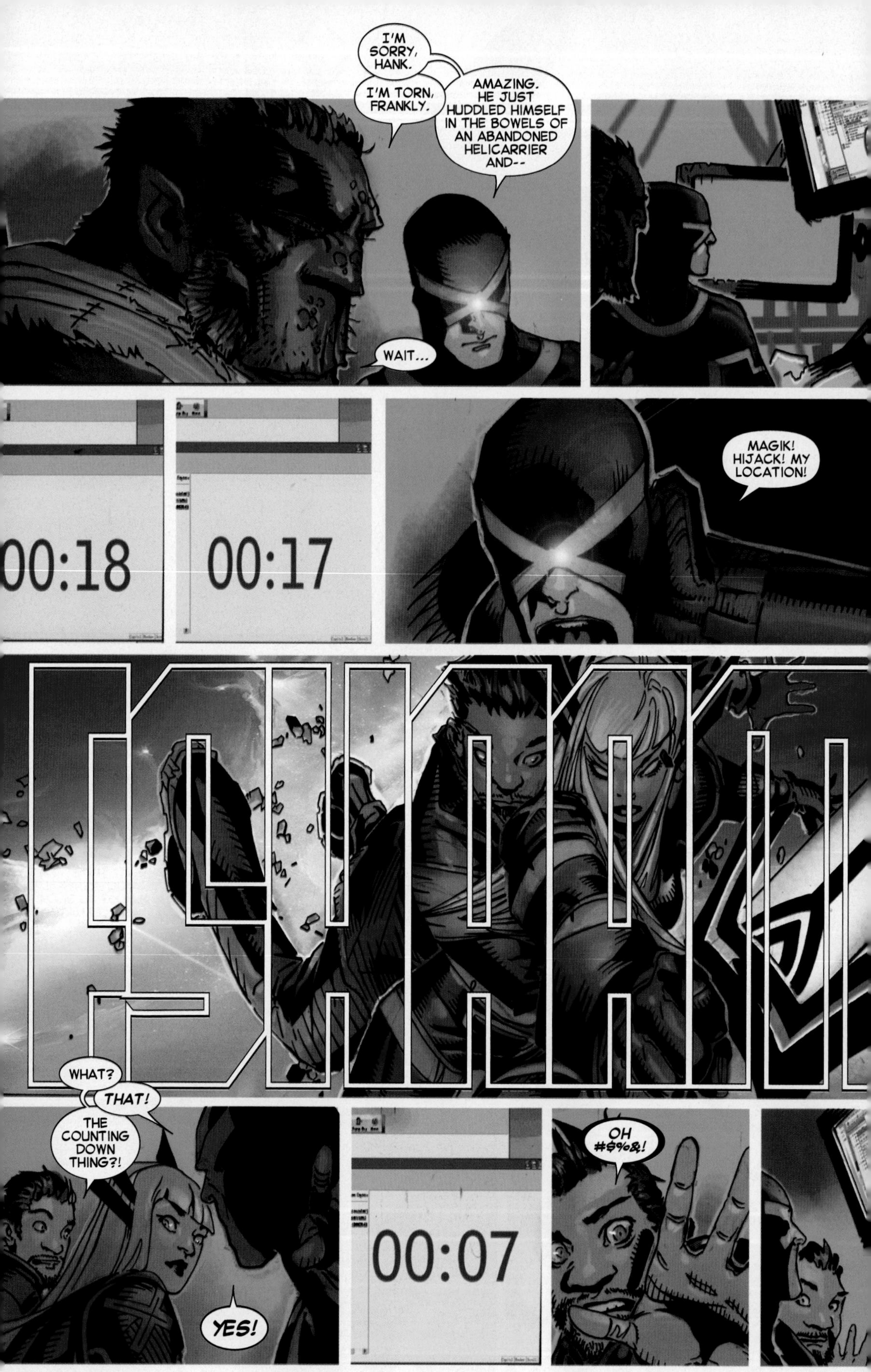
I'M SORRY, HANK.
I'M TORN, FRANKLY.
AMAZING. HE JUST HUDDLED HIMSELF IN THE BOWELS OF AN ABANDONED HELICARRIER AND--
WAIT...
00:18
00:17
MAGIK! HIJACK! MY LOCATION!
WHAT?
THAT!
THE COUNTING DOWN THING?!
YES!
00:07
OH #$%&!

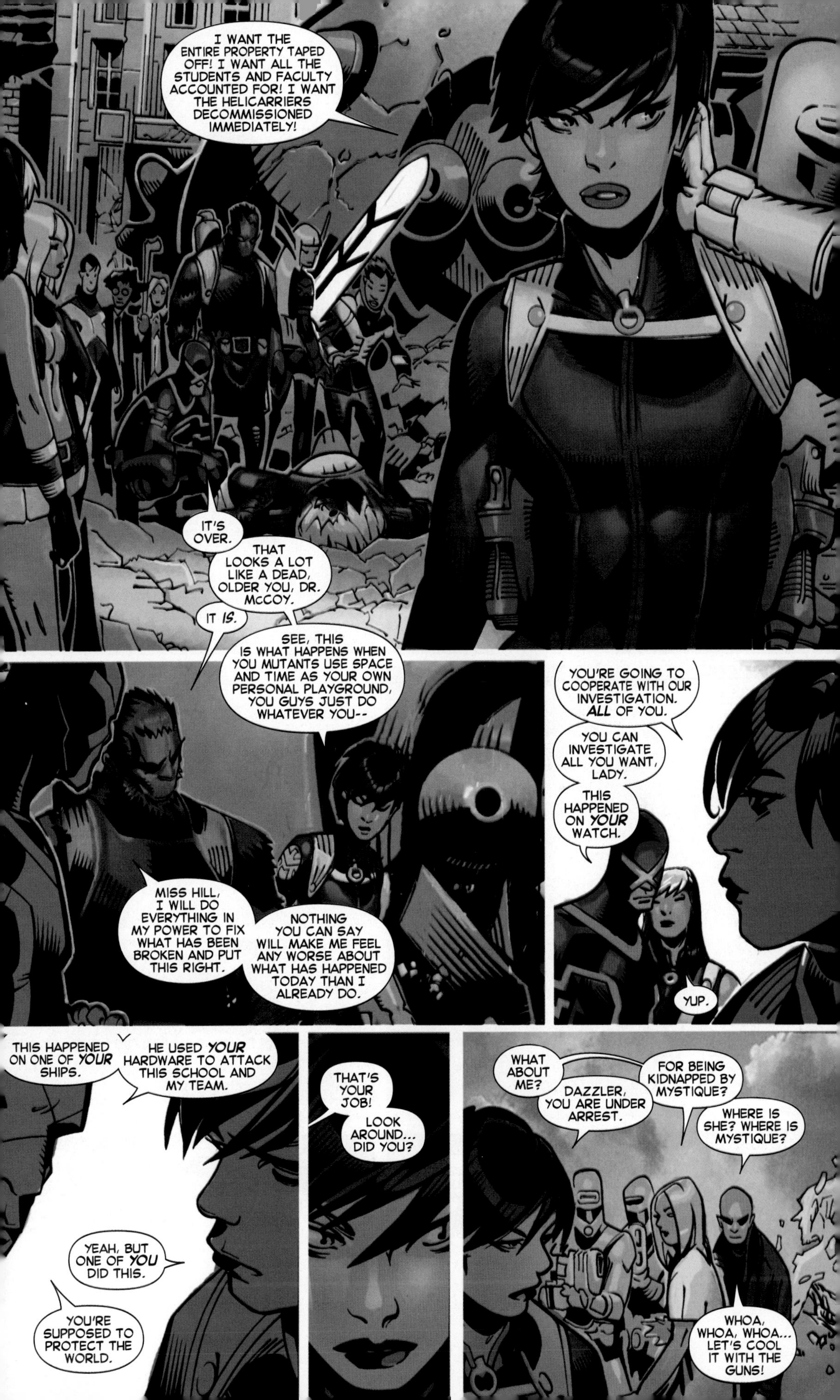
I WANT THE ENTIRE PROPERTY TAPED OFF! I WANT ALL THE STUDENTS AND FACULTY ACCOUNTED FOR! I WANT THE HELICARRIERS DECOMMISSIONED IMMEDIATELY!
IT'S OVER.
THAT LOOKS A LOT LIKE A DEAD, OLDER YOU, DR. McCOY.
IT IS.
SEE, THIS IS WHAT HAPPENS WHEN YOU MUTANTS USE SPACE AND TIME AS YOUR OWN PERSONAL PLAYGROUND, YOU GUYS JUST DO WHATEVER YOU--
MISS HILL, I WILL DO EVERYTHING IN MY POWER TO FIX WHAT HAS BEEN BROKEN AND PUT THIS RIGHT.
NOTHING YOU CAN SAY WILL MAKE ME FEEL ANY WORSE ABOUT WHAT HAS HAPPENED TODAY THAN I ALREADY DO.
YOU'RE GOING TO COOPERATE WITH OUR INVESTIGATION. ALL OF YOU.
YOU CAN INVESTIGATE ALL YOU WANT, LADY.
THIS HAPPENED ON YOUR WATCH.
YUP.
THIS HAPPENED ON ONE OF YOUR SHIPS.
HE USED YOUR HARDWARE TO ATTACK THIS SCHOOL AND MY TEAM.
YEAH, BUT ONE OF YOU DID THIS.
YOU'RE SUPPOSED TO PROTECT THE WORLD.
THAT'S YOUR JOB!
LOOK AROUND... DID YOU?
WHAT ABOUT ME?
FOR BEING KIDNAPPED BY MYSTIQUE?
DAZZLER, YOU ARE UNDER ARREST.
WHERE IS SHE? WHERE IS MYSTIQUE?
WHOA, WHOA, WHOA... LET'S COOL IT WITH THE GUNS!

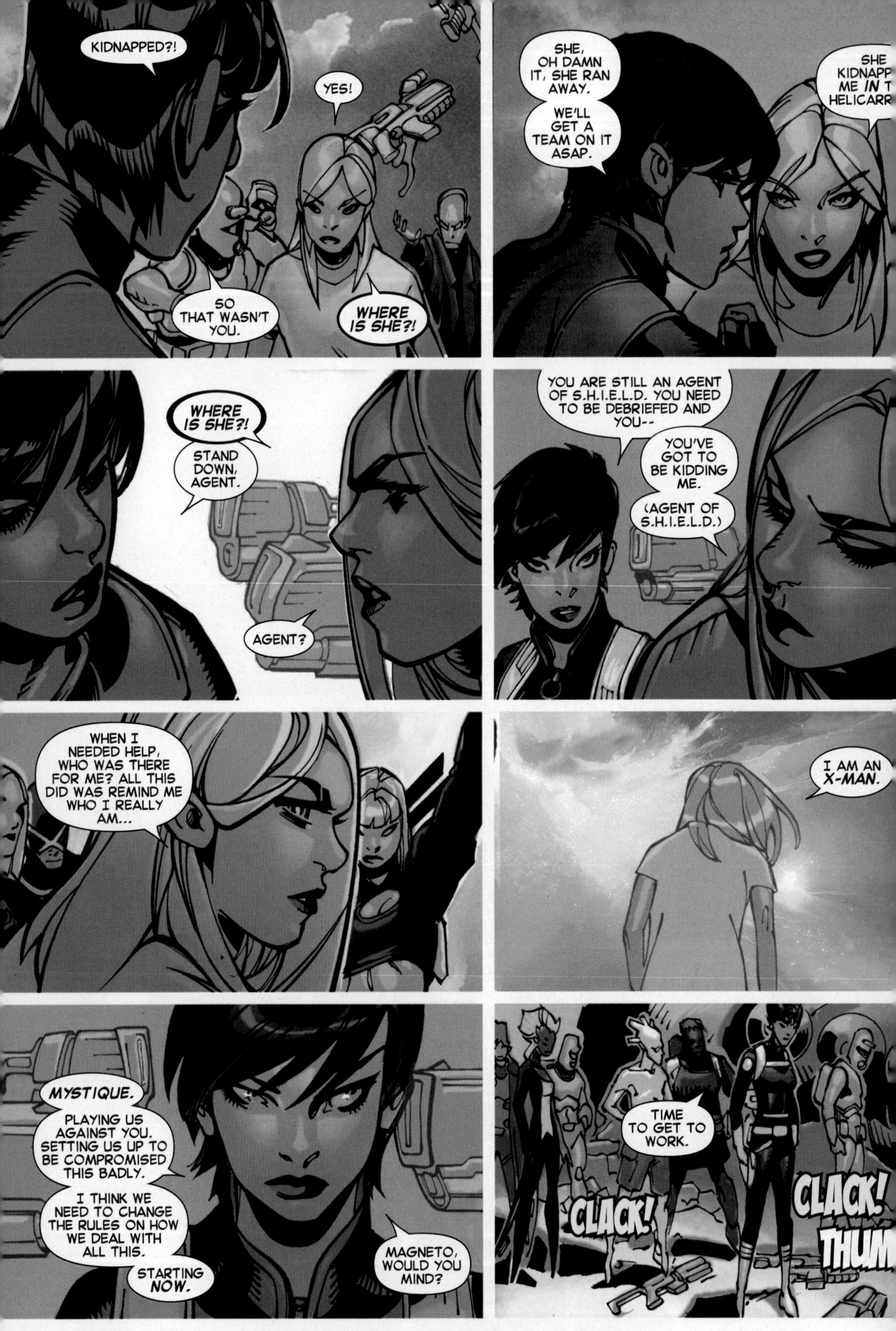
KIDNAPPED?!
YES!
SO THAT WASN'T YOU.
WHERE IS SHE?!
SHE, OH DAMN IT, SHE RAN AWAY.
WE'LL GET A TEAM ON IT ASAP.
SHE KIDNAPP ME IN T HELICARR
WHERE IS SHE?!
STAND DOWN, AGENT.
AGENT?
YOU ARE STILL AN AGENT OF S.H.I.E.L.D. YOU NEED TO BE DEBRIEFED AND YOU--
YOU'VE GOT TO BE KIDDING ME.
(AGENT OF S.H.I.E.L.D.)
WHEN I NEEDED HELP, WHO WAS THERE FOR ME? ALL THIS DID WAS REMIND ME WHO I REALLY AM...
I AM AN X-MAN.
MYSTIQUE.
PLAYING US AGAINST YOU. SETTING US UP TO BE COMPROMISED THIS BADLY.
I THINK WE NEED TO CHANGE THE RULES ON HOW WE DEAL WITH ALL THIS.
STARTING NOW.
MAGNETO, WOULD YOU MIND?
TIME TO GET TO WORK.
CLACK!
CLACK!
THUM

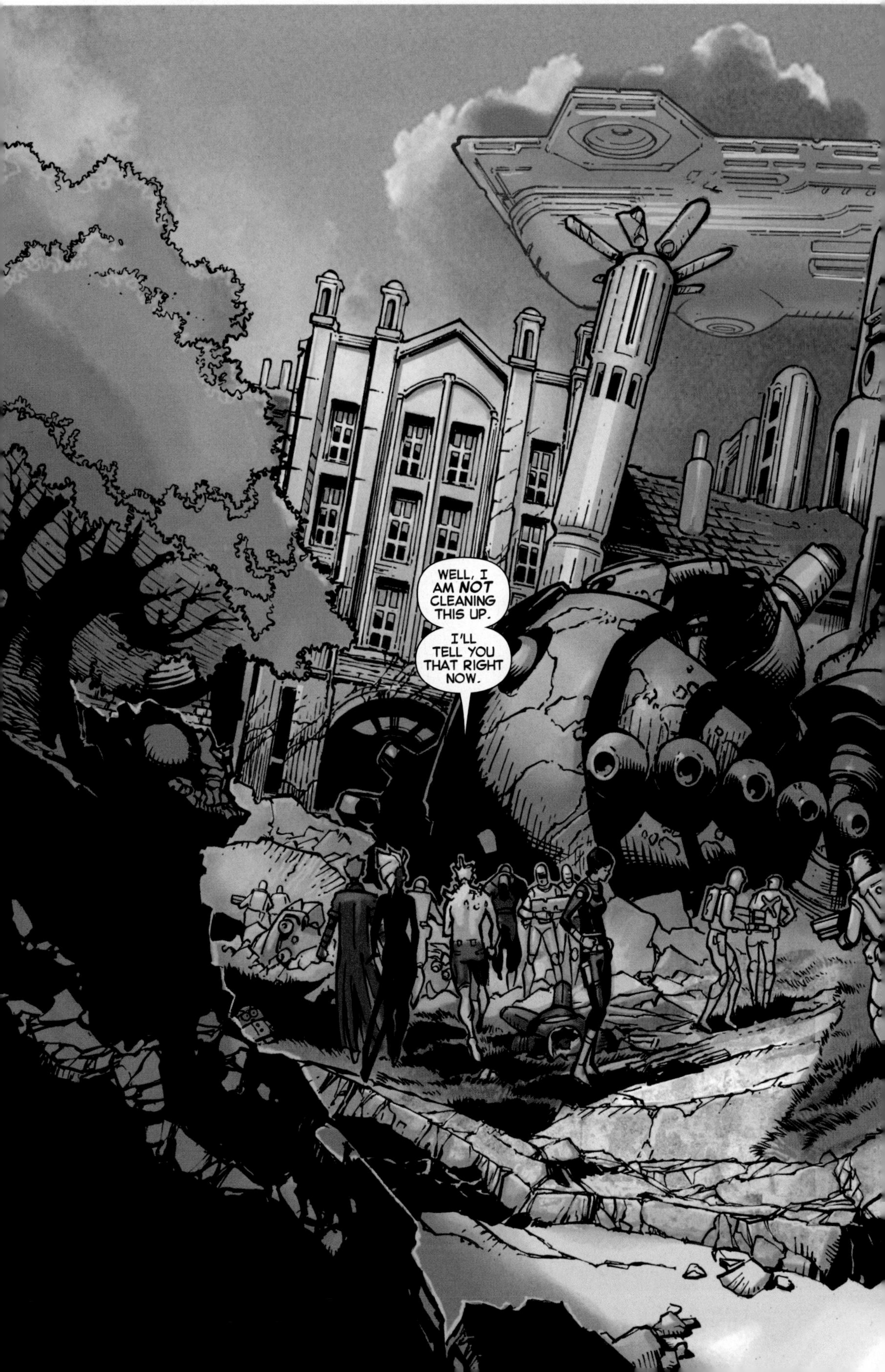
WELL, I AM NOT CLEANING THIS UP.
I'LL TELL YOU THAT RIGHT NOW.

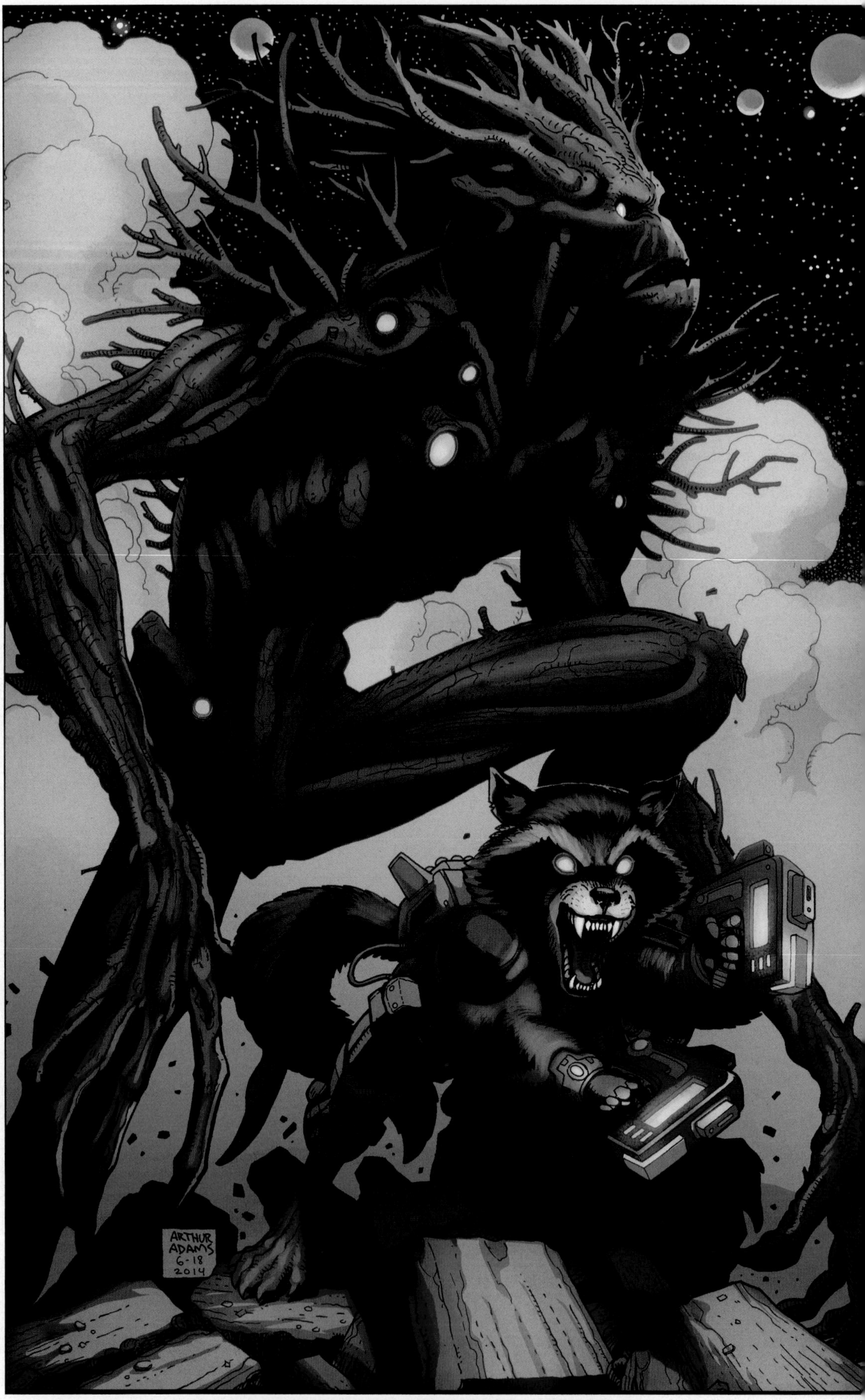
ARTHUR
ADAMS
6-18
2014

UNCANNY X-MEN #23 GUARDIANS OF THE GALAXY VARIANT
BY ARTHUR ADAMS & JASON KEITH

THE LAST WILL AND TESTAMENT OF CHARLES XAVIER

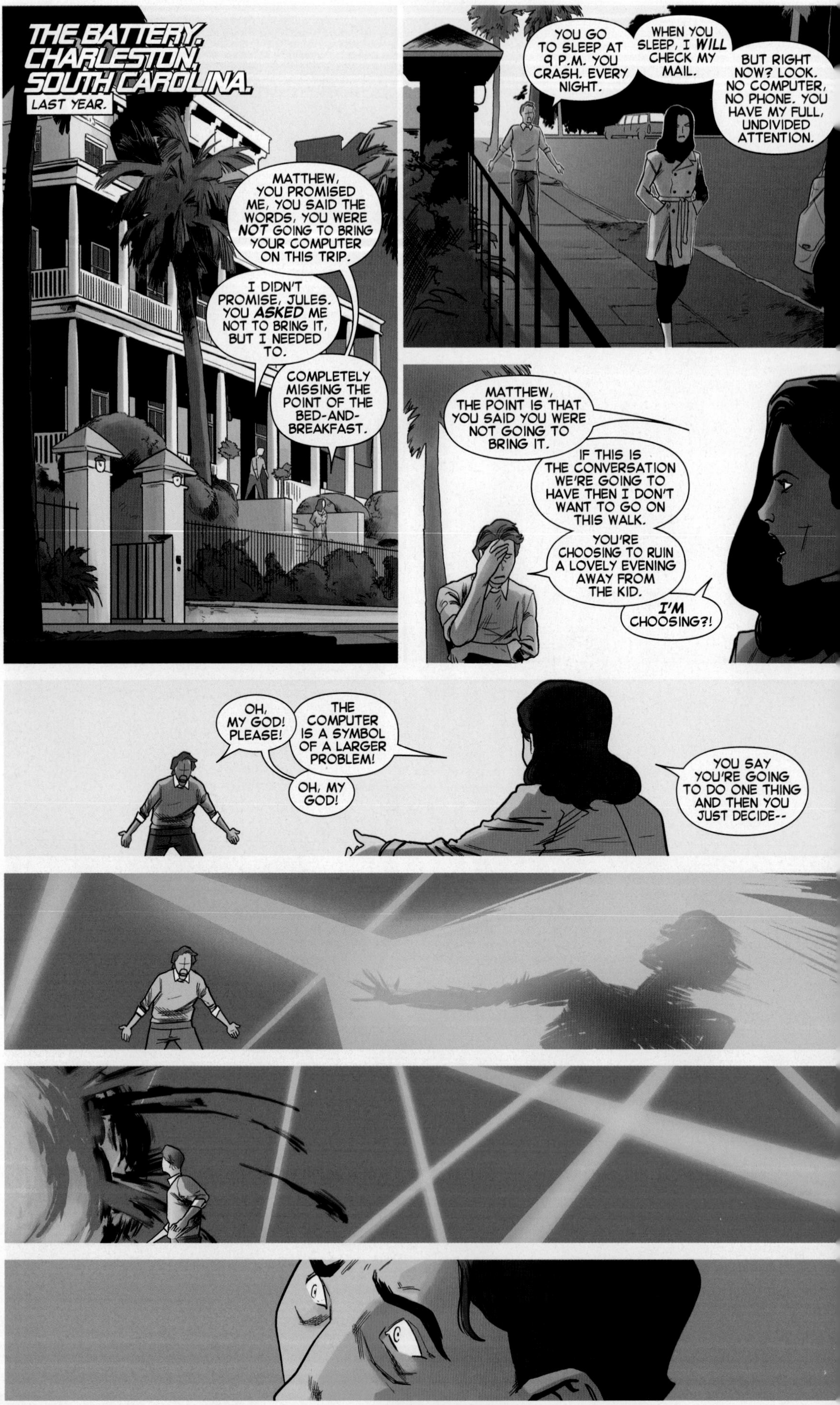
THE BATTERY. CHARLESTON, SOUTH CAROLINA.
LAST YEAR.
MATTHEW, YOU PROMISED ME, YOU SAID THE WORDS, YOU WERE NOT GOING TO BRING YOUR COMPUTER ON THIS TRIP.
I DIDN'T PROMISE, JULES. YOU ASKED ME NOT TO BRING IT, BUT I NEEDED TO.
COMPLETELY MISSING THE POINT OF THE BED-AND-BREAKFAST.
YOU GO TO SLEEP AT 9 P.M. YOU CRASH. EVERY NIGHT.
WHEN YOU SLEEP, I WILL CHECK MY MAIL.
BUT RIGHT NOW? LOOK. NO COMPUTER, NO PHONE. YOU HAVE MY FULL, UNDIVIDED ATTENTION.
MATTHEW, THE POINT IS THAT YOU SAID YOU WERE NOT GOING TO BRING IT.
IF THIS IS THE CONVERSATION WE'RE GOING TO HAVE THEN I DON'T WANT TO GO ON THIS WALK.
YOU'RE CHOOSING TO RUIN A LOVELY EVENING AWAY FROM THE KID.
I'M CHOOSING?!
OH, MY GOD! PLEASE!
THE COMPUTER IS A SYMBOL OF A LARGER PROBLEM!
OH, MY GOD!
YOU SAY YOU'RE GOING TO DO ONE THING AND THEN YOU JUST DECIDE--

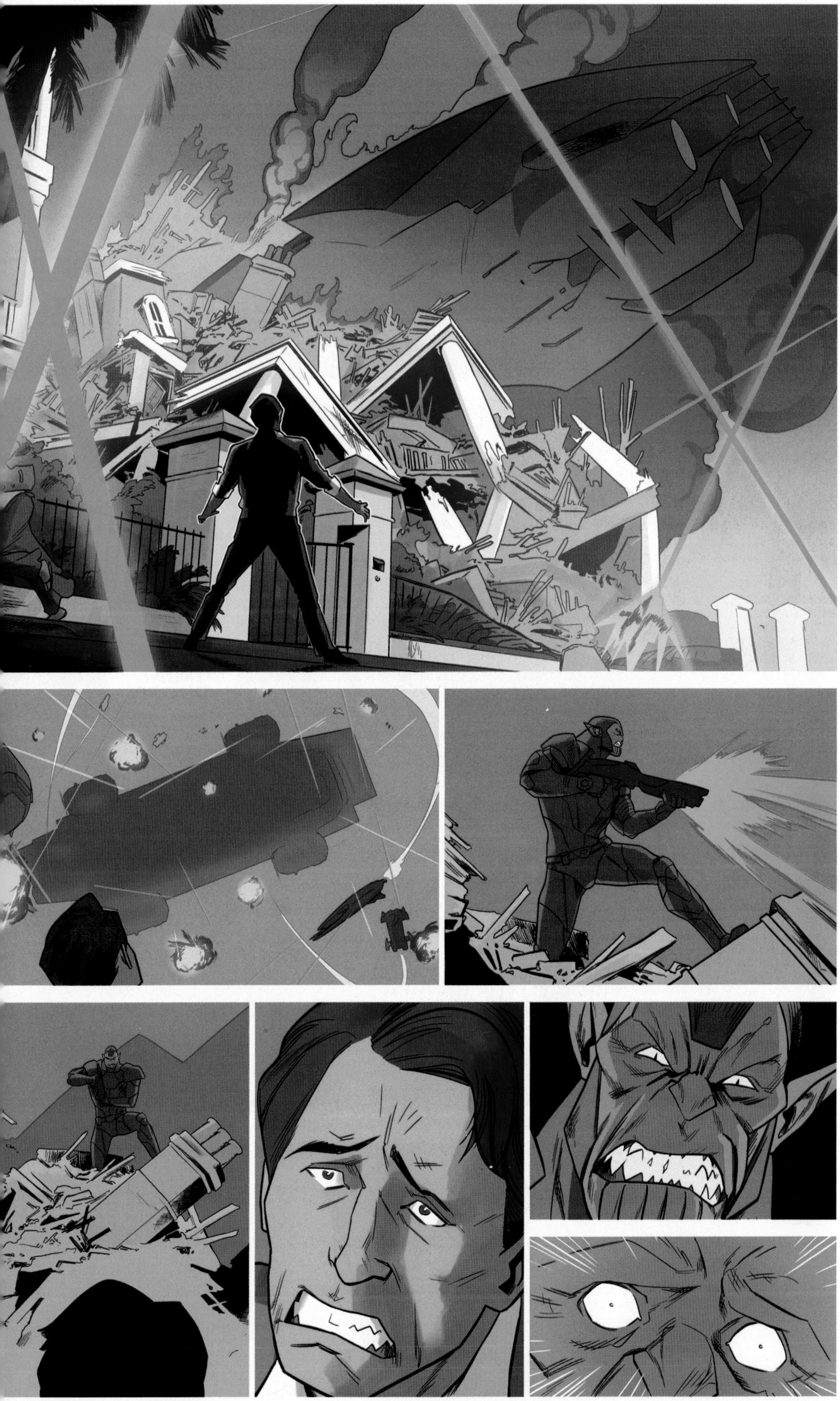

CITIZENS, THIS IS S.H.I.E.L.D. COMMAND!

WE ARE UNDER SKRULL ATTACK.

PLEASE STAY IN YOUR HOMES!

DO NOT TRUST ANYONE!

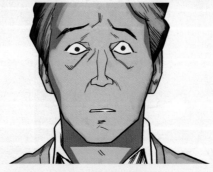

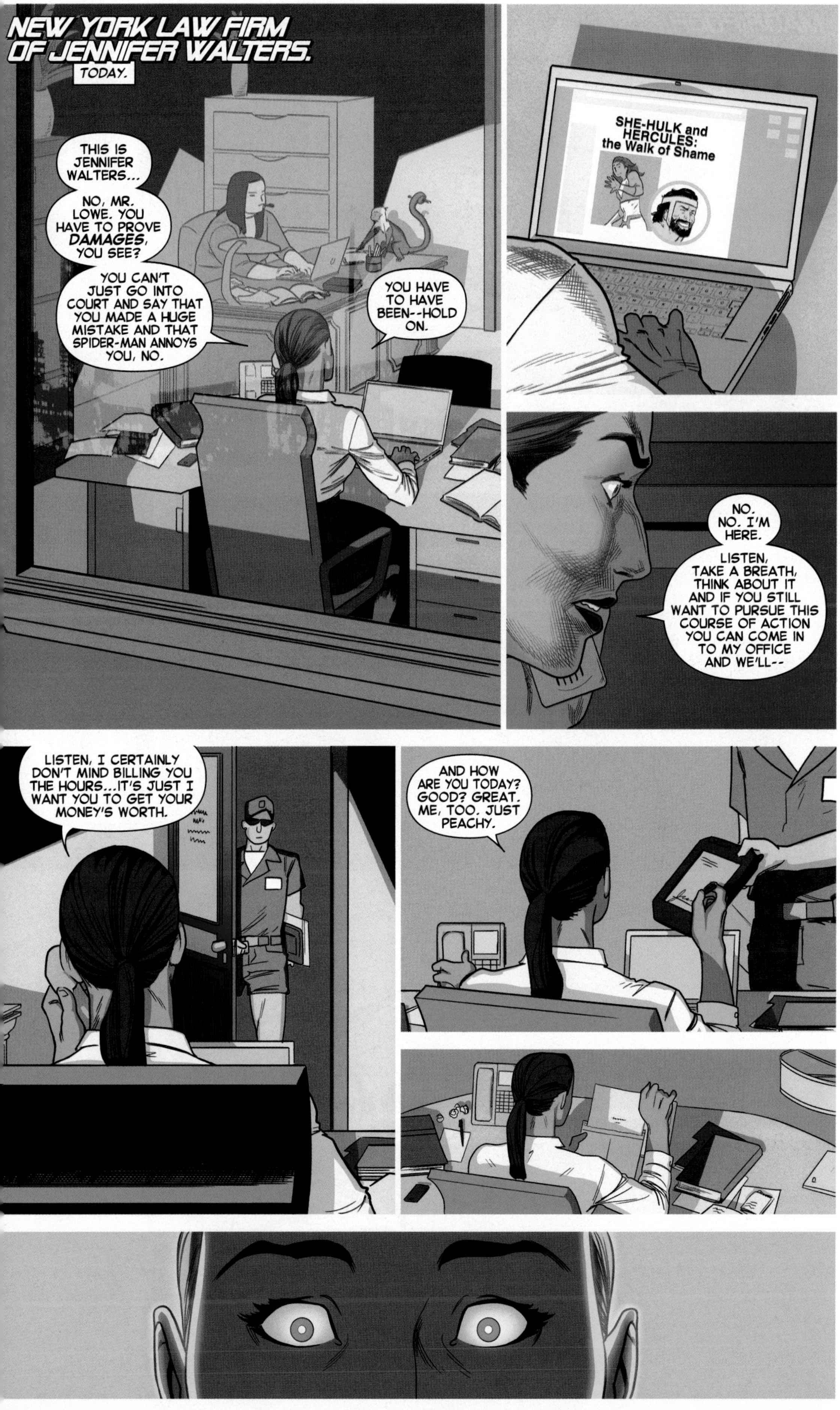

NEW YORK LAW FIRM OF JENNIFER WALTERS.
TODAY.
THIS IS JENNIFER WALTERS...
NO, MR. LOWE. YOU HAVE TO PROVE *DAMAGES*, YOU SEE?
YOU CAN'T JUST GO INTO COURT AND SAY THAT YOU MADE A HUGE MISTAKE AND THAT SPIDER-MAN ANNOYS YOU, NO.
YOU HAVE TO HAVE BEEN--HOLD ON.
SHE-HULK and HERCULES: the Walk of Shame
NO. NO. I'M HERE.
LISTEN, TAKE A BREATH, THINK ABOUT IT AND IF YOU STILL WANT TO PURSUE THIS COURSE OF ACTION YOU CAN COME IN TO MY OFFICE AND WE'LL--
LISTEN, I CERTAINLY DON'T MIND BILLING YOU THE HOURS...IT'S JUST I WANT YOU TO GET YOUR MONEY'S WORTH.
AND HOW ARE YOU TODAY? GOOD? GREAT. ME, TOO. JUST PEACHY.

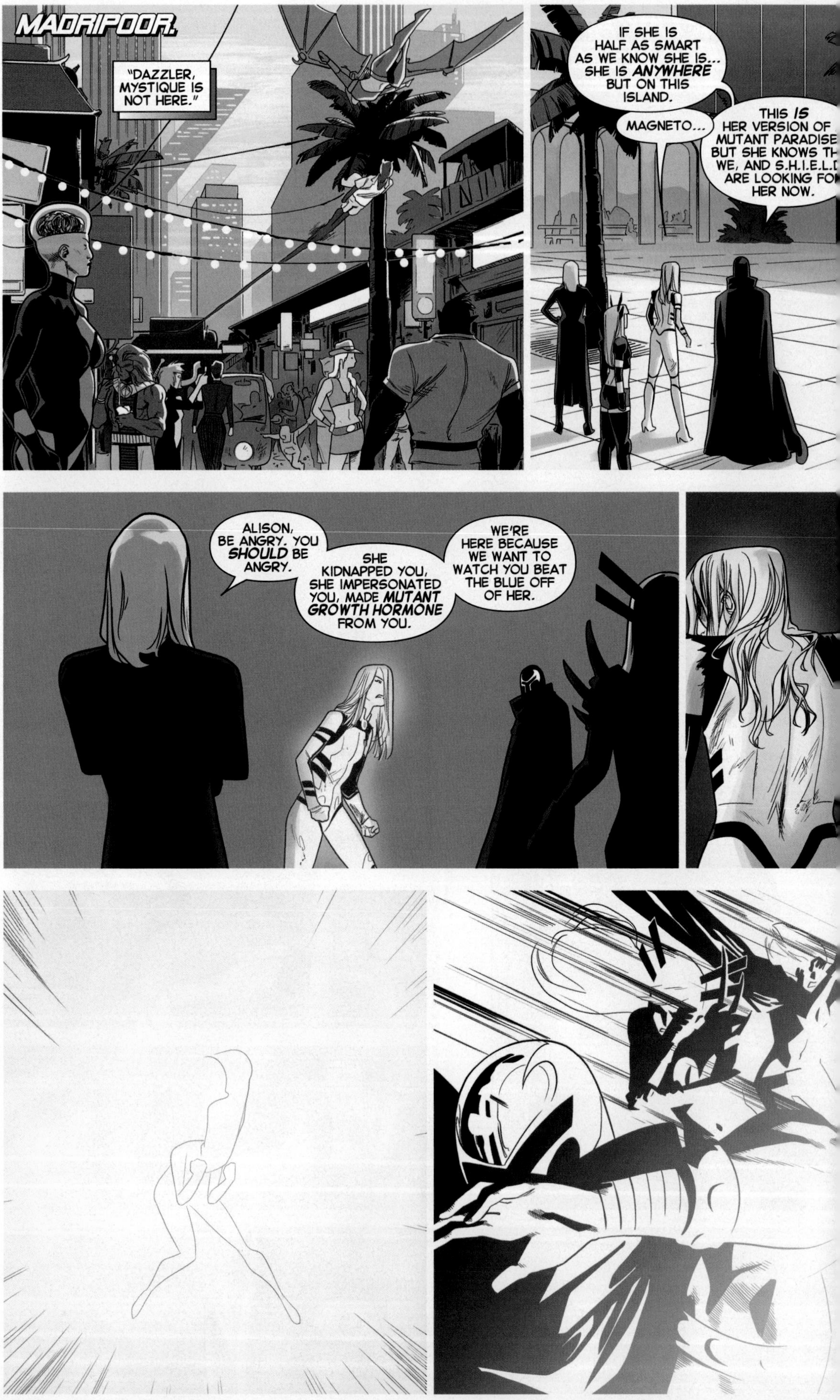
MADRIPOOR.
"DAZZLER, MYSTIQUE IS NOT HERE."
IF SHE IS HALF AS SMART AS WE KNOW SHE IS... SHE IS ANYWHERE BUT ON THIS ISLAND.
MAGNETO...
THIS IS HER VERSION OF MUTANT PARADISE BUT SHE KNOWS TH WE, AND S.H.I.E.L.D ARE LOOKING FO HER NOW.
ALISON, BE ANGRY. YOU SHOULD BE ANGRY.
SHE KIDNAPPED YOU, SHE IMPERSONATED YOU, MADE MUTANT GROWTH HORMONE FROM YOU.
WE'RE HERE BECAUSE WE WANT TO WATCH YOU BEAT THE BLUE OFF OF HER.

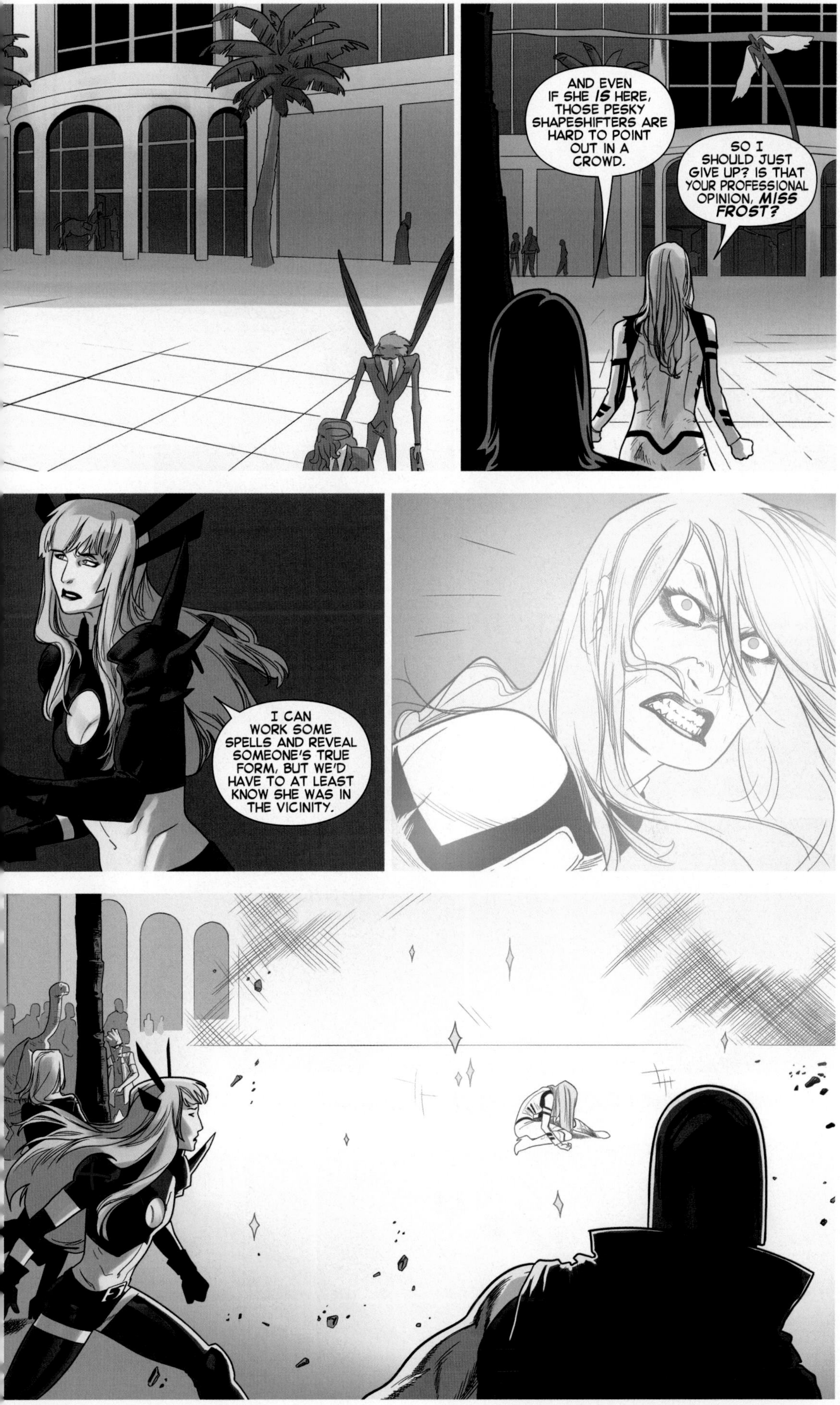
AND EVEN IF SHE IS HERE, THOSE PESKY SHAPESHIFTERS ARE HARD TO POINT OUT IN A CROWD.
SO I SHOULD JUST GIVE UP? IS THAT YOUR PROFESSIONAL OPINION, MISS FROST?
I CAN WORK SOME SPELLS AND REVEAL SOMEONE'S TRUE FORM, BUT WE'D HAVE TO AT LEAST KNOW SHE WAS IN THE VICINITY.

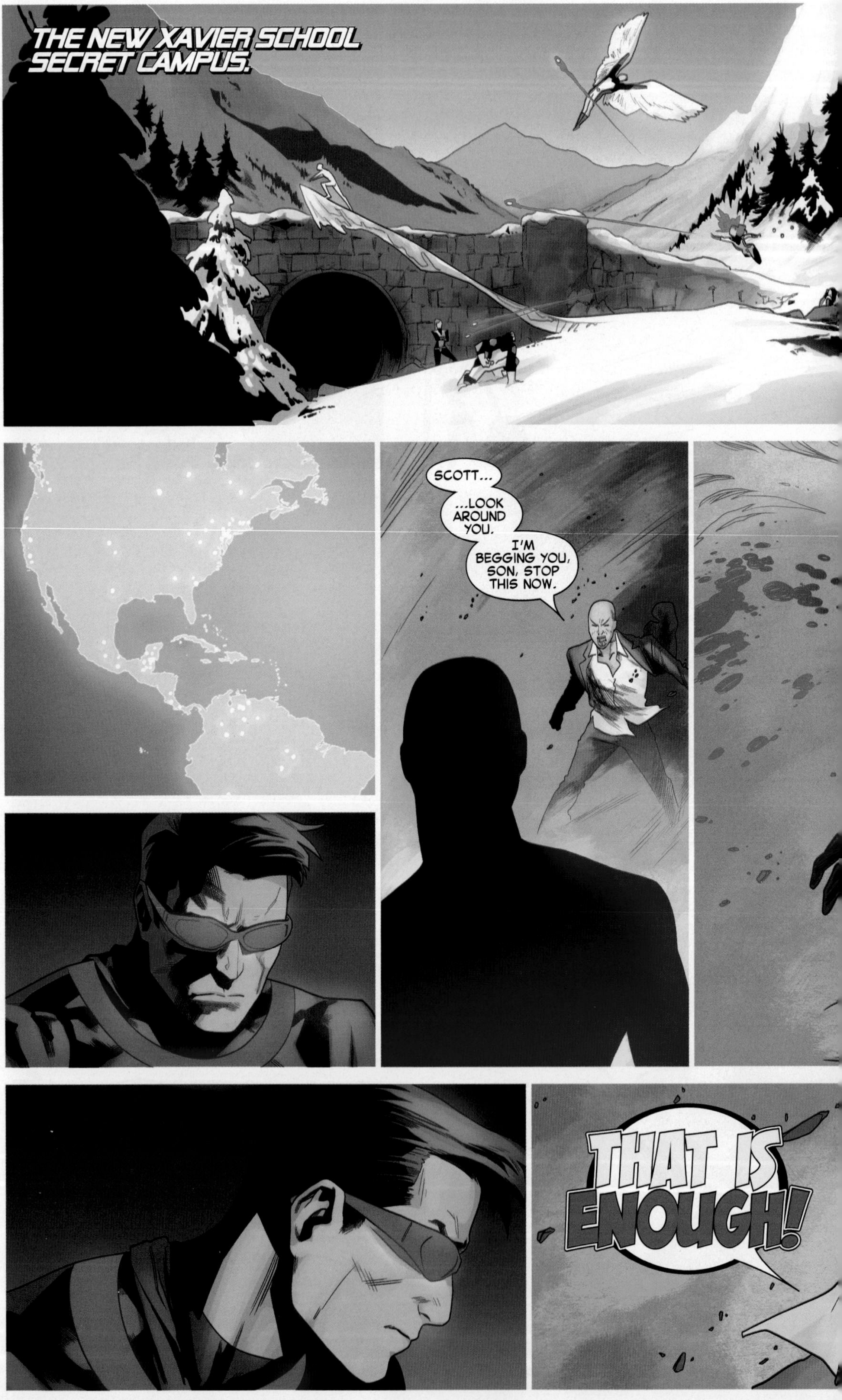
THE NEW XAVIER SCHOOL SECRET CAMPUS.
SCOTT...
...LOOK AROUND YOU.
I'M BEGGING YOU, SON, STOP THIS NOW.
THAT IS ENOUGH!

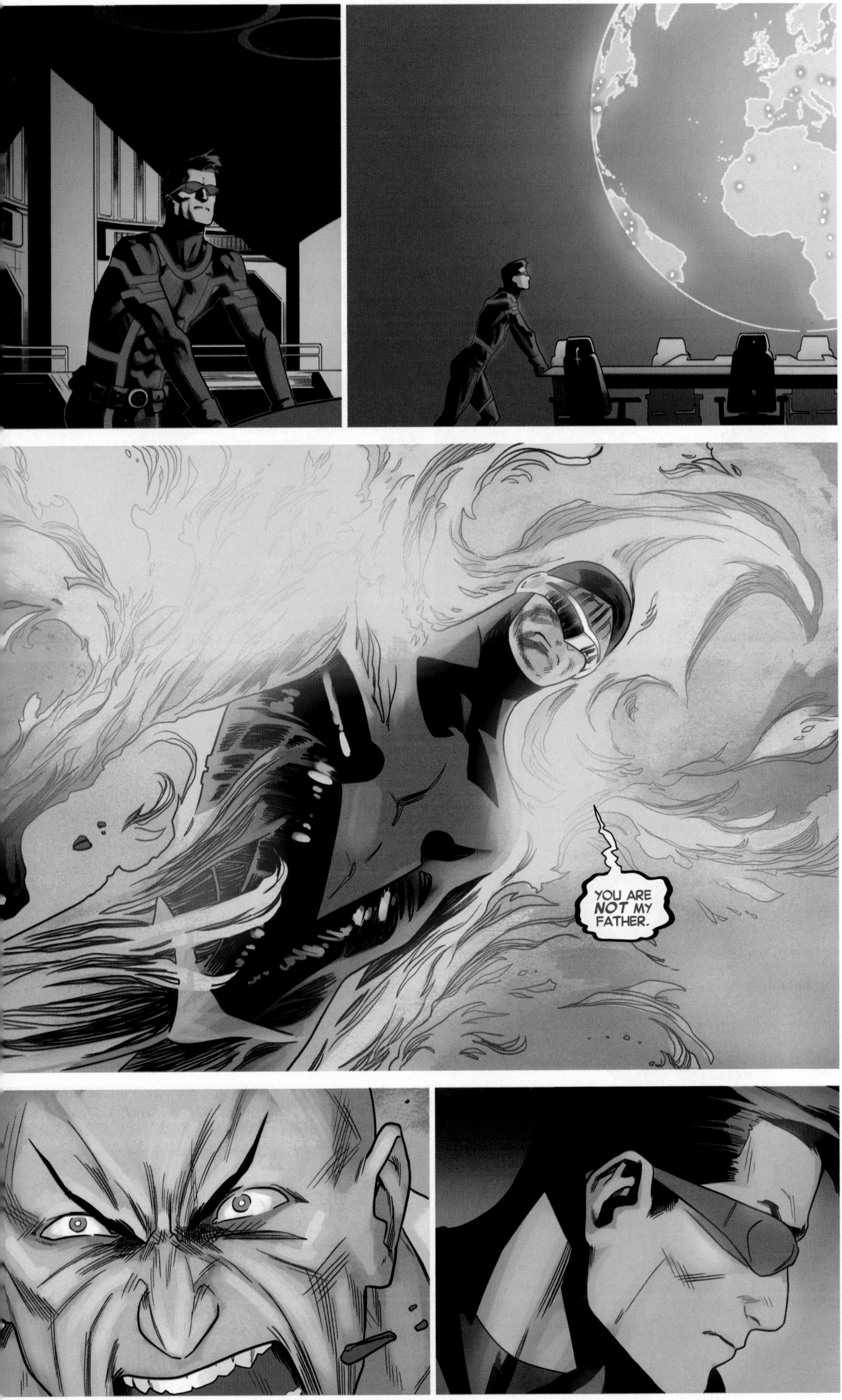
YOU ARE NOT MY FATHER.

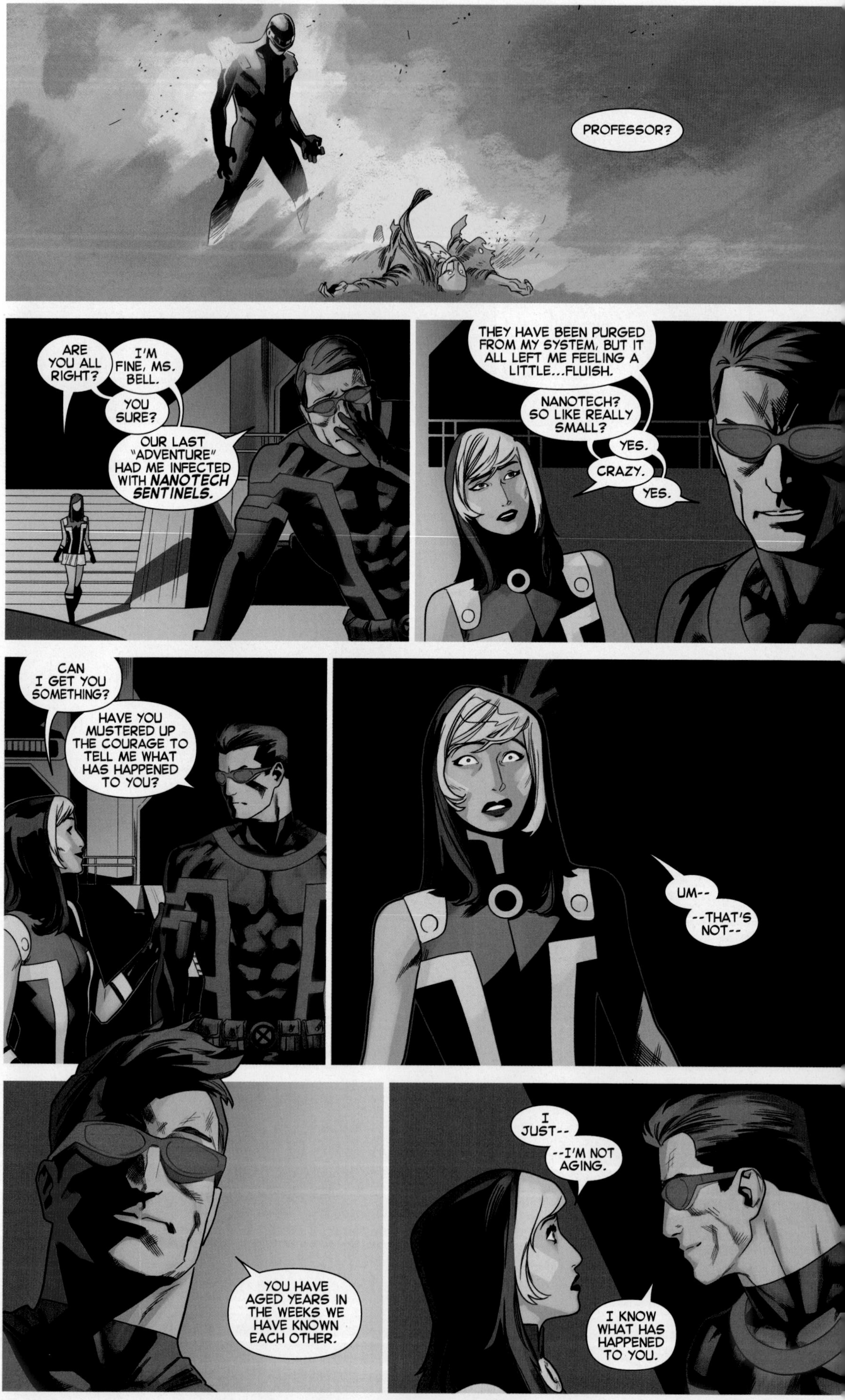
PROFESSOR?
ARE YOU ALL RIGHT?
I'M FINE, MS. BELL.
YOU SURE?
OUR LAST "ADVENTURE" HAD ME INFECTED WITH NANOTECH SENTINELS.
THEY HAVE BEEN PURGED FROM MY SYSTEM, BUT IT ALL LEFT ME FEELING A LITTLE...FLUISH.
NANOTECH? SO LIKE REALLY SMALL?
YES.
CRAZY.
YES.
CAN I GET YOU SOMETHING?
HAVE YOU MUSTERED UP THE COURAGE TO TELL ME WHAT HAS HAPPENED TO YOU?
UM--
--THAT'S NOT--
YOU HAVE AGED YEARS IN THE WEEKS WE HAVE KNOWN EACH OTHER.
I JUST--
--I'M NOT AGING.
I KNOW WHAT HAS HAPPENED TO YOU.

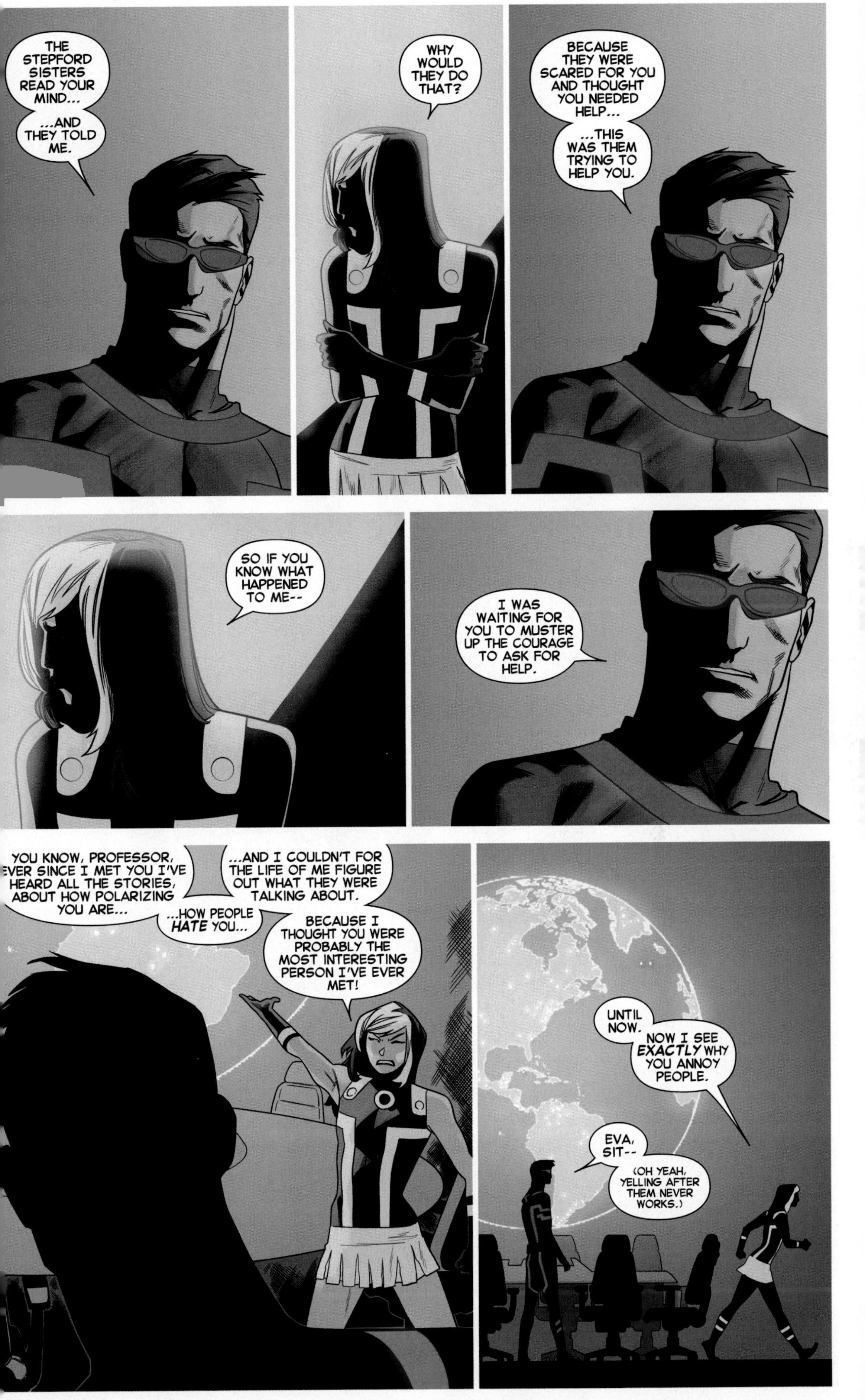
THE STEPFORD SISTERS READ YOUR MIND...
...AND THEY TOLD ME.
WHY WOULD THEY DO THAT?
BECAUSE THEY WERE SCARED FOR YOU AND THOUGHT YOU NEEDED HELP...
...THIS WAS THEM TRYING TO HELP YOU.
SO IF YOU KNOW WHAT HAPPENED TO ME--
I WAS WAITING FOR YOU TO MUSTER UP THE COURAGE TO ASK FOR HELP.
YOU KNOW, PROFESSOR, EVER SINCE I MET YOU I'VE HEARD ALL THE STORIES, ABOUT HOW POLARIZING YOU ARE...
...HOW PEOPLE HATE YOU...
...AND I COULDN'T FOR THE LIFE OF ME FIGURE OUT WHAT THEY WERE TALKING ABOUT.
BECAUSE I THOUGHT YOU WERE PROBABLY THE MOST INTERESTING PERSON I'VE EVER MET!
UNTIL NOW.
NOW I SEE EXACTLY WHY YOU ANNOY PEOPLE.
EVA, SIT--
(OH YEAH, YELLING AFTER THEM NEVER WORKS.)

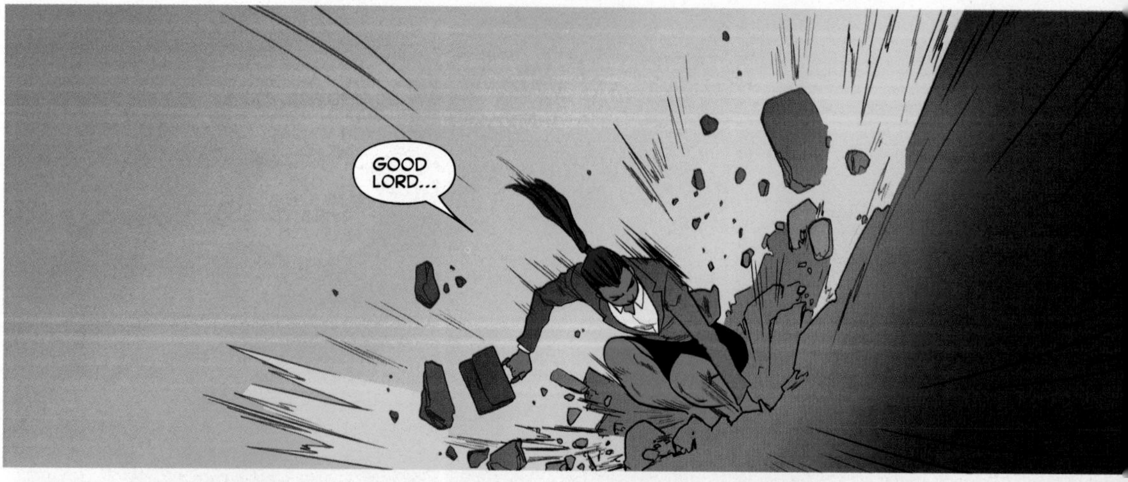
GOOD LORD...

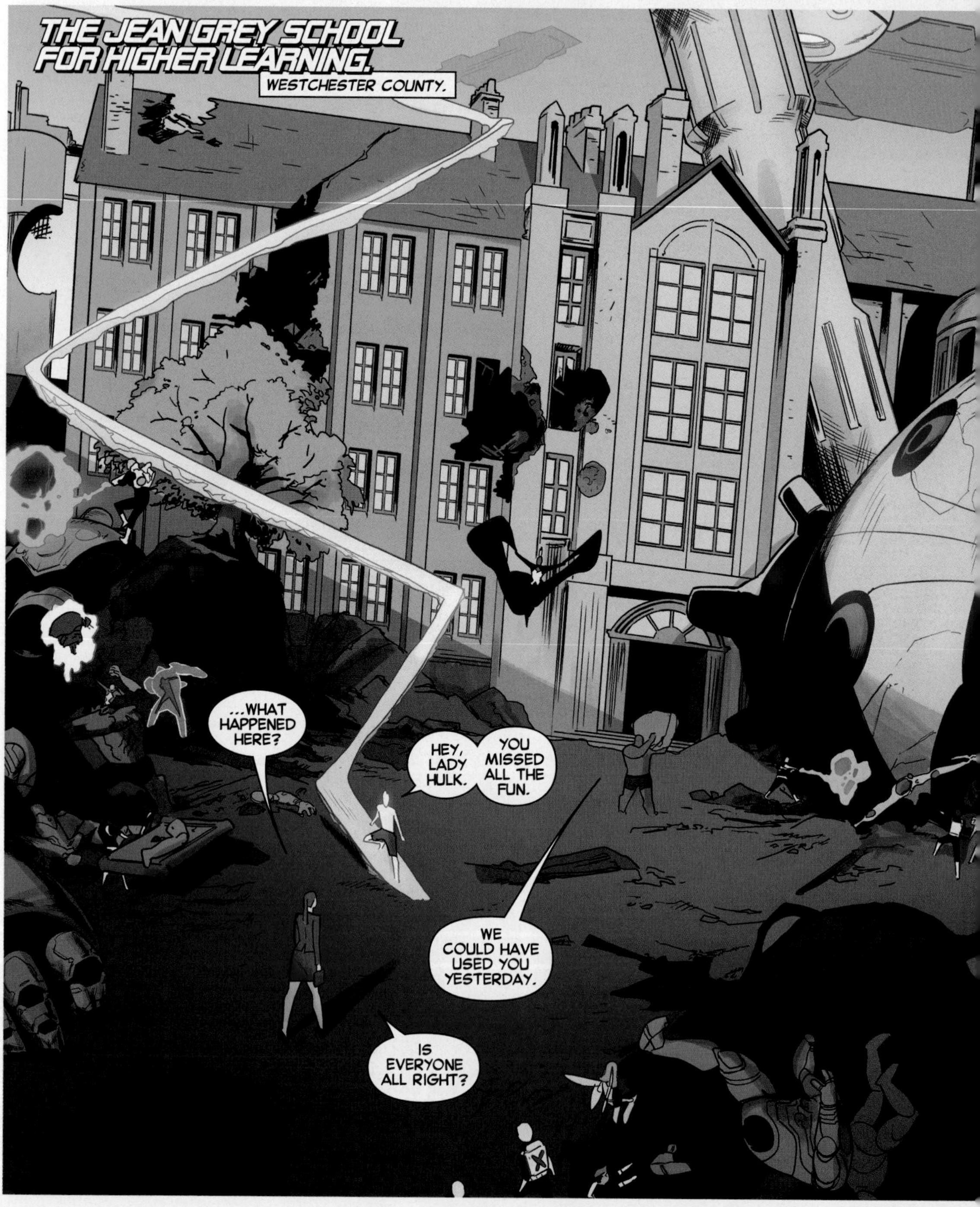
THE JEAN GREY SCHOOL FOR HIGHER LEARNING.
WESTCHESTER COUNTY.
...WHAT HAPPENED HERE?
HEY, LADY HULK.
YOU MISSED ALL THE FUN.
WE COULD HAVE USED YOU YESTERDAY.
IS EVERYONE ALL RIGHT?

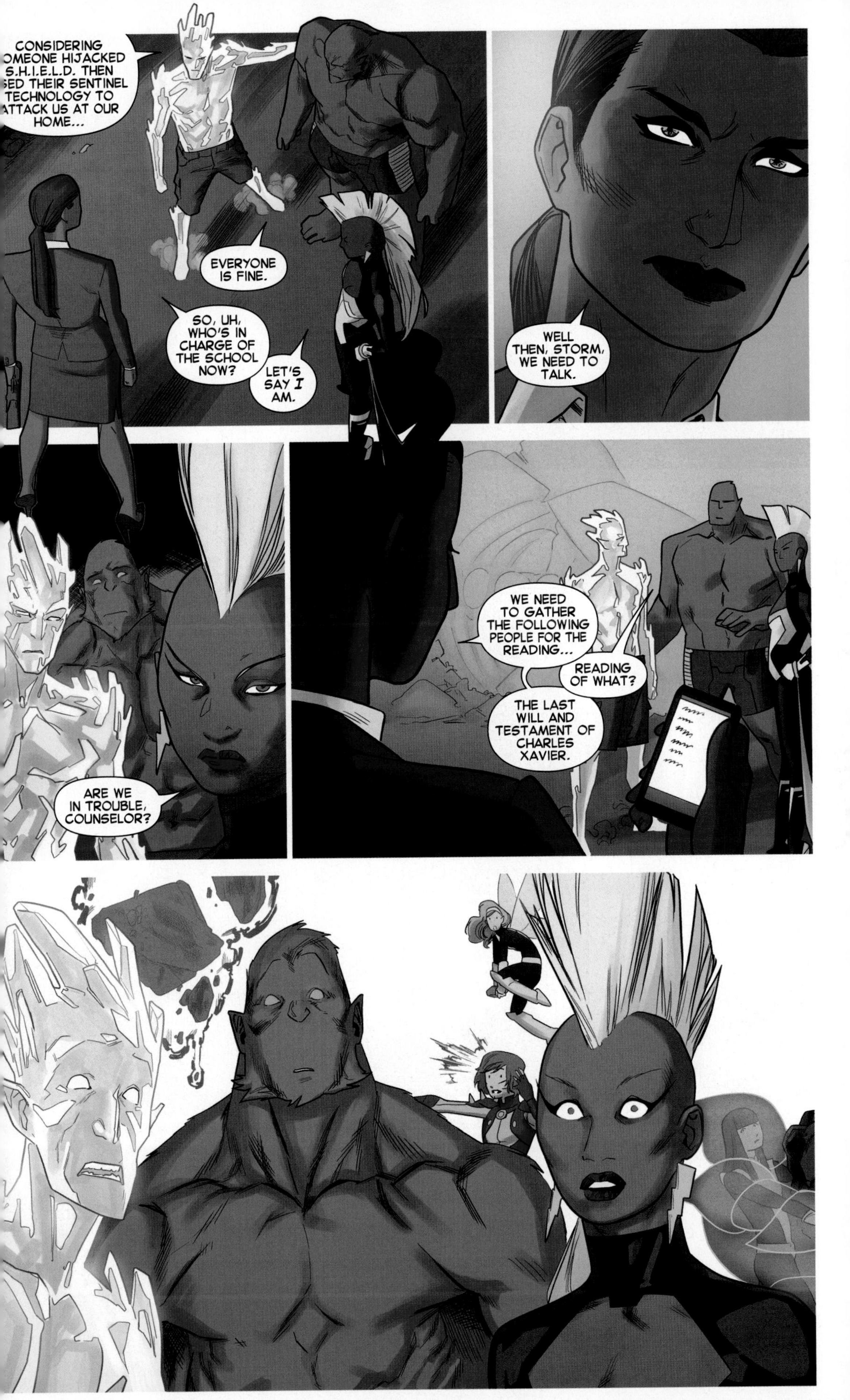

CONSIDERING OMEONE HIJACKED S.H.I.E.L.D. THEN SED THEIR SENTINEL TECHNOLOGY TO ATTACK US AT OUR HOME...
EVERYONE IS FINE.
SO, UH, WHO'S IN CHARGE OF THE SCHOOL NOW?
LET'S SAY I AM.
WELL THEN, STORM, WE NEED TO TALK.
ARE WE IN TROUBLE, COUNSELOR?
WE NEED TO GATHER THE FOLLOWING PEOPLE FOR THE READING...
READING OF WHAT?
THE LAST WILL AND TESTAMENT OF CHARLES XAVIER.

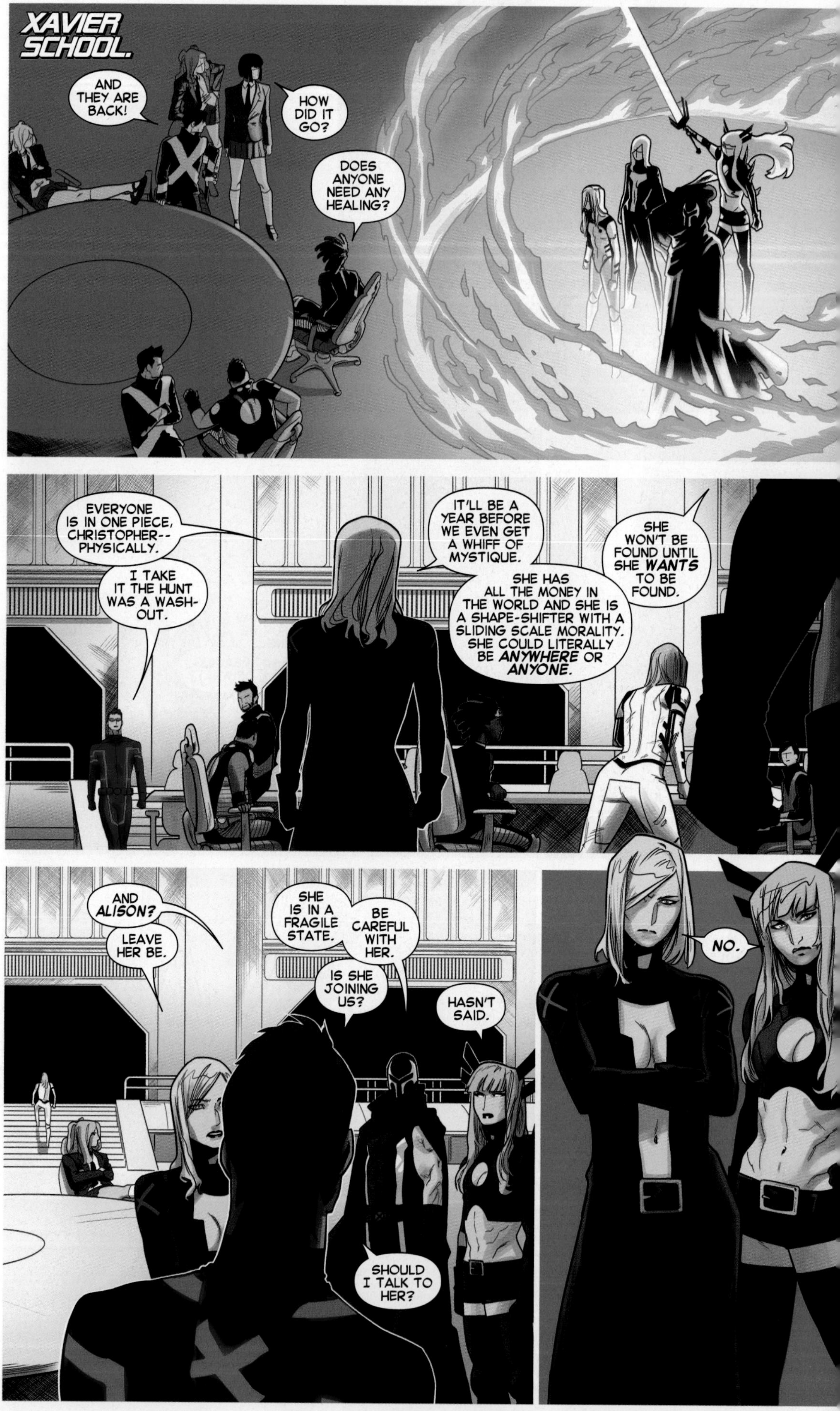
XAVIER SCHOOL.
AND THEY ARE BACK!
HOW DID IT GO?
DOES ANYONE NEED ANY HEALING?
EVERYONE IS IN ONE PIECE, CHRISTOPHER-- PHYSICALLY.
I TAKE IT THE HUNT WAS A WASH-OUT.
IT'LL BE A YEAR BEFORE WE EVEN GET A WHIFF OF MYSTIQUE.
SHE HAS ALL THE MONEY IN THE WORLD AND SHE IS A SHAPE-SHIFTER WITH A SLIDING SCALE MORALITY. SHE COULD LITERALLY BE ANYWHERE OR ANYONE.
SHE WON'T BE FOUND UNTIL SHE WANTS TO BE FOUND.
AND ALISON?
LEAVE HER BE.
SHE IS IN A FRAGILE STATE.
BE CAREFUL WITH HER.
IS SHE JOINING US?
HASN'T SAID.
SHOULD I TALK TO HER?
NO.

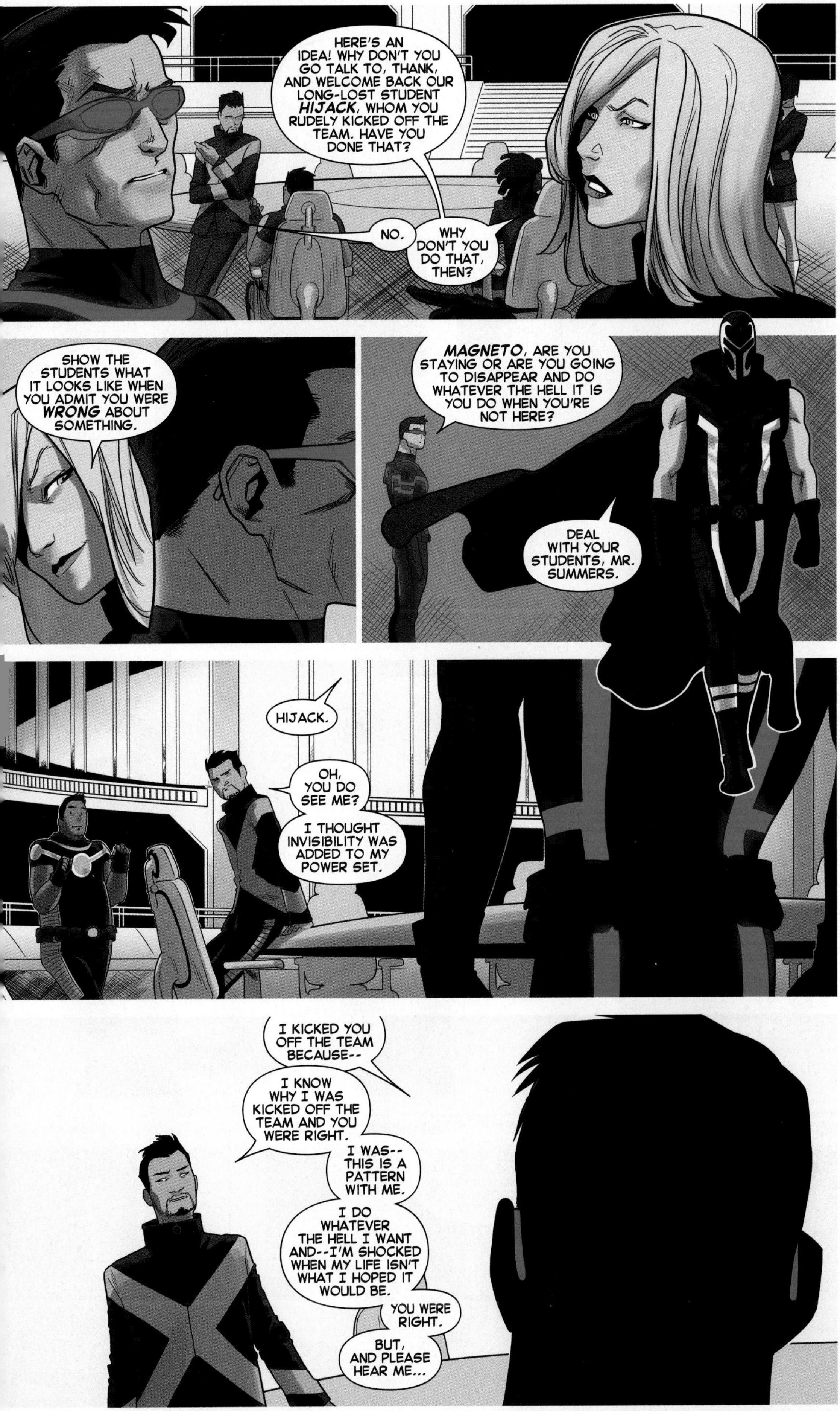
HERE'S AN IDEA! WHY DON'T YOU GO TALK TO, THANK, AND WELCOME BACK OUR LONG-LOST STUDENT HIJACK, WHOM YOU RUDELY KICKED OFF THE TEAM. HAVE YOU DONE THAT?
NO.
WHY DON'T YOU DO THAT, THEN?
SHOW THE STUDENTS WHAT IT LOOKS LIKE WHEN YOU ADMIT YOU WERE WRONG ABOUT SOMETHING.
MAGNETO, ARE YOU STAYING OR ARE YOU GOING TO DISAPPEAR AND DO WHATEVER THE HELL IT IS YOU DO WHEN YOU'RE NOT HERE?
DEAL WITH YOUR STUDENTS, MR. SUMMERS.
HIJACK.
OH, YOU DO SEE ME?
I THOUGHT INVISIBILITY WAS ADDED TO MY POWER SET.
I KICKED YOU OFF THE TEAM BECAUSE--
I KNOW WHY I WAS KICKED OFF THE TEAM AND YOU WERE RIGHT.
I WAS-- THIS IS A PATTERN WITH ME.
I DO WHATEVER THE HELL I WANT AND--I'M SHOCKED WHEN MY LIFE ISN'T WHAT I HOPED IT WOULD BE.
YOU WERE RIGHT.
BUT, AND PLEASE HEAR ME...

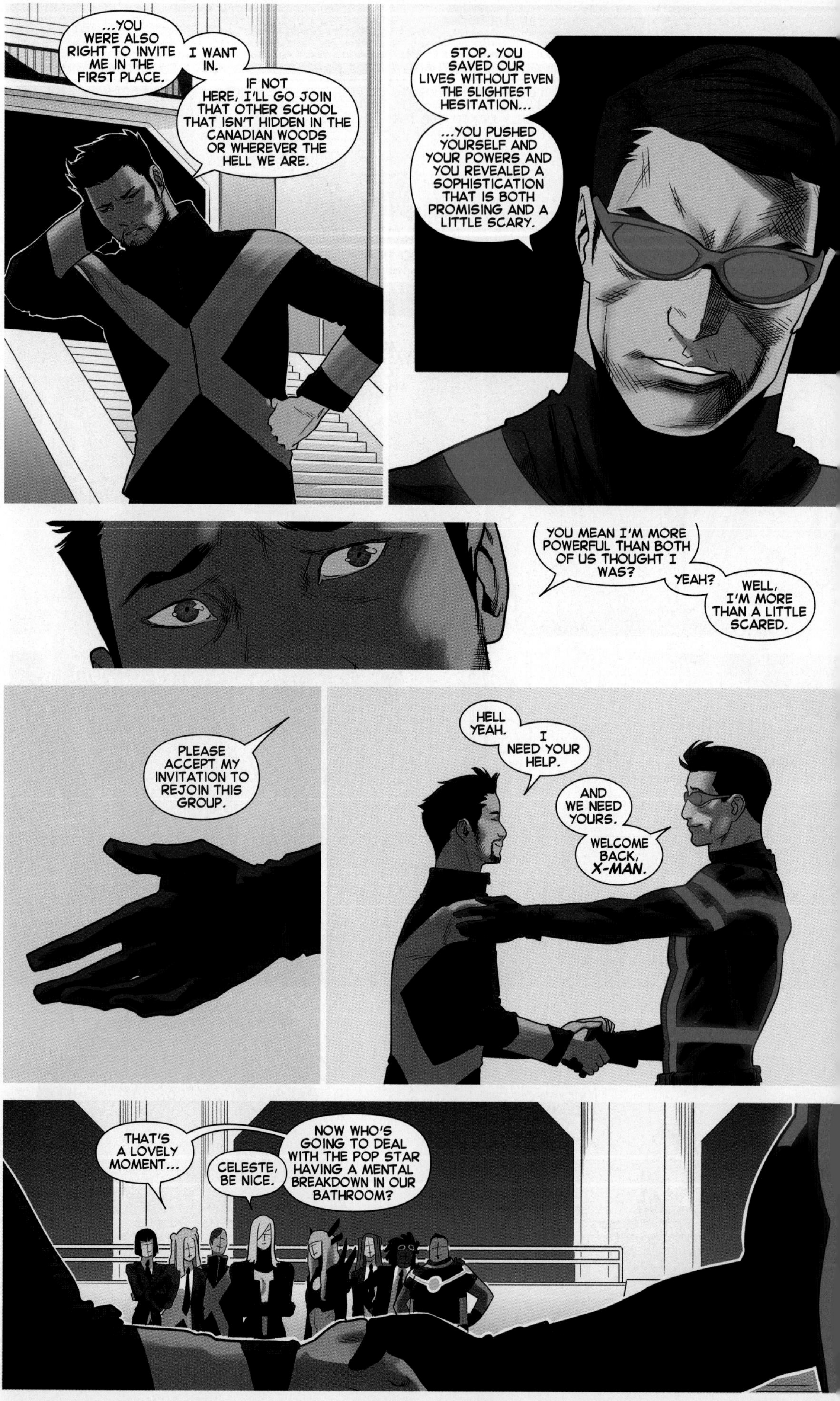
...YOU WERE ALSO RIGHT TO INVITE ME IN THE FIRST PLACE.
I WANT IN.
IF NOT HERE, I'LL GO JOIN THAT OTHER SCHOOL THAT ISN'T HIDDEN IN THE CANADIAN WOODS OR WHEREVER THE HELL WE ARE.
STOP. YOU SAVED OUR LIVES WITHOUT EVEN THE SLIGHTEST HESITATION...
...YOU PUSHED YOURSELF AND YOUR POWERS AND YOU REVEALED A SOPHISTICATION THAT IS BOTH PROMISING AND A LITTLE SCARY.
YOU MEAN I'M MORE POWERFUL THAN BOTH OF US THOUGHT I WAS?
YEAH?
WELL, I'M MORE THAN A LITTLE SCARED.
PLEASE ACCEPT MY INVITATION TO REJOIN THIS GROUP.
HELL YEAH.
I NEED YOUR HELP.
AND WE NEED YOURS.
WELCOME BACK, X-MAN.
THAT'S A LOVELY MOMENT...
NOW WHO'S GOING TO DEAL WITH THE POP STAR HAVING A MENTAL BREAKDOWN IN OUR BATHROOM?
CELESTE, BE NICE.

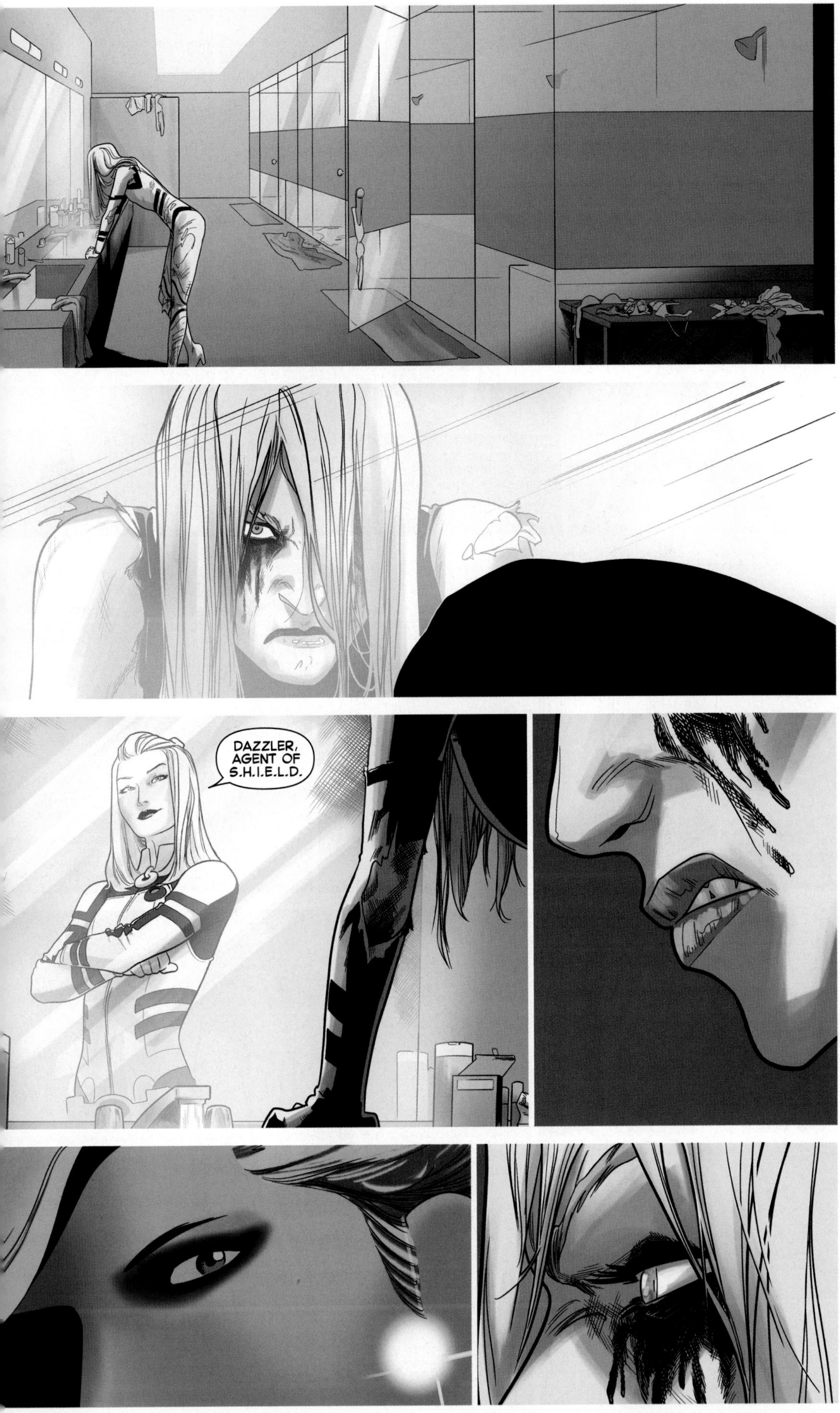
DAZZLER, AGENT OF S.H.I.E.L.D.

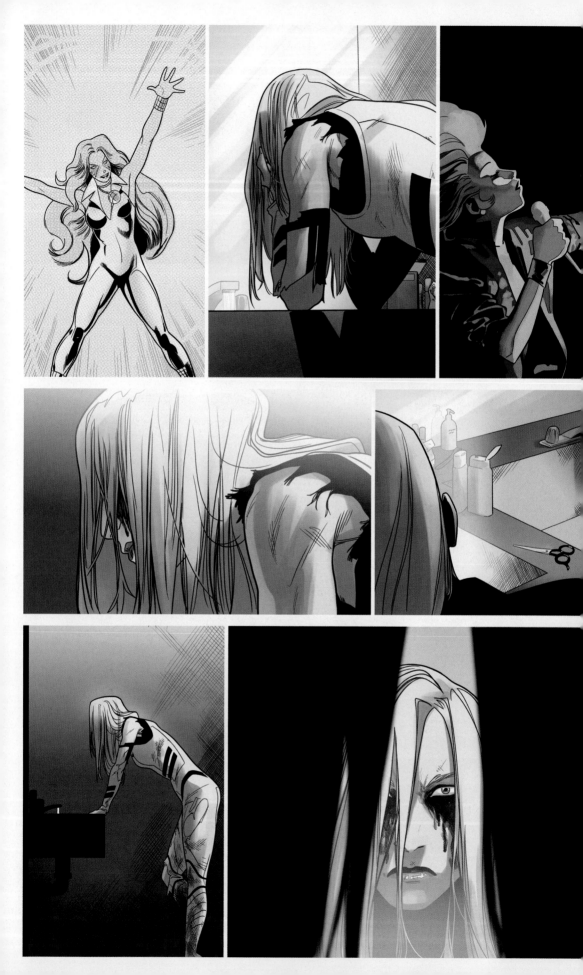

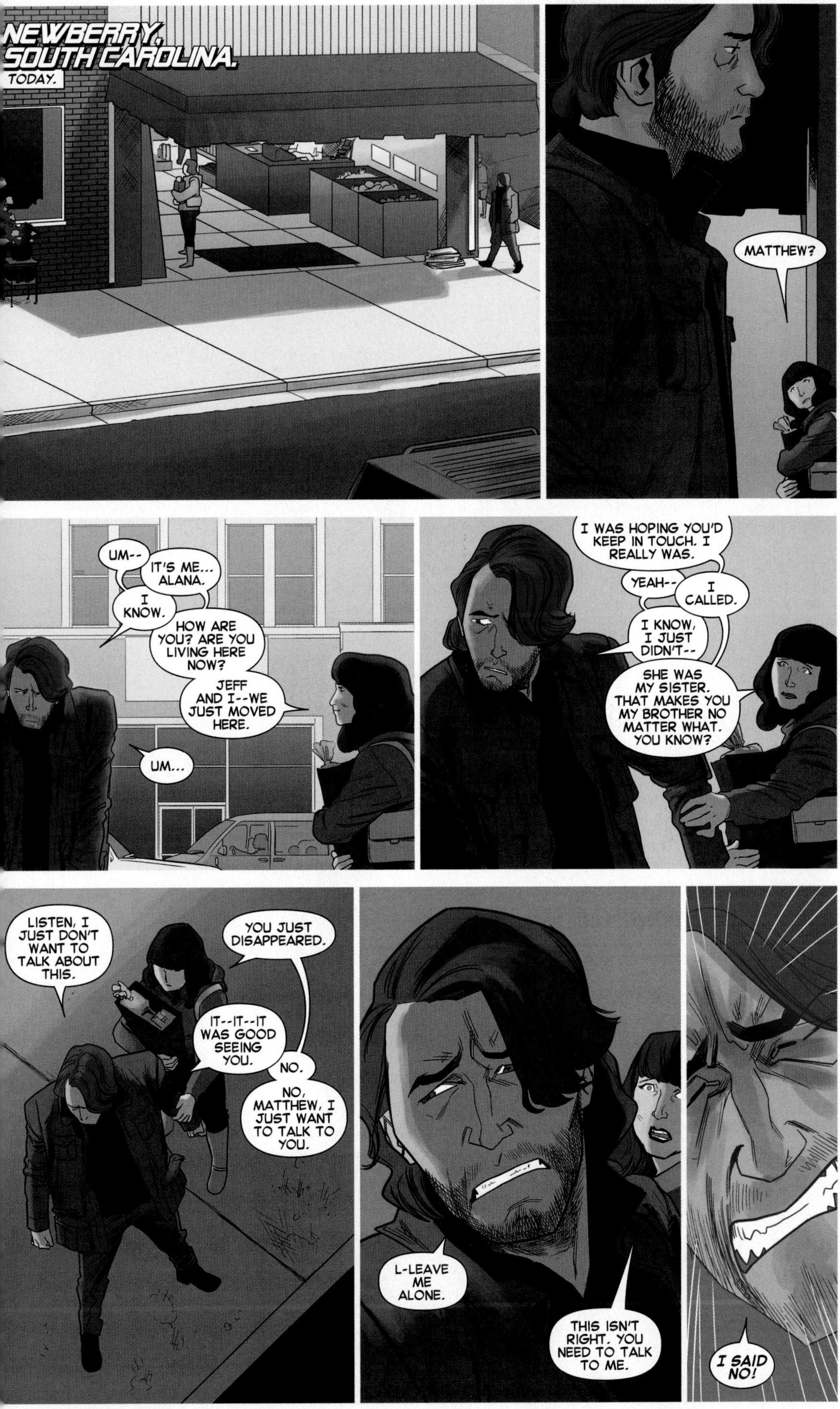
NEWBERRY, SOUTH CAROLINA.
TODAY.
MATTHEW?
UM--
IT'S ME... ALANA.
I KNOW.
HOW ARE YOU? ARE YOU LIVING HERE NOW?
JEFF AND I--WE JUST MOVED HERE.
UM...
I WAS HOPING YOU'D KEEP IN TOUCH. I REALLY WAS.
YEAH--
I CALLED.
I KNOW, I JUST DIDN'T--
SHE WAS MY SISTER. THAT MAKES YOU MY BROTHER NO MATTER WHAT. YOU KNOW?
LISTEN, I JUST DON'T WANT TO TALK ABOUT THIS.
YOU JUST DISAPPEARED.
IT--IT--IT WAS GOOD SEEING YOU.
NO.
NO, MATTHEW, I JUST WANT TO TALK TO YOU.
L-LEAVE ME ALONE.
THIS ISN'T RIGHT. YOU NEED TO TALK TO ME.
I SAID NO!

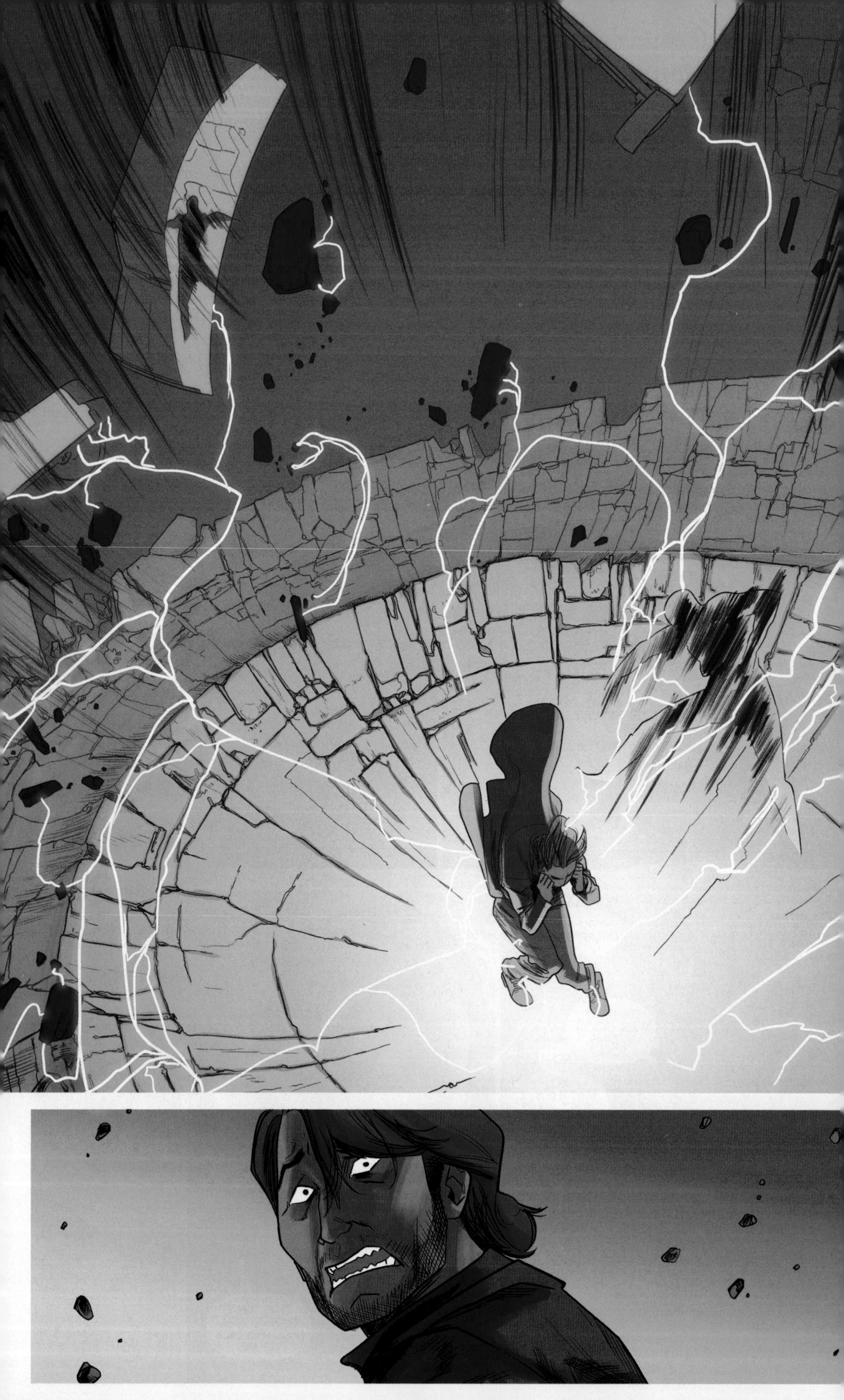

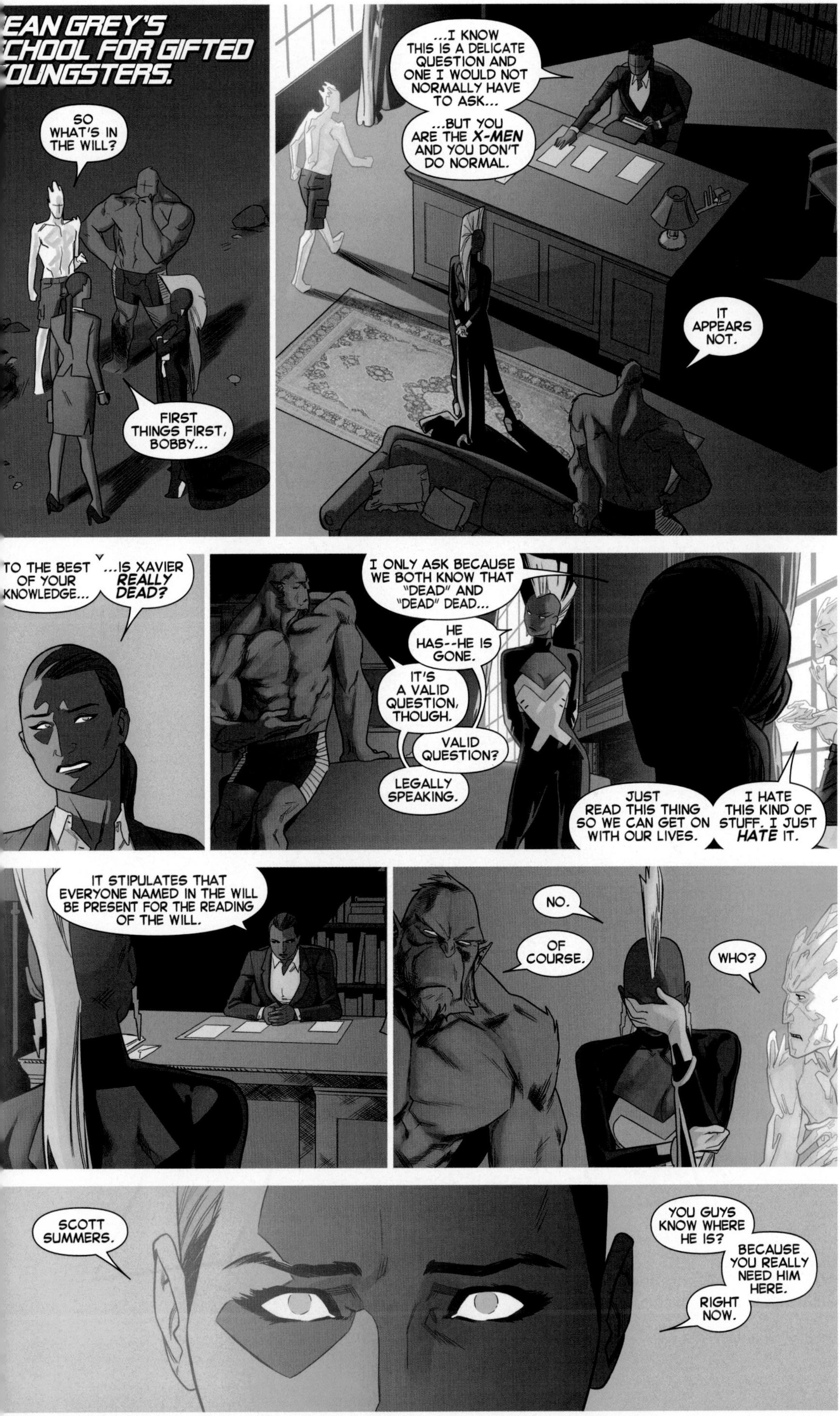

EAN GREY'S
CHOOL FOR GIFTED
OUNGSTERS.
SO WHAT'S IN THE WILL?
FIRST THINGS FIRST, BOBBY...
...I KNOW THIS IS A DELICATE QUESTION AND ONE I WOULD NOT NORMALLY HAVE TO ASK...
...BUT YOU ARE THE X-MEN AND YOU DON'T DO NORMAL.
IT APPEARS NOT.
TO THE BEST OF YOUR KNOWLEDGE...
...IS XAVIER REALLY DEAD?
I ONLY ASK BECAUSE WE BOTH KNOW THAT "DEAD" AND "DEAD" DEAD...
HE HAS--HE IS GONE.
IT'S A VALID QUESTION, THOUGH.
VALID QUESTION?
LEGALLY SPEAKING.
JUST READ THIS THING SO WE CAN GET ON WITH OUR LIVES.
I HATE THIS KIND OF STUFF. I JUST HATE IT.
IT STIPULATES THAT EVERYONE NAMED IN THE WILL BE PRESENT FOR THE READING OF THE WILL.
NO.
OF COURSE.
WHO?
SCOTT SUMMERS.
YOU GUYS KNOW WHERE HE IS?
BECAUSE YOU REALLY NEED HIM HERE.
RIGHT NOW.

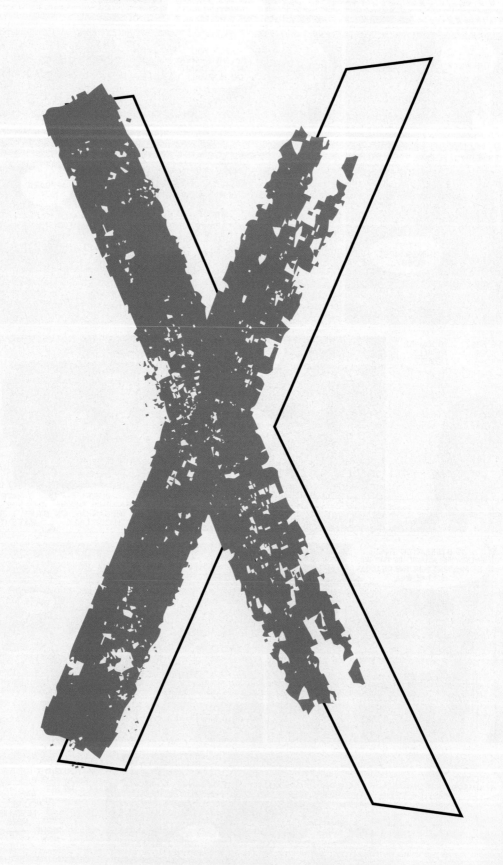

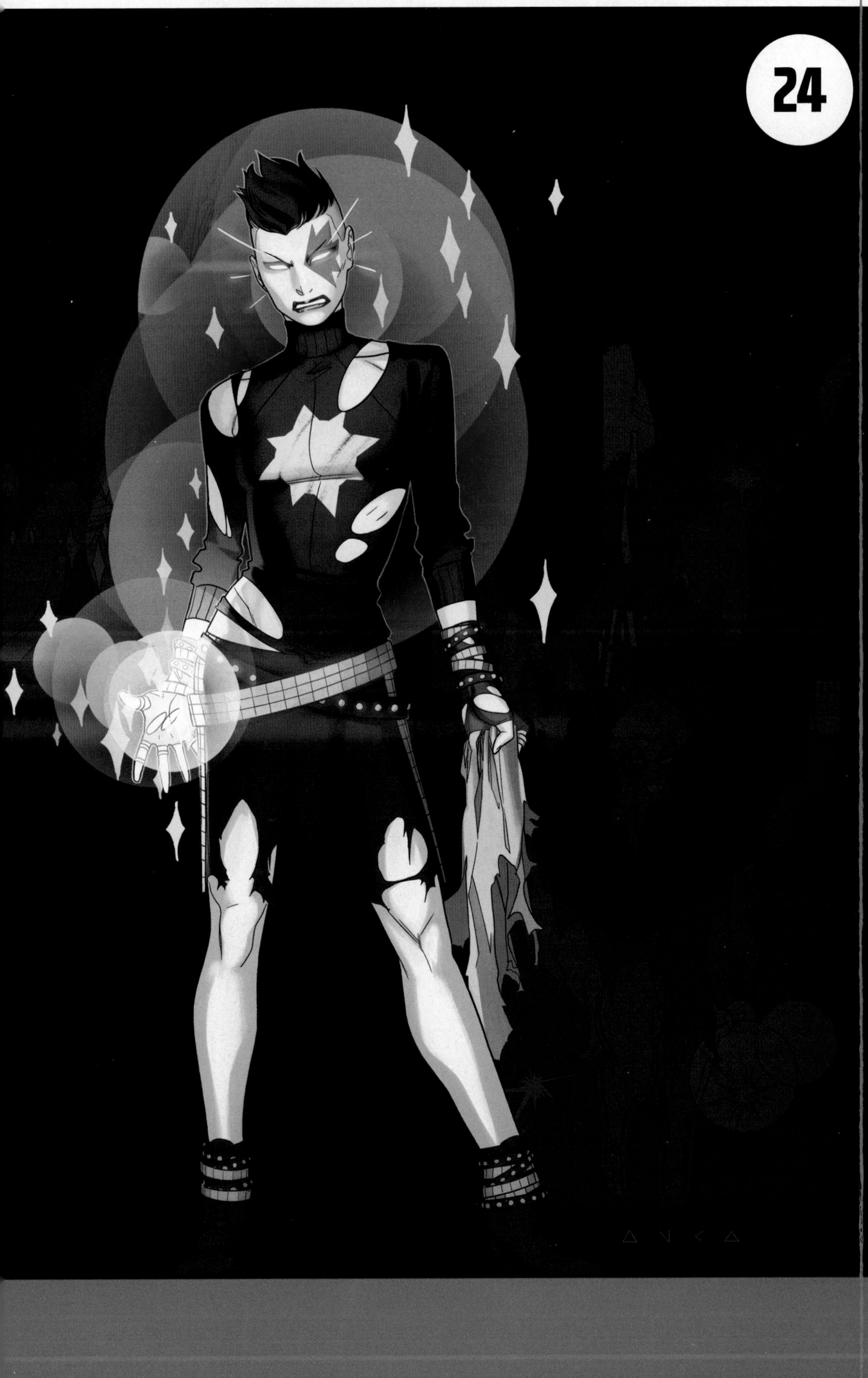
24

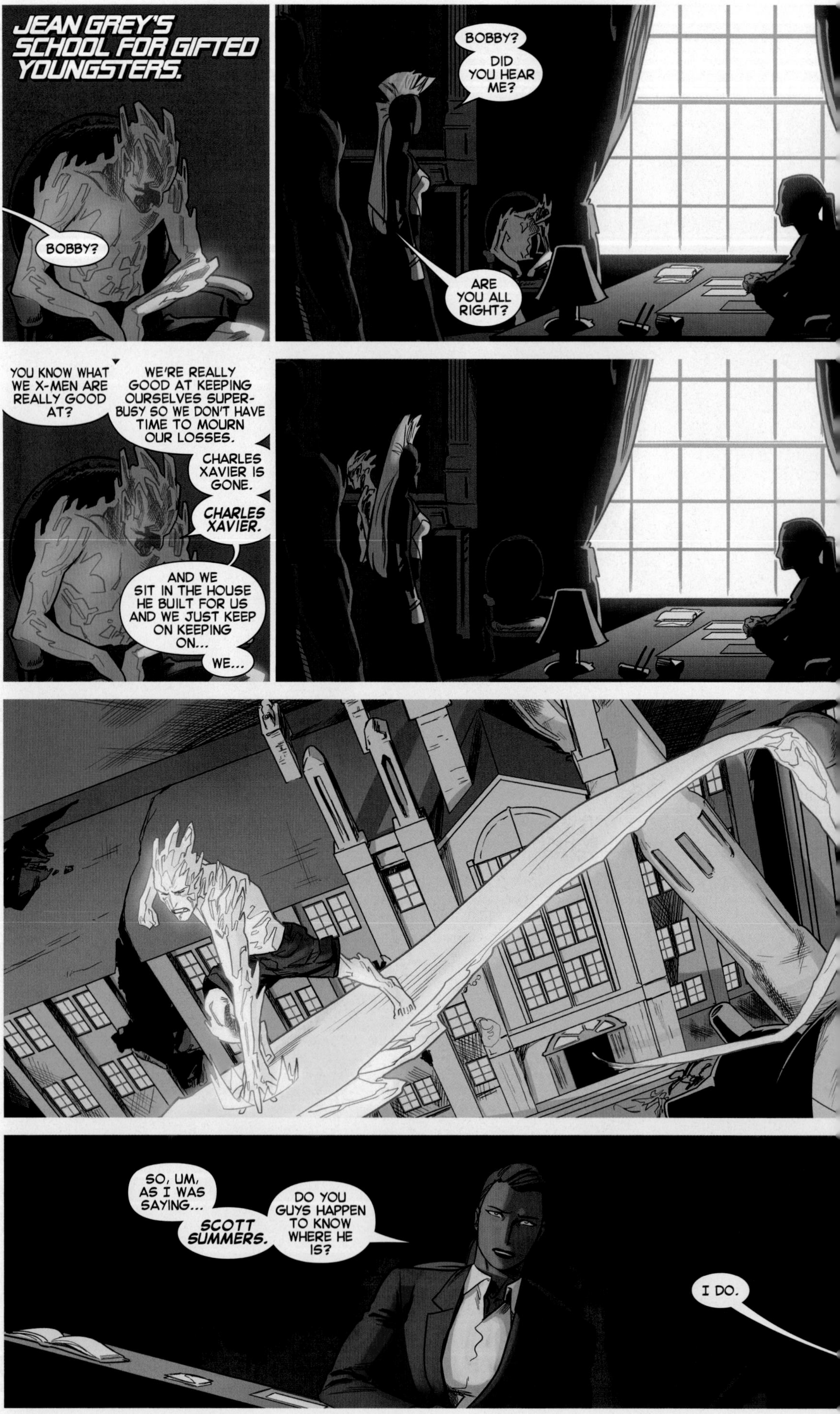
JEAN GREY'S SCHOOL FOR GIFTED YOUNGSTERS.
BOBBY?
BOBBY?
DID YOU HEAR ME?
ARE YOU ALL RIGHT?
YOU KNOW WHAT WE X-MEN ARE REALLY GOOD AT?
WE'RE REALLY GOOD AT KEEPING OURSELVES SUPER-BUSY SO WE DON'T HAVE TIME TO MOURN OUR LOSSES.
CHARLES XAVIER IS GONE.
CHARLES XAVIER.
AND WE SIT IN THE HOUSE HE BUILT FOR US AND WE JUST KEEP ON KEEPING ON...
WE...
SO, UM, AS I WAS SAYING...
SCOTT SUMMERS.
DO YOU GUYS HAPPEN TO KNOW WHERE HE IS?
I DO.

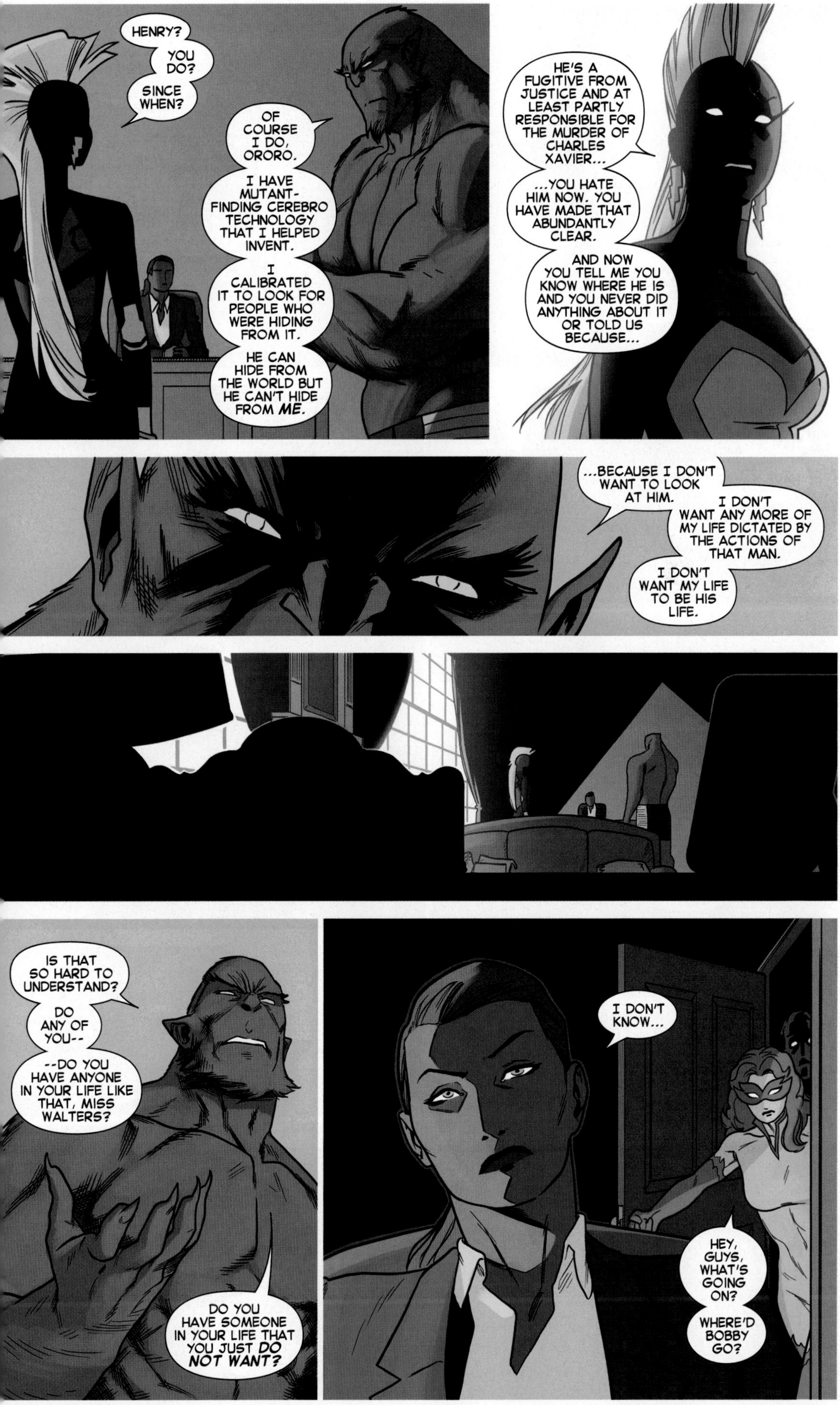
HENRY?
YOU DO?
SINCE WHEN?
OF COURSE I DO, ORORO.
I HAVE MUTANT-FINDING CEREBRO TECHNOLOGY THAT I HELPED INVENT.
I CALIBRATED IT TO LOOK FOR PEOPLE WHO WERE HIDING FROM IT.
HE CAN HIDE FROM THE WORLD BUT HE CAN'T HIDE FROM ME.
HE'S A FUGITIVE FROM JUSTICE AND AT LEAST PARTLY RESPONSIBLE FOR THE MURDER OF CHARLES XAVIER...
...YOU HATE HIM NOW. YOU HAVE MADE THAT ABUNDANTLY CLEAR.
AND NOW YOU TELL ME YOU KNOW WHERE HE IS AND YOU NEVER DID ANYTHING ABOUT IT OR TOLD US BECAUSE...
...BECAUSE I DON'T WANT TO LOOK AT HIM.
I DON'T WANT ANY MORE OF MY LIFE DICTATED BY THE ACTIONS OF THAT MAN.
I DON'T WANT MY LIFE TO BE HIS LIFE.
IS THAT SO HARD TO UNDERSTAND?
DO ANY OF YOU--
--DO YOU HAVE ANYONE IN YOUR LIFE LIKE THAT, MISS WALTERS?
DO YOU HAVE SOMEONE IN YOUR LIFE THAT YOU JUST DO NOT WANT?
I DON'T KNOW...
HEY, GUYS, WHAT'S GOING ON?
WHERE'D BOBBY GO?

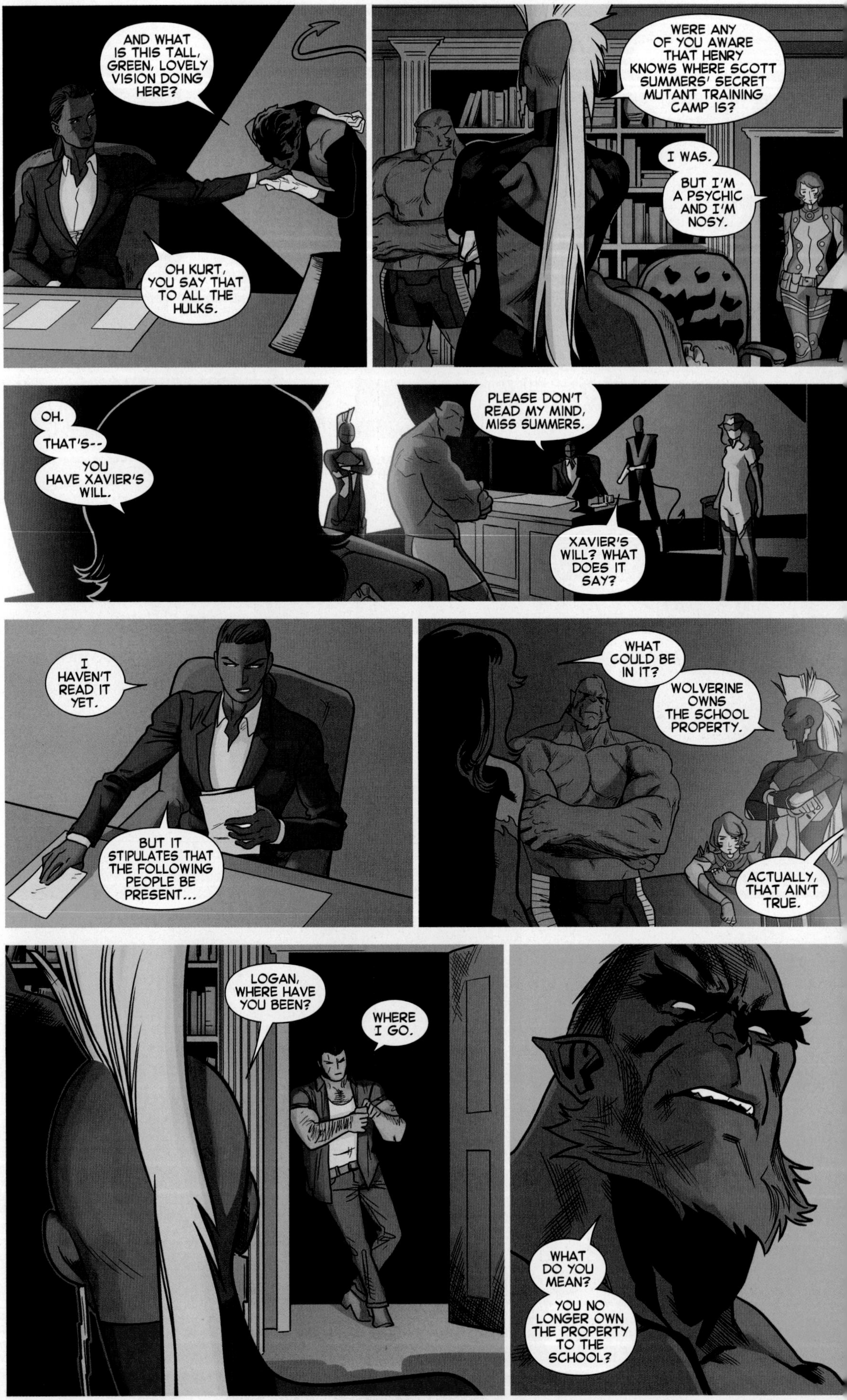
AND WHAT IS THIS TALL, GREEN, LOVELY VISION DOING HERE?
OH KURT, YOU SAY THAT TO ALL THE HULKS.
WERE ANY OF YOU AWARE THAT HENRY KNOWS WHERE SCOTT SUMMERS' SECRET MUTANT TRAINING CAMP IS?
I WAS.
BUT I'M A PSYCHIC AND I'M NOSY.
OH.
THAT'S--
YOU HAVE XAVIER'S WILL.
PLEASE DON'T READ MY MIND, MISS SUMMERS.
XAVIER'S WILL? WHAT DOES IT SAY?
I HAVEN'T READ IT YET.
BUT IT STIPULATES THAT THE FOLLOWING PEOPLE BE PRESENT...
WHAT COULD BE IN IT?
WOLVERINE OWNS THE SCHOOL PROPERTY.
ACTUALLY, THAT AIN'T TRUE.
LOGAN, WHERE HAVE YOU BEEN?
WHERE I GO.
WHAT DO YOU MEAN?
YOU NO LONGER OWN THE PROPERTY TO THE SCHOOL?

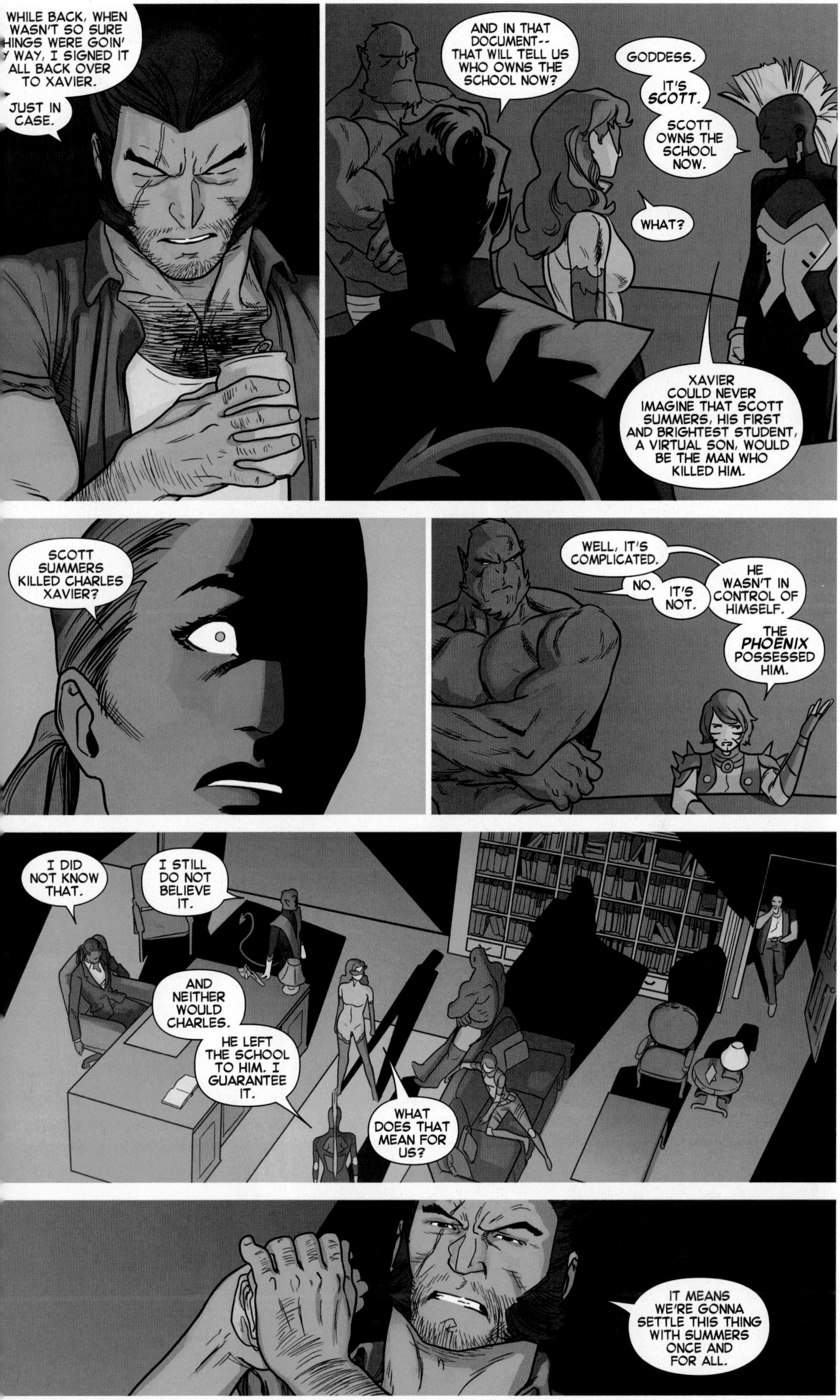
WHILE BACK, WHEN WASN'T SO SURE HINGS WERE GOIN' Y WAY, I SIGNED IT ALL BACK OVER TO XAVIER.
JUST IN CASE.
AND IN THAT DOCUMENT-- THAT WILL TELL US WHO OWNS THE SCHOOL NOW?
GODDESS.
IT'S SCOTT.
SCOTT OWNS THE SCHOOL NOW.
WHAT?
XAVIER COULD NEVER IMAGINE THAT SCOTT SUMMERS, HIS FIRST AND BRIGHTEST STUDENT, A VIRTUAL SON, WOULD BE THE MAN WHO KILLED HIM.
SCOTT SUMMERS KILLED CHARLES XAVIER?
WELL, IT'S COMPLICATED.
NO.
IT'S NOT.
HE WASN'T IN CONTROL OF HIMSELF.
THE PHOENIX POSSESSED HIM.
I DID NOT KNOW THAT.
I STILL DO NOT BELIEVE IT.
AND NEITHER WOULD CHARLES.
HE LEFT THE SCHOOL TO HIM. I GUARANTEE IT.
WHAT DOES THAT MEAN FOR US?
IT MEANS WE'RE GONNA SETTLE THIS THING WITH SUMMERS ONCE AND FOR ALL.

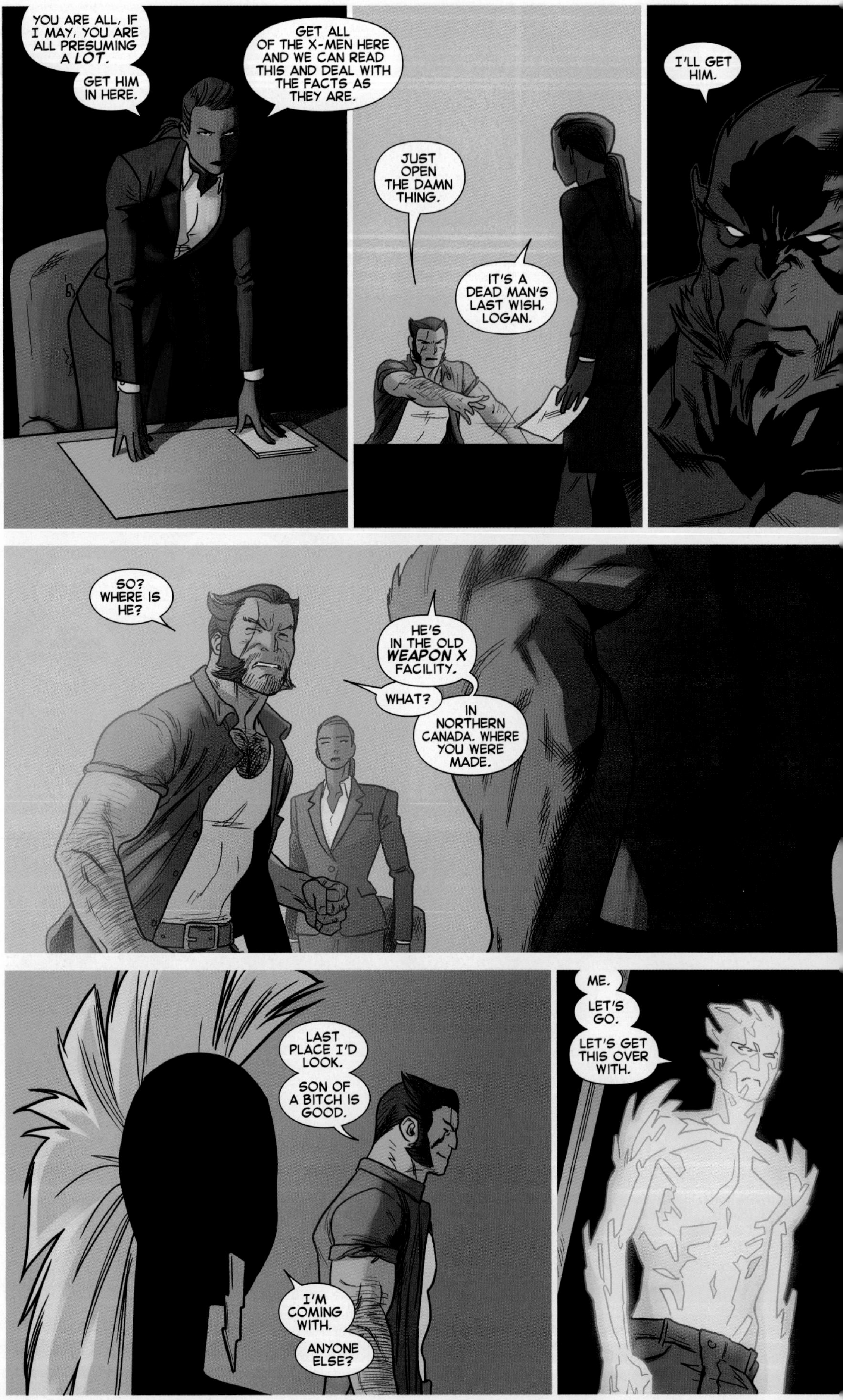
YOU ARE ALL, IF I MAY, YOU ARE ALL PRESUMING A LOT.
GET HIM IN HERE.
GET ALL OF THE X-MEN HERE AND WE CAN READ THIS AND DEAL WITH THE FACTS AS THEY ARE.
JUST OPEN THE DAMN THING.
IT'S A DEAD MAN'S LAST WISH, LOGAN.
I'LL GET HIM.
SO? WHERE IS HE?
HE'S IN THE OLD WEAPON X FACILITY.
WHAT?
IN NORTHERN CANADA. WHERE YOU WERE MADE.
LAST PLACE I'D LOOK.
SON OF A BITCH IS GOOD.
I'M COMING WITH.
ANYONE ELSE?
ME.
LET'S GO.
LET'S GET THIS OVER WITH.

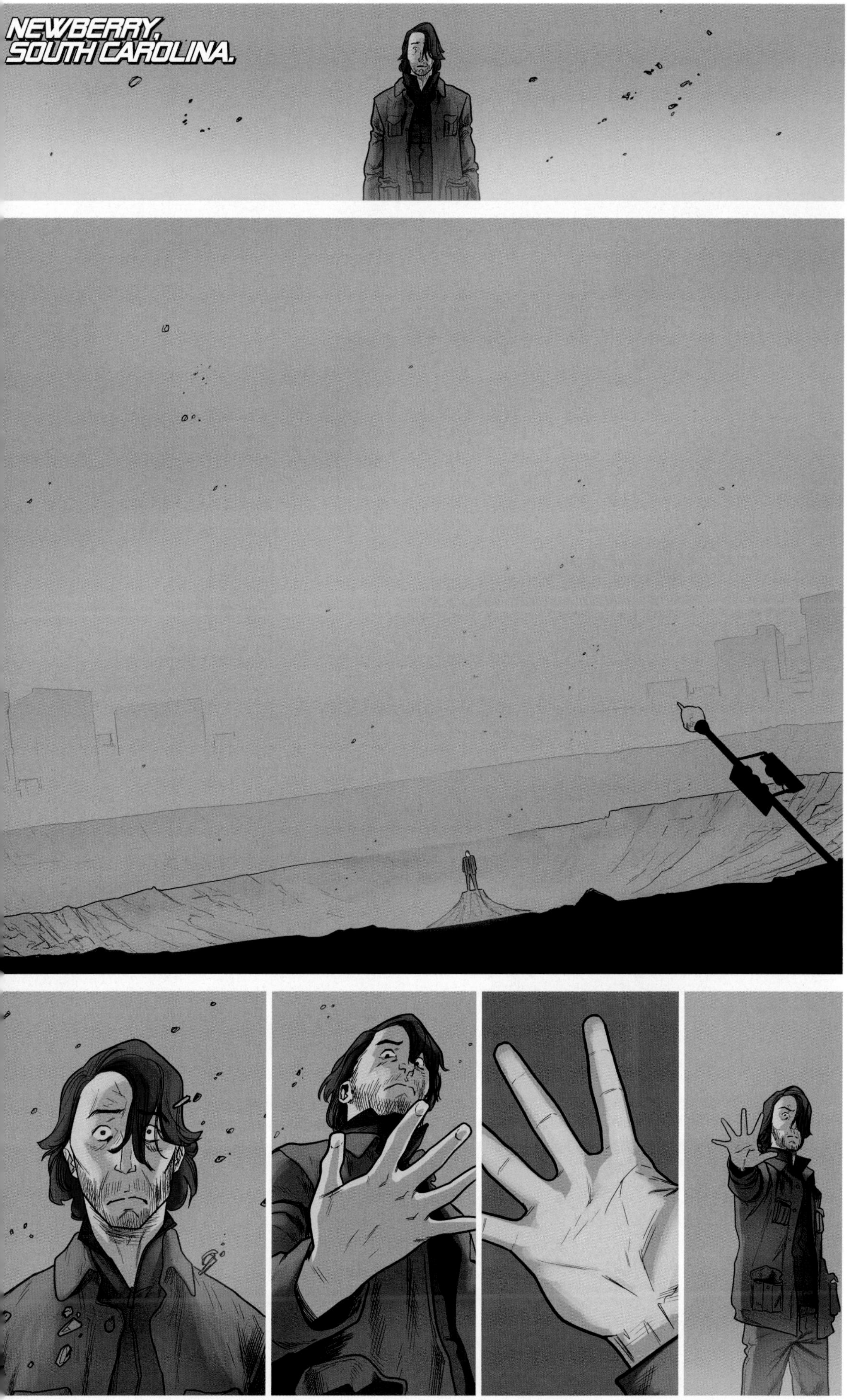
NEWBERRY, SOUTH CAROLINA.

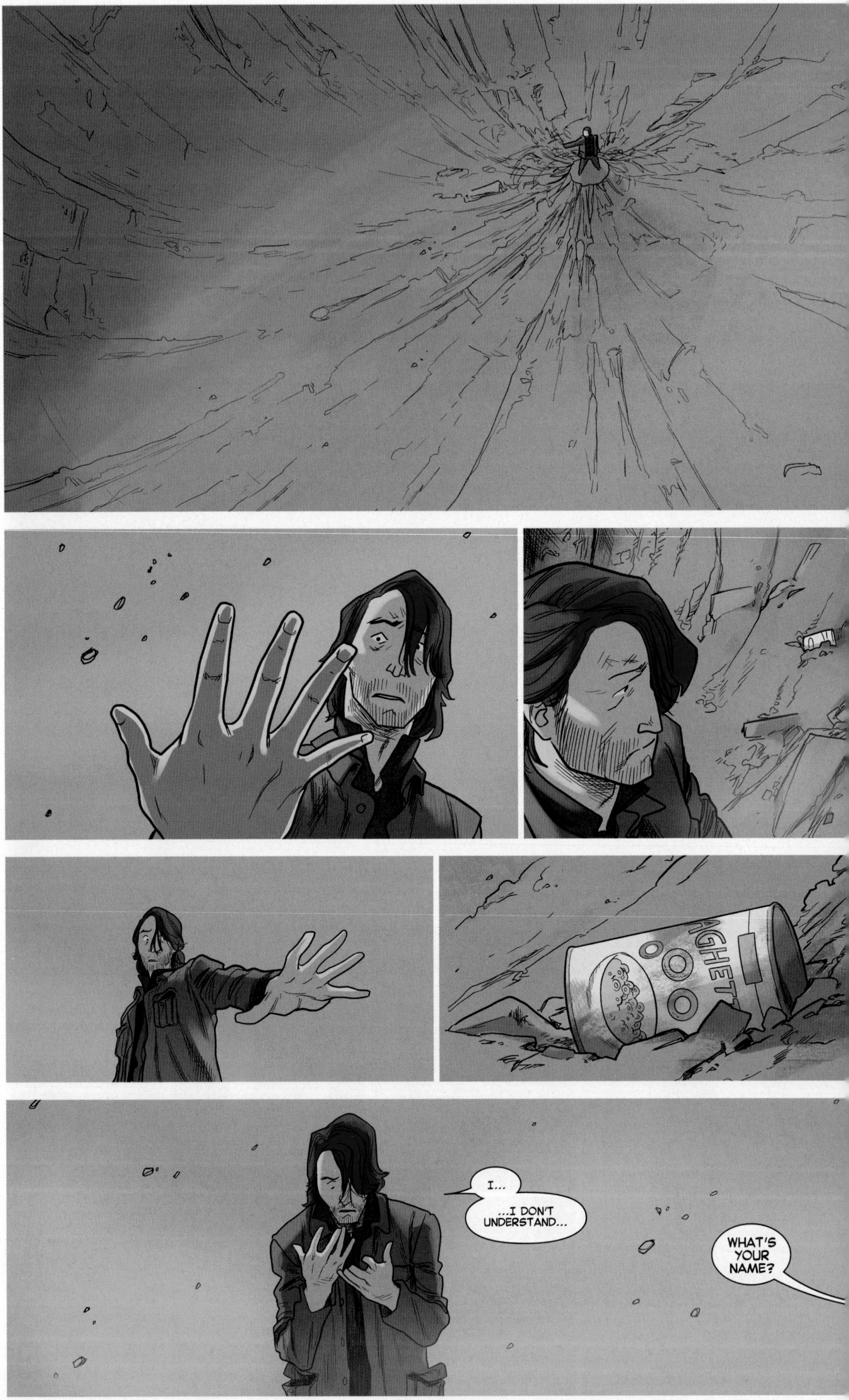

AGHETT
I...
...I DON'T UNDERSTAND...
WHAT'S YOUR NAME?

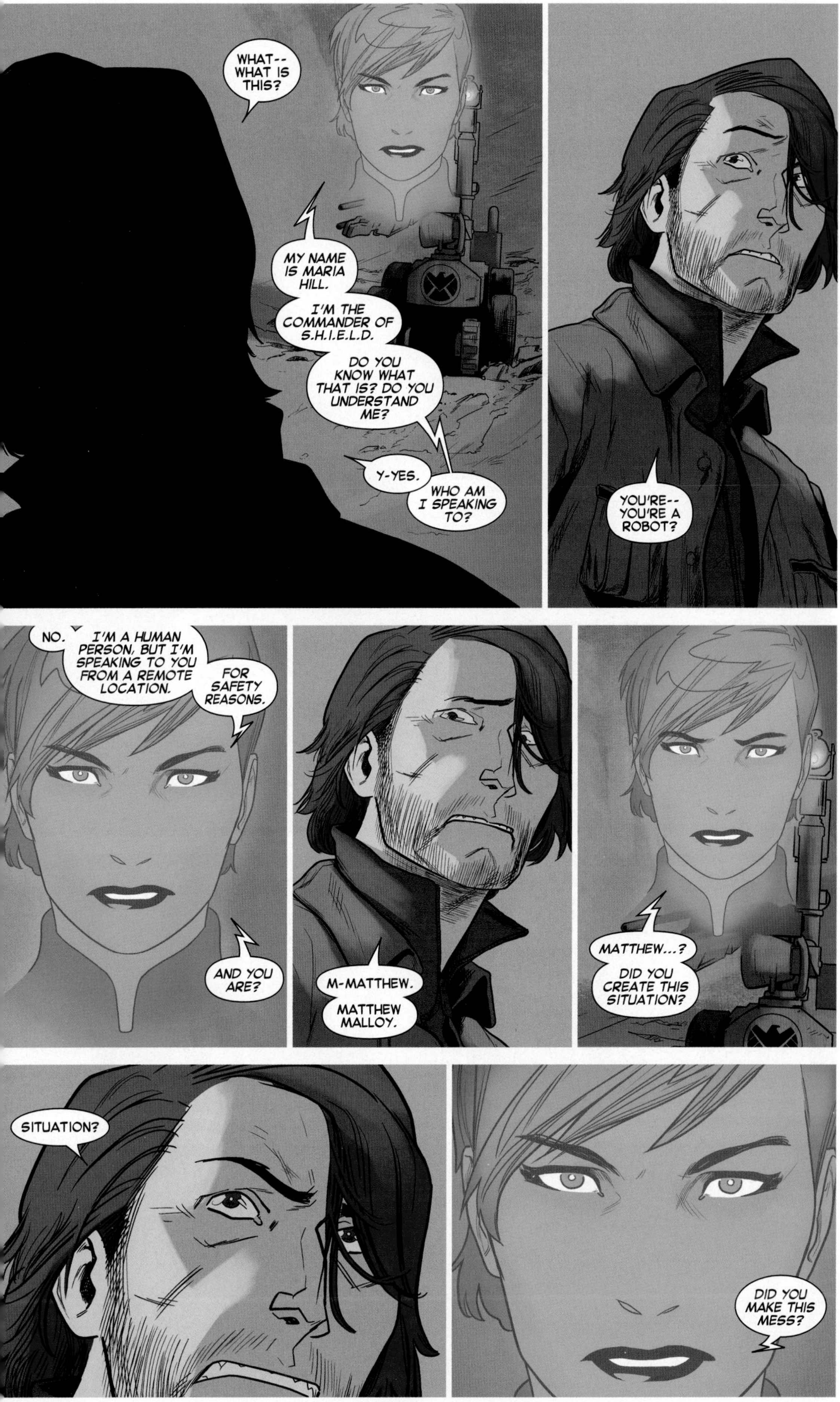
WHAT-- WHAT IS THIS?
MY NAME IS MARIA HILL.
I'M THE COMMANDER OF S.H.I.E.L.D.
DO YOU KNOW WHAT THAT IS? DO YOU UNDERSTAND ME?
Y-YES.
WHO AM I SPEAKING TO?
YOU'RE-- YOU'RE A ROBOT?
NO.
I'M A HUMAN PERSON, BUT I'M SPEAKING TO YOU FROM A REMOTE LOCATION.
FOR SAFETY REASONS.
AND YOU ARE?
M-MATTHEW.
MATTHEW MALLOY.
MATTHEW...?
DID YOU CREATE THIS SITUATION?
SITUATION?
DID YOU MAKE THIS MESS?

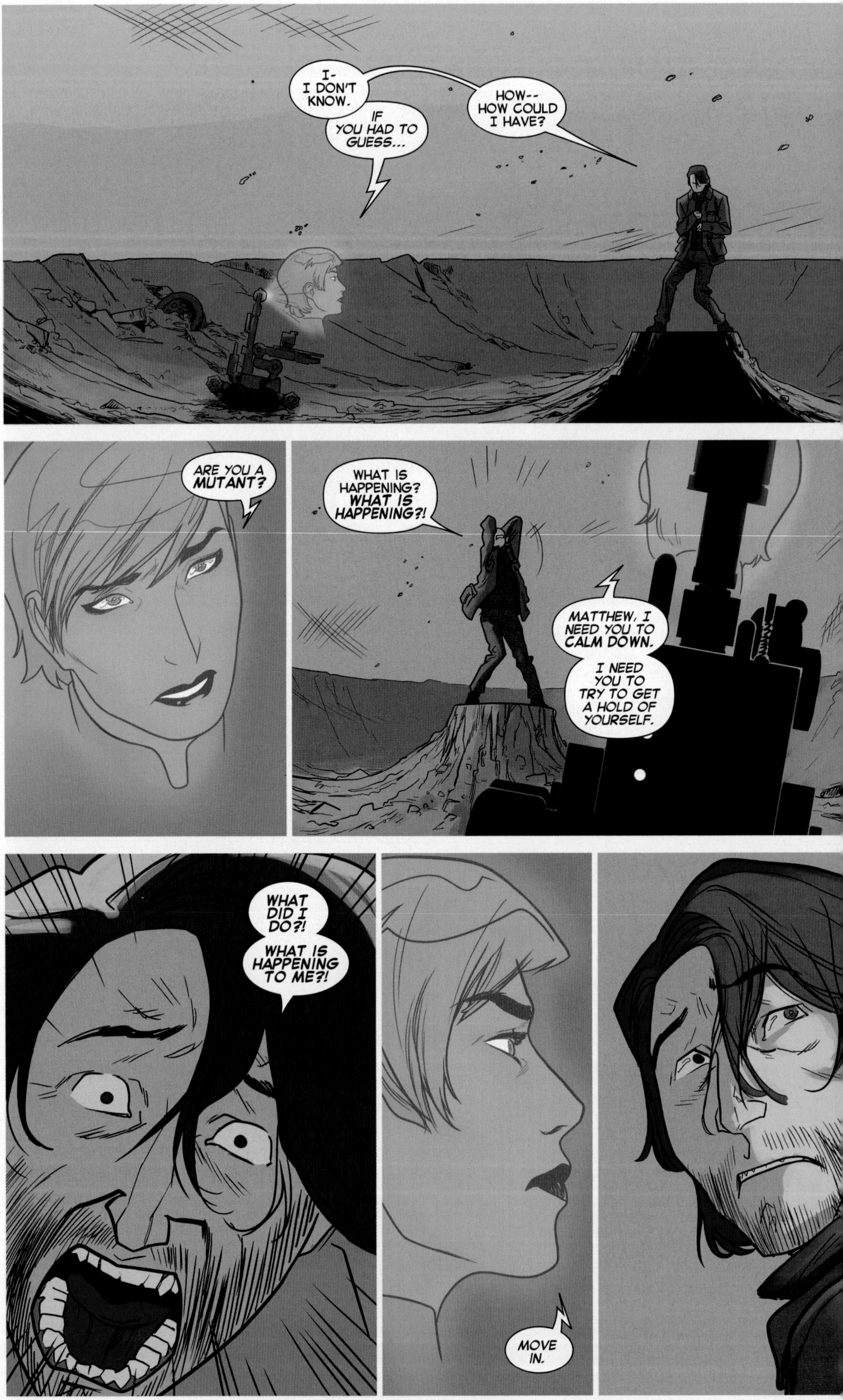

I-
I DON'T KNOW.
IF YOU HAD TO GUESS...
HOW--
HOW COULD I HAVE?
ARE YOU A MUTANT?
WHAT IS HAPPENING? WHAT IS HAPPENING?!
MATTHEW, I NEED YOU TO CALM DOWN.
I NEED YOU TO TRY TO GET A HOLD OF YOURSELF.
WHAT DID I DO?!
WHAT IS HAPPENING TO ME?!
MOVE IN.

DO YOU HAVE-- ARE YOU A POWER?

A POWER?

YOU'RE NOT IN TROUBLE, I JUST WANT TO TALK--

DID I KILL THESE PEOPLE?!

THERE WERE PEOPLE.

HAVE YOU EVER DONE ANYTHING LIKE THIS BEFORE?

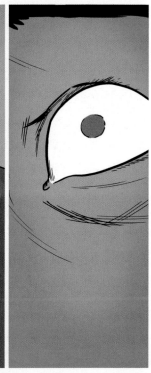

MATTHEW, IT WOULD BE WONDERFUL IF YOU WOULD CALMLY SIT DOWN.

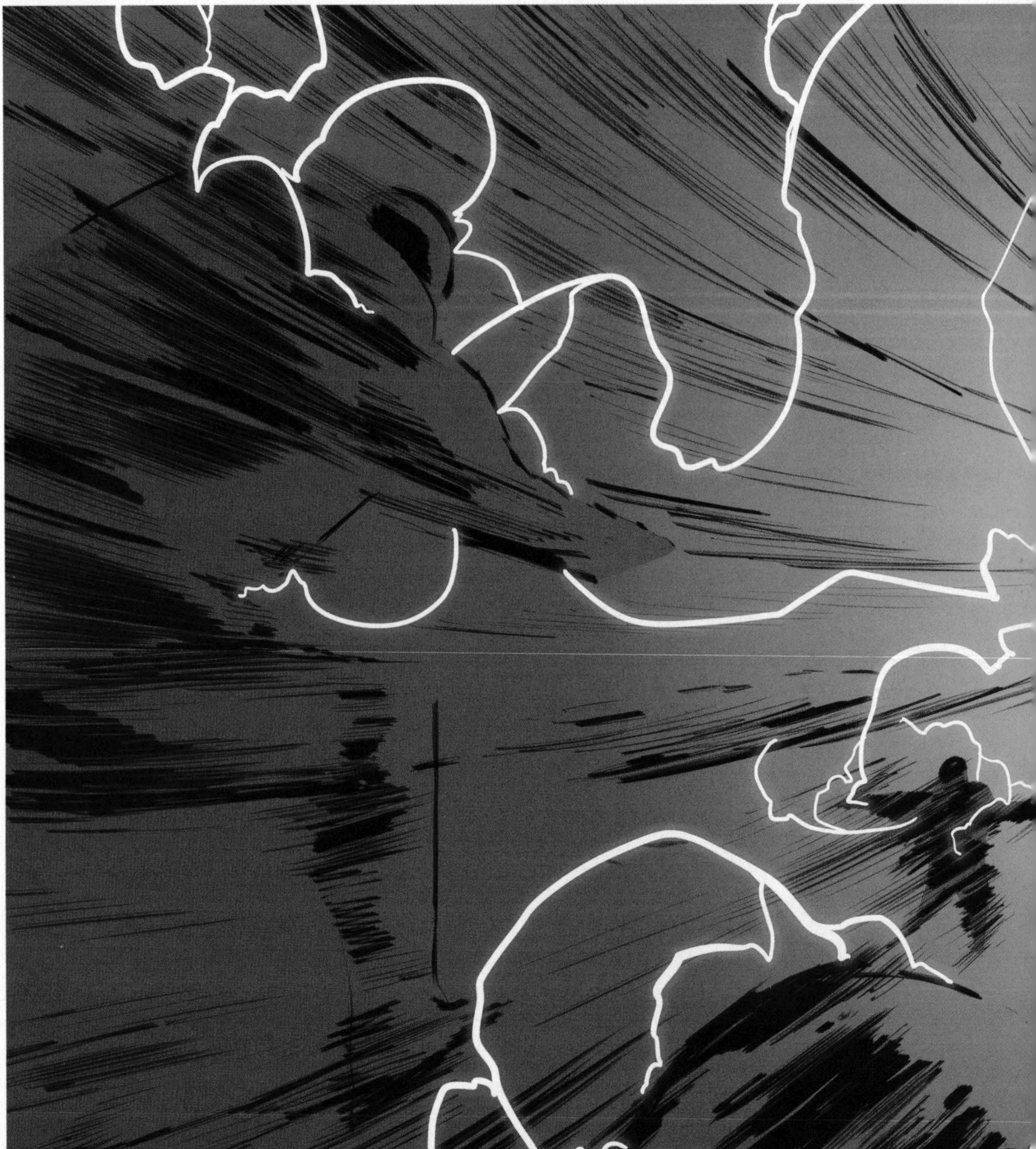

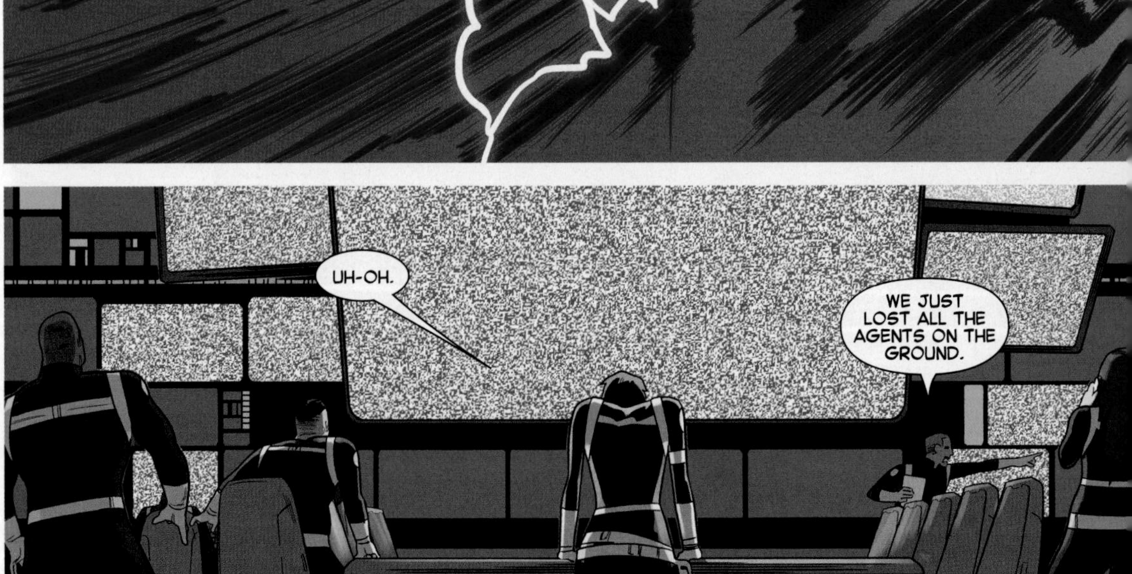
UH-OH.
WE JUST LOST ALL THE AGENTS ON THE GROUND.

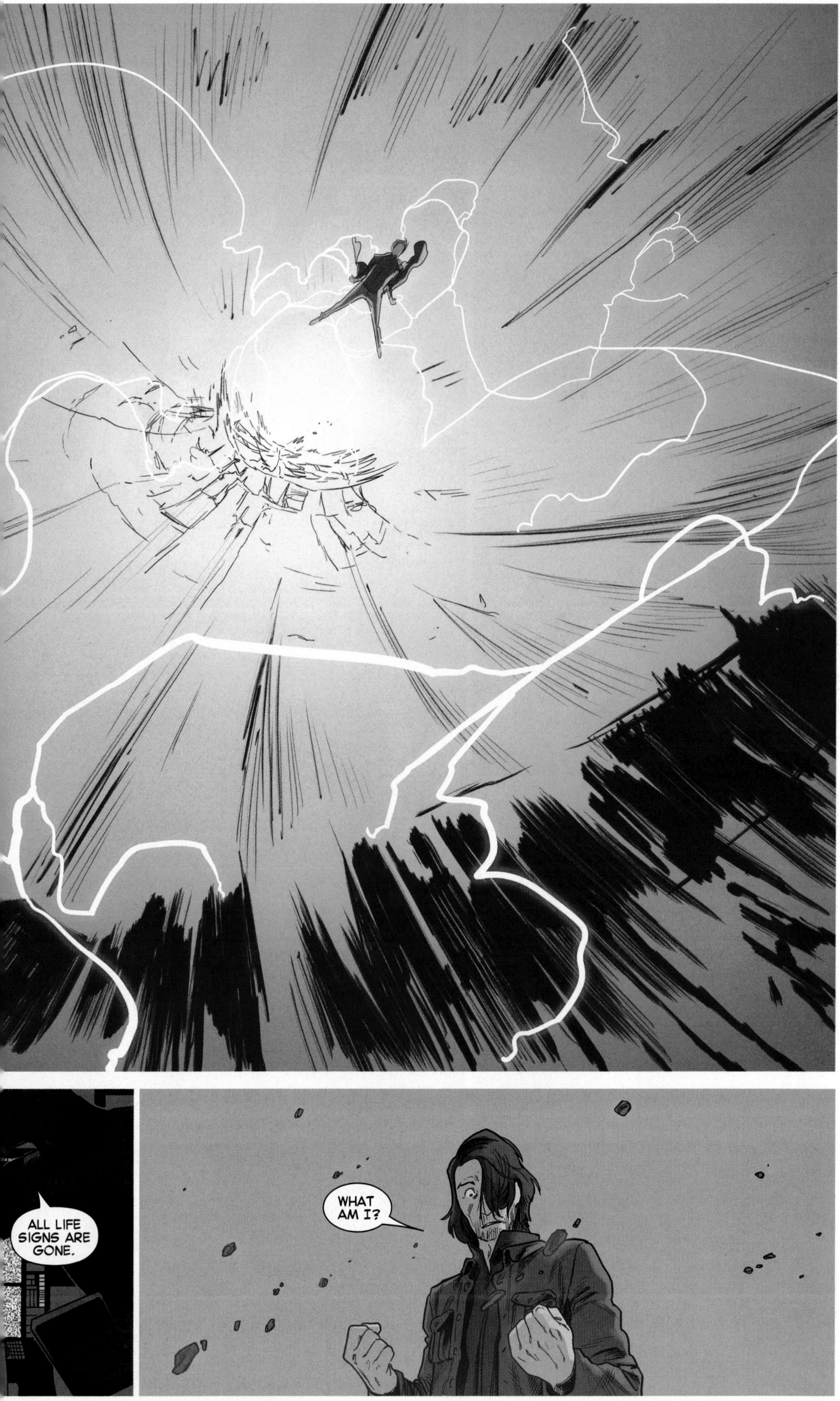
ALL LIFE SIGNS ARE GONE.
WHAT AM I?

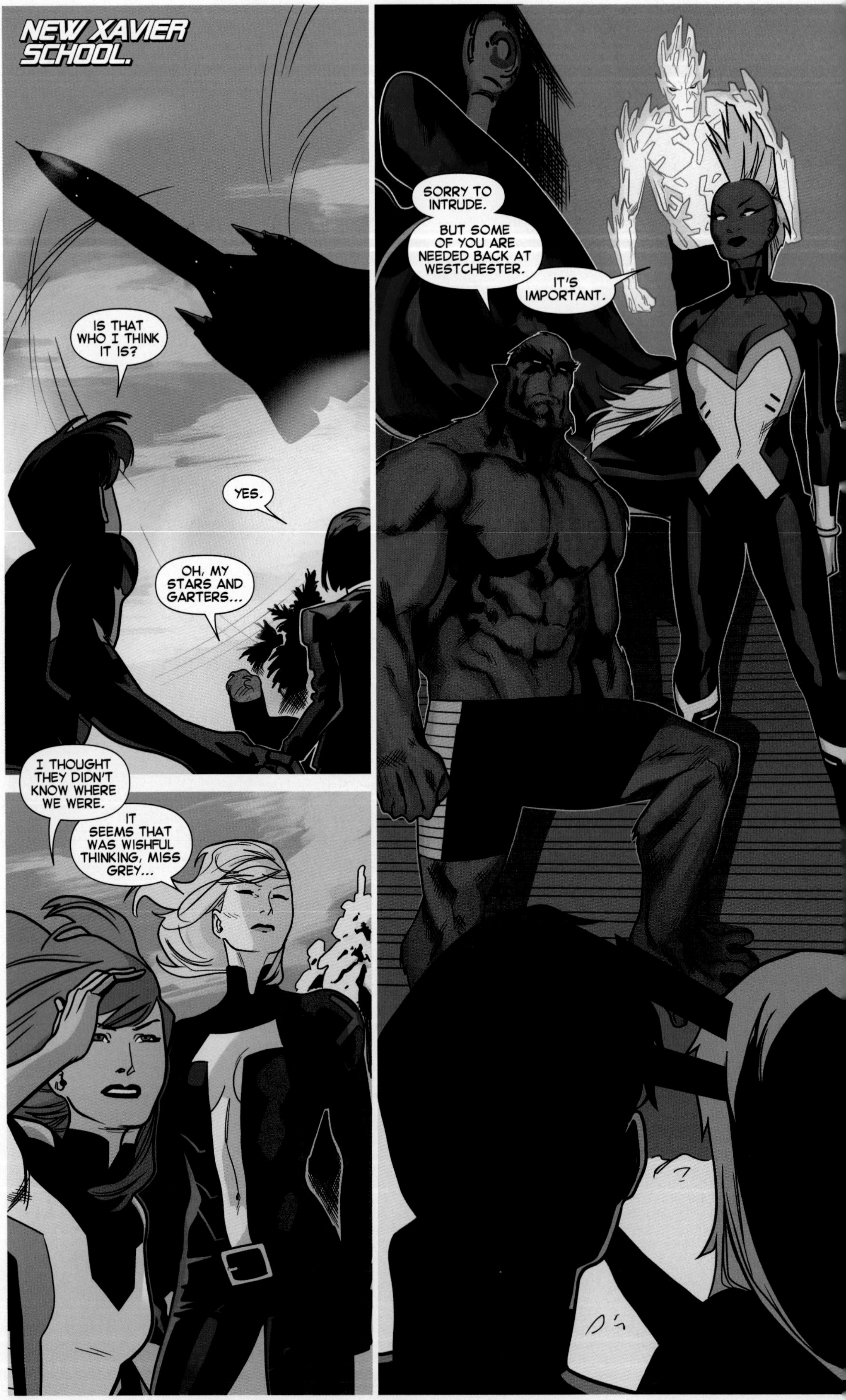
NEW XAVIER SCHOOL.
IS THAT WHO I THINK IT IS?
YES.
OH, MY STARS AND GARTERS...
I THOUGHT THEY DIDN'T KNOW WHERE WE WERE.
IT SEEMS THAT WAS WISHFUL THINKING, MISS GREY...
SORRY TO INTRUDE.
BUT SOME OF YOU ARE NEEDED BACK AT WESTCHESTER.
IT'S IMPORTANT.

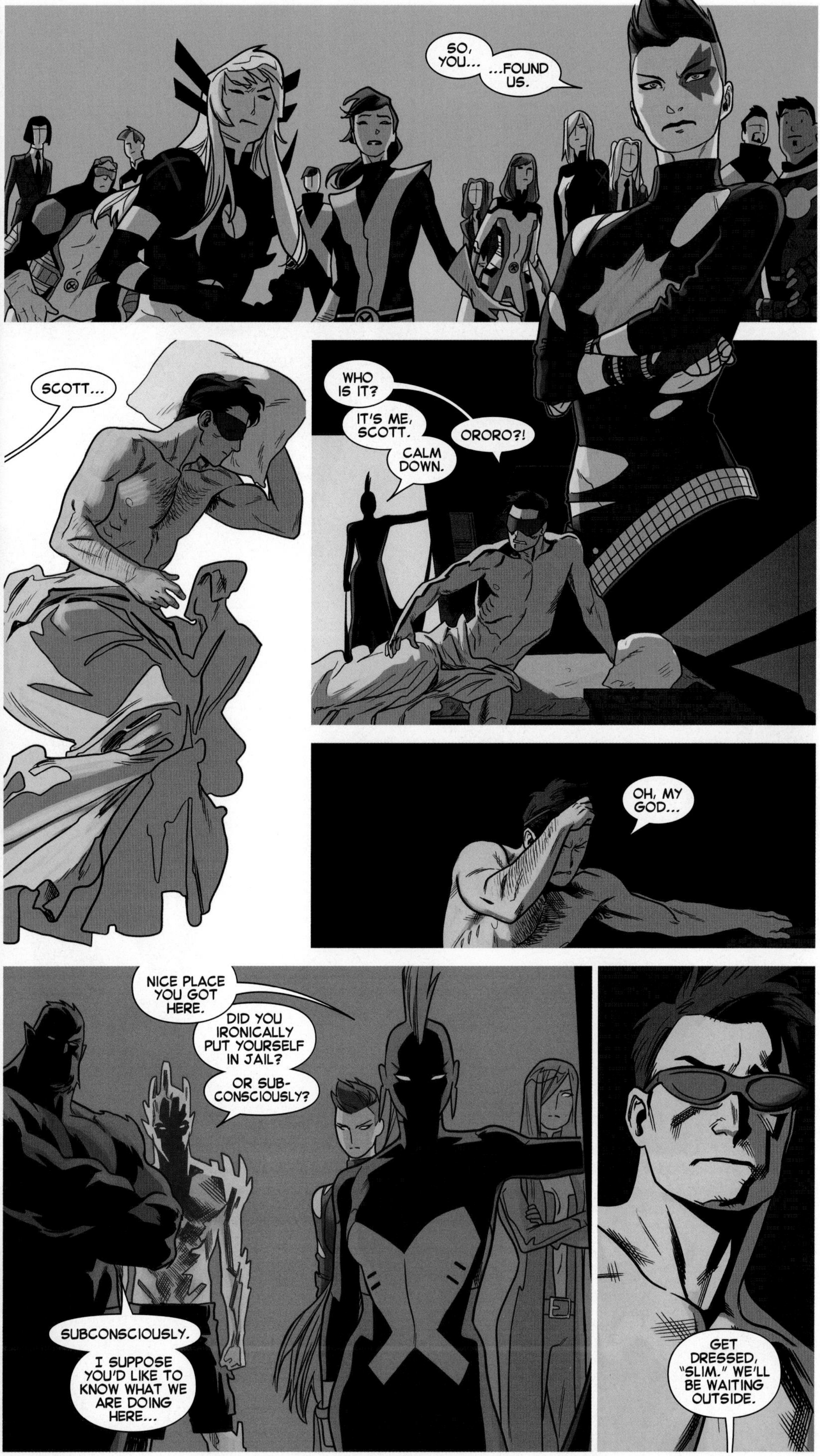
SO, YOU...
...FOUND US.
SCOTT...
WHO IS IT?
IT'S ME, SCOTT.
CALM DOWN.
ORORO?!
OH, MY GOD...
NICE PLACE YOU GOT HERE.
DID YOU IRONICALLY PUT YOURSELF IN JAIL?
OR SUB-CONSCIOUSLY?
SUBCONSCIOUSLY.
I SUPPOSE YOU'D LIKE TO KNOW WHAT WE ARE DOING HERE...
GET DRESSED, "SLIM." WE'LL BE WAITING OUTSIDE.

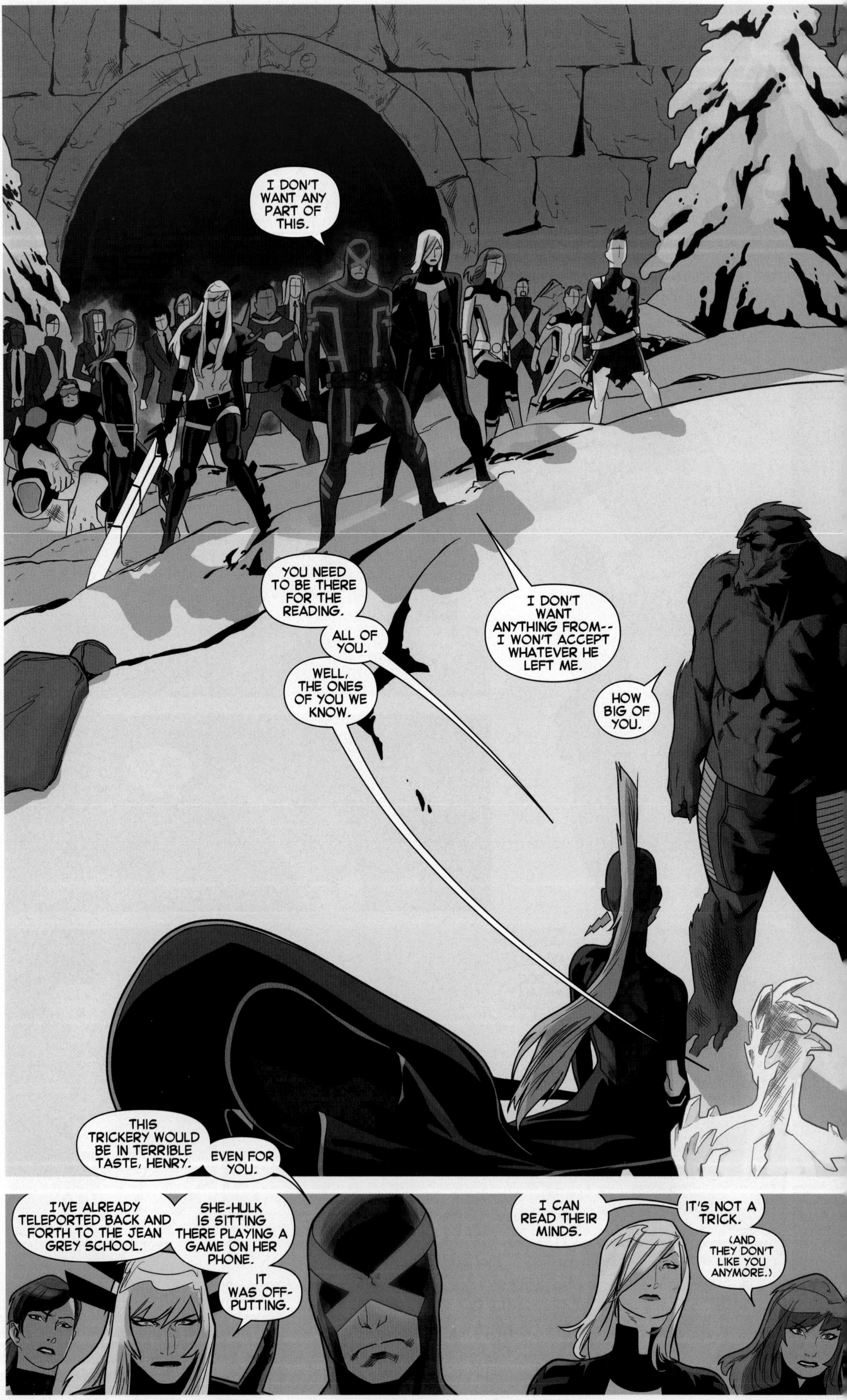

I DON'T WANT ANY PART OF THIS.
YOU NEED TO BE THERE FOR THE READING.
ALL OF YOU.
WELL, THE ONES OF YOU WE KNOW.
I DON'T WANT ANYTHING FROM-- I WON'T ACCEPT WHATEVER HE LEFT ME.
HOW BIG OF YOU.
THIS TRICKERY WOULD BE IN TERRIBLE TASTE, HENRY.
EVEN FOR YOU.
I'VE ALREADY TELEPORTED BACK AND FORTH TO THE JEAN GREY SCHOOL.
SHE-HULK IS SITTING THERE PLAYING A GAME ON HER PHONE.
IT WAS OFF-PUTTING.
I CAN READ THEIR MINDS.
IT'S NOT A TRICK.
(AND THEY DON'T LIKE YOU ANYMORE.)

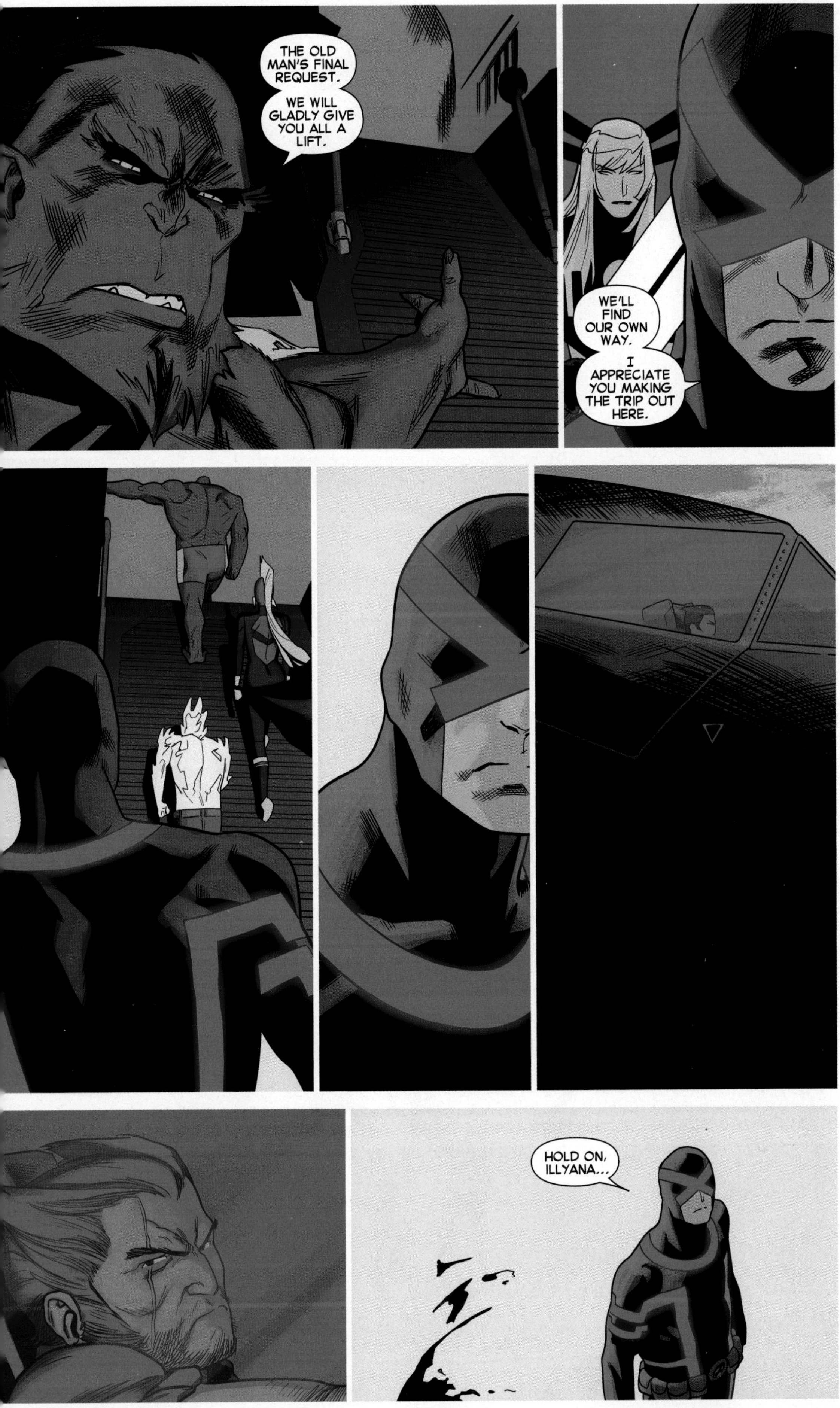
THE OLD MAN'S FINAL REQUEST.
WE WILL GLADLY GIVE YOU ALL A LIFT.
WE'LL FIND OUR OWN WAY.
I APPRECIATE YOU MAKING THE TRIP OUT HERE.
HOLD ON, ILLYANA...

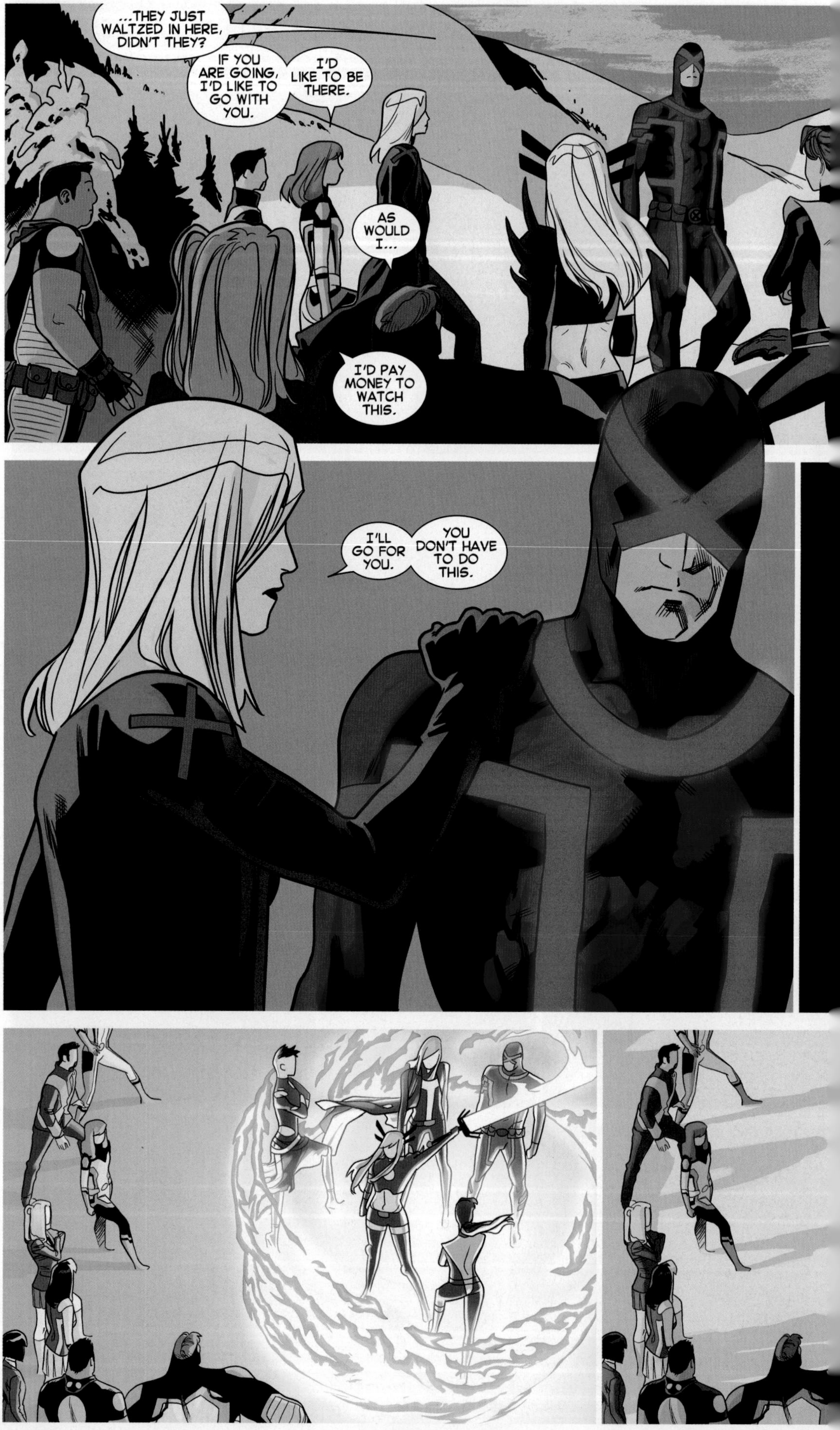
...THEY JUST WALTZED IN HERE, DIDN'T THEY?
IF YOU ARE GOING, I'D LIKE TO GO WITH YOU.
I'D LIKE TO BE THERE.
AS WOULD I...
I'D PAY MONEY TO WATCH THIS.
I'LL GO FOR YOU.
YOU DON'T HAVE TO DO THIS.

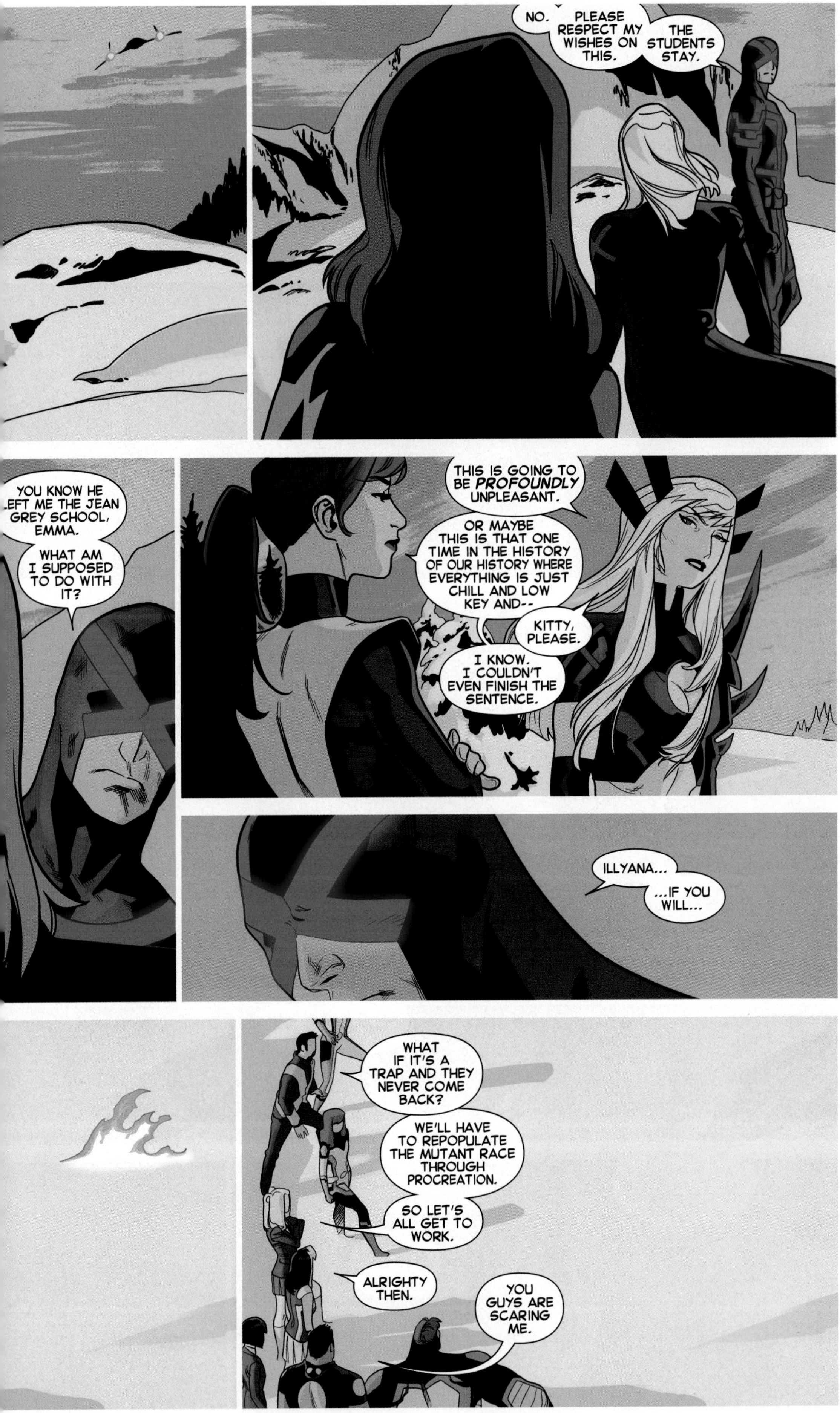
NO.
PLEASE RESPECT MY WISHES ON THIS.
THE STUDENTS STAY.
YOU KNOW HE LEFT ME THE JEAN GREY SCHOOL, EMMA.
WHAT AM I SUPPOSED TO DO WITH IT?
THIS IS GOING TO BE PROFOUNDLY UNPLEASANT.
OR MAYBE THIS IS THAT ONE TIME IN THE HISTORY OF OUR HISTORY WHERE EVERYTHING IS JUST CHILL AND LOW KEY AND--
KITTY, PLEASE.
I KNOW. I COULDN'T EVEN FINISH THE SENTENCE.
ILLYANA...
...IF YOU WILL...
WHAT IF IT'S A TRAP AND THEY NEVER COME BACK?
WE'LL HAVE TO REPOPULATE THE MUTANT RACE THROUGH PROCREATION.
SO LET'S ALL GET TO WORK.
ALRIGHTY THEN.
YOU GUYS ARE SCARING ME.

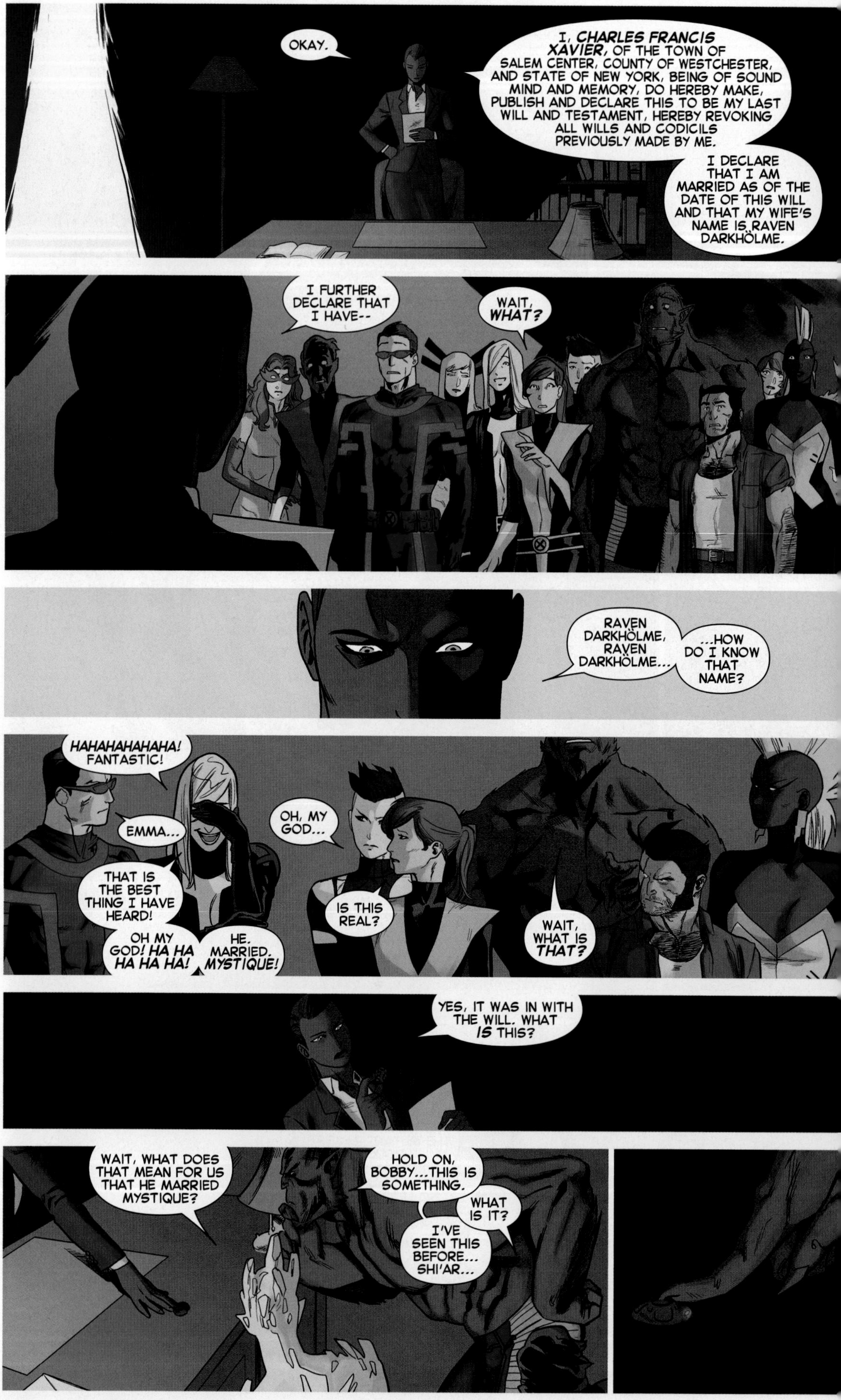

OKAY.
I, *CHARLES FRANCIS XAVIER,* OF THE TOWN OF SALEM CENTER, COUNTY OF WESTCHESTER, AND STATE OF NEW YORK, BEING OF SOUND MIND AND MEMORY, DO HEREBY MAKE, PUBLISH AND DECLARE THIS TO BE MY LAST WILL AND TESTAMENT, HEREBY REVOKING ALL WILLS AND CODICILS PREVIOUSLY MADE BY ME.
I DECLARE THAT I AM MARRIED AS OF THE DATE OF THIS WILL AND THAT MY WIFE'S NAME IS RAVEN DARKHÖLME.
I FURTHER DECLARE THAT I HAVE--
WAIT, *WHAT?*
RAVEN DARKHÖLME, RAVEN DARKHÖLME...
...HOW DO I KNOW THAT NAME?
HAHAHAHAHAHA! FANTASTIC!
EMMA...
THAT IS THE BEST THING I HAVE HEARD!
OH MY GOD! *HA HA HA HA HA!*
HE. MARRIED. *MYSTIQUE!*
OH, MY GOD...
IS THIS REAL?
WAIT, WHAT IS *THAT?*
YES, IT WAS IN WITH THE WILL. WHAT *IS* THIS?
WAIT, WHAT DOES THAT MEAN FOR US THAT HE MARRIED MYSTIQUE?
HOLD ON, BOBBY...THIS IS SOMETHING.
WHAT IS IT?
I'VE SEEN THIS BEFORE... SHI'AR...

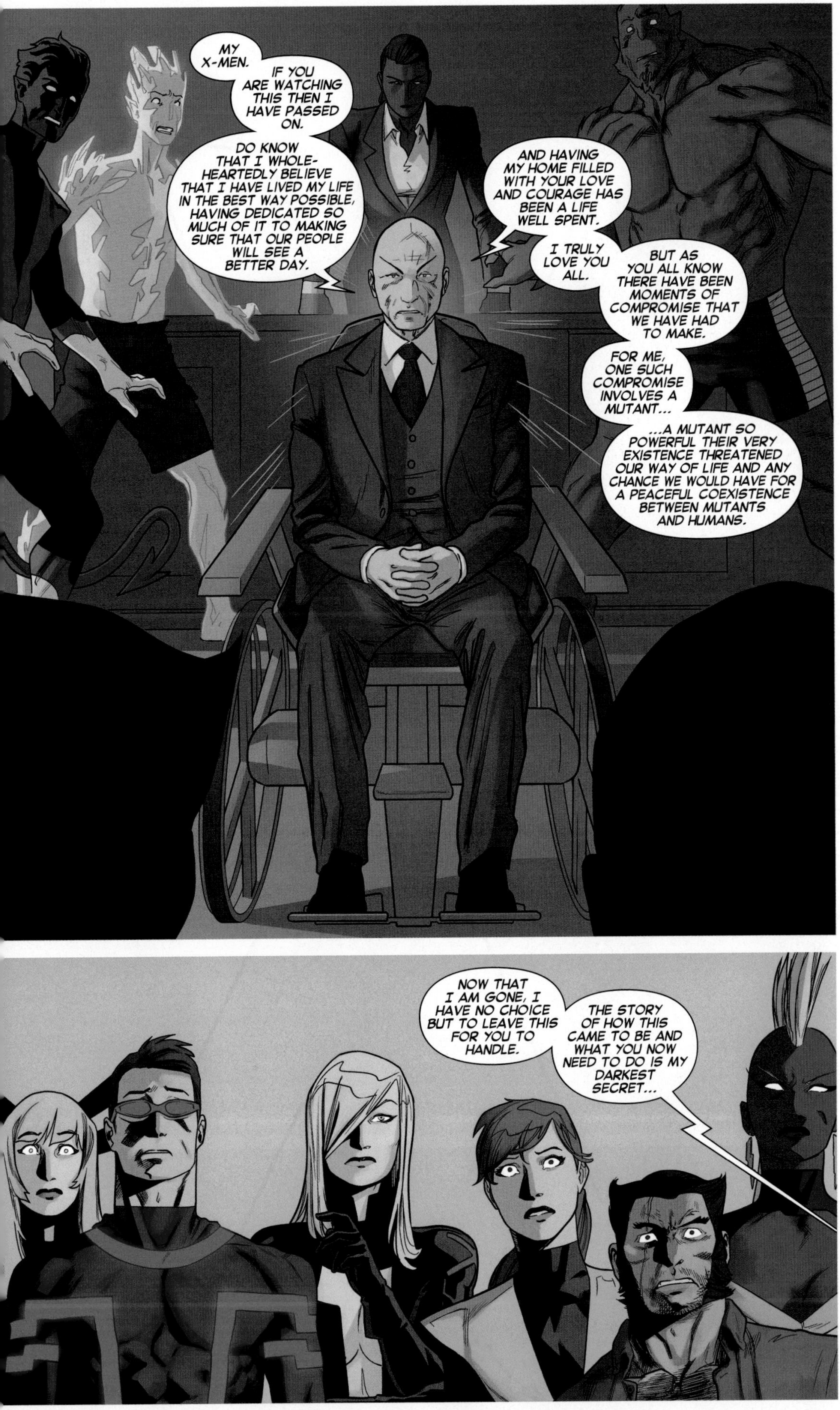
MY X-MEN.
IF YOU ARE WATCHING THIS THEN I HAVE PASSED ON.
DO KNOW THAT I WHOLE-HEARTEDLY BELIEVE THAT I HAVE LIVED MY LIFE IN THE BEST WAY POSSIBLE, HAVING DEDICATED SO MUCH OF IT TO MAKING SURE THAT OUR PEOPLE WILL SEE A BETTER DAY.
AND HAVING MY HOME FILLED WITH YOUR LOVE AND COURAGE HAS BEEN A LIFE WELL SPENT.
I TRULY LOVE YOU ALL.
BUT AS YOU ALL KNOW THERE HAVE BEEN MOMENTS OF COMPROMISE THAT WE HAVE HAD TO MAKE.
FOR ME, ONE SUCH COMPROMISE INVOLVES A MUTANT...
...A MUTANT SO POWERFUL THEIR VERY EXISTENCE THREATENED OUR WAY OF LIFE AND ANY CHANCE WE WOULD HAVE FOR A PEACEFUL COEXISTENCE BETWEEN MUTANTS AND HUMANS.
NOW THAT I AM GONE, I HAVE NO CHOICE BUT TO LEAVE THIS FOR YOU TO HANDLE.
THE STORY OF HOW THIS CAME TO BE AND WHAT YOU NOW NEED TO DO IS MY DARKEST SECRET...

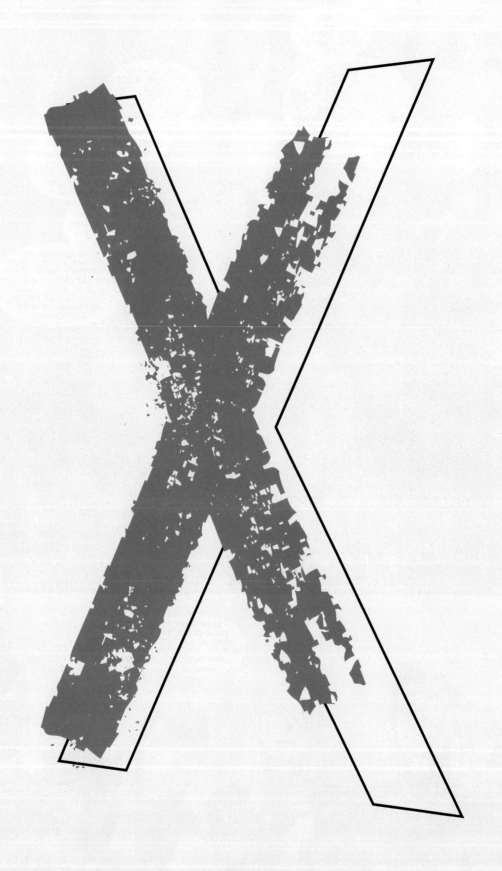

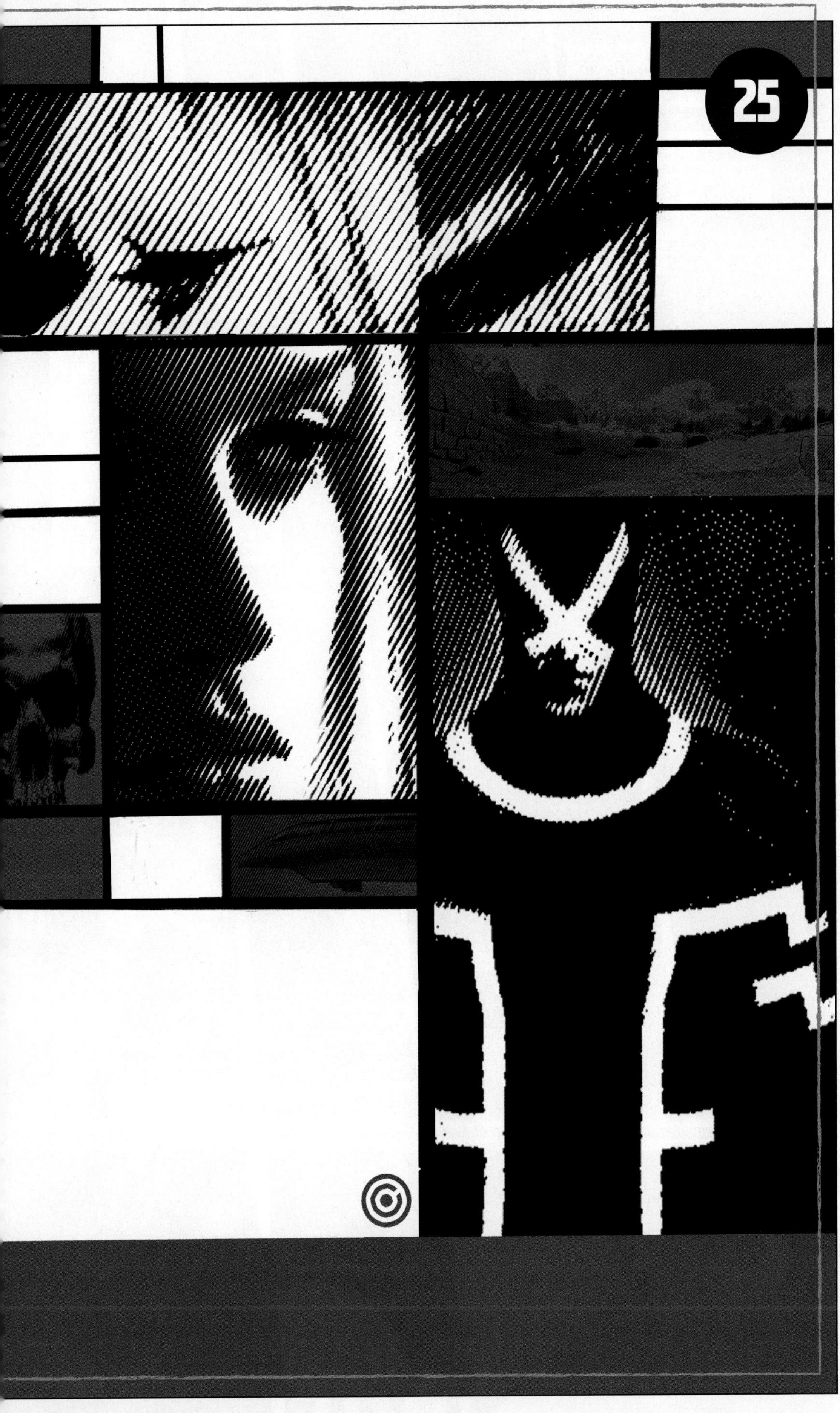
25

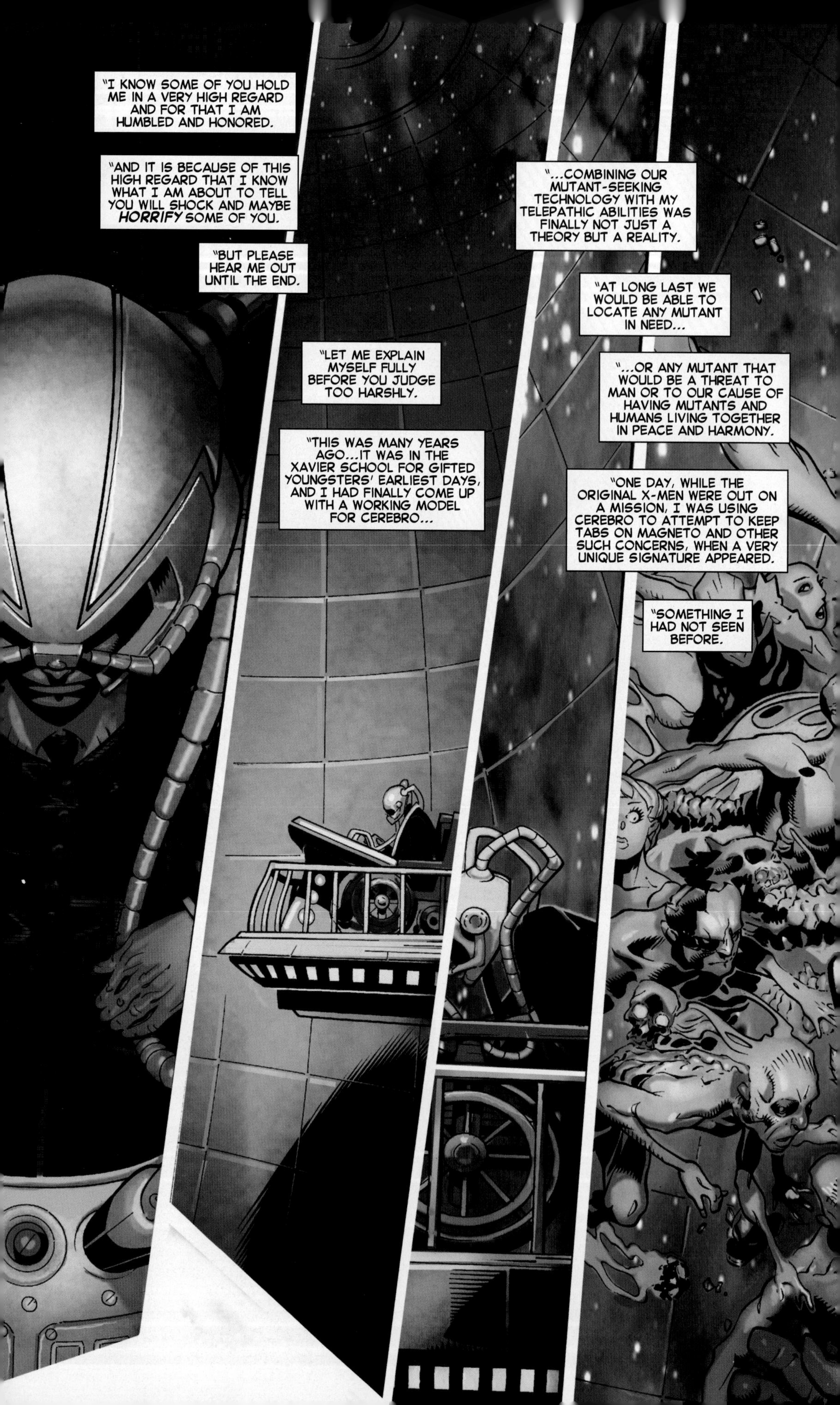
"I KNOW SOME OF YOU HOLD ME IN A VERY HIGH REGARD AND FOR THAT I AM HUMBLED AND HONORED.
"AND IT IS BECAUSE OF THIS HIGH REGARD THAT I KNOW WHAT I AM ABOUT TO TELL YOU WILL SHOCK AND MAYBE *HORRIFY* SOME OF YOU.
"BUT PLEASE HEAR ME OUT UNTIL THE END.
"LET ME EXPLAIN MYSELF FULLY BEFORE YOU JUDGE TOO HARSHLY.
"THIS WAS MANY YEARS AGO...IT WAS IN THE XAVIER SCHOOL FOR GIFTED YOUNGSTERS' EARLIEST DAYS, AND I HAD FINALLY COME UP WITH A WORKING MODEL FOR CEREBRO...
"...COMBINING OUR MUTANT-SEEKING TECHNOLOGY WITH MY TELEPATHIC ABILITIES WAS FINALLY NOT JUST A THEORY BUT A REALITY.
"AT LONG LAST WE WOULD BE ABLE TO LOCATE ANY MUTANT IN NEED...
"...OR ANY MUTANT THAT WOULD BE A THREAT TO MAN OR TO OUR CAUSE OF HAVING MUTANTS AND HUMANS LIVING TOGETHER IN PEACE AND HARMONY.
"ONE DAY, WHILE THE ORIGINAL X-MEN WERE OUT ON A MISSION, I WAS USING CEREBRO TO ATTEMPT TO KEEP TABS ON MAGNETO AND OTHER SUCH CONCERNS, WHEN A VERY UNIQUE SIGNATURE APPEARED.
"SOMETHING I HAD NOT SEEN BEFORE.

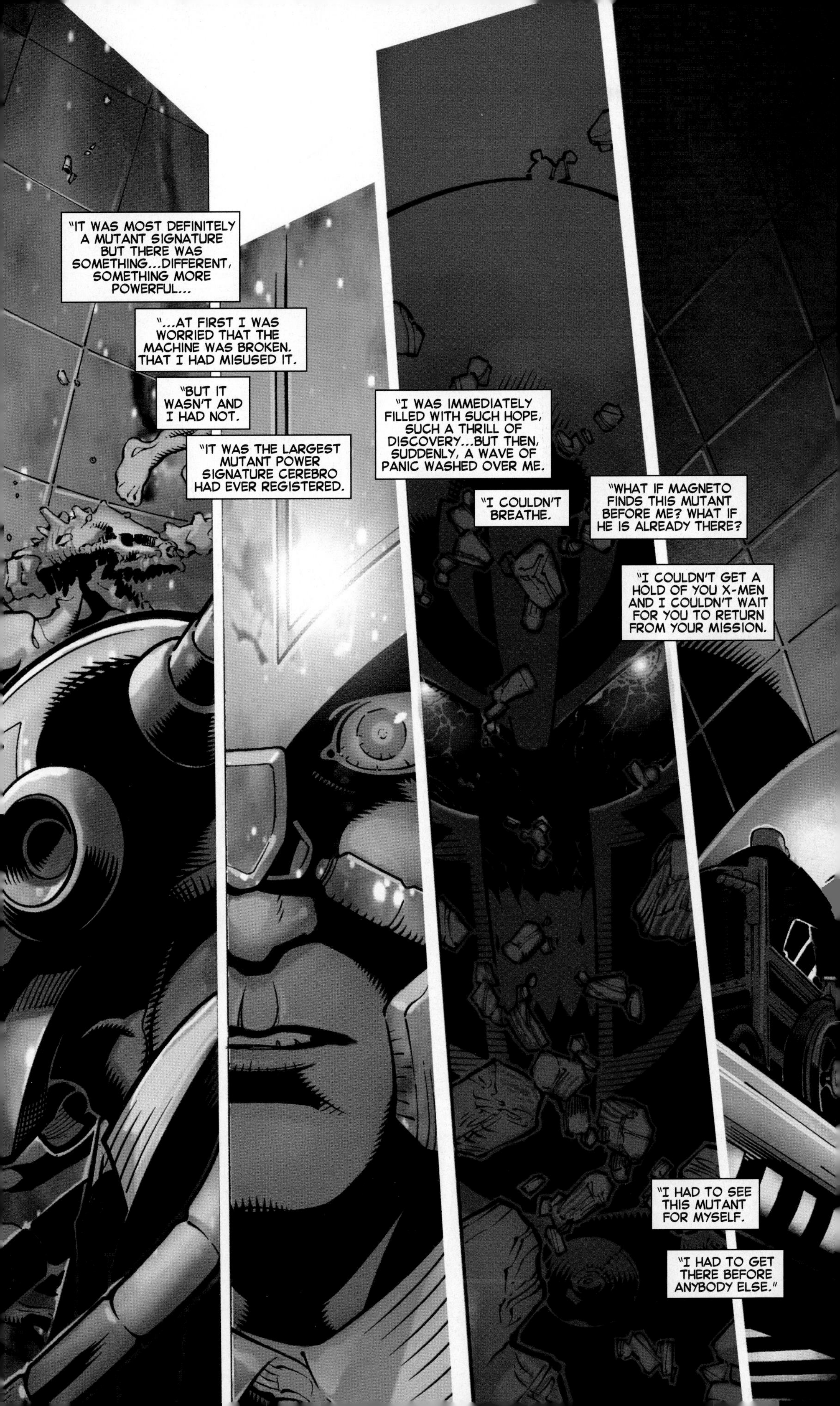
"IT WAS MOST DEFINITELY A MUTANT SIGNATURE BUT THERE WAS SOMETHING...DIFFERENT, SOMETHING MORE POWERFUL...
"...AT FIRST I WAS WORRIED THAT THE MACHINE WAS BROKEN. THAT I HAD MISUSED IT.
"BUT IT WASN'T AND I HAD NOT.
"IT WAS THE LARGEST MUTANT POWER SIGNATURE CEREBRO HAD EVER REGISTERED.
"I WAS IMMEDIATELY FILLED WITH SUCH HOPE, SUCH A THRILL OF DISCOVERY...BUT THEN, SUDDENLY, A WAVE OF PANIC WASHED OVER ME.
"I COULDN'T BREATHE.
"WHAT IF MAGNETO FINDS THIS MUTANT BEFORE ME? WHAT IF HE IS ALREADY THERE?
"I COULDN'T GET A HOLD OF YOU X-MEN AND I COULDN'T WAIT FOR YOU TO RETURN FROM YOUR MISSION.
"I HAD TO SEE THIS MUTANT FOR MYSELF.
"I HAD TO GET THERE BEFORE ANYBODY ELSE."

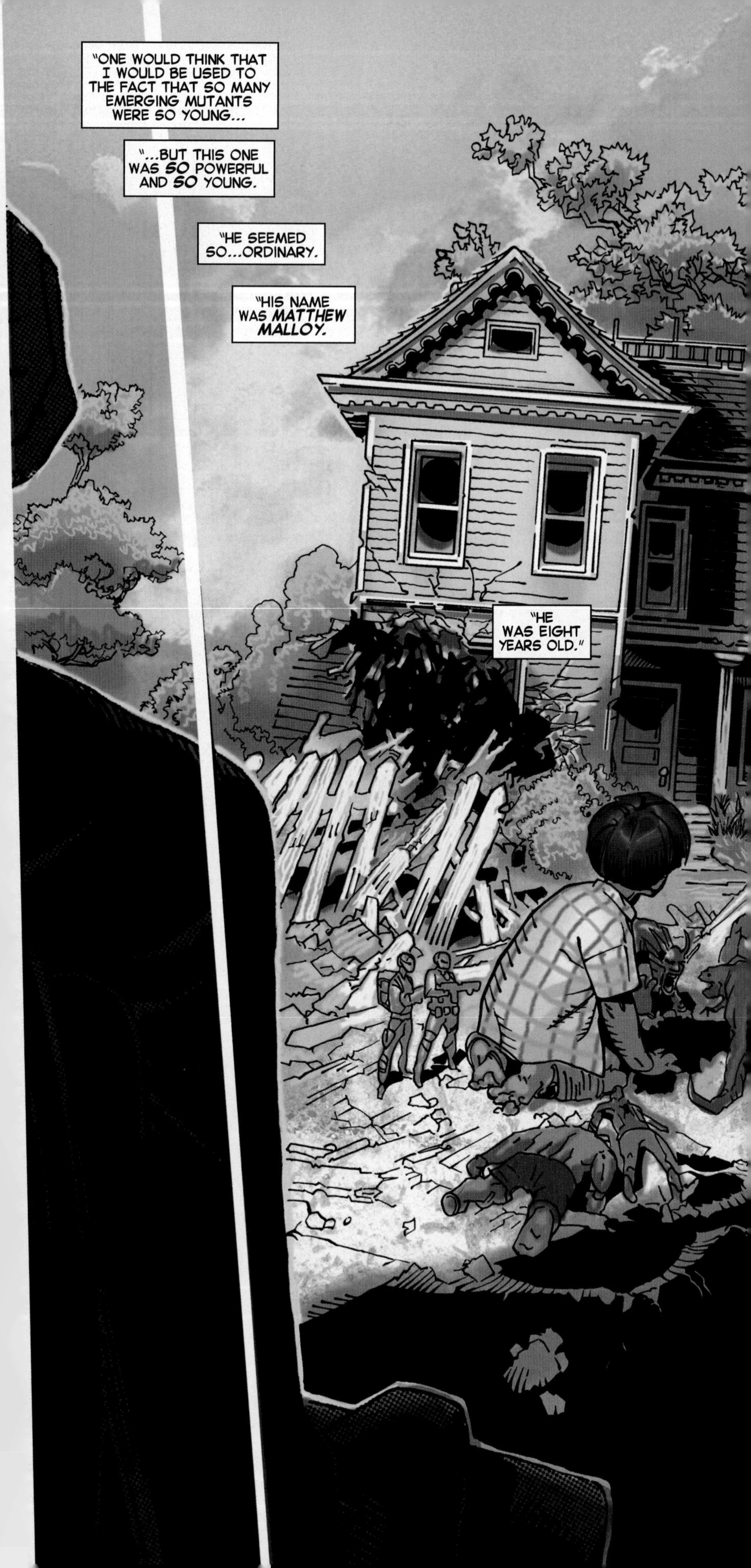
"ONE WOULD THINK THAT I WOULD BE USED TO THE FACT THAT SO MANY EMERGING MUTANTS WERE SO YOUNG...
"...BUT THIS ONE WAS SO POWERFUL AND SO YOUNG.
"HE SEEMED SO...ORDINARY.
"HIS NAME WAS MATTHEW MALLOY.
"HE WAS EIGHT YEARS OLD."

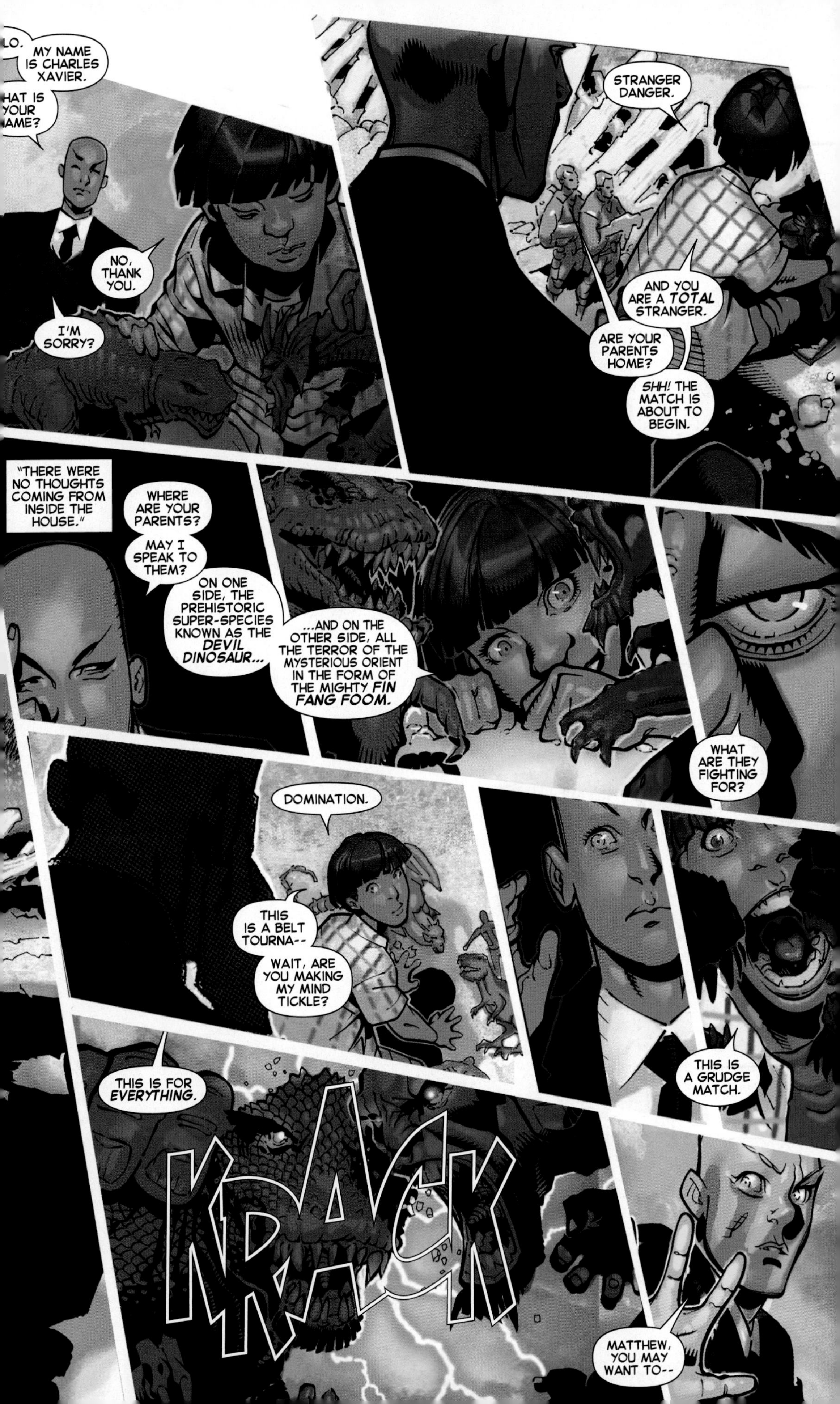

LO.
MY NAME IS CHARLES XAVIER.
HAT IS YOUR AME?
NO, THANK YOU.
I'M SORRY?
STRANGER DANGER.
AND YOU ARE A *TOTAL* STRANGER.
ARE YOUR PARENTS HOME?
SHH! THE MATCH IS ABOUT TO BEGIN.
"THERE WERE NO THOUGHTS COMING FROM INSIDE THE HOUSE."
WHERE ARE YOUR PARENTS?
MAY I SPEAK TO THEM?
ON ONE SIDE, THE PREHISTORIC SUPER-SPECIES KNOWN AS THE *DEVIL DINOSAUR...*
...AND ON THE OTHER SIDE, ALL THE TERROR OF THE MYSTERIOUS ORIENT IN THE FORM OF THE MIGHTY *FIN FANG FOOM.*
WHAT ARE THEY FIGHTING FOR?
DOMINATION.
THIS IS A BELT TOURNA--
WAIT, ARE YOU MAKING MY MIND TICKLE?
THIS IS A GRUDGE MATCH.
THIS IS FOR *EVERYTHING.*
KRACK
MATTHEW, YOU MAY WANT TO--

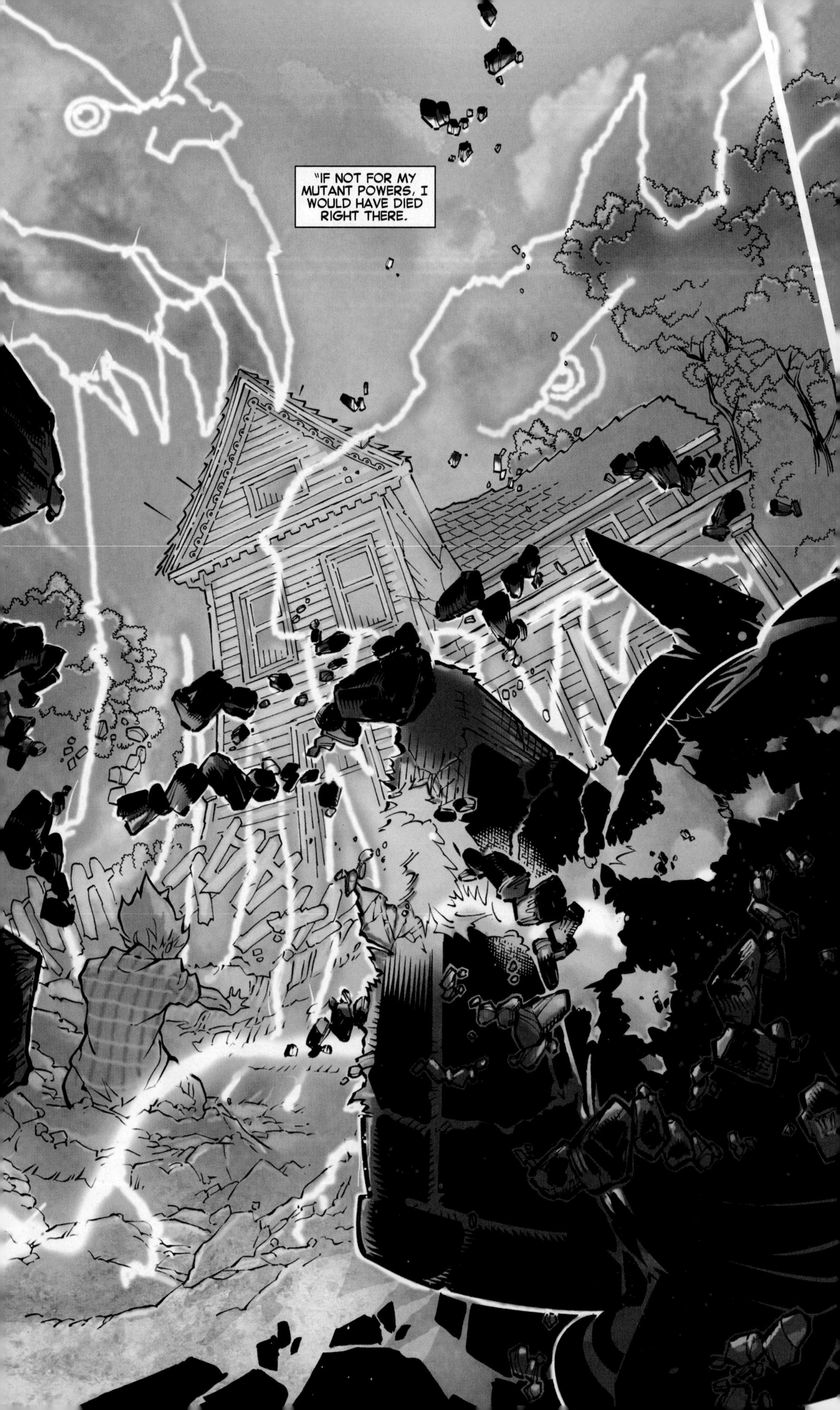
"IF NOT FOR MY MUTANT POWERS, I WOULD HAVE DIED RIGHT THERE.

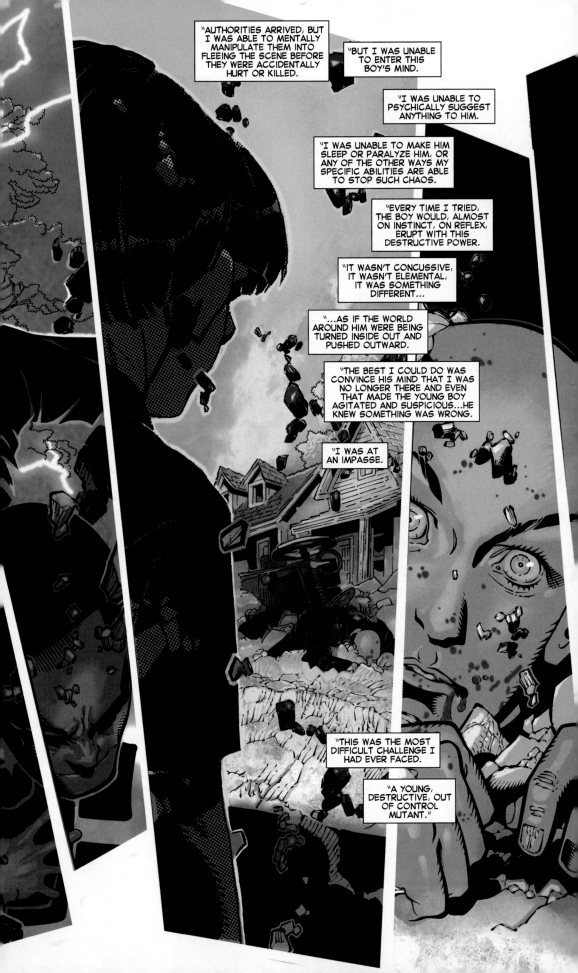

"AUTHORITIES ARRIVED, BUT I WAS ABLE TO MENTALLY MANIPULATE THEM INTO FLEEING THE SCENE BEFORE THEY WERE ACCIDENTALLY HURT OR KILLED.

"BUT I WAS UNABLE TO ENTER THIS BOY'S MIND.

"I WAS UNABLE TO PSYCHICALLY SUGGEST ANYTHING TO HIM.

"I WAS UNABLE TO MAKE HIM SLEEP OR PARALYZE HIM, OR ANY OF THE OTHER WAYS MY SPECIFIC ABILITIES ARE ABLE TO STOP SUCH CHAOS.

"EVERY TIME I TRIED, THE BOY WOULD, ALMOST ON INSTINCT, ON REFLEX, ERUPT WITH THIS DESTRUCTIVE POWER.

"IT WASN'T CONCUSSIVE, IT WASN'T ELEMENTAL, IT WAS SOMETHING DIFFERENT...

"...AS IF THE WORLD AROUND HIM WERE BEING TURNED INSIDE OUT AND PUSHED OUTWARD.

"THE BEST I COULD DO WAS CONVINCE HIS MIND THAT I WAS NO LONGER THERE AND EVEN THAT MADE THE YOUNG BOY AGITATED AND SUSPICIOUS...HE KNEW SOMETHING WAS WRONG.

"I WAS AT AN IMPASSE.

"THIS WAS THE MOST DIFFICULT CHALLENGE I HAD EVER FACED.

"A YOUNG, DESTRUCTIVE, OUT OF CONTROL MUTANT."

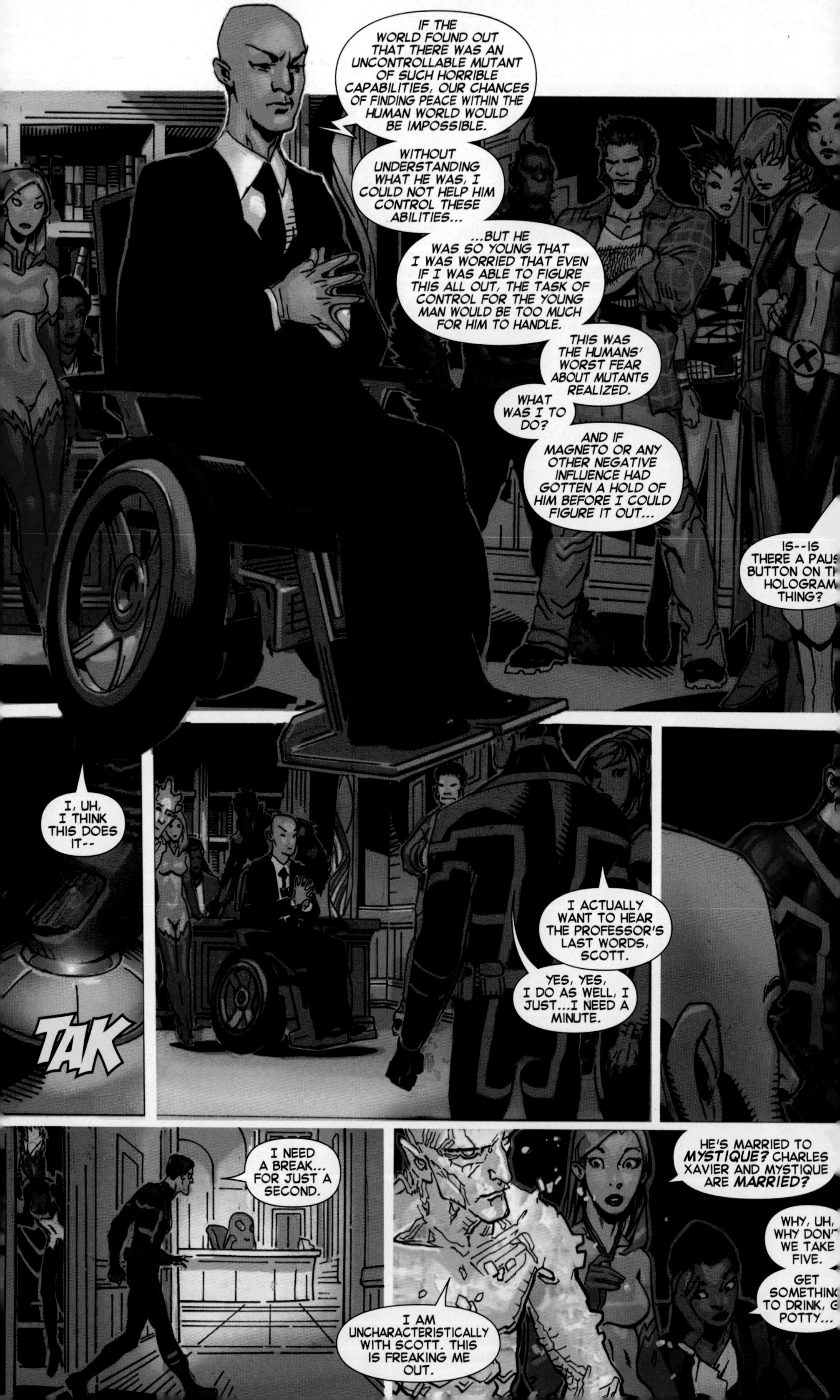
IF THE WORLD FOUND OUT THAT THERE WAS AN UNCONTROLLABLE MUTANT OF SUCH HORRIBLE CAPABILITIES, OUR CHANCES OF FINDING PEACE WITHIN THE HUMAN WORLD WOULD BE IMPOSSIBLE.
WITHOUT UNDERSTANDING WHAT HE WAS, I COULD NOT HELP HIM CONTROL THESE ABILITIES...
...BUT HE WAS SO YOUNG THAT I WAS WORRIED THAT EVEN IF I WAS ABLE TO FIGURE THIS ALL OUT, THE TASK OF CONTROL FOR THE YOUNG MAN WOULD BE TOO MUCH FOR HIM TO HANDLE.
THIS WAS THE HUMANS' WORST FEAR ABOUT MUTANTS REALIZED.
WHAT WAS I TO DO?
AND IF MAGNETO OR ANY OTHER NEGATIVE INFLUENCE HAD GOTTEN A HOLD OF HIM BEFORE I COULD FIGURE IT OUT...
IS--IS THERE A PAUS BUTTON ON T HOLOGRAM THING?
I, UH, I THINK THIS DOES IT--
TAK
I ACTUALLY WANT TO HEAR THE PROFESSOR'S LAST WORDS, SCOTT.
YES, YES, I DO AS WELL, I JUST...I NEED A MINUTE.
I NEED A BREAK... FOR JUST A SECOND.
HE'S MARRIED TO MYSTIQUE? CHARLES XAVIER AND MYSTIQUE ARE MARRIED?
WHY, UH, WHY DON' WE TAKE FIVE.
GET SOMETHIN TO DRINK, G POTTY...
I AM UNCHARACTERISTICALLY WITH SCOTT. THIS IS FREAKING ME OUT.

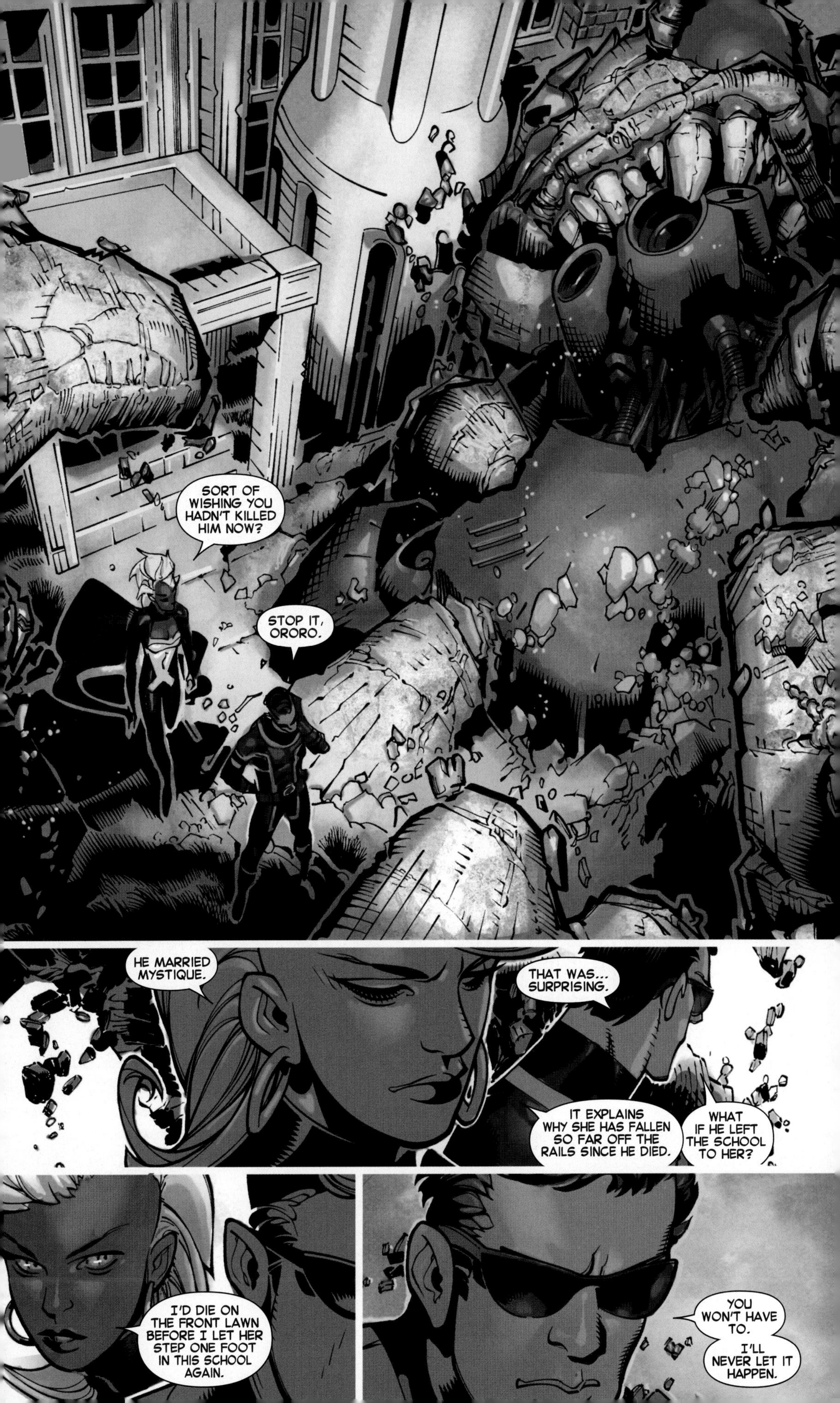
SORT OF WISHING YOU HADN'T KILLED HIM NOW?
STOP IT, ORORO.
HE MARRIED MYSTIQUE.
THAT WAS... SURPRISING.
IT EXPLAINS WHY SHE HAS FALLEN SO FAR OFF THE RAILS SINCE HE DIED.
WHAT IF HE LEFT THE SCHOOL TO HER?
I'D DIE ON THE FRONT LAWN BEFORE I LET HER STEP ONE FOOT IN THIS SCHOOL AGAIN.
YOU WON'T HAVE TO.
I'LL NEVER LET IT HAPPEN.

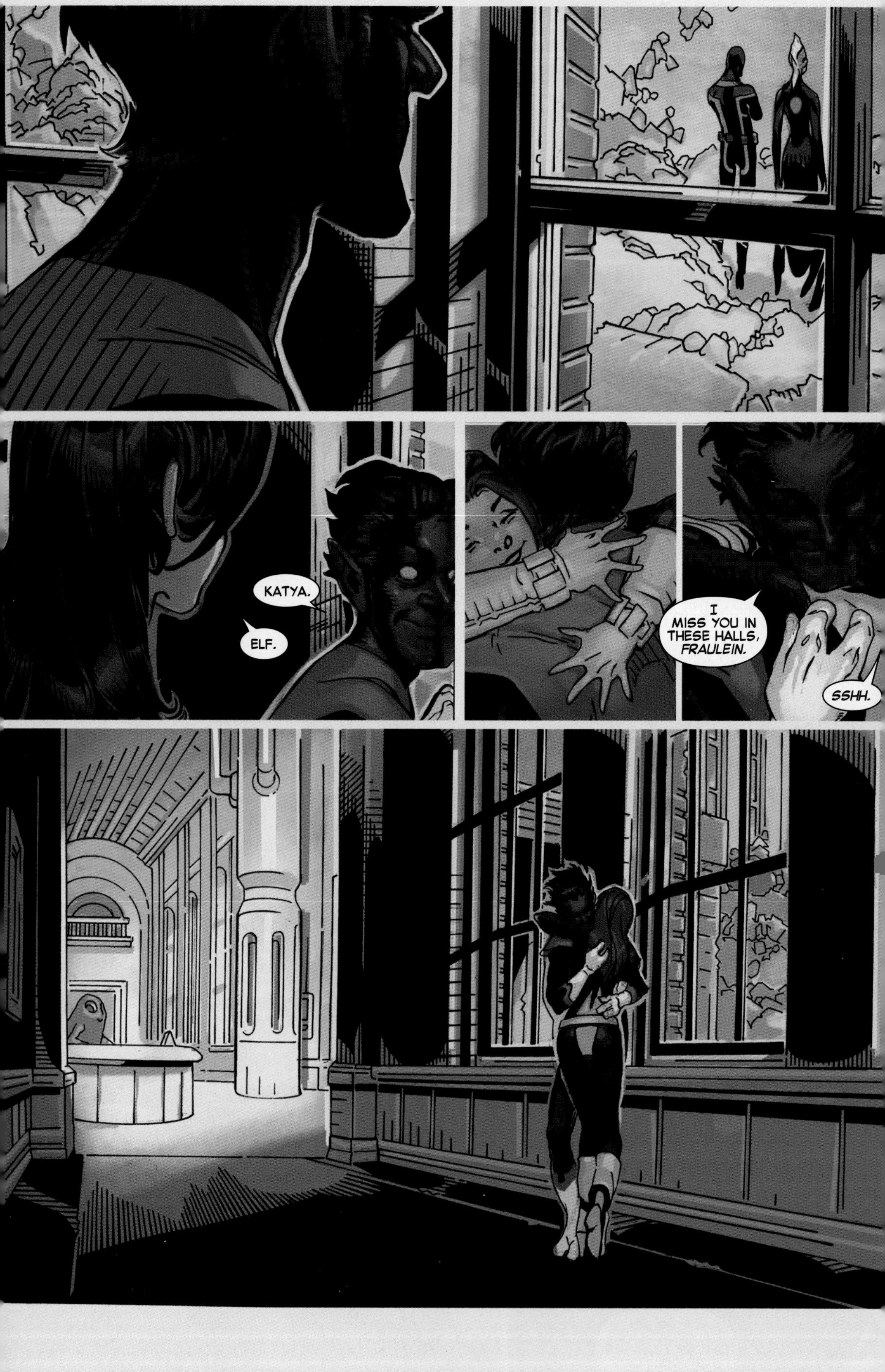
KATYA.
ELF.
I MISS YOU IN THESE HALLS, FRAULEIN.
SSHH.

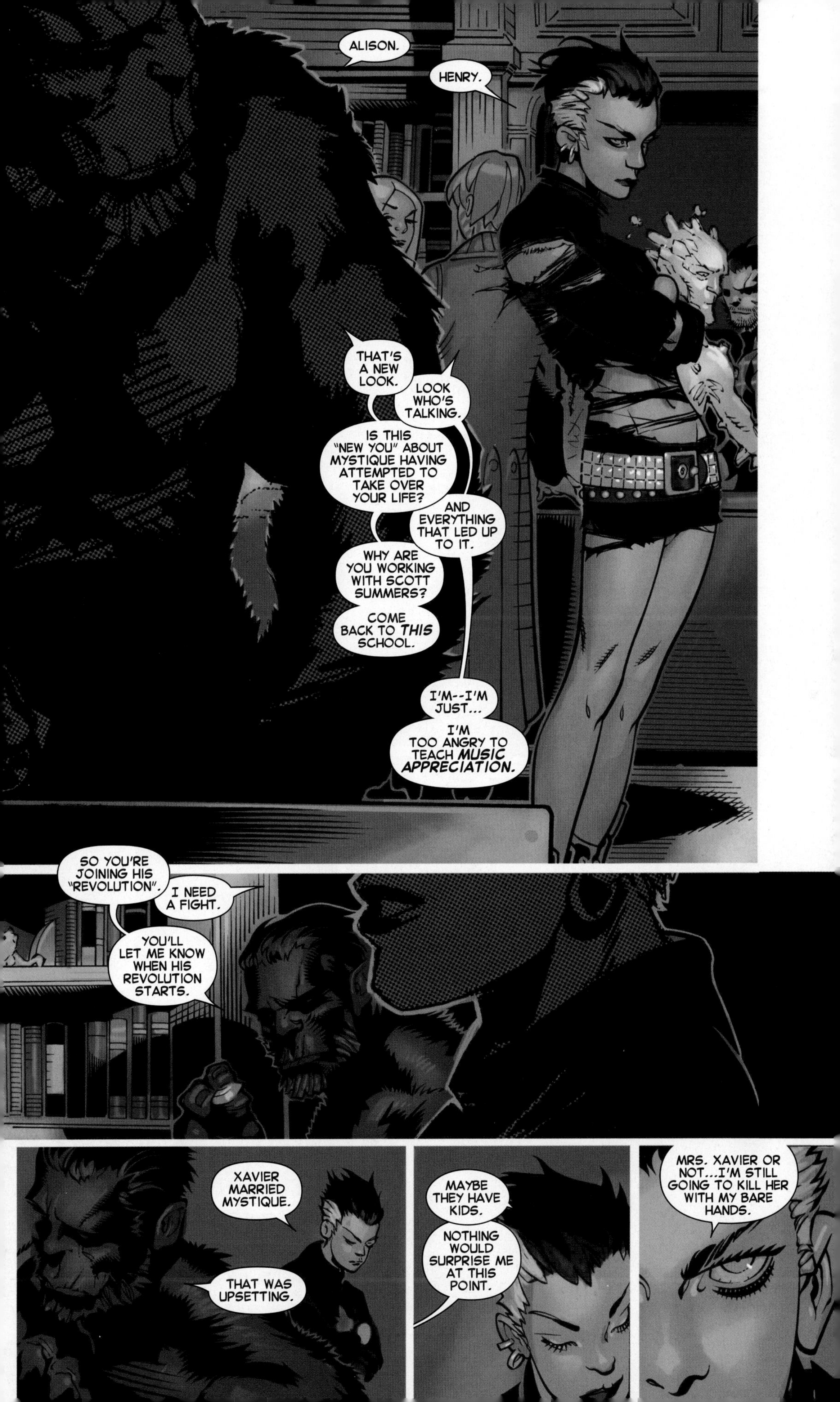
ALISON.
HENRY.
THAT'S A NEW LOOK.
LOOK WHO'S TALKING.
IS THIS "NEW YOU" ABOUT MYSTIQUE HAVING ATTEMPTED TO TAKE OVER YOUR LIFE?
AND EVERYTHING THAT LED UP TO IT.
WHY ARE YOU WORKING WITH SCOTT SUMMERS?
COME BACK TO *THIS* SCHOOL.
I'M--I'M JUST...
I'M TOO ANGRY TO TEACH *MUSIC APPRECIATION.*
SO YOU'RE JOINING HIS "REVOLUTION".
I NEED A FIGHT.
YOU'LL LET ME KNOW WHEN HIS REVOLUTION STARTS.
XAVIER MARRIED MYSTIQUE.
THAT WAS UPSETTING.
MAYBE THEY HAVE KIDS.
NOTHING WOULD SURPRISE ME AT THIS POINT.
MRS. XAVIER OR NOT...I'M STILL GOING TO KILL HER WITH MY BARE HANDS.

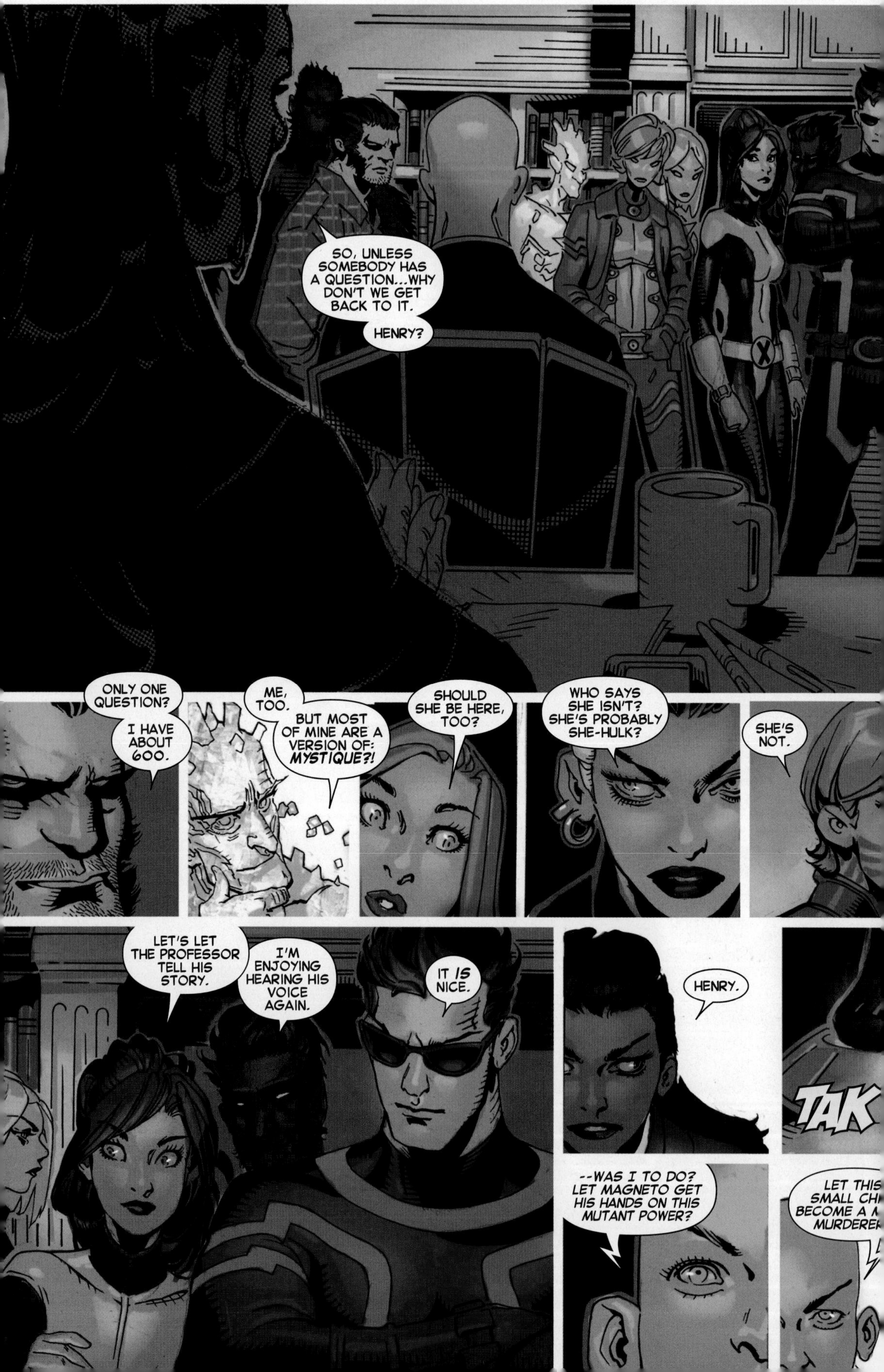
SO, UNLESS SOMEBODY HAS A QUESTION...WHY DON'T WE GET BACK TO IT.
HENRY?
ONLY ONE QUESTION?
I HAVE ABOUT 600.
ME, TOO.
BUT MOST OF MINE ARE A VERSION OF: MYSTIQUE?!
SHOULD SHE BE HERE, TOO?
WHO SAYS SHE ISN'T? SHE'S PROBABLY SHE-HULK?
SHE'S NOT.
LET'S LET THE PROFESSOR TELL HIS STORY.
I'M ENJOYING HEARING HIS VOICE AGAIN.
IT IS NICE.
HENRY.
TAK
--WAS I TO DO? LET MAGNETO GET HIS HANDS ON THIS MUTANT POWER?

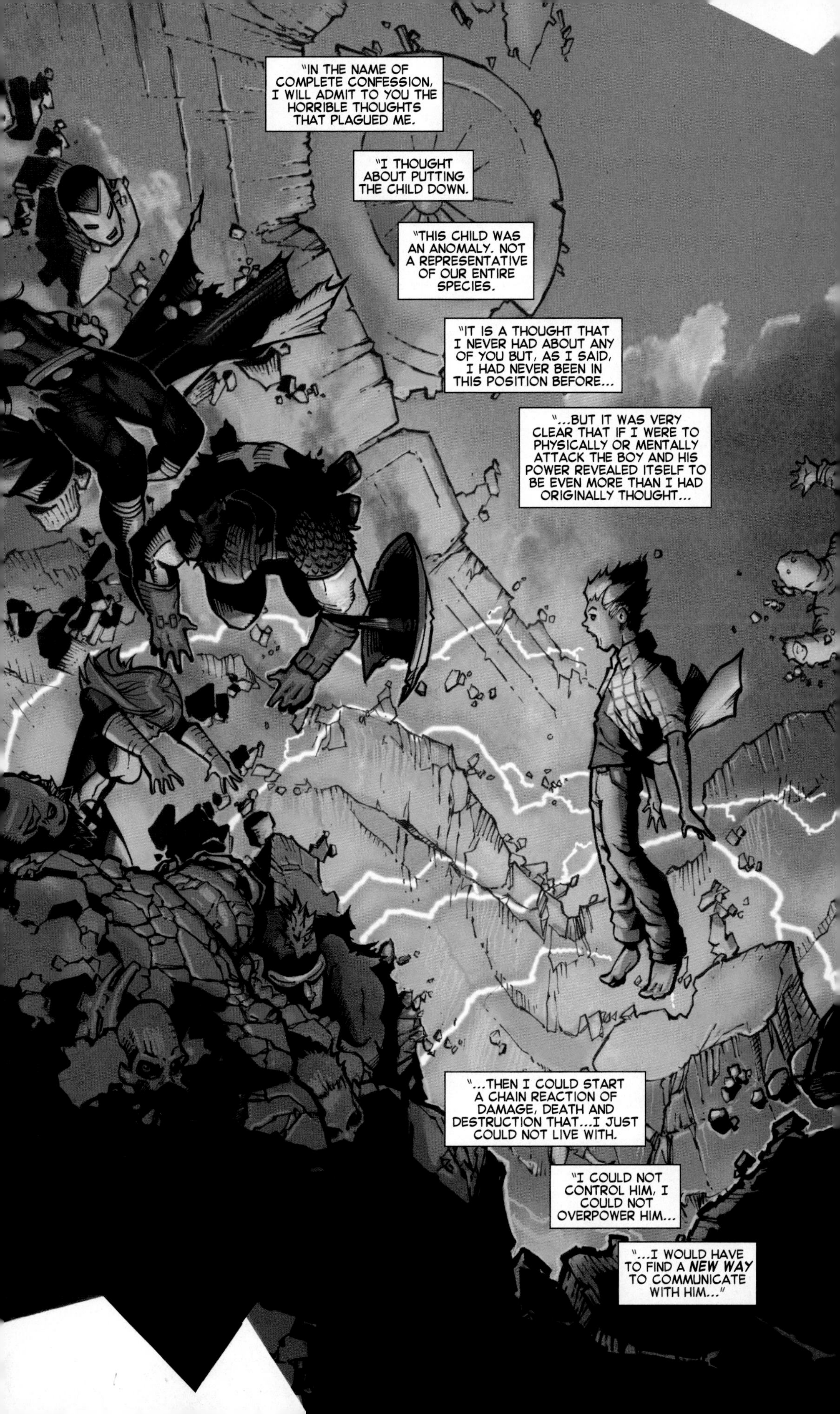
"IN THE NAME OF COMPLETE CONFESSION, I WILL ADMIT TO YOU THE HORRIBLE THOUGHTS THAT PLAGUED ME.
"I THOUGHT ABOUT PUTTING THE CHILD DOWN.
"THIS CHILD WAS AN ANOMALY. NOT A REPRESENTATIVE OF OUR ENTIRE SPECIES.
"IT IS A THOUGHT THAT I NEVER HAD ABOUT ANY OF YOU BUT, AS I SAID, I HAD NEVER BEEN IN THIS POSITION BEFORE...
"...BUT IT WAS VERY CLEAR THAT IF I WERE TO PHYSICALLY OR MENTALLY ATTACK THE BOY AND HIS POWER REVEALED ITSELF TO BE EVEN MORE THAN I HAD ORIGINALLY THOUGHT...
"...THEN I COULD START A CHAIN REACTION OF DAMAGE, DEATH AND DESTRUCTION THAT...I JUST COULD NOT LIVE WITH.
"I COULD NOT CONTROL HIM, I COULD NOT OVERPOWER HIM...
"...I WOULD HAVE TO FIND A ***NEW WAY*** TO COMMUNICATE WITH HIM..."

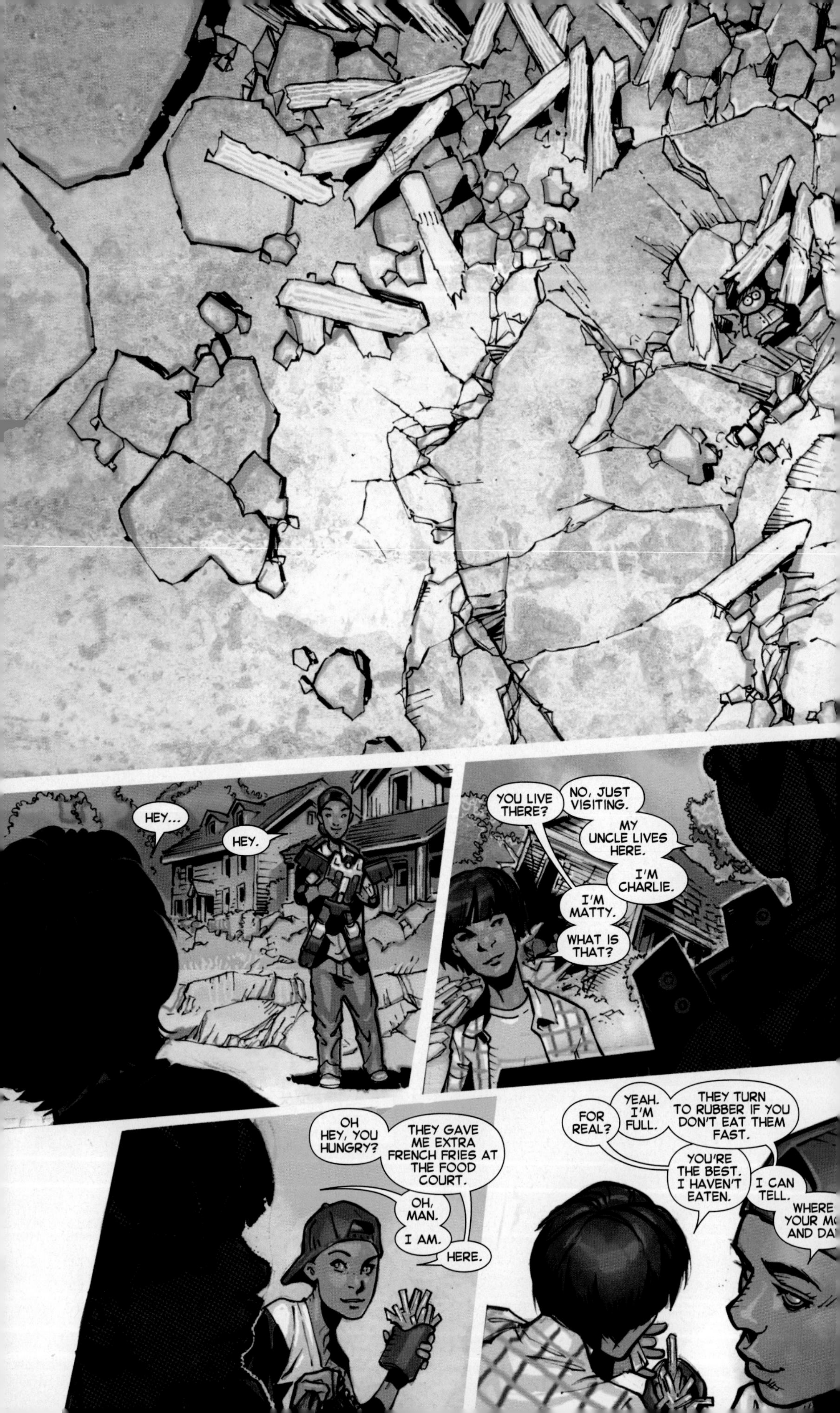
HEY...
HEY.
YOU LIVE THERE?
NO, JUST VISITING.
MY UNCLE LIVES HERE.
I'M CHARLIE.
I'M MATTY.
WHAT IS THAT?
OH HEY, YOU HUNGRY?
THEY GAVE ME EXTRA FRENCH FRIES AT THE FOOD COURT.
OH, MAN.
I AM.
HERE.
FOR REAL?
YEAH. I'M FULL.
THEY TURN TO RUBBER IF YOU DON'T EAT THEM FAST.
YOU'RE THE BEST. I HAVEN'T EATEN.
I CAN TELL.
WHERE

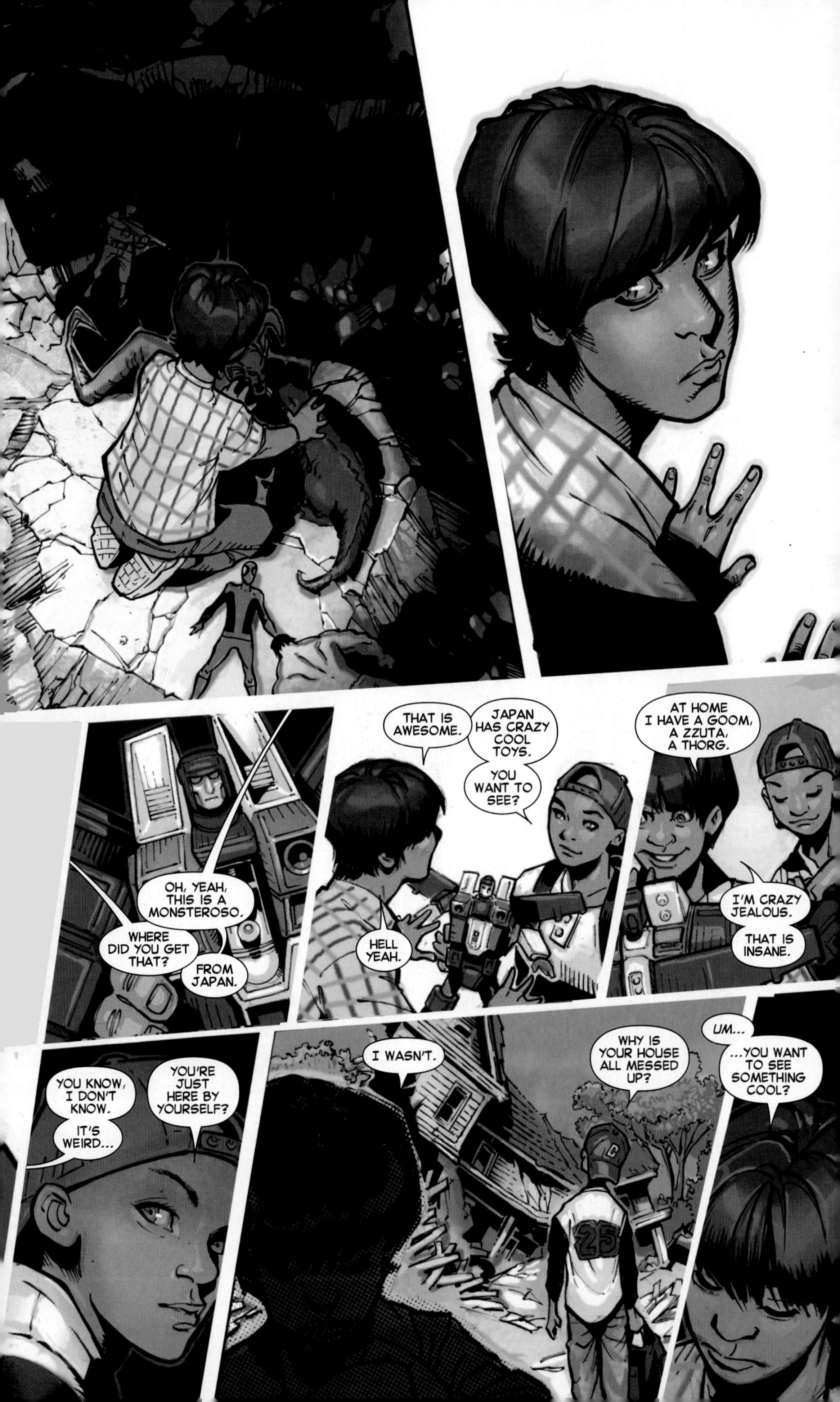

THAT IS AWESOME.
JAPAN HAS CRAZY COOL TOYS.
YOU WANT TO SEE?
AT HOME I HAVE A GOOM, A ZZUTA, A THORG.
OH, YEAH, THIS IS A MONSTEROSO.
WHERE DID YOU GET THAT?
FROM JAPAN.
HELL YEAH.
I'M CRAZY JEALOUS.
THAT IS INSANE.
YOU KNOW, I DON'T KNOW.
IT'S WEIRD...
YOU'RE JUST HERE BY YOURSELF?
I WASN'T.
WHY IS YOUR HOUSE ALL MESSED UP?
UM...
...YOU WANT TO SEE SOMETHING COOL?

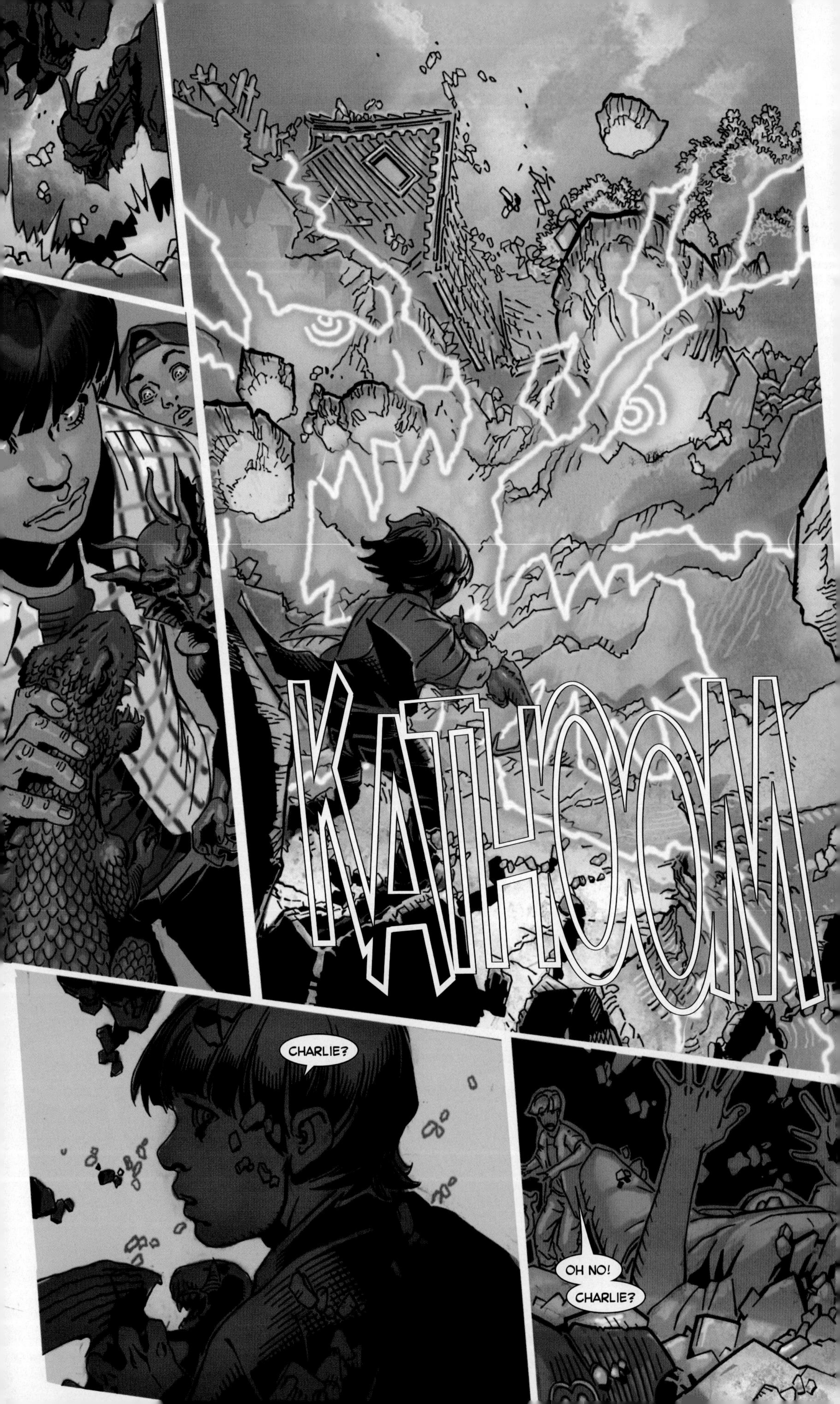
KATHOOM
CHARLIE?
OH NO!
CHARLIE?

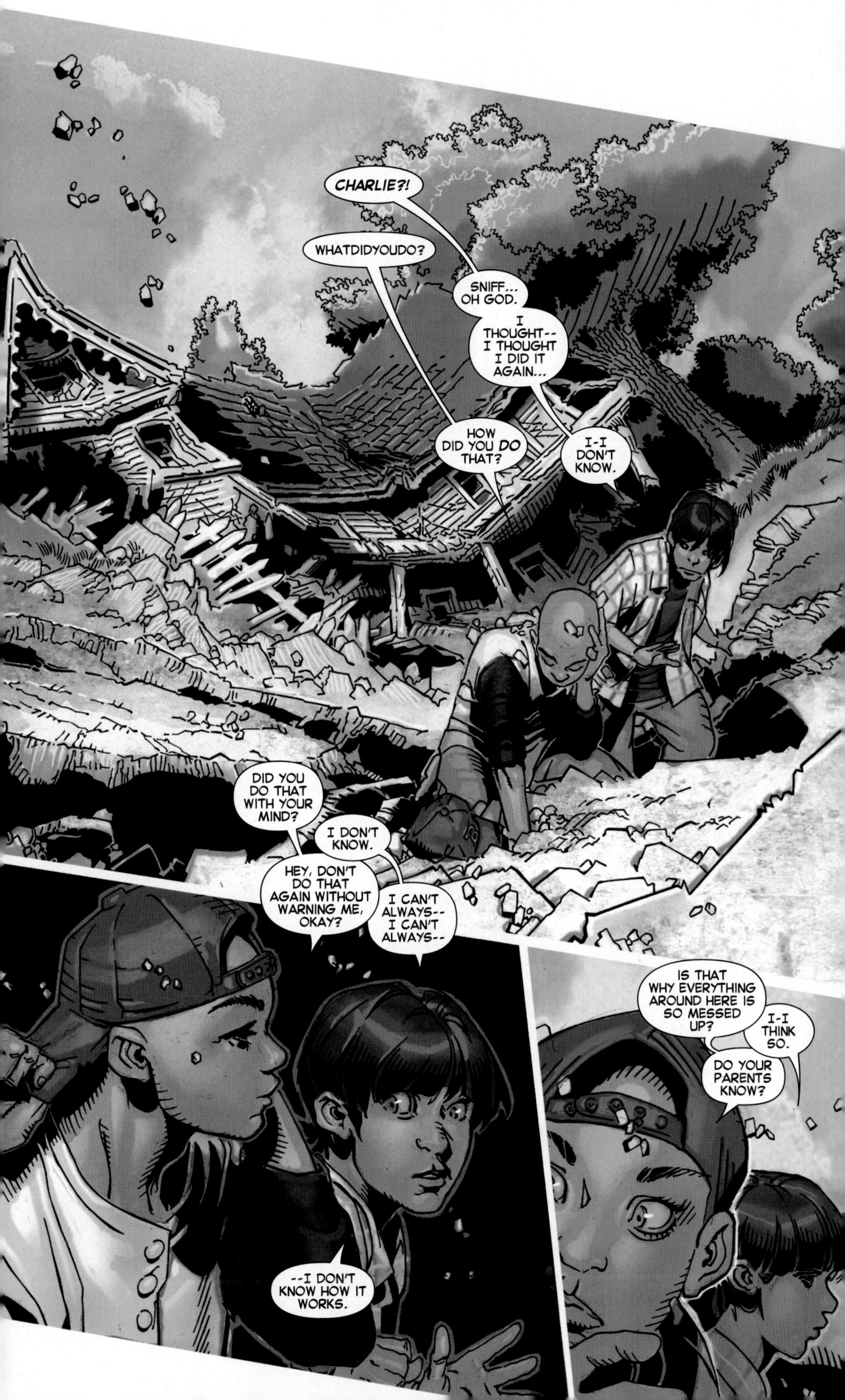
CHARLIE?!
WHATDIDYOUDO?
SNIFF... OH GOD.
I THOUGHT-- I THOUGHT I DID IT AGAIN...
HOW DID YOU DO THAT?
I-I DON'T KNOW.
DID YOU DO THAT WITH YOUR MIND?
I DON'T KNOW.
HEY, DON'T DO THAT AGAIN WITHOUT WARNING ME, OKAY?
I CAN'T ALWAYS-- I CAN'T ALWAYS--
--I DON'T KNOW HOW IT WORKS.
IS THAT WHY EVERYTHING AROUND HERE IS SO MESSED UP?
I-I THINK SO.
DO YOUR PARENTS KNOW?

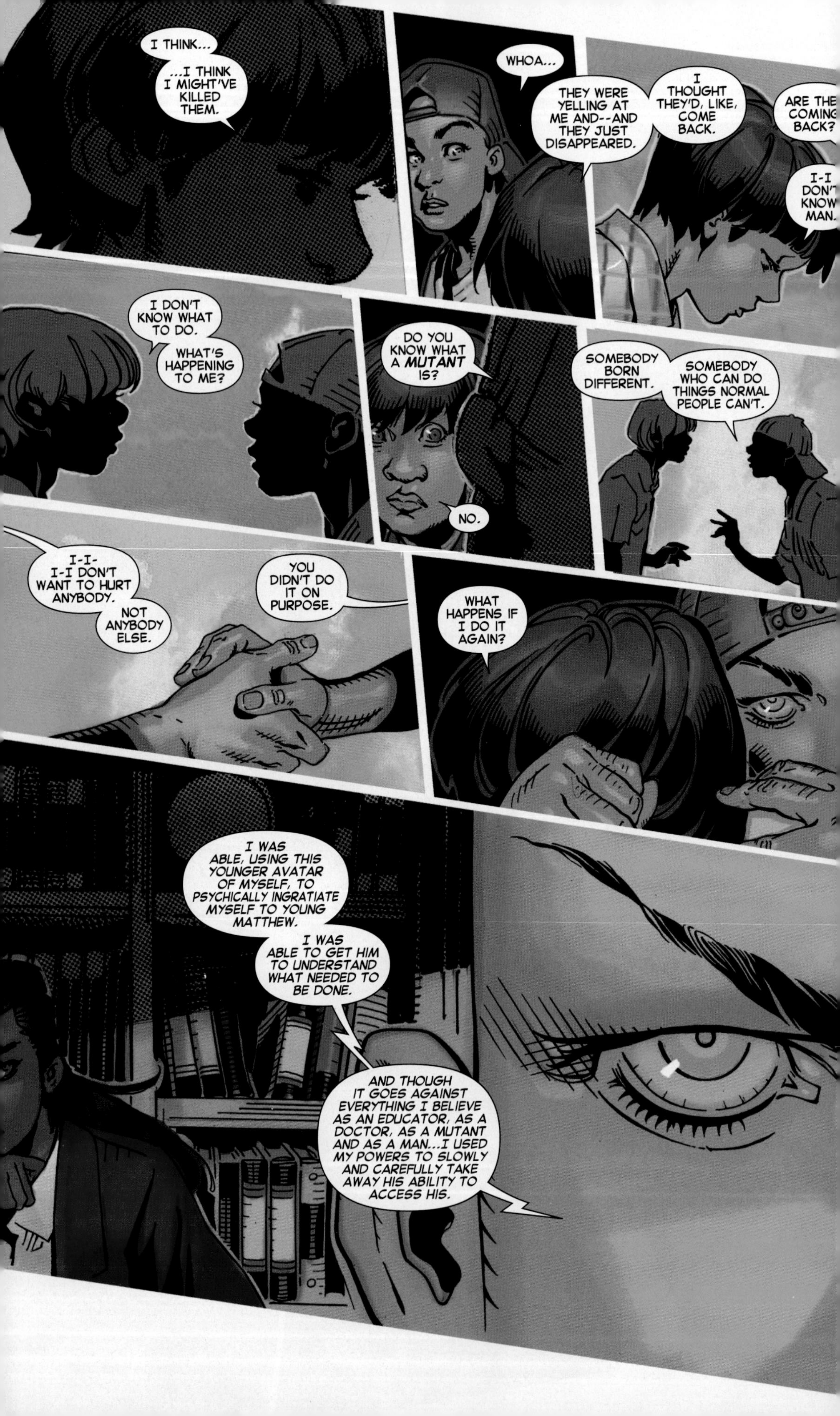
I THINK...
...I THINK I MIGHT'VE KILLED THEM.
WHOA...
THEY WERE YELLING AT ME AND--AND THEY JUST DISAPPEARED.
I THOUGHT THEY'D, LIKE, COME BACK.
ARE THE COMING BACK?
I-I DON'T KNOW MAN.
I DON'T KNOW WHAT TO DO.
WHAT'S HAPPENING TO ME?
DO YOU KNOW WHAT A MUTANT IS?
NO.
SOMEBODY BORN DIFFERENT.
SOMEBODY WHO CAN DO THINGS NORMAL PEOPLE CAN'T.
I-I- I-I DON'T WANT TO HURT ANYBODY.
NOT ANYBODY ELSE.
YOU DIDN'T DO IT ON PURPOSE.
WHAT HAPPENS IF I DO IT AGAIN?
I WAS ABLE, USING THIS YOUNGER AVATAR OF MYSELF, TO PSYCHICALLY INGRATIATE MYSELF TO YOUNG MATTHEW.
I WAS ABLE TO GET HIM TO UNDERSTAND WHAT NEEDED TO BE DONE.
AND THOUGH IT GOES AGAINST EVERYTHING I BELIEVE AS AN EDUCATOR, AS A DOCTOR, AS A MUTANT AND AS A MAN...I USED MY POWERS TO SLOWLY AND CAREFULLY TAKE AWAY HIS ABILITY TO ACCESS HIS.

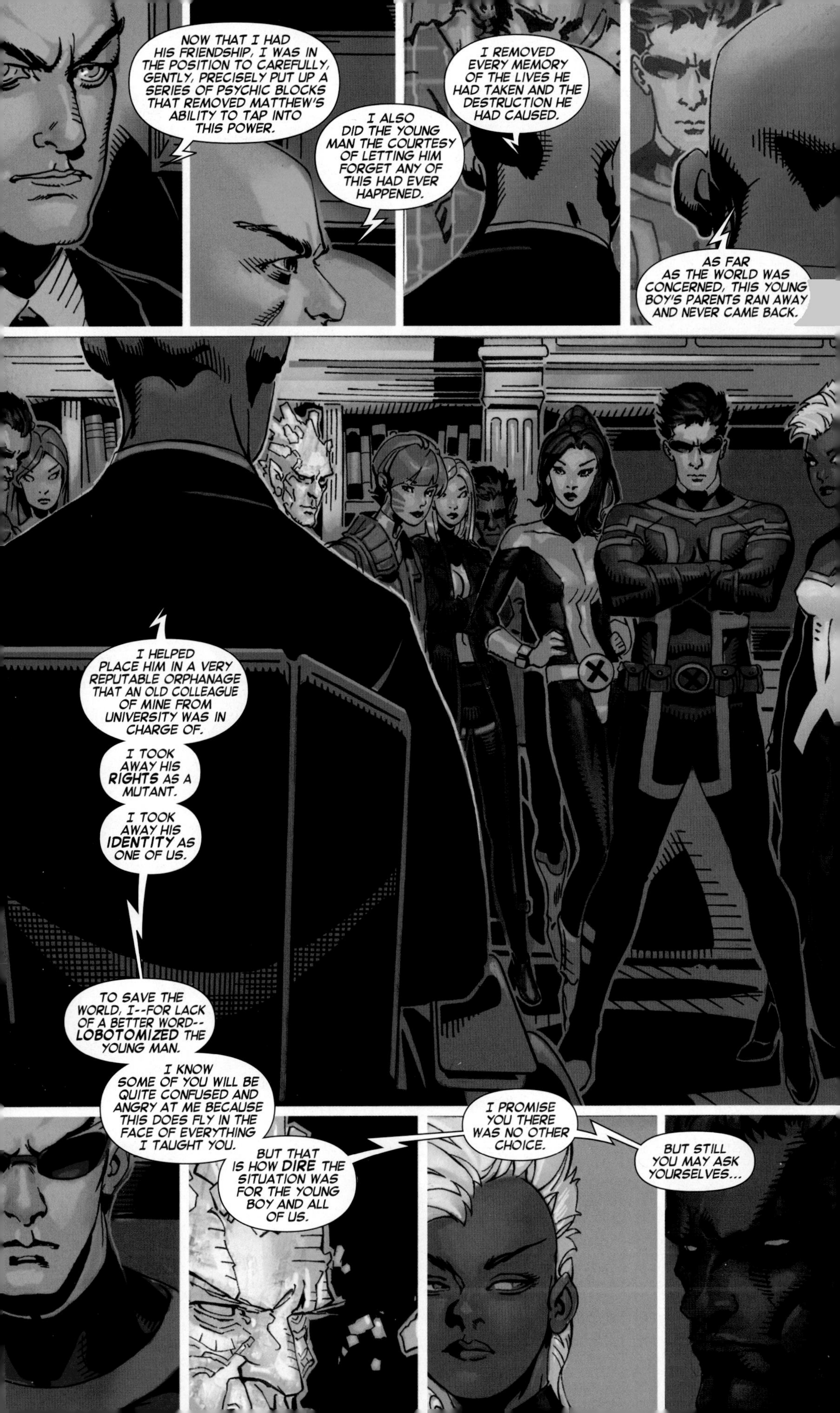
NOW THAT I HAD HIS FRIENDSHIP, I WAS IN THE POSITION TO CAREFULLY, GENTLY, PRECISELY PUT UP A SERIES OF PSYCHIC BLOCKS THAT REMOVED MATTHEW'S ABILITY TO TAP INTO THIS POWER.
I ALSO DID THE YOUNG MAN THE COURTESY OF LETTING HIM FORGET ANY OF THIS HAD EVER HAPPENED.
I REMOVED EVERY MEMORY OF THE LIVES HE HAD TAKEN AND THE DESTRUCTION HE HAD CAUSED.
AS FAR AS THE WORLD WAS CONCERNED, THIS YOUNG BOY'S PARENTS RAN AWAY AND NEVER CAME BACK.
I HELPED PLACE HIM IN A VERY REPUTABLE ORPHANAGE THAT AN OLD COLLEAGUE OF MINE FROM UNIVERSITY WAS IN CHARGE OF.
I TOOK AWAY HIS RIGHTS AS A MUTANT.
I TOOK AWAY HIS IDENTITY AS ONE OF US.
TO SAVE THE WORLD, I--FOR LACK OF A BETTER WORD--LOBOTOMIZED THE YOUNG MAN.
I KNOW SOME OF YOU WILL BE QUITE CONFUSED AND ANGRY AT ME BECAUSE THIS DOES FLY IN THE FACE OF EVERYTHING I TAUGHT YOU.
BUT THAT IS HOW DIRE THE SITUATION WAS FOR THE YOUNG BOY AND ALL OF US.
I PROMISE YOU THERE WAS NO OTHER CHOICE.
BUT STILL YOU MAY ASK YOURSELVES...

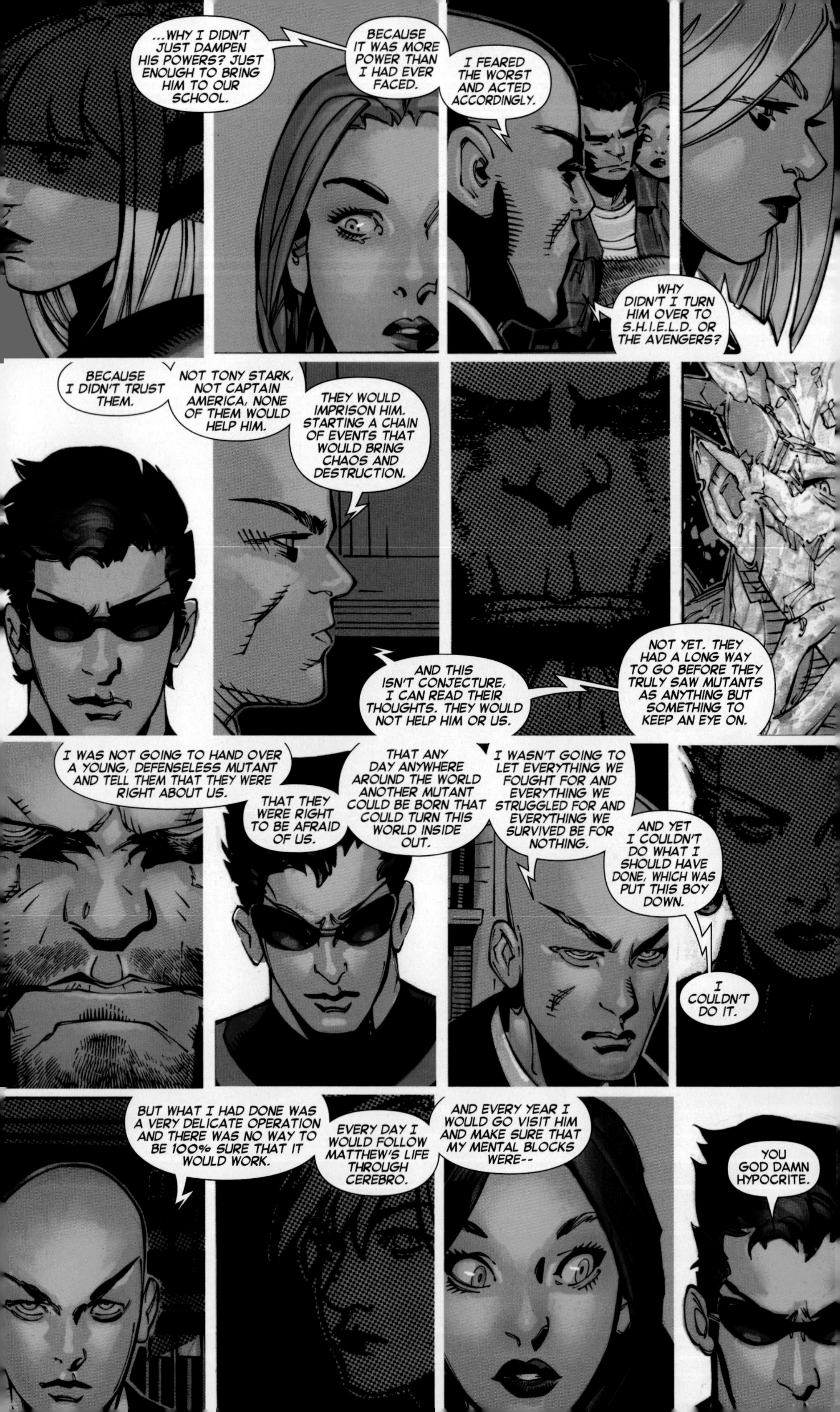
...WHY I DIDN'T JUST DAMPEN HIS POWERS? JUST ENOUGH TO BRING HIM TO OUR SCHOOL.
BECAUSE IT WAS MORE POWER THAN I HAD EVER FACED.
I FEARED THE WORST AND ACTED ACCORDINGLY.
WHY DIDN'T I TURN HIM OVER TO S.H.I.E.L.D. OR THE AVENGERS?
BECAUSE I DIDN'T TRUST THEM.
NOT TONY STARK, NOT CAPTAIN AMERICA, NONE OF THEM WOULD HELP HIM.
THEY WOULD IMPRISON HIM. STARTING A CHAIN OF EVENTS THAT WOULD BRING CHAOS AND DESTRUCTION.
AND THIS ISN'T CONJECTURE, I CAN READ THEIR THOUGHTS. THEY WOULD NOT HELP HIM OR US.
NOT YET. THEY HAD A LONG WAY TO GO BEFORE THEY TRULY SAW MUTANTS AS ANYTHING BUT SOMETHING TO KEEP AN EYE ON.
I WAS NOT GOING TO HAND OVER A YOUNG, DEFENSELESS MUTANT AND TELL THEM THAT THEY WERE RIGHT ABOUT US.
THAT THEY WERE RIGHT TO BE AFRAID OF US.
THAT ANY DAY ANYWHERE AROUND THE WORLD ANOTHER MUTANT COULD BE BORN THAT COULD TURN THIS WORLD INSIDE OUT.
I WASN'T GOING TO LET EVERYTHING WE FOUGHT FOR AND EVERYTHING WE STRUGGLED FOR AND EVERYTHING WE SURVIVED BE FOR NOTHING.
AND YET I COULDN'T DO WHAT I SHOULD HAVE DONE, WHICH WAS PUT THIS BOY DOWN.
I COULDN'T DO IT.
BUT WHAT I HAD DONE WAS A VERY DELICATE OPERATION AND THERE WAS NO WAY TO BE 100% SURE THAT IT WOULD WORK.
EVERY DAY I WOULD FOLLOW MATTHEW'S LIFE THROUGH CEREBRO.
AND EVERY YEAR I WOULD GO VISIT HIM AND MAKE SURE THAT MY MENTAL BLOCKS WERE--
YOU GOD DAMN HYPOCRITE.

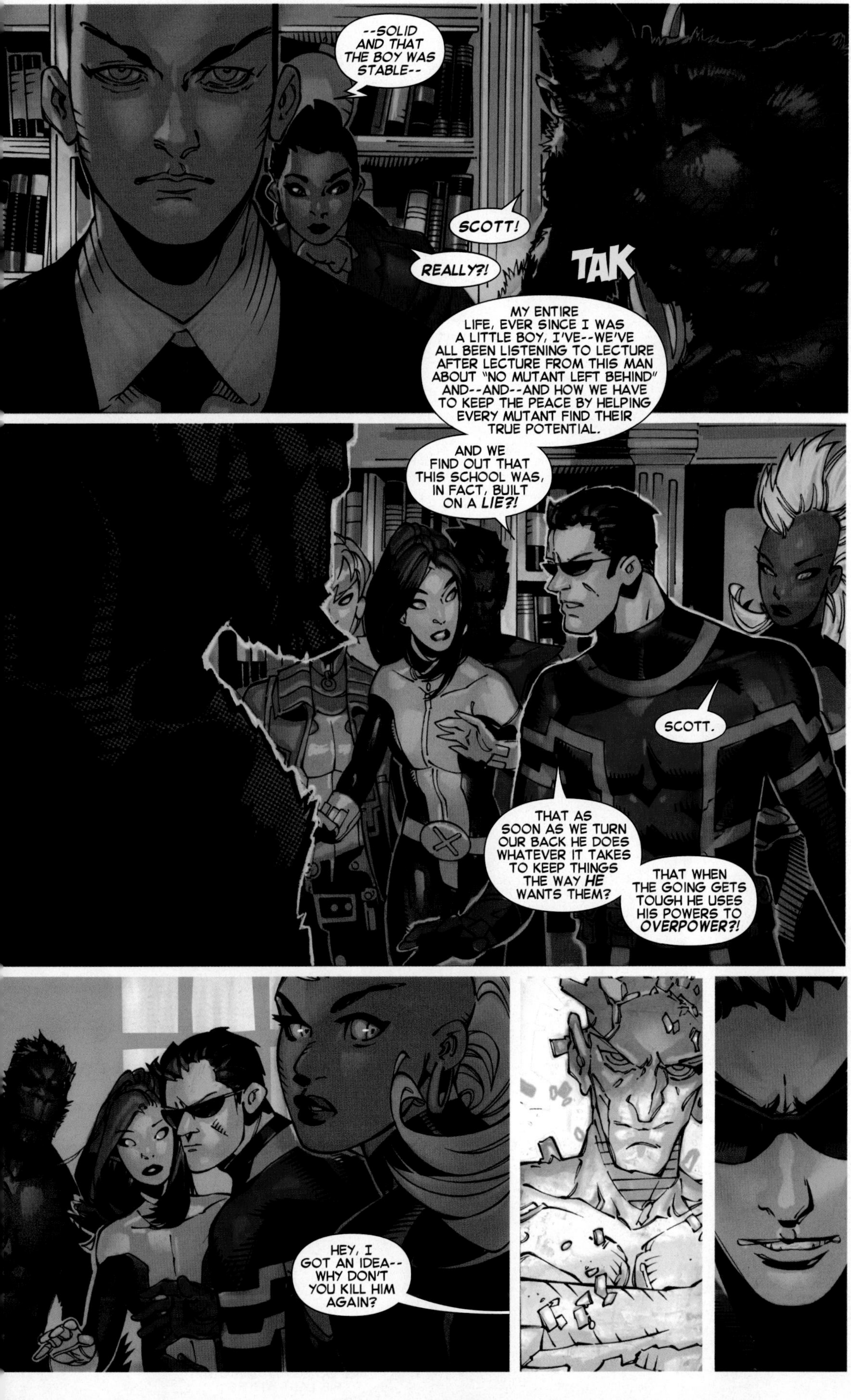
--SOLID AND THAT THE BOY WAS STABLE--
SCOTT!
REALLY?!
TAK
MY ENTIRE LIFE, EVER SINCE I WAS A LITTLE BOY, I'VE--WE'VE ALL BEEN LISTENING TO LECTURE AFTER LECTURE FROM THIS MAN ABOUT "NO MUTANT LEFT BEHIND" AND--AND--AND HOW WE HAVE TO KEEP THE PEACE BY HELPING EVERY MUTANT FIND THEIR TRUE POTENTIAL.
AND WE FIND OUT THAT THIS SCHOOL WAS, IN FACT, BUILT ON A LIE?!
SCOTT.
THAT AS SOON AS WE TURN OUR BACK HE DOES WHATEVER IT TAKES TO KEEP THINGS THE WAY HE WANTS THEM?
THAT WHEN THE GOING GETS TOUGH HE USES HIS POWERS TO OVERPOWER?!
HEY, I GOT AN IDEA--WHY DON'T YOU KILL HIM AGAIN?

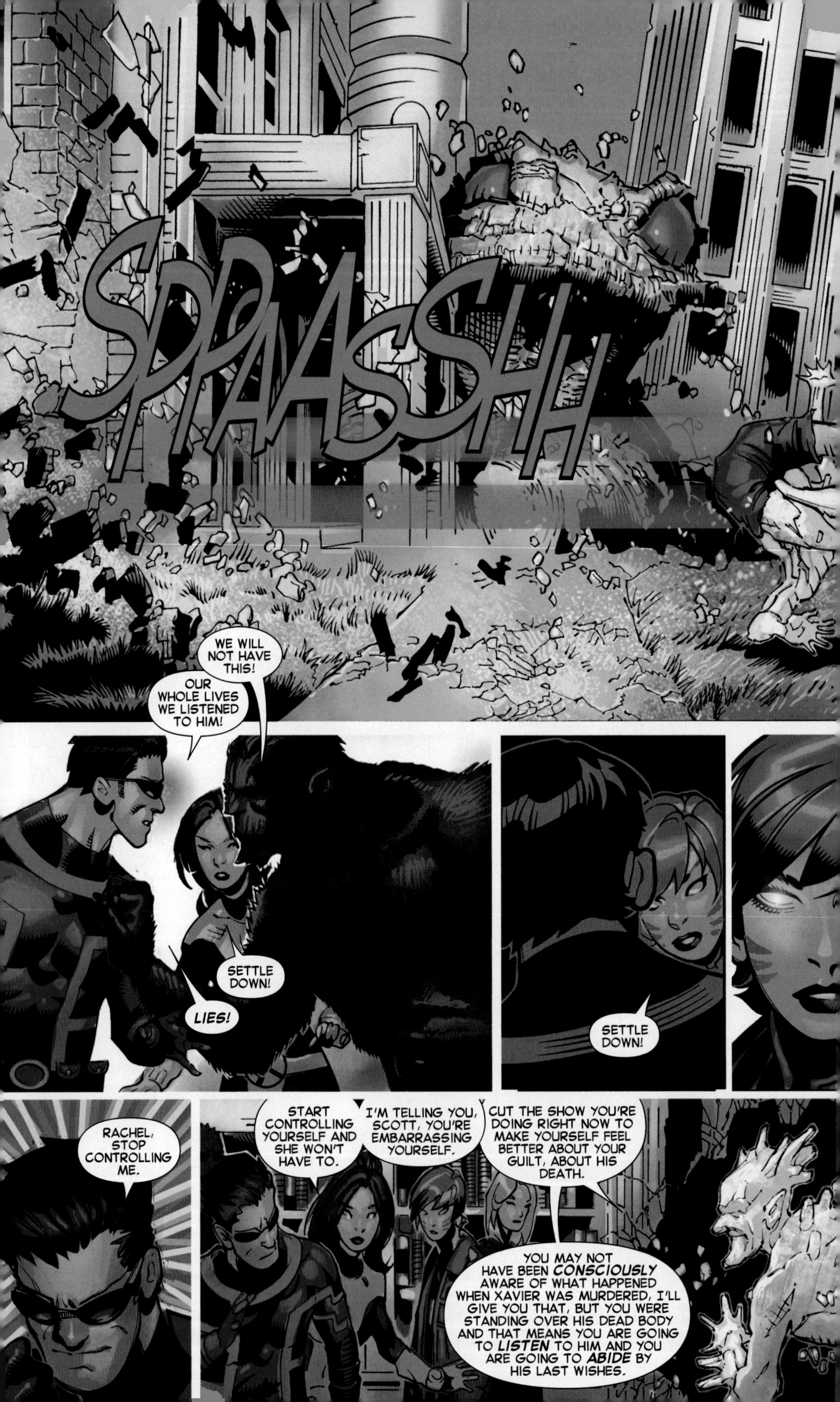
SPPAASSHH
WE WILL NOT HAVE THIS!
OUR WHOLE LIVES WE LISTENED TO HIM!
SETTLE DOWN!
LIES!
SETTLE DOWN!
RACHEL, STOP CONTROLLING ME.
START CONTROLLING YOURSELF AND SHE WON'T HAVE TO.
I'M TELLING YOU, SCOTT, YOU'RE EMBARRASSING YOURSELF.
CUT THE SHOW YOU'RE DOING RIGHT NOW TO MAKE YOURSELF FEEL BETTER ABOUT YOUR GUILT, ABOUT HIS DEATH.
YOU MAY NOT HAVE BEEN CONSCIOUSLY AWARE OF WHAT HAPPENED WHEN XAVIER WAS MURDERED, I'LL GIVE YOU THAT, BUT YOU WERE STANDING OVER HIS DEAD BODY AND THAT MEANS YOU ARE GOING TO LISTEN TO HIM AND YOU ARE GOING TO ABIDE BY HIS LAST WISHES.

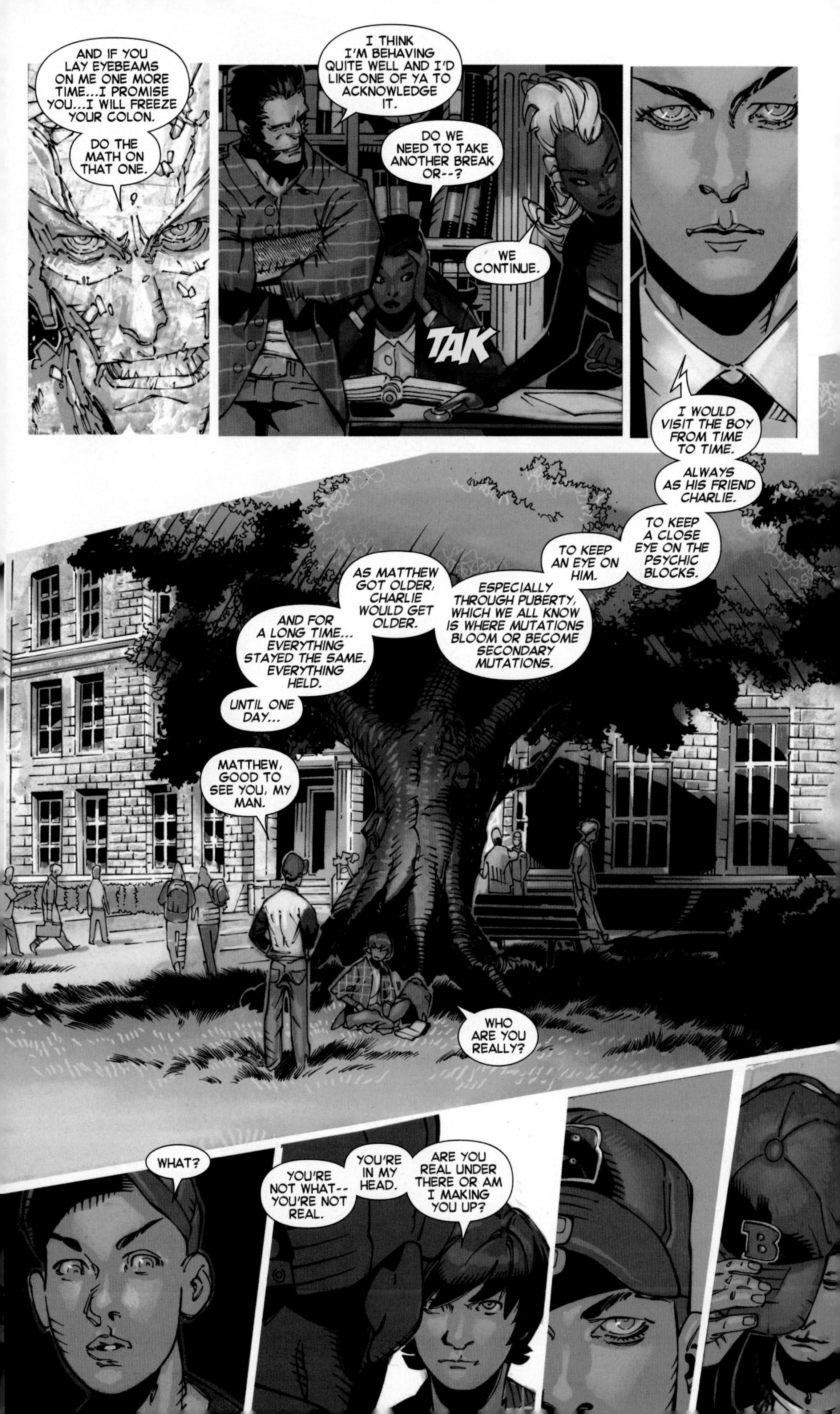
AND IF YOU LAY EYEBEAMS ON ME ONE MORE TIME...I PROMISE YOU...I WILL FREEZE YOUR COLON.
DO THE MATH ON THAT ONE.
I THINK I'M BEHAVING QUITE WELL AND I'D LIKE ONE OF YA TO ACKNOWLEDGE IT.
DO WE NEED TO TAKE ANOTHER BREAK OR--?
WE CONTINUE.
TAK
I WOULD VISIT THE BOY FROM TIME TO TIME.
ALWAYS AS HIS FRIEND CHARLIE.
TO KEEP A CLOSE EYE ON THE PSYCHIC BLOCKS.
TO KEEP AN EYE ON HIM.
ESPECIALLY THROUGH PUBERTY, WHICH WE ALL KNOW IS WHERE MUTATIONS BLOOM OR BECOME SECONDARY MUTATIONS.
AS MATTHEW GOT OLDER, CHARLIE WOULD GET OLDER.
AND FOR A LONG TIME... EVERYTHING STAYED THE SAME. EVERYTHING HELD.
UNTIL ONE DAY...
MATTHEW, GOOD TO SEE YOU, MY MAN.
WHO ARE YOU REALLY?
WHAT?
YOU'RE NOT WHAT-- YOU'RE NOT REAL.
YOU'RE IN MY HEAD.
ARE YOU REAL UNDER THERE OR AM I MAKING YOU UP?

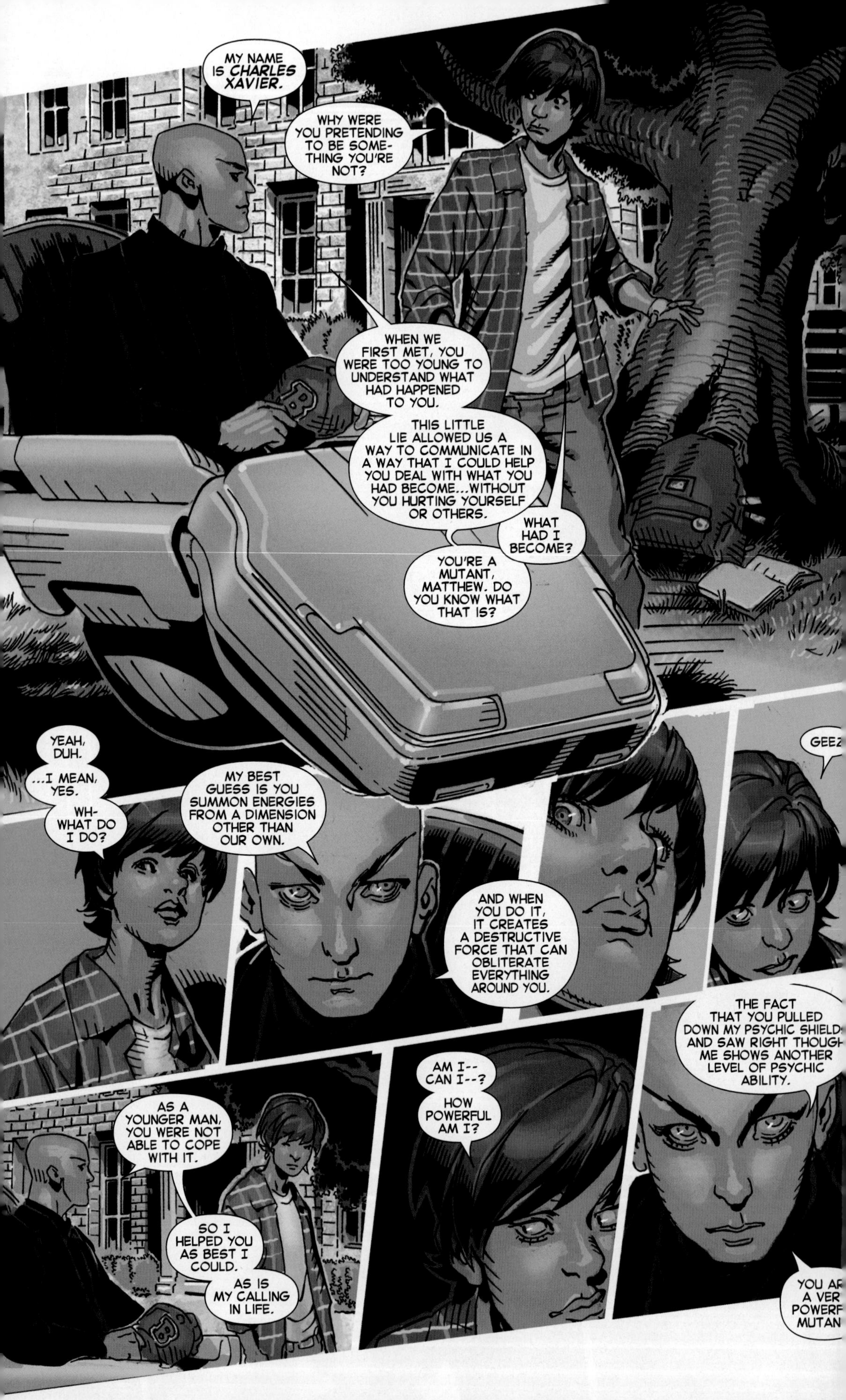

MY NAME IS CHARLES XAVIER.
WHY WERE YOU PRETENDING TO BE SOME-THING YOU'RE NOT?
WHEN WE FIRST MET, YOU WERE TOO YOUNG TO UNDERSTAND WHAT HAD HAPPENED TO YOU.
THIS LITTLE LIE ALLOWED US A WAY TO COMMUNICATE IN A WAY THAT I COULD HELP YOU DEAL WITH WHAT YOU HAD BECOME...WITHOUT YOU HURTING YOURSELF OR OTHERS.
WHAT HAD I BECOME?
YOU'RE A MUTANT, MATTHEW. DO YOU KNOW WHAT THAT IS?
YEAH, DUH.
...I MEAN, YES.
WH- WHAT DO I DO?
MY BEST GUESS IS YOU SUMMON ENERGIES FROM A DIMENSION OTHER THAN OUR OWN.
AND WHEN YOU DO IT, IT CREATES A DESTRUCTIVE FORCE THAT CAN OBLITERATE EVERYTHING AROUND YOU.
GEEZ
AS A YOUNGER MAN, YOU WERE NOT ABLE TO COPE WITH IT.
SO I HELPED YOU AS BEST I COULD.
AS IS MY CALLING IN LIFE.
AM I-- CAN I--?
HOW POWERFUL AM I?
THE FACT THAT YOU PULLED DOWN MY PSYCHIC SHIELD AND SAW RIGHT THOUGH ME SHOWS ANOTHER LEVEL OF PSYCHIC ABILITY.
YOU AR A VER POWERF MUTAN

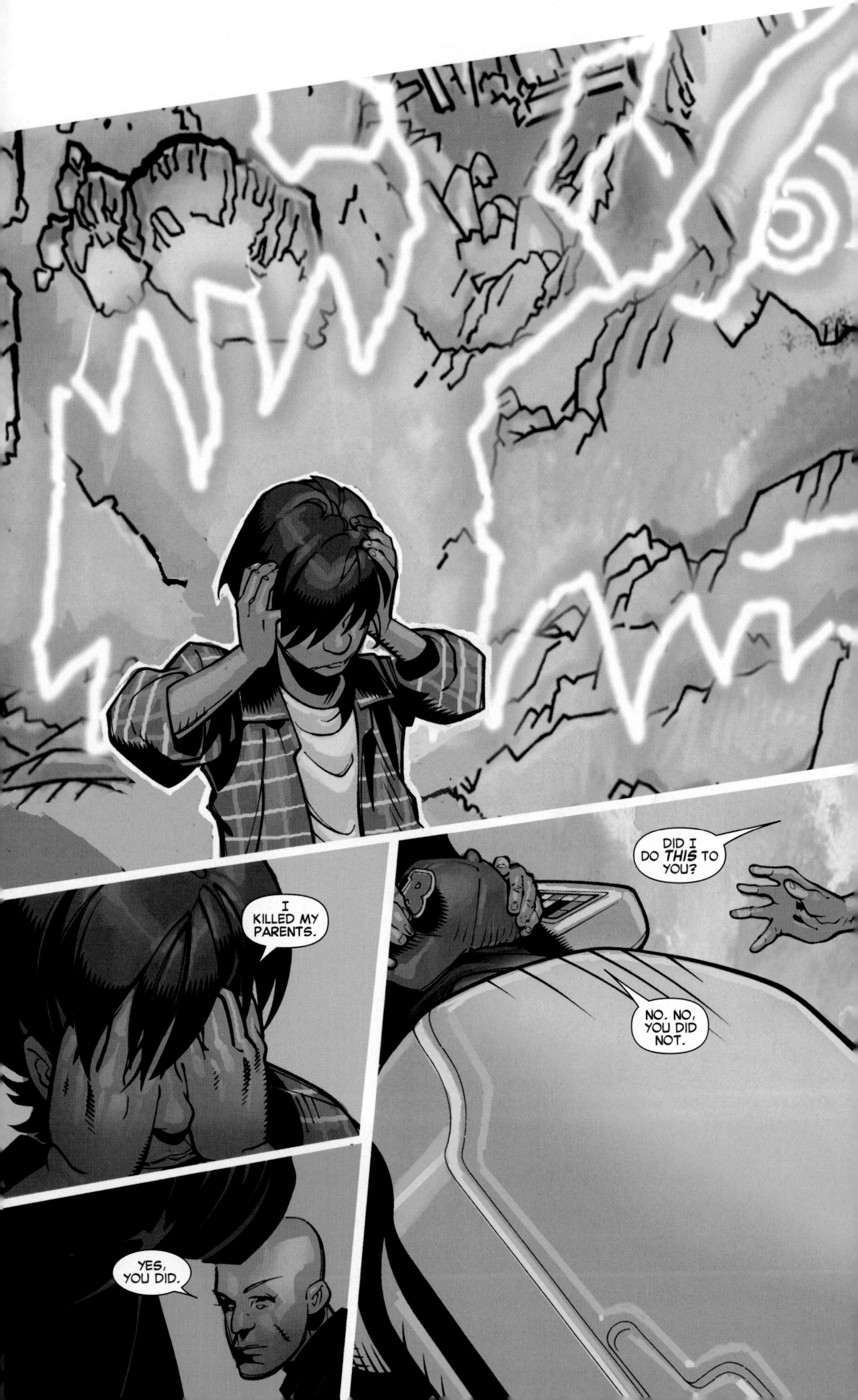

I KILLED MY PARENTS.
DID I DO THIS TO YOU?
NO. NO, YOU DID NOT.
YES, YOU DID.

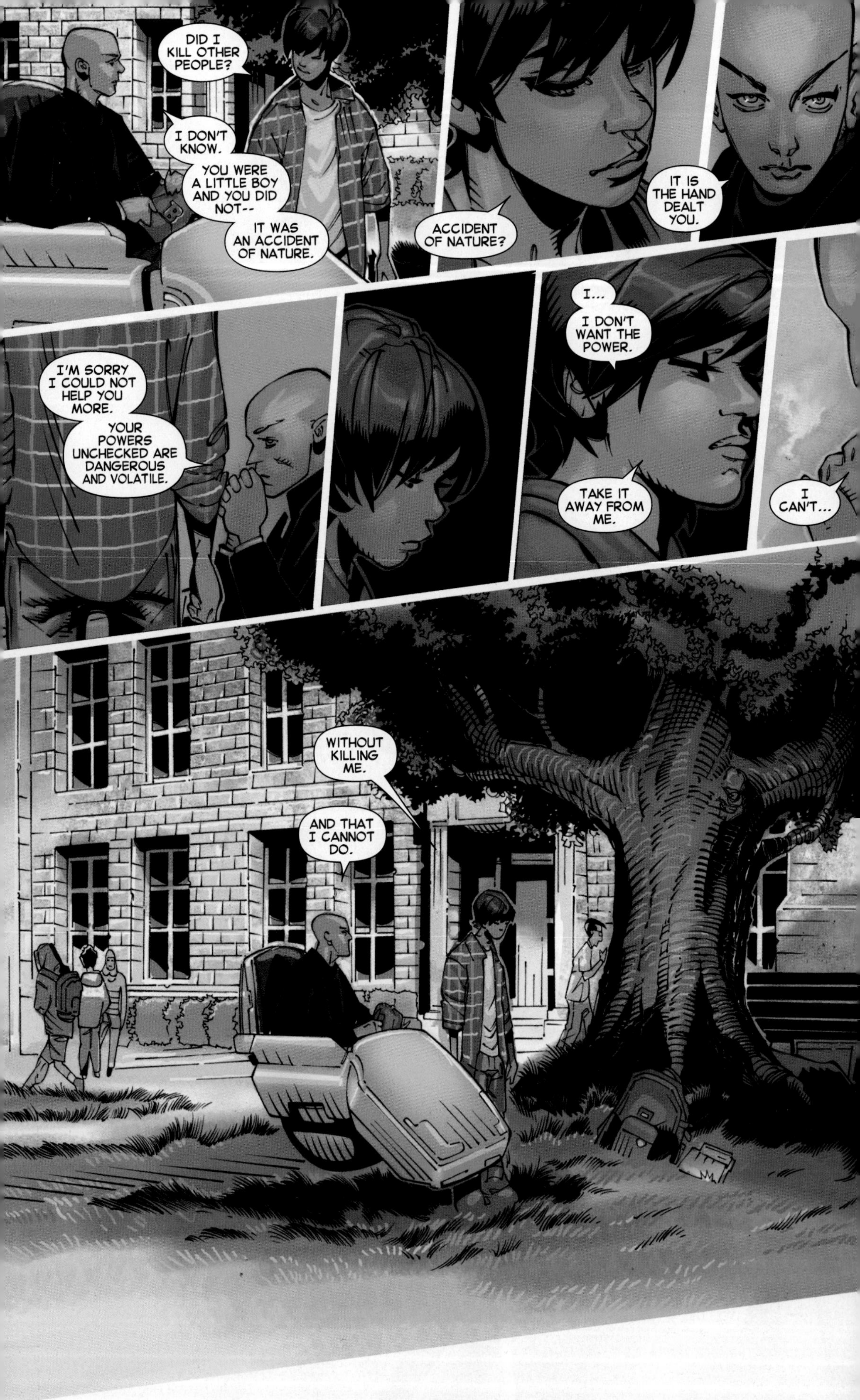
DID I KILL OTHER PEOPLE?
I DON'T KNOW.
YOU WERE A LITTLE BOY AND YOU DID NOT--
IT WAS AN ACCIDENT OF NATURE.
ACCIDENT OF NATURE?
IT IS THE HAND DEALT YOU.
I'M SORRY I COULD NOT HELP YOU MORE.
YOUR POWERS UNCHECKED ARE DANGEROUS AND VOLATILE.
I...
I DON'T WANT THE POWER.
TAKE IT AWAY FROM ME.
I CAN'T...
WITHOUT KILLING ME.
AND THAT I CANNOT DO.

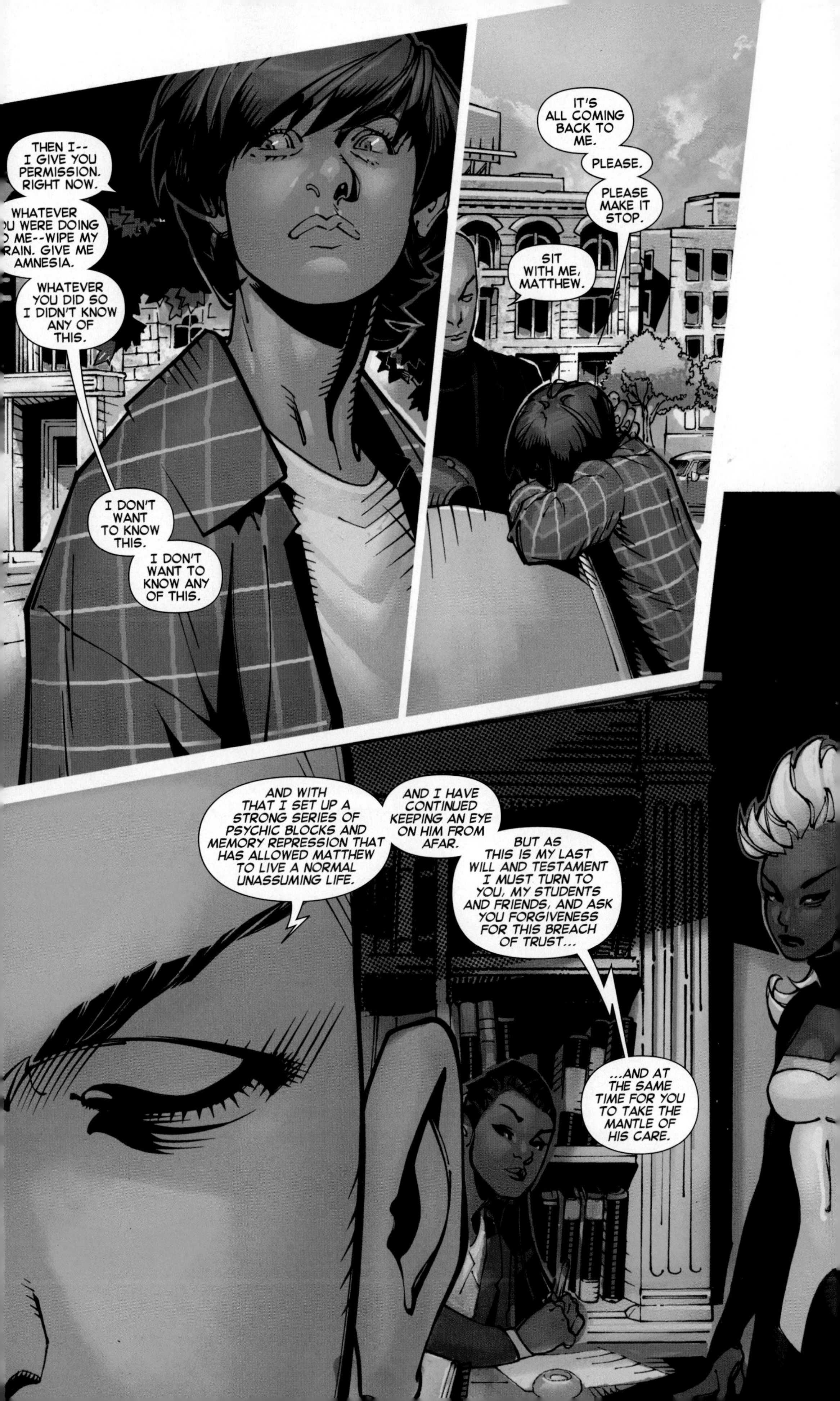
THEN I-- I GIVE YOU PERMISSION. RIGHT NOW.
WHATEVER OU WERE DOING O ME--WIPE MY RAIN. GIVE ME AMNESIA.
WHATEVER YOU DID SO I DIDN'T KNOW ANY OF THIS.
I DON'T WANT TO KNOW THIS.
I DON'T WANT TO KNOW ANY OF THIS.
IT'S ALL COMING BACK TO ME.
PLEASE.
PLEASE MAKE IT STOP.
SIT WITH ME, MATTHEW.
AND WITH THAT I SET UP A STRONG SERIES OF PSYCHIC BLOCKS AND MEMORY REPRESSION THAT HAS ALLOWED MATTHEW TO LIVE A NORMAL UNASSUMING LIFE.
AND I HAVE CONTINUED KEEPING AN EYE ON HIM FROM AFAR.
BUT AS THIS IS MY LAST WILL AND TESTAMENT I MUST TURN TO YOU, MY STUDENTS AND FRIENDS, AND ASK YOU FORGIVENESS FOR THIS BREACH OF TRUST...
...AND AT THE SAME TIME FOR YOU TO TAKE THE MANTLE OF HIS CARE.

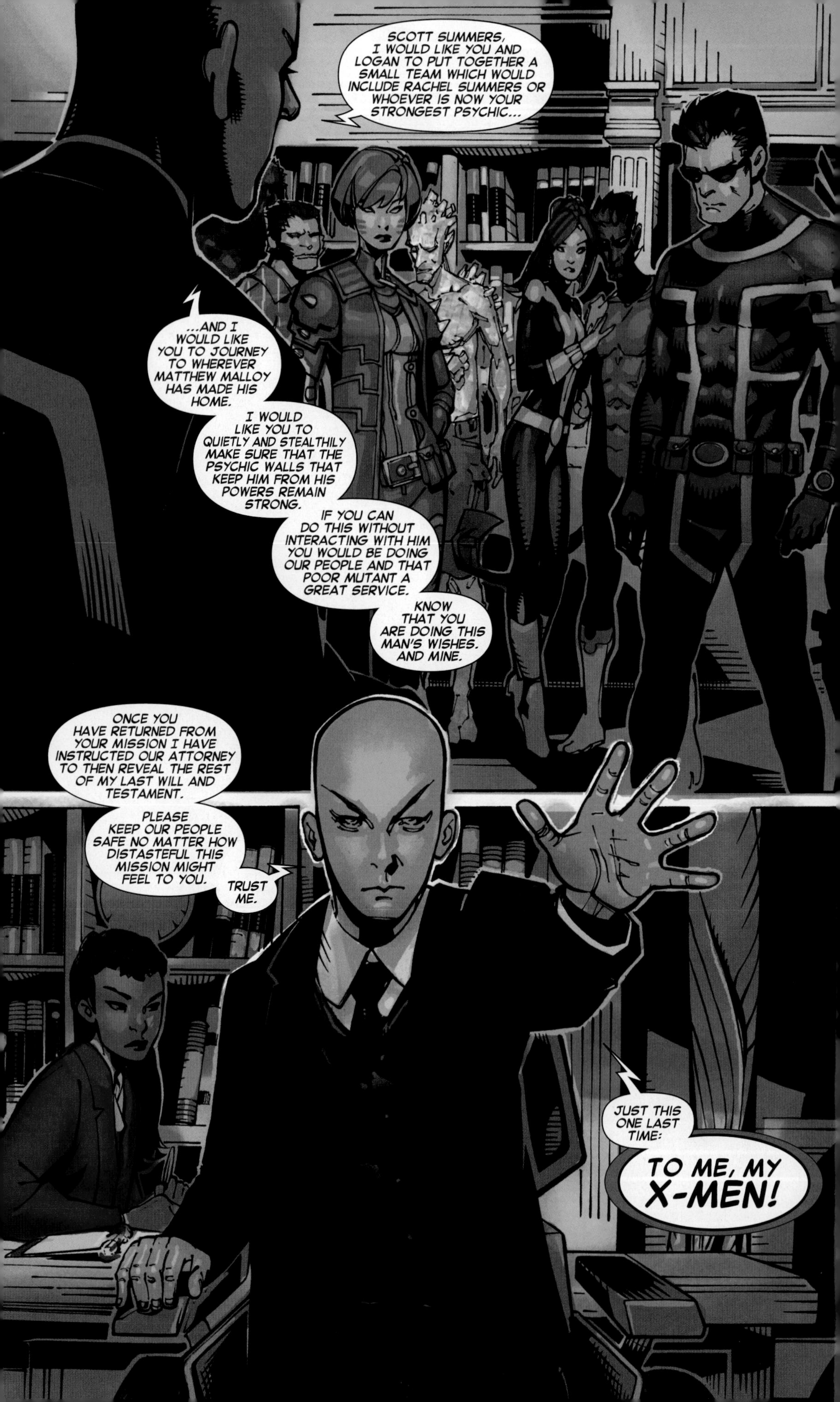
SCOTT SUMMERS, I WOULD LIKE YOU AND LOGAN TO PUT TOGETHER A SMALL TEAM WHICH WOULD INCLUDE RACHEL SUMMERS OR WHOEVER IS NOW YOUR STRONGEST PSYCHIC...
...AND I WOULD LIKE YOU TO JOURNEY TO WHEREVER MATTHEW MALLOY HAS MADE HIS HOME.
I WOULD LIKE YOU TO QUIETLY AND STEALTHILY MAKE SURE THAT THE PSYCHIC WALLS THAT KEEP HIM FROM HIS POWERS REMAIN STRONG.
IF YOU CAN DO THIS WITHOUT INTERACTING WITH HIM YOU WOULD BE DOING OUR PEOPLE AND THAT POOR MUTANT A GREAT SERVICE.
KNOW THAT YOU ARE DOING THIS MAN'S WISHES. AND MINE.
ONCE YOU HAVE RETURNED FROM YOUR MISSION I HAVE INSTRUCTED OUR ATTORNEY TO THEN REVEAL THE REST OF MY LAST WILL AND TESTAMENT.
PLEASE KEEP OUR PEOPLE SAFE NO MATTER HOW DISTASTEFUL THIS MISSION MIGHT FEEL TO YOU.
TRUST ME.
JUST THIS ONE LAST TIME:
TO ME, MY X-MEN!

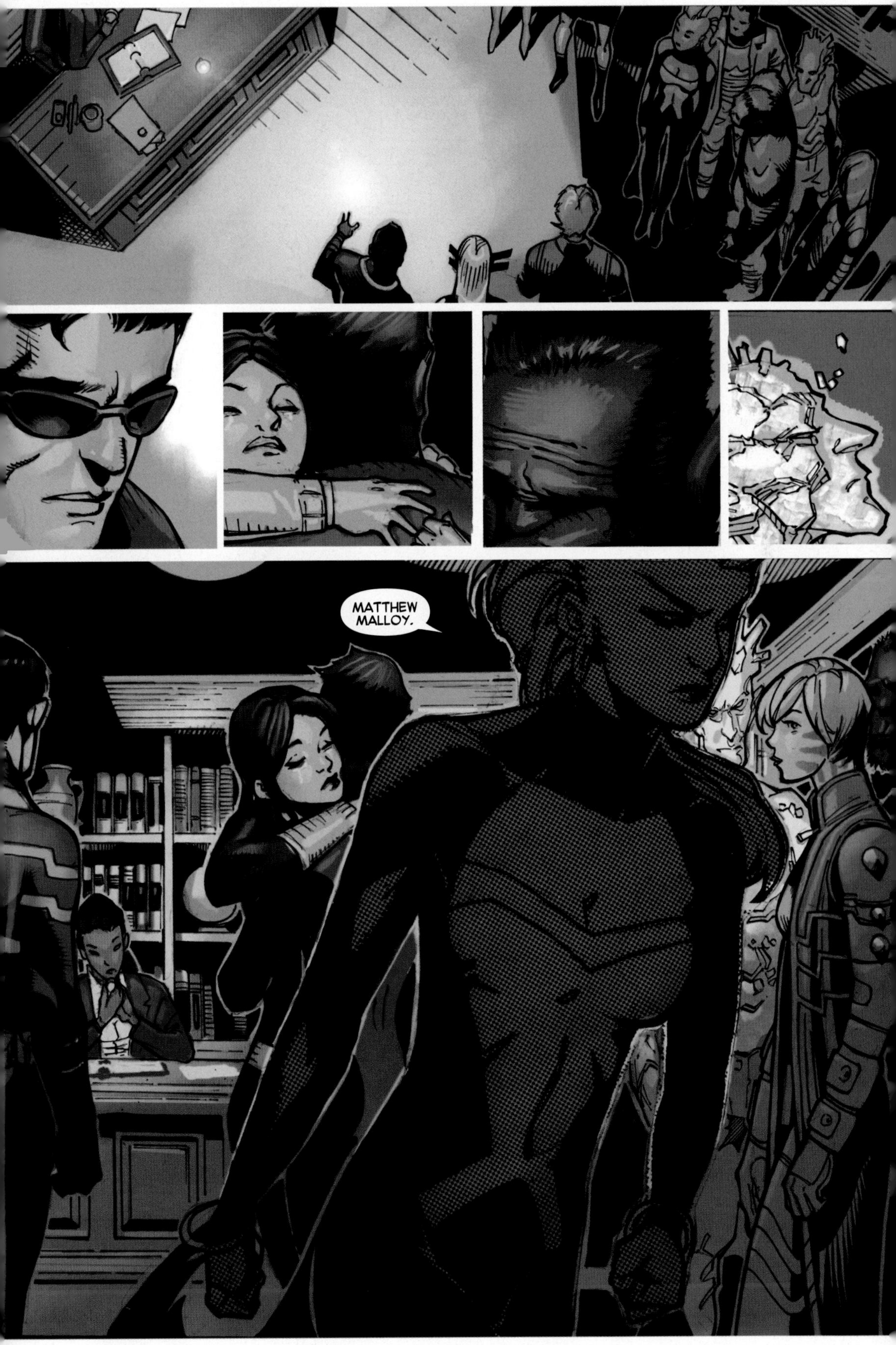
MATTHEW MALLOY.

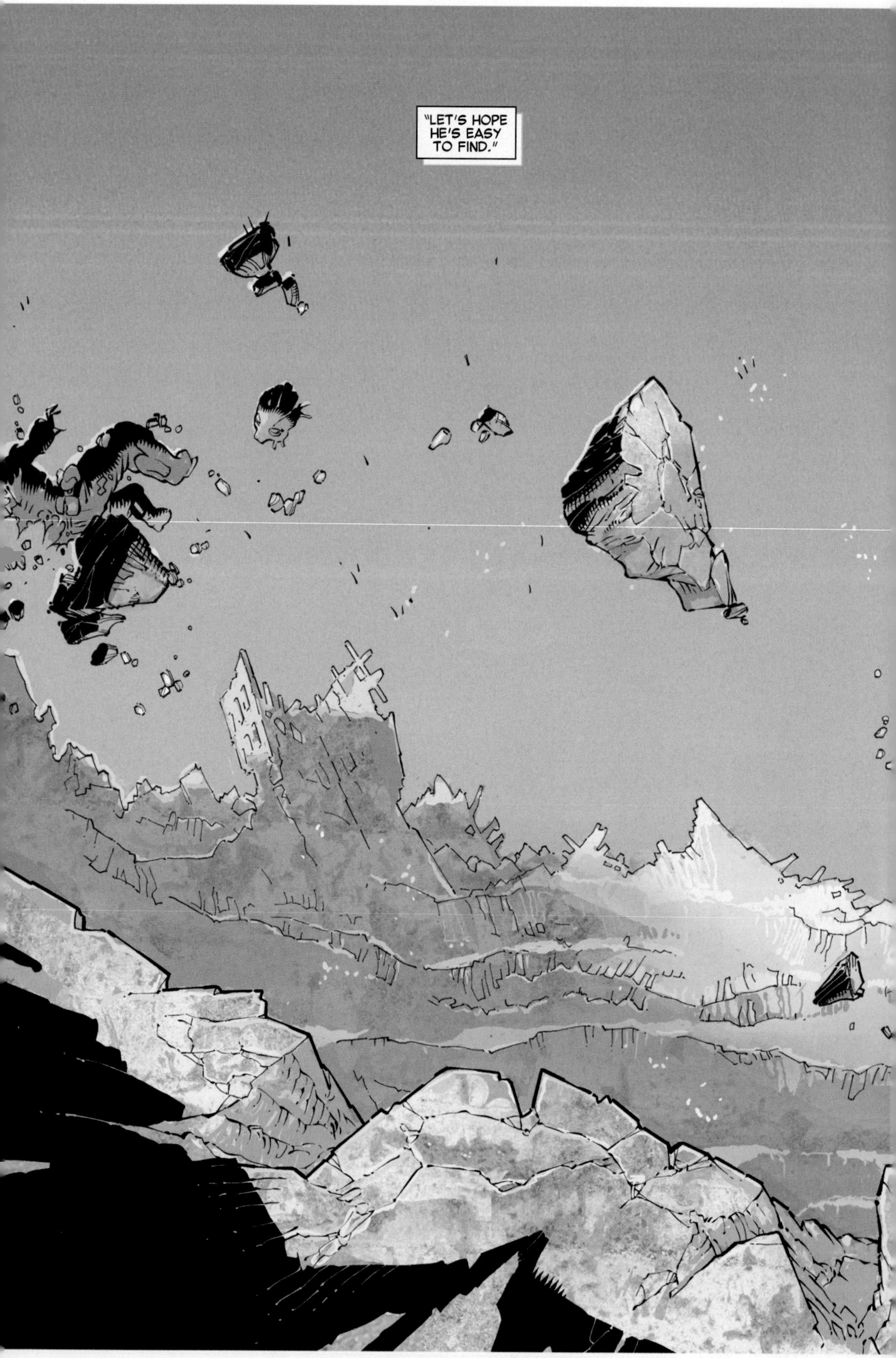
"LET'S HOPE HE'S EASY TO FIND."

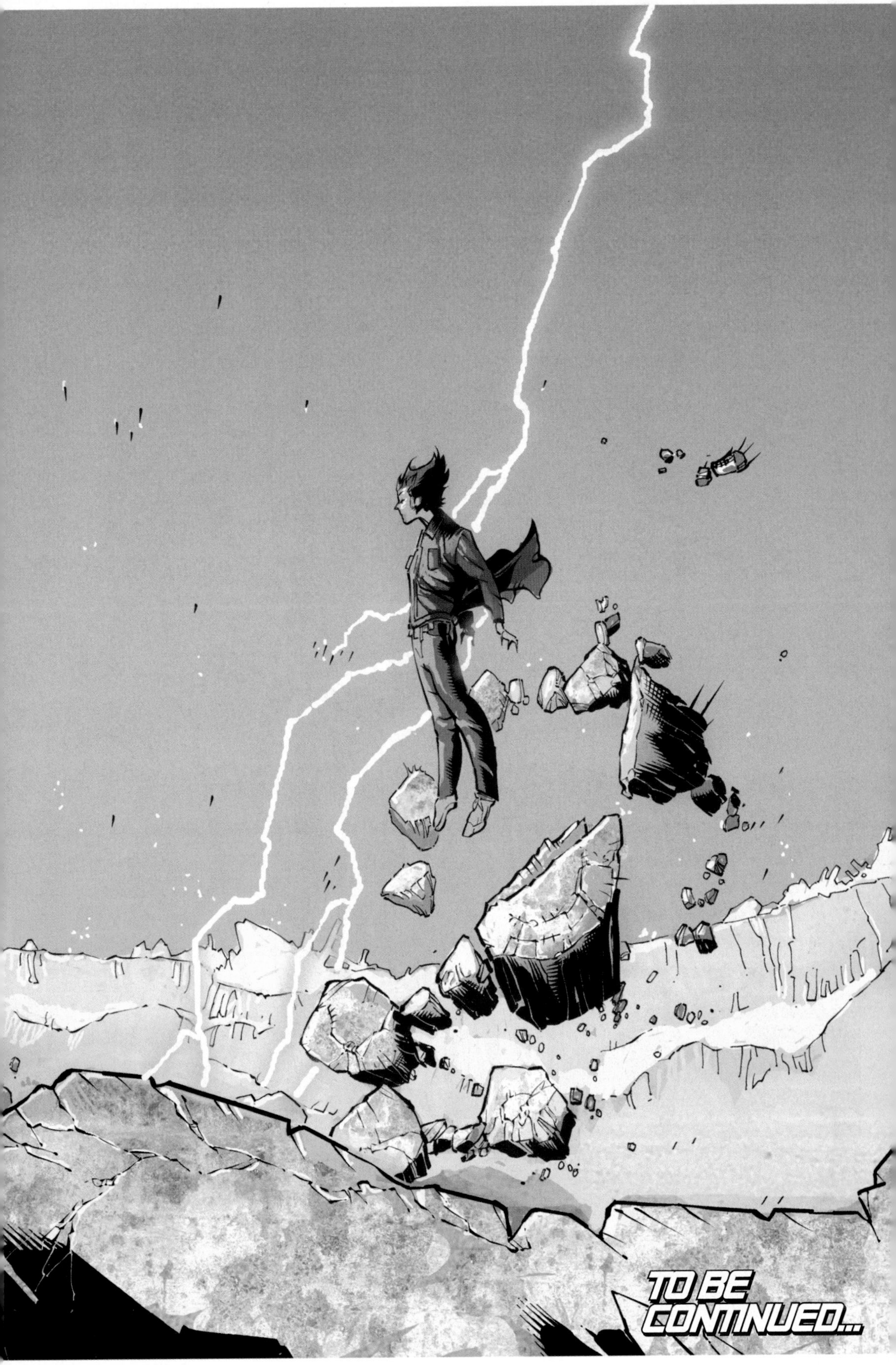
TO BE
CONTINUED...

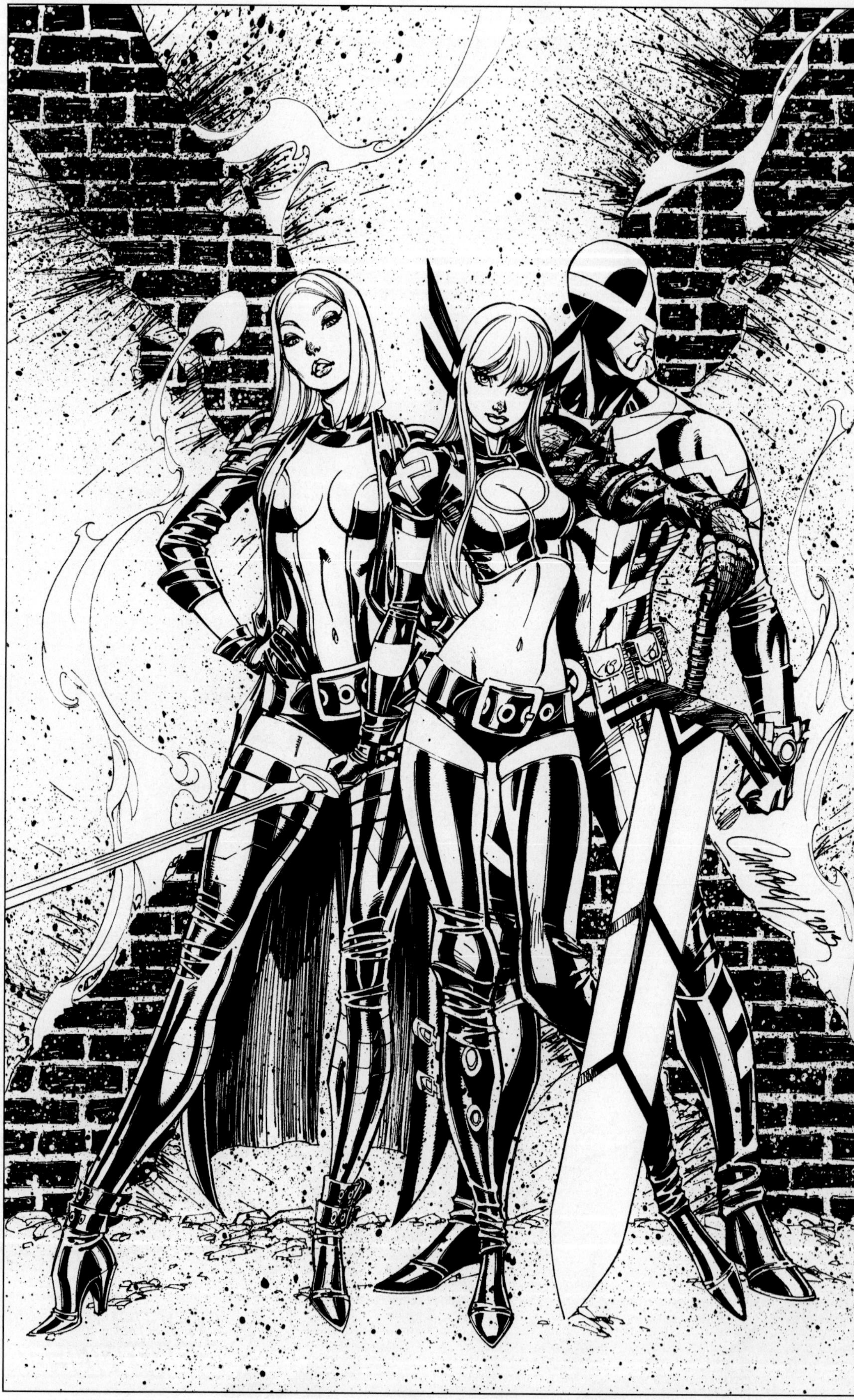

UNCANNY X-MEN #19 SKETCH VARIANT

BY J. SCOTT CAMPBELL

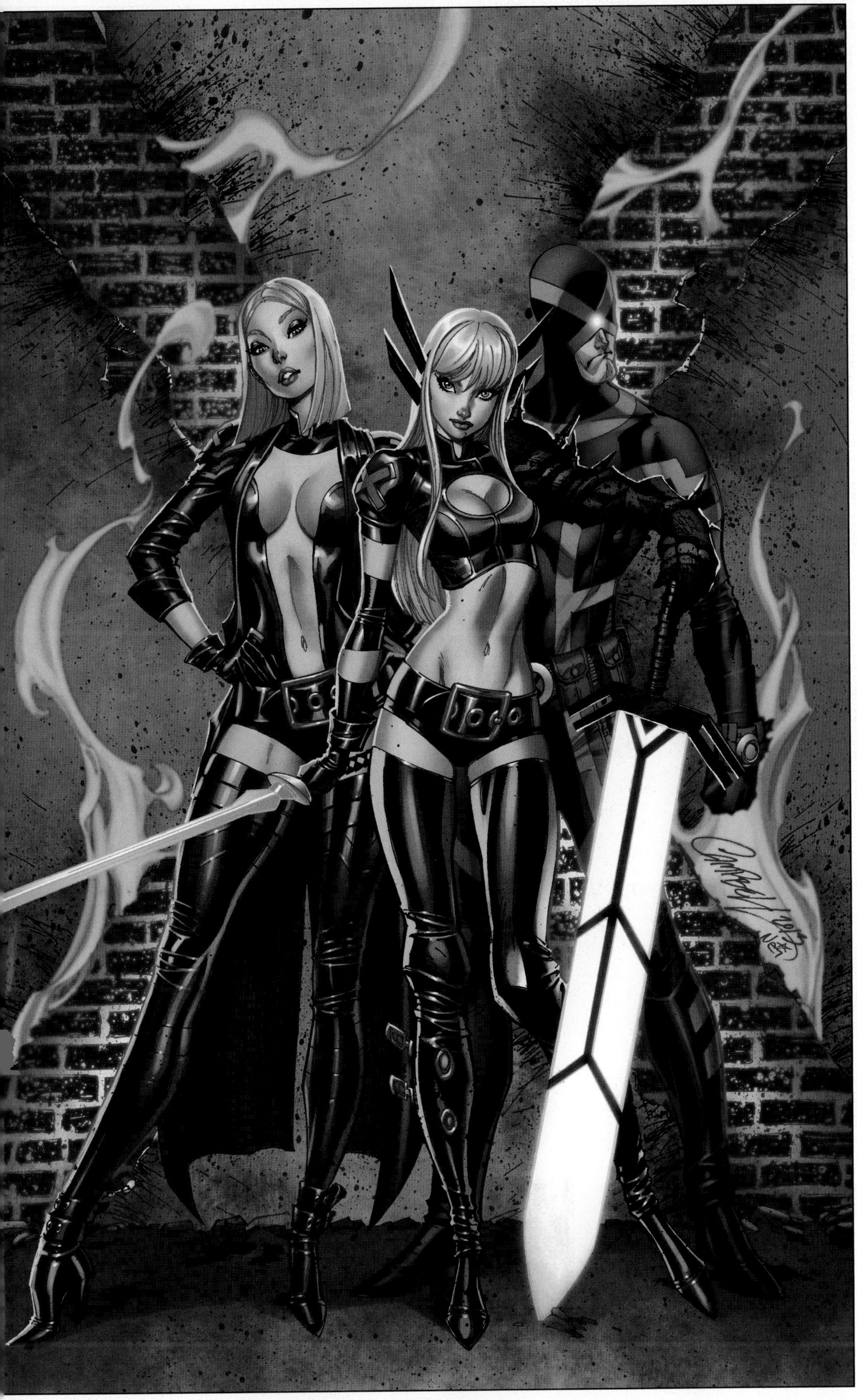

UNCANNY X-MEN #19 VARIANT
BY J. SCOTT CAMPBELL & NEI RUFFINO

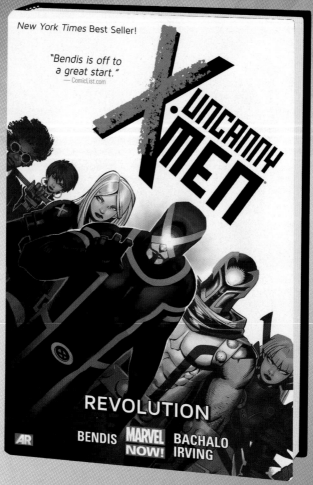